SIGILL : COLL : CARLETON
DECLARATIO SERMONUM TUORUM ILLUMINAT
NORTHFIELD, MINN. A.D. 1866

A Treatise on Mystical Love

Journal of Arabic and Islamic Studies Monograph Series 1

A Treatise on Mystical Love

Abū ʾl-Ḥasan ʿAlī b. Muḥammad al-Daylamī

Translated by

Joseph Norment Bell and
Hassan Mahmood Abdul Latif Al Shafie

Edinburgh University Press

Edinburgh University Press Ltd
22 George Square, Edinburgh

Printed and bound in Great Britain by
by MPG Books Ltd, Bodmin, Cornwall

A CIP record for this book is available from the
British Library

ISBN 0 7486 1915 1 (hardback)

CONTENTS

To the memory of Florence Willis Crallé Bell

ACKNOWLEDGMENTS

This translation and the edition from which it was made were supported by two grants from the American Research Center in Egypt, a Title F grant from the State University of New York, and research and travel funds from the University of Bergen. Publication of the translation was supported by the Norwegian Research Council and the University of Bergen. Numerous friends and colleagues have helped us in the course of our work, and we have acknowledged the assistance of some of them in the notes. We should like to mention in particular Muhsin Mahdi, who encouraged us to undertake this project. The many others who have helped us include El-Said Badawi, Diana deTreville, Carl W. Ernst, Josef van Ess, Ellen Finamore, Angelika Hartmann, Waltraud Hartje, Abd al-Fattah al-Hilw, John O. Hunwick, Ahmed Mahmoud Ibrahim, David A. King, E. Kümmerer, Father Régis Morelon, Albrecht Noth, Richard Holton Pierce, David Pingree, Bernd Radtke, George Saliba, Fuat Sezgin, Abdel Bari Taher, Hamed Taher, Manfred Ullmann, and Ali Ashri Zayed. Their assistance or their advice and support at various stages of our work we have not forgotten. Wilferd Madelung kindly reviewed drafts of the introduction and the text of the translation. Further we wish to acknowledge our debt to Jean-Claude Vadet, many aspects of whose previous edition and translation of al-Daylamī's treatise are reflected in ours, and to Florian Sobieroj, who allowed us to consult his doctoral dissertation on Ibn Khafīf before its publication and who provided us with information that allowed us to improve or correct our arguments in the Introduction at a number of places. At this point we should also mention our indebtedness to the efforts of Louis Massignon, Hellmut Ritter, Richard Walzer, Franz Rosenthal, Hans Hinrich Biesterfeldt, and Dimitri Gutas, whose previous work on various passages of the *Kitāb ᶜaṭf al-alif* has made our task easier. Thanks are likewise due to Helen Miles, whose careful reading of our draft helped us eliminate a number of mistakes and infelicities of style. We are also especially indebted to our departed friend and colleague Father G. C. Anawati and to the library of the Institut Dominicain d'Études Orientales in Cairo.

ACKNOWLEDGEMENTS

INTRODUCTION

As nearly as can be determined, the major literary activity of Abū ʾl-Ḥasan ʿAlī b. Muḥammad al-Daylamī belongs to the latter quarter of the tenth century A.D. His *Kitāb ʿaṭf al-alif al-maʾlūf ʿalā al-lām al-maʿṭūf* is one of the earliest extant treatises on mystical love in Arabic literature. The work represents a Sunni spirituality grounded in the teachings of al-Daylamī's master Ibn Khafīf of Shiraz (d. 371/982), but it reveals what may be the remnants of Shiite influence in certain of the author's expressions.[1] In some of its theoretical passages the work is indebted to the doctrine of the extremist mystic al-Ḥusayn b. Manṣūr al-Ḥallāj, who was executed for his controversial teachings in 309/922. Although al-Daylamī's text propounds a mysticism that includes Ḥallājian elements and makes room for a certain notion of union of the mystical lover with God, it seems to repudiate outright al-Ḥallāj's ecstatic claims to identity with the divine essence.[2] The book gives a well-rounded picture of the religious, philosophical, and literary trends of the author's time as these are reflected in theoretical discussions about love, both sacred and profane, and in the author's selection of anecdotes, poetry, and hagiographical literature relevant to the topic. In addition, through its many valuable citations of authorities from prior generations, the text helps explain how the ideas it deals with developed in early Islamic society.

Although now surviving in only one known manuscript, the work appears to have exercised a profound and continued influence, directly and indirectly, on the later mystical tradition in Shiraz. This influence is most clearly evident in the writings of Rūzbihān Baqlī, who died in 606/1209, or some two hundred years after al-Daylamī.[3] Perhaps al-Daylamī's work was also of some significance for the subsequent literary flowering of Persian mysticism, a matter continuing research on Rūzbihān Baqlī

[1] The author refers to the family of the Prophet as "our leaders" or "our *imams*" in his preface (cf. MS, p. 2 and n. 6 there), and on occasion he uses, or retains when narrating, the benediction "may God bless him and grant him peace" after the name of ʿAlī (cf. chapter five, MS, pp. 65 and n. 53, and MS, pp. 138, 282) and the similar formula "upon whom be peace" after the names of ʿAlī and of his son al-Ḥasan (MS, pp. 151, 282). (Page references after the abbreviation MS, here and in subsequent notes, are to pages of the manuscript given in boldface between brackets in the text of this translation at the beginning of each manuscript page and on the margins of our edition.)

[2] Cf. chapter seven, MS p. 108 and n. 15 there.

[3] See n. 4.

may help to elucidate.[4]

THE AUTHOR

Life and Times

Biographer of his teacher Ibn Khafīf and perpetuator of the memory of many scholars and mystics whose names would otherwise have remained unknown, al-Daylamī himself, though repeatedly cited by later biographers of the city of Shiraz, ironically receives no biographical notice in any of the published biographical works we have consulted. A few facts about the life of our author and the subsequent transmission of his treatise on love can be gleaned from other sources. Most of these have been collected or pointed out by Jean-Claude Vadet in the introduction to his French translation of the *Kitāb ᶜatf al-alif.*[5]

As a consequence of the silence of the biographers, we do not know when al-Daylamī was born, but we may assume that he was relatively young, possibly still a boy or a youth, when he became a disciple of Ibn Khafīf. This was at the latest in or around 352/963–64, or some eighteen years before Ibn Khafīf died.[6] We are also ignorant regarding the date of

[4] On an initiatic chain connecting the great poet Ḥāfiẓ of Shiraz (d. 791/1389 or 792/1390) to Rūzbihān Baqlī and for a view of the affinity between Rūzbihān and the poet, see Rūzbihān Baqlī, *Kitāb-i ᶜabhar al-ᶜāshiqīn,* ed. Henry Corbin and Moh. Mo'in, French intro., pp. 56–63. For further discussion of this question, and of the legacy of Rūzbihān Baqlī in general, and thus to some extent of that of al-Daylamī, see Carl W. Ernst, *Rūzbihān Baqlī: Mysticism and the Rhetoric of Sainthood in Persian Sufism,* pp. 6–15, 111–41, esp. pp. 9–10. For an inquiry into a specific example of al-Daylamī's influence on Rūzbihān Baqlī, see Masataka Takeshita, "Continuity and Change in the Tradition of Shirazi Love Mysticism—A Comparison between Daylamī's *ᶜAtf al-Alif* and Rūzbihān Baqlī's *ᶜAbhar al-ᶜĀshiqīn,*" pp. 113–31.

[5] Jean-Claude Vadet, *Le traité d'amour mystique d'al-Daylami* (Geneva: Librairie Droz, 1980), pp. 1–23, and especially, on al-Daylamī's biography, pp. 4–6. A number of points we touch on here are developed more fully by Vadet. In particular, Vadet gives a much fuller sketch of the memory of al-Daylamī in the Shiraz school and the transmission of his work to Rūzbihān than we have attempted here (ibid., pp. 6–23). In this connection the critical review of Vadet's suggestions by Florian Sobieroj should also be consulted ("Ibn Ḫafīf aš-Šīrāzī," pp. 26–27). Vadet's translation was made from his edition of the Arabic text, *Kitāb ᶜatf al-alif al-maʾlūf ᶜalā al-lām al-maᶜṭūf,* Cairo: Imprimerie de l'Institut Français d'Archéologie Orientale, 1962. As a rule we refer in our annotations to Vadet's edition and translation simply as Vadet, edition, and Vadet, trans.

[6] Ibn Khafīf died in 371/982. Abū Aḥmad al-Kabīr, the servant and companion of Ibn Khafīf, died in 377/987–88. Al-Daylamī claims he saw this servant,

al-Daylamī's death. The best we can hope for is a date at which, and perhaps for some time after which, he was still active. A rather uncertain identification with an Abū ʾl-Ḥasan al-Daylamī said by al-Qifṭī to have visited the vizicr Abū ʿAlī Muʾayyad al-Mulk would suggest 392/1001–1002, the year of the vizier's investiture.[7] If the identification is false,

---

who always wore a coarse woolen cloak, for some twenty-five years, thus from approximately 352 (377 minus 25) at the latest, perhaps already earlier (Junayd Shīrāzī, *Shadd al-izār,* p. 46; the parallel text from the *Shīrāznāma* of Zarkūb Shīrāzī, cited by Vadet, trans., p. 9, has a hiatus that doubles al-Daylamī's claim from twenty-five to fifty years). According to this reckoning al-Daylamī must have been in the company of Ibn Khafīf at least nineteen years (352–371). Moreover, on one occasion (if the subject of the verb *qāla* introducing the report is al-Daylamī himself and not someone he is quoting) al-Daylamī saw Abū Aḥmad al-Kabīr when he (al-Daylamī) was in the company of Abū ʿAbd Allāh al-Bayṭār, Abū Naṣr al-Ṭūsī (whom the editors of the *Shadd,* Muḥammad Qazvīnī and ʿAbbās Iqbāl, identify as the author of the *Kitāb al-lumaʿ* [pp. 47, n. 2, and 49, n. 1]), and a certain al-Ḥasan al-Jawāliqī or al-Jawālīqī. This event occurred presumably after 352 and definitely before 27 Ramaḍān 363/974, when Abū ʿAbd Allāh al-Ḥusayn b. Aḥmad, known as al-Bayṭār, died. Al-Bayṭār was a disciple of Ibn Khafīf. Al-Daylamī is said to have claimed in his *mashyakha* that he never *saw* (*ma raʾaytu*) anyone more cultured (*akmal adaban*) than him (*Shadd al-izār,* p. 104, cited by Vadet, trans., pp. 7–8) and that he heard Abū Ḥayyān, whom the editor of the *Shadd* considers definitely to be the philosopher al-Tawḥīdī, tell of his having seen him in Ahvaz. The important element in the dates we have is that they fit together and thus tend to confirm one another. A quotation from al-Daylamī in the *Shadd al-izār* suggests that Ibn Khafīf, who is said to havc lived one hundred and five or one hundred and fourteen lunar years (al-Daylamī, *Sīrat,* p. 218), was considerably older than al-Daylamī, and that al-Daylamī must have been rather young when he became the sheikh's follower, presumably ca. 352, when he also began to observe Ibn Khafīf's follower Abū Aḥmad al-Kabīr. "If God had not been gracious to us by granting him [Ibn Khafīf] long life so that we could come into contact with him (*adraknāhu*) and benefit from him," al-Daylamī is reported to have said, "he would have been numbered in the second class" (*Shadd*, pp. 38–39). Regarding the age of Ibn Khafīf at his death, subtracting the birth date 268 suggested below (p. xxiv and n. 42) from the generally accepted death date 371, one arrives at a maximum life span of one hundred and three lunar years. A life span of one hundred and four years is mentioned at the end of Ibn ʿAsākir's biographical notice on Ibn Khafīf on the authority of a person who claimed to have calculated it based on the date of the sheikh's birth written over a door in his house in his own hand (*Taʾrīkh madinat Dimashq,* XV, p. 301).

[7] The Abū ʾl-Ḥasan al-Daylamī mentioned by al-Qifṭī visited the vizier Abū ʿAlī Muʾayyad al-Mulk with some companions, presumably after the latter's

then 385/995–96, the year of the death of Ibn Khafīf's servant and follower Abū Aḥmad al-Ṣaghīr, is the latest date at and for a time after which our author must have been active.[8]

If we accept the date based on al-Qifṭī, then the minimum range for al-Daylamī's active career is some forty years, from about 352/963–64, when he first began to frequent Ibn Khafīf, until 392/1001–1002. Projecting arbitrarily fifteen years before he became Ibn Khafīf's disciple, we arrive at an approximate minimum life span of some fifty-five lunar years extending from about 337 to about 392.

Al-Daylamī's life span, insofar as we have been able to approximate its limits, corresponds roughly to the reigns of the caliph al-Muṭīᶜ (334/946–363/974) and his son al-Ṭāᵓiᶜ (363/974–381/991) and to the beginning of the reign of al-Qādir (381/991–422/1031). The author of the *ᶜAṭf* thus lived during the first half century of Buwayhid dominion in western Persia and Iraq, years during which the Buwayhids were the most powerful force in the central Islamic world.

The original Buwayhids came from Daylam, the area of Iran to which our author's family, as the *nisba* al-Daylamī implies, traced its origin. Unfortunately we can only speculate regarding the relevance of al-Daylamī's genealogy for his literary production. The name Daylam is applied loosely to the mountainous region between Gīlān on the Caspian coast and the plain of Qazvīn, but it refers more properly to the valleys of the Shāh-rūd before this river joins the Safīd-rūd to break through the Alburz range to the Caspian. In Daylam stand the ruins of the remote

---

investiture in 392, after consulting a blind astrologer named Shakaḥ (Vadet, trans., p. 5, citing al-Qifṭī, *Taᵓrīkh al-ḥukamāᵓ* [Leipzig, 1903], pp. 211–12, and al-Ṣābiᵓ, *Kitāb tuḥfat al-umarāᵓ fī taᵓrīkh al-wuzarāᵓ* [Beirut, 1904], p. 467). This questionable date appears to be the latest we have for al-Daylamī's activity. Al-Tawḥīdī's dates (he died in 414/1023) are not particularly helpful, as we do not know how long al-Daylamī was in contact with the philosopher.

[8] Junayd Shīrāzī, *Shadd al-izār,* pp. 46–47. The date of Abū Aḥmad al-Ṣaghīr's death would seem to be the latest death date in the *Shadd* that unquestionably comes from al-Daylamī. Al-Daylamī says of him: "I never knew him during his entire life (*ṭūla ᶜumrihi*) to be guilty of any slip or lapse" (ibid., p. 47). Massignon (*Passion*, trans. Mason, II, p. 409) seems to suggest that al-Daylamī may have been involved in the Khafīfiya's recognizing Abū Ḥayyān al-Tawḥīdī as a mystic after his death in Shiraz in 414/1023. We have not been able to confirm this undocumented implication. Perhaps it is the result of a confusion of the *kunya* of *Abū ᵓl-Ḥusayn* Aḥmad b. Muḥammad, known as Ibn Sālbih (Sāliba), with al-Daylamī's *kunya Abū ᵓl-Ḥasan.* See *Shadd,* p. 54 and n. 6.

fortress of Alamūt, originally built by a Daylamite ruler but later famous as the headquarters of the Order of Assassins. The mountaineers of Daylam made good foot soldiers. Already in pre-Islamic times the region was known as the home of rugged mercenary infantrymen armed with swords, shields, and javelins.[9]

During the first two centuries or so after the Islamic conquest of Iran, as earlier under the Sassanids, the Daylamites remained largely independent, both politically and culturally. But in the latter part of the ninth century and particularly at the beginning of the tenth, as a result of the missionary efforts of the Caspian Zaydī sayyids, with whom the Daylamites for most of the period were in alliance, Zaydī Shiism gained a strong foothold in Daylam. When during this same period, for reasons that are not clear, large numbers of Daylamite men began to migrate from their homeland and enlist as mercenaries in the armies of the powers that surrounded them, it was often the Shiite faith, though not necessarily in Zaydī form, that they took with them.

In 319/931, after the Sāmānid lieutenant Mākān had suffered several defeats at the hands of Mardāwīj b. Ziyār, the founder of the Ziyārid dynasty, three brothers from Daylam, ᶜAlī, al-Ḥasan, and Aḥmad, who were commanders in Mākān's army, deserted to the forces of the victor. Following a series of conquests by Mardāwīj in central and western Persia, ᶜAlī, the eldest of the three brothers, turned against him. Setting himself up in Arrajān in 321/933, he took Fārs, including Shiraz, the next year. As was the usual practice for successful rebels, he took the precaution of having his authority over the area recognized by the Abbasid caliphate. A series of confused events ended with his brother al-Ḥasan, although not unchallenged, in control of most of Djibāl, and his brother Aḥmad in control of Kirmān and Khūzistān and poised to enter Baghdad. Aḥmad took the city in 334/945, thus bringing the caliphate under his control. The three brothers then had bestowed on themselves the honorific titles by which they were thenceforth to be known: ᶜImād al-Dawla (ᶜAlī), Rukn al-Dawla (al-Ḥasan), and Muᶜizz al-Dawla (Aḥmad).[10] The dynasty they had founded would be called by the name of their father Buwayh (Būyah).[11]

---

[9] See V. Minorsky, *EI²,* II, p. 190a–b, s.v. "Daylam," citing the description of the "Dolomites" given by Procopius, the historian of the wars of Justinian.

[10] Cf. Cl. Cahen, *EI²,* I, pp. 1350a–b, s.v. "Buwayhids or Būyids."

[11] On the rise and fall of the Buwayhids, see, in addition to the articles by Cahen and Minorsky mentioned above, the articles "ᶜImād al-Dawla" (Cl. Cahen), "Mardāwīdj" (C. E. Bosworth), "Mākān b. Kākī" (C. E. Bosworth),

Buwayhid rule, which lasted in the Abbasid capital for 110 years, was an interlude of Iranian Shiite resurgence between the end of Arab domination in the early tenth century and the nearly universal ascendancy achieved by Turkic groups by the middle of the eleventh. It came to an end with the Seljuk seizure of Baghdad in 447/1055. In a sense the Buwayhids brought the seeds of their downfall with them from Daylam. First, their system of succession made it difficult for them to hold their dominions together after a strong prince had died. Second, their Daylamite army, consisting primarily of foot soldiers, was insufficient alone to meet the military requirements of the time and had to be supplemented with Turkish cavalry. Moreover, recruitment from Daylam fell off with time, and the last reigning descendants of the Buwayhid princes, as Claude Cahen has remarked, "were surrounded almost entirely by Turkish soldiers."[12]

Although al-Daylamī may conceivably have been old enough to witness from Shiraz much of the confusion that preceded the Buwayhid occupation of Baghdad in 334/945, the dominant political facts of his lifetime were the relative stability of Buwayhid rule over Iraq and most of western Iran, albeit with intermittent infighting, and the Shiite Buwayhid tutelage over the Sunni Abbasid caliphs. Though he cannot have been unaware of some of the quarrels among the princes of the dynasty, he also saw active princes like ᶜAḍud al-Dawla and Bahāᵓ al-Dawla unite for a time under their authority Iraq, Fārs, and Kirmān, which constituted the major part of the Buwayhid dominions.[13]

The news he heard from other parts of the Islamic world can hardly have been encouraging for the Sunni cause, even if the reports revealed a severely split Shiite camp. By 327/939 the Abbasids had indeed been able to buy "protection" for the pilgrimage routes from the Ismaili Qarmaṭīs of Bahrain, who had previously sacked southern Iraq and had been robbing pilgrimage caravans. Some twelve years later, in 339/951, by this time under Buwayhid tutelage, they had also managed to buy back the Black Stone of the Kaaba, which the Bahrain Qarmaṭīs had carried off two decades earlier. But a more formidable Ismaili threat was rising in the West. In 358/969 the rival Fatimid caliphs conquered Egypt.

"Muᶜizz al-Dawla" (K. V. Zetterstéen/H. Busse), and "Rukn al-Dawla" (Harold Bowen/C. E. Bosworth) in *EI²,* and "Mardāwidj" (M. Nazim) and "Mākān b. Kākī" (M. Nazim) in *EI¹*.

[12] *EI²,* I, p. 1355b. s.v. "Buwayhids or Būyids."

[13] ᶜAḍud al-Dawla, according to a report in Zarkūb's *Shīrāznāma,* one questioned however by Sobieroj, was a devoted follower of al-Daylamī's teacher Ibn Khafīf. See Sobieroj, "Ibn Ḫafīf aš-Šīrāzī," p. 158. Cf. also below, p. xlii.

Notwithstanding the failure of the Fatimids to win over their fellow Ismailis in Bahrain, and despite the periods of outright hostility between the two groups, the Qarmaṭīs became at best extremely unreliable allies of the Abbasid/Buwayhid center.[14]

Likewise distressing for those Sunnis who had not become reconciled to the Buwayhid order must have been the news of the successive misfortunes of the Sāmānids, the Buwayhids' main Sunni rival in Iran. Al-Daylamī most likely lived to hear of the eventual division of the Sāmānid domains in Transoxiana and Khurasan between the Turkic Qarakhānids and Ghaznavids in 389/999. On the other hand, the beginning of the end of the power of the Buwayhids themselves, the occupation of Rayy by the son of the Sunni Maḥmūd of Ghazna in 420/1029, may have come after his time.

In comparison with the Qarmaṭīs and the Fatimids, the Buwayhids represented a moderate and accommodating form of Shiism. Although they were apparently originally Zaydīs, the conqueror of Baghdad, Muᶜizz al-Dawla Aḥmad, rejected the opportunity to place a Zaydī Alid claimant on the caliphal throne. Adopting a policy of pragmatic tolerance, the Buwayhids maintained close ties with the larger Twelver Shiite group, while at the same time they legitimized their rule by presenting it as derived from the authority of the Sunni Abbasid caliphs.

Despite the religious strife that raged around the domains of the Buwayhids, tolerance and intellectual inquiry seem to have been to a striking degree the hallmark of the central Islamic regions under their control. The pagan Sabaean Abū Isḥāq Ibrāhīm b. Hilāl al-Ṣābiᵓ (d. 384/994) was appointed chief secretary of the *Dīwān al-Inshāᵓ* (Department of Letters and State Documents, previously the *Dīwān al-Rasāᵓil*) in 349 by Muᶜizz al-Dawla, and although he resisted to the end the prince's attempts to convert him to Islam, it was a dynastic squabble between ᶜIzz al-Dawla, the son and heir of Muᶜizz, and the ambitious ᶜAḍud al-Dawla that led to his downfall, not his loyalty to his pagan faith.[15] The Buwayhids were the benefactors of some of the most celebrated figures in Islamic cultural history. The author of the voluminous literary collec-

---

[14] See Wilferd Madelung, *EI²,* IV, pp. 660b–64a, s.v. "Ḳarmaṭī."

[15] See F. Krenkow, *EI¹,* VII, pp. 19b–20b, s.v. "al-Ṣābiᵓ." The pagan Sabaeans, with few exceptions, experienced considerable tolerance on the part of their Muslim rulers. They shared the name al-Ṣābiᵓīn/al-Ṣābiᵓa with the Judaeo-Christian Mandaean sect mentioned in the Koran among "the People of the Book" (B. Carra de Vaux, *EI¹,* VII, pp. 21b–22a, s.v. "al-Ṣābiᵓa"; cf. Koran 2:62, 22:17).

tion *Kitāb al-aghānī,* the Shiite Abū ʾl-Faraj al-Iṣfahānī (d. 356/967), who lived for many years in Baghdad and died there, was among the recipients of Buwayhid patronage. As a sign of their support for science and culture, the Buwayhids were active library builders, although their libraries could naturally also be used to spread Shiite doctrine. (The library at Rayy was burnt by the Sunni Ghaznavids after they took the city in 420.) In al-Daylamī's own city Shiraz a great library was established by ᶜAḍud al-Dawla.[16]

Perhaps representative of the age were the Twelver Shiite brothers al-Sharīf al-Raḍī (d. 406/1016) and al-Sharīf al-Murtaḍā (d. 436/1044). Al-Sharīf al-Raḍī succeeded his father as *naqīb* of the Ṭālibids (formal head of the descendants of ᶜAlī through Fāṭima) in Baghdad, and on his death his brother al-Murtaḍā followed in his footsteps. The two men were as a rule on cordial terms not only with the Shiite Buwayhid sultans but also with the Sunni caliphs. Recognized as both scholars and poets, they authored odes in praise of their Abbasid rivals, and the intellectual and literary gatherings they held were open to men of more or less every persuasion.[17] Al-Sharīf al-Raḍī, who is generally considered the compiler of the sayings of ᶜAlī contained in the *Nahj al-balāgha,* wrote elegies on the secretary Abū Isḥāq al-Ṣābiʾ, whom he considered a close friend, his pagan belief notwithstanding.[18]

Al-Daylamī, despite the possible traces of Shiite expressions referred to at the beginning of this introduction, appears in our text as a firm adherent of Sunnism.[19] We can do no more than surmise that any propensities for Shiism he may have had owed their origin to the Daylamite background that he had in common with the Buwayhids. In any event, he shared the cosmopolitan spirit of his times, and it was presumably not a difficult task for him to accommodate himself to the fact of the Buwayhids' relatively tolerant rule and to the cultural symbiosis they encouraged, a civilization greatly enriched by the contribution of Shiite intellectuals and to a very great extent under Shiite control, but still deriving its ultimate legitimacy from the authority of the recog-

---

[16] See D. Sourdel, *EI²,* II, p. 127a–b, s.v. "Dār al-ᶜIlm."

[17] Cf., e.g., al-Sharīf al-Murtaḍā, *Dīwān al-Sharīf al-Murtaḍā,* I, introduction by Muḥammad Riḍā al-Shaybī, pp. 8–9, and introduction by Rashīd al-Ṣaffār, pp. 55–58, 80–81, 94–96.

[18] The poems did arouse some misgivings on the part of his brother. See F. Krenkow, *EI¹,* VII, p. 330b, s.v. "al-Sharīf al-Raḍī."

[19] See MS, pp. 281–82 (on the caliph ᶜUthmān), the author's preface, n. 6, and chapter five, n. 53.

nized Sunni establishment.

Intellectual Personality

Of al-Daylamī's intellectual personality we know little more than what can be gleaned from the few passages we have already made use of and the internal evidence provided by his two extant works, particularly the treatise at hand, and the citations from him in later compilations. His devotion to the mystical teaching of his master Ibn Khafīf and his particular interest in aspects of the doctrine of al-Ḥallāj were accompanied by an eclectic curiosity that expressed itself in a wide range of other concerns. The references we have to his activity are too few and too uncertain to give a reliable picture of the man and his immediate milieu. But the outline they suggest is confirmed by numerous passages in our text.

We may never know to what extent, or in some cases even whether, he was in fact influenced by figures named in the sources like the philosopher Abū Ḥayyān al-Tawḥīdī (d. 414/1023), the blind astrologer Shakaḥ, and the polymath Abū ᶜAbd Allāh al-Bayṭār (d. 363/974). Al-Tawḥīdī is apparently cited by al-Daylamī directly in the *ᶜAṭf,*[20] and he is also almost certainly the Abū Ḥayyān whom al-Daylamī is cited quoting directly in the *Shadd al-izār.*[21] The connection with Shakaḥ, however, depends upon a text in which the identification with al-Daylamī himself is uncertain and which in any case implies no more than that al-Daylamī together with others consulted him before a visit to the vizier Abū ᶜAlī Muᵓayyad al-Mulk.[22] Regarding al-Bayṭār, who was definitely a student of Ibn Khafīf and who is said to have mastered numerous branches of learning, including belles-lettres, asceticism, mysticism, Koranic criticism and exegesis, medicine, and law, the text of the *Shadd* leaves little room for doubt that al-Daylamī actually saw him and admired his learning.[23] Moreover, while al-Bayṭār himself is not cited in the text of the *ᶜAṭf,* a hagiographic work by his father, his *mashyakha,* is apparently cited twice in the last chapter of the treatise.[24] Al-Bayṭār's father, Abū ᵓl-ᶜAbbās Aḥmad b. Manṣūr (d. 382/992), was according to the *Shadd* learned in jurisprudence, grammar, and medicine,[25] and appears to have

---

[20] MS, p. 56. Cf. below, p. lxiv.

[21] *Shadd al-izār,* pp. 104–5. Cf. n. 6.

[22] See n. 7.

[23] See n. 6.

[24] MS, pp. 287, 299–300 (the last report recorded in the *ᶜAṭf*).

[25] Junayd Shīrāzī, *Shadd al-izār,* p. 104. Al-Bayṭār was a Ẓāhirite in law before turning to Shāfiᶜism, and it is reasonable to assume that his father was also a Ẓāhirite, although he had a number of Shāfiᶜite connections. Ẓāhirism, more-

set an example for his son. He and his son may also have served as models for al-Daylamī. Evidently a generous benefactor of the Sufis of Shiraz, Abū ʾl-ʿAbbās Aḥmad contracted numerous debts in his efforts to support them. When he allowed a student of his suspected of radical Shiism (*rafḍ*) to settle a debt for him, he was obliged by the Sufis to leave the city and moved to Ahvaz, where he lived until his death.[26]

Whatever the nature of al-Daylamī's contacts with these men, the text of his treatise reflects aspects of most of the sciences in which they specialized. We see an instance of his eclecticism in the *ʿAṭf* when he concludes a series of prophetic sayings on beauty with the words "Beauty is the breaking forth of the light of the rational soul on the physical form," which he ascribes to "a certain philosopher."[27] Chapter four of the *ʿAṭf* provides numerous examples of al-Daylamī's lexicographical and linguistic learning and of his awareness of the importance of linguistic science for mystical theology and psychology. Another example of the variety of disciplines on which he draws is his inclusion in his treatise of a long pseudo-Aristotelian medical dialogue that represents an expanded version of what has been called "the most systematic and consistent account of the malady of love given in humoral medicine."[28]

Travels

Al-Daylamī's intellectual curiosity seems to have led him to travel in

---

over, was especially prominent in Shiraz in this period (Sobieroj, "Ibn Ḫafīf aš-Šīrāzī, pp. 163–66, 169). We are not in a position to speculate about the significance of a possible Ẓāhirite influence (an influence of Muḥammad b. Dāwūd [d. 297/910]) on al-Daylamī's doctrine of love, however, beyond the references to Ibn Dāwūd in the text (MS, pp. 116, 124–25, 143). These are no more numerous than might be expected in a medieval Muslim treatise on love. It should be added, perhaps, that the *ẓarf* ideal of refined, "courtly" love of which Ibn Dāwūd was a hero and for which al-Washshāʾ (d. 325/936) wrote the textbook (*al-Muwashshā*) is not quite the same thing as the mystical eros al-Daylamī was investigating, even if the loaded word *ʿishq* is often used for both. Cf. Bell, "Avicenna's *Treatise on Love* and the Nonphilosophical Muslim Tradition," pp. 85–89.

26 Junayd Shīrāzī, *Shadd al-izār,* p. 104.

27 MS, p. 14.

28 Hans Hinrich Biesterfeldt and Dimitri Gutas, "The Malady of Love," *Journal of the American Oriental Society* 104 (1984), p. 55, referring to the pseudo-Aristotelian passages in MS, pp. 59–61, 156–60, 241–42. Sobieroj mentions in some detail the discussions of mystical love that took place in or close to the circle of Ibn Khafīf in "Ibn Ḫafīf aš-Šīrāzī," pp. 144–49, esp. pp. 144–45. Cf. n. 159 below.

search of knowledge. In this he would have been following the example of his master Ibn Khafīf, who was a great traveler, despite the considerable discomfort and many perils associated with travel at the time. Ibn Khafīf, according to the *Sīrat,* made the pilgrimage at least four, and perhaps as many as six or more times, taking his mother with him on his fourth pilgrimage.[29] In the *ᶜAṭf,* al-Daylamī refers to a trip, or trips, of his own to Mecca,[30] as well as a visit to the closer by Arrajān,[31] perhaps while he was on his way to Mecca. Moreover, if the text is to be understood as implying that al-Daylamī himself was present, a visit to the "Elephant House," mentioned in chapter nineteen, would seem to have taken place in Baghdad.[32] Likewise the visit to the vizier Muᵓayyad al-Mulk mentioned above must have taken place in the Abbasid capital. From al-Qushayrī, assuming once again that our author is identical with an Abū ᵓl-Ḥasan al-Daylamī mentioned in the *Risāla,* we hear of a trip to Antioch in Syria. He visited Antioch in order to meet a gnostic of black race of whom he had heard, and he stayed there until the man came down from Mount Lukkām, a favorite place of retreat for ascetics, to sell a few edibles. Al-Daylamī wished to see something of the man's clairvoyance, and the story reveals a little of his technique in dealing with such saintly recluses. Although he had not eaten for two days and apparently had no money, he pretended to bargain with the man over the price of the food in order to achieve his purpose.[33]

In order to derive a more complete picture of al-Daylamī's life, it would be necessary, in view of the scarcity of information on him in the sources, to describe the last years of the life of his master Ibn Khafīf, about whom, to a great extent thanks to al-Daylamī himself, much more is known. However this would involve a separate study, the scope of which would exceed the ambitions of this introduction.

---

[29] al-Daylamī, *Sīrat-i Ibn al-Ḫafīf,* pp. 44, 46. Al-Daylamī does not know for certain how many times Ibn Khafīf went on the pilgrimage. For a reconstruction of the chronology of Ibn Khafīf's pilgrimages, see Sobieroj, "Ibn Ḫafīf aš-Šīrāzī," pp. 108–9.

[30] Al-Daylamī relates the behavior of two courting pigeons he saw while he was in the Holy Mosque in Mecca and the story of a camel he had observed, when he was in the desert with the pilgrims, that died of love (MS, pp. 227–28).

[31] In Arrajān al-Daylamī heard a story that a sheikh related from an old woman in Mecca (MS, pp. 244–49).

[32] See MS, p. 229 and n. 4.

[33] al-Qushayrī, *Risāla* (Cairo: Muḥammad ᶜAlī Ṣubayḥ, 1386/1966), p. 181. Cited by Vadet (using another edition), trans., pp. 4–5.

Works

Two of al-Daylamī's works are extant. The present treatise, which as mentioned above survives in only one known manuscript,[34] was first published by Jean-Claude Vadet in 1962 and subsequently translated by him into French.[35] Al-Daylamī's biography of his celebrated teacher Ibn Khafīf has reached us only in Persian translation, the Arabic original having disappeared. It has been edited by Annemarie Schimmel under the title *Sīrat-i Abū ᶜAbdullāh İbn al-Ḫafīf aş-Şīrāzī.*[36] Many fragments of a work by al-Daylamī on the lives of scholars and Sufi masters—his *mashyakha*—and perhaps of other biographical works by him, have been cited in published biographical compilations.[37] Another work, which is mentioned by al-Daylamī himself in the *ᶜAṭf,* his *Asrār al-maᶜārif* (The secrets of knowledge),[38] has been lost.

TEACHERS AND SOURCES

Ibn Khafīf and al-Ḥallāj

Al-Daylamī's spiritual master in Shiraz, Abū ᶜAbd Allāh Muḥammad b. Khafīf b. Iskafshādh?[39] al-Shīrāzī (268/882?–371/982), although he is among the authorities most often cited in the *ᶜAṭf,* does not appear to have been the author's single most important source for material on love. He may nevertheless be assumed to have had a profound influence on al-Daylamī's spiritual and intellectual development and thus also on the theoretical concerns reflected in his treatise on love and the selection of material it includes. More specifically, it seems that Ibn Khafīf himself

---

34 Tübingen, Ma VI 82.

35 See n. 5 and the Bibliography. Our edition, from which the present translation has been made, is forthcoming.

36 Persian translation by Ibn Junayd al-Shīrāzī, edited by Annemarie Schimmel Tarı, Ankara Üniversitesi İlâhiyat Fakültesi Yayınlarından, vol. 12, Ankara: Türk Tarih Kurumu Basımevi, 1955.

37 Notably Junayd Shīrāzī, *Shadd al-izār,* ed. Muḥammad Qazvīnī and ᶜAbbās Iqbāl, and Zarkūb Shīrāzī, *Shīrāznāma,* ed. Bahman Karīmī. See the Bibliography.

38 MS, p. 281. Sezgin (*GAS,* I, p. 664) mentions no such work. In addition to the works we have mentioned here, Ritter, in his introduction to the *Mashāriq anwār al-qulūb* of Ibn al-Dabbāgh (p. *hā'*), ascribes a *Risālat al-ᶜaqīda al-ṣaḥīḥa* to al-Daylamī, but he does not name his source.

39 Various spellings of this name are given. The form we have adopted here is that given in the text of Qazvīnī's edition of Junayd Shīrāzī's *Shadd al-izār* (p. 38). Cf. ibid., n. 1, and al-Sulamī, *Ṭabaqāt al-ṣūfiya* (ed. Pedersen), p. 485, n. 3.

authored at least two short works as well as a tract on the subject of love, and there can be little doubt that one or more of these compositions, all now lost, influenced the content, if not necessarily the form, of the *ᶜAṭf*.

Partly because of his significance for studies on al-Ḥallāj, and partly because of his importance for the later history of mysticism in Shiraz and thus in the Persian- and Turkish-speaking world generally, Ibn Khafīf has attracted the attention of a number of western scholars. The most complete exposition of his life and teaching is now the study prepared by Florian Sobieroj in connection with his edition and translation of Ibn Khafīf's *Kitāb al-iqtiṣād*.[40] Sobieroj's valuable study adds significantly to the information collected earlier by Annemarie Schimmel in the introduction and copious appendix to her edition of al-Daylamī's biography of the mystic.[41]

---

[40] "Ibn Ḫafīf aš-Šīrāzī und seine Schrift zur Novizenerziehung (Kitāb al-Iqtiṣād)," doctoral dissertation, Albert-Ludwigs-Universität zu Freiburg, Freiburg, 1992. The study has since been published in the series Beiruter Texte und Studien. Sobieroj's study was not available to us at the time the main body of this introduction was being written. The few facts about Ibn Khafīf for which we have made space here are therefore based in large part on Schimmel's work. Later, however, Sobieroj kindly provided us with a copy of his dissertation, and we were thus able to make use of his work while revising our original draft.

[41] Earlier contributions to our knowledge of Ibn Khafīf are discussed in some detail by Schimmel in her introduction (pp. 3–5). Notable among these are the studies of Louis Massignon on al-Ḥallāj, which situate Ibn Khafīf primarily in the context of the prosecution of al-Ḥallāj for heresy, Fritz Meier's introduction to his edition of the *Vita* of the later Shirazi mystic Abū Isḥāq al-Kāzarūnī (d. 426/1035), and the edition with copious footnotes of *Shadd al-izār* by Muḥammad Qazvīnī and ᶜAbbās Iqbāl. Schimmel also deals at length with other Oriental primary sources for the life and teaching of Ibn Khafīf (intro., pp. 5–12), many of which are reproduced in the appendix to her edition. Her introduction is given in both German and Turkish versions in the edition. There are some problems with Schimmel's references to the places she has made use of in the sources, and our references may therefore not always agree with hers. The Persian text of al-Daylamī's biography of Ibn Khafīf, along with Schimmel's introduction, has been translated into Arabic by Ibrāhīm al-Dusūqī Shitā (see the Bibliography), and there also exists an Iranian issue based on Schimmel's edition that has not been available to us (*Sīrat al-Shaykh al-Kabīr Abū ᶜAbd Allāh ibn al-Khafīf al-Shīrāzī*, ed. A. Shimīl-Ṭārī, *bi-kūshish-i* Tawfīq Subḥānī, Tehran: Intishārāt-i Bābak, 1363 [1984]). See also the article on Ibn Khafīf by Jean-Claude Vadet in *EI*², III, pp. 823a–24a, s.v. "Ibn Khafīf," and the comments on the arguments presented there in Sobieroj, "Ibn Ḫafīf aš-Šīrāzī," pp. 25–26.

If one accepts the information provided by al-Daylamī, Ibn Khafīf was born in Shiraz in or not long after 268/882, when the Ṣaffārid ᶜAmr b. al-Layth of Sijistān occupied the city.[42] Ibn Khafīf's father was a Daylamite commander in the service of ᶜAmr. Sometime during or after ᶜAmr's campaign to reoccupy Fārs he had brought his wife to Shiraz. Ibn Khafīf's roots thus lay in the Daylamite warrior class that within his lifetime would come to dominate the central Islamic world. As we have already noted, the *nisba* of his disciple ᶜAlī b. Muḥammad, the author of the *ᶜAṭf,* suggests that he descended from this same stock. Al-Hujwīrī's *Kashf* and some other sources state that Ibn Khafīf belonged to the "sons of kings" (*abnā-yi mulūk*) but that God granted him repentance and he forsook worldly concerns. According to Schimmel this allusion to the mystic's exalted lineage reflects his Daylamite origins.[43] It can thus be reconciled, at least in part, with what Schimmel considers to be more reliable reports to the effect that Ibn Khafīf's family suffered considerable poverty during his childhood and that his ascetic tendencies—perhaps encouraged by his mother, who was from the pietistic Karrāmīya sect[44]—were evident from a tender age.[45] Whatever the age at which Ibn Khafīf began to show his saintliness, it is in any event not unlikely that the mixed fortunes of his father's master ᶜAmr b. al-Layth, who lost control over Fārs in 274/887, influenced the material situation of his family when he was a child.[46]

---

42 Most of al-Daylamī's report is presented as Ibn Khafīf's own words. His source for the report, whom he considers trustworthy, adds that, according to Ibn Khafīf's mother, her son was eight months old when ᶜAmr b. al-Layth returned to Khurasan (*Sīrat,* p. 9). Schimmel opts for 268/882 as the year of the mystic's birth (ibid., intro., p. 13). The latest date that can conceivably be reconciled with al-Daylamī's report is late 278/891–92 or 279/892–93, not long before ᶜAmr, in Ramaḍān of the latter year, was invested for the third time with the governorship of Khurasan. Sobieroj, arguing that there are no established dates for Ibn Khafīf's contacts with his *ḥadīth* authorities prior to 298 and that the mystic is known to have begun his travels while he was young, regards 280 as the earliest likely year of birth ("Ibn Ḫafīf aš-Šīrāzī," p. 221).

43 al-Hujwīrī, *Kashf al-mahjūb,* ed. V. A. Zhukovskii, p. 199; trans. Nicholson, p. 158; *Sīrat,* intro., p. 14.

44 *Sīrat,* p. 9.

45 Ibid., intro., p. 14.

46 Cf. W. Barthold, *EI²,* I, pp. 452b–53a, s.v. "ᶜAmr b. al-Layth." ᶜAmr succeeded his brother Yaᶜqūb, the founder of the Ṣaffārid dynasty, in 265/879. He was executed in Baghdad in 289/902, a year after having been defeated by the Sāmānid Ismāᶜīl and sent in captivity to the Abbasid capital.

Ibn Khafīf's early education in mysticism took place in Shiraz under the guidance of the extravagant ecstatic Aḥmad b. Yaḥyā, whom he names as his first master. Aḥmad b. Yaḥyā and his associates practiced the spiritual concert (*samā*ᶜ), and Ibn Khafīf was on occasion witness to some extraordinary things during these performances. Once having gone into a state of ecstasy (*vajd, ḥālat*), Aḥmad picked up some burning coals with his hands, drew his sleeves over them, and held them under his shirt until they went out. Afterwards, apparently unhurt, he went to the mosque and performed the prayer until morning. Another time, one of his fellow sheikhs who was in attendance had laughed with a follower of his at Aḥmad's behavior when the singer began to sing. Aḥmad threw a candlestick at the man and knocked him unconscious. When the man came to himself, Aḥmad reprimanded him for not observing the etiquette required of dervishes. "I have seen many ecstatics," al-Daylamī quotes Ibn Khafīf as saying, "but I have never seen anyone like him."[47]

In Shiraz Ibn Khafīf unquestionably came in contact with authorities who exercised a more moderate influence, in particular traditionists with Ḥanbalite connections or under Ḥanbalite influence[48] and students of the comparatively restrained mystic al-Junayd.[49] The sheikh who seems to have been the most important among the latter was the illiterate Muᵓammil b. Muḥammad al-Jaṣṣāṣ (d. 322/933–34). Muᵓammil, who incidentally is not cited in the ᶜAṭf, was a great admirer of the ecstatic Abū Yazīd al-Bisṭāmī,[50] whose doctrine of intoxication (*sukr*) al-Hujwīrī contrasts with al-Junayd's stress on sobriety (*ṣaḥw*).[51] Muᵓammil's leanings are apparently reflected in Ibn Khafīf's own special attachment to mystics like al-Bisṭāmī and Shāh al-Kirmānī.[52]

Also in Shiraz, Ibn Khafīf had the opportunity to study law under the noted Shāfiᶜite jurist Abū ᵓl-ᶜAbbās Aḥmad b. ᶜUmar b. Surayj (d. 306/918–9 in Baghdad), who had been a student in mysticism of both al-Muḥāsibī and al-Junayd. Ibn Surayj was judge in Shiraz from 296 or 297 to 301.[53] According to Ibn Khafīf, as cited by al-Daylamī in the *Sīrat,* he used his influence with the religious scholars of Shiraz, who before his

---

[47] *Sīrat,* pp. 129–30.

[48] Sobieroj, "Ibn Ḫafīf aš-Šīrāzī," pp. 130–32.

[49] Ibid., pp. 133–34.

[50] Ibid., pp. 68, 70, 138.

[51] al-Hujwīrī, *Kashf al-maḥjūb,* ed. Zhukovskii, pp. 228–32; trans. Nicholson, pp. 184–86.

[52] Sobieroj, "Ibn Ḫafīf aš-Šīrāzī," p. 142.

[53] Ibid., p. 175.

coming had been contemptuous of the Sufi sheikhs of the city, to convince them to respect the mystics.[54] The fact that Ibn Khafīf studied under Ibn Surayj, along with other perhaps not entirely conclusive pieces of evidence, supports the statement of al-Sulamī, recorded by Junayd Shīrāzī, that he was a follower of al-Shāfiᶜī in jurisprudence.[55]

Wishing to learn from the spiritual masters in other places, Ibn Khafīf undertook a number of long journeys. Our information on his travels, however, is rather unsatisfactory. Reports given in some sources of trips to Egypt and Asia Minor are not confirmed in al-Daylamī's biography, while tales of trips to such distant places as Ceylon are almost certainly legends. More reliable, we may assume, is the information contained in the *Sīrat.* Ibn Khafīf, as has been mentioned above, made the pilgrimage to Mecca at least four and possibly six or more times. On one of his trips—the story is told by the master himself—he had the misfortune of being arrested on suspicion of theft and would have lost his hand, had he not been recognized by the local ruler, who had earlier been in the service of his father.[56]

While in Basra during the earlier part of his life he met the theologian Abū ᵓl-Ḥasan al-Ashᶜarī (d. 324/935–36?). The reports of their meeting differ somewhat. That in the *Sīrat,* which is attributed by al-Daylamī to Ibn Khafīf himself, asserts that it was al-Ashᶜarī who first came up to Ibn Khafīf with questions, although the latter likewise wished to hear the theologian.[57] According to the reports related by al-Subkī, on the other hand, Ibn Khafīf went to Basra specifically to meet al-Ashᶜarī.[58] Despite discrepancies of this kind, the upshot of the various reports is that Ibn Khafīf came away from the meeting with a positive assessment of al-Ashᶜarī. According to one tradition, when towards the very end of the mystic's life the Ashᶜarite theologian al-Bāqillānī was in Shiraz, he visited Ibn Khafīf and found him teaching his disciples

---

[54] Cf. ibid., pp. 89–90, 175, al-Daylamī, *Sīrat,* pp. 175–76, and Sezgin, *GAS,* I, p. 495. On Ibn Surayj, see also MS, pp. 124–25.

[55] Cf. *Shadd al-izār,* p. 41. It is only in the later Shāfiᶜite biographical literature, however, as Sobieroj has pointed out, that Ibn Khafīf is listed among the followers of the Shāfiᶜite school ("Ibn Ḫafīf aš-Šīrāzī," pp. 170–71).

[56] *Sīrat,* intro., p 15; cf. *Sīrat,* pp. 47–49, on Ibn Khafīf's arrest.

[57] Ibid., pp. 109–11; intro., p. 16.

[58] Ibid., appendix, pp. 241–42, 242–47, the passages cited by Schimmel from al-Subkī's *Ṭabaqāt al-Shāfiᶜīya* (II, pp. 277 and 155–59). On the various reports concerning Ibn Khafīf's meeting with al-Ashᶜarī and the question of his relation to him, see Sobieroj, "Ibn Ḫafīf aš-Šīrāzī," pp. 56–57, 217–18.

from al-Ashᶜarī's *Lumaᶜ*.[59]

Al-Daylamī devotes separate chapters in the *Sīrat* to the teachers Ibn Khafīf met in Mecca, those he met in Iraq, and those he met in Fārs. Of interest here are those whom al-Daylamī also names in his treatise on love. From the list given in the *Sīrat* of the teachers Ibn Khafīf met in Mecca, those cited or mentioned in the *ᶜAṭf* are Abū ᶜAlī al-Rūdhbārī, who is quoted three times, in each case for his verse,[60] ᶜAlī b. Muḥammad al-Muzayyin (the Barber), who despite his importance in the *Sīrat* is quoted only once in the *ᶜAṭf,*[61] and Abū Yaᶜqūb al-Aqṭaᶜ, the story of whose death al-Muzayyin relates.[62] Also among the masters Ibn Khafīf met in Mecca was Abu Saᶜīd b. al-Aᶜrābī, who, however, is not listed in the chapter in the *Sīrat* on Ibn Khafīf's Meccan sheikhs. As we shall see later on, Abu Saᶜīd was among the chief sources used by al-Daylamī in the *ᶜAṭf.*[63] From the list of the teachers Ibn Khafīf met in Iraq, those cited in the *ᶜAṭf* include Abū Muḥammad Ruwaym, who according to Ibn Khafīf's own words was his first master there,[64] Abū ᵓl-ᶜAbbās Aḥmad b. ᶜAṭāᵓ,[65] Abū Bakr al-Shiblī,[66] and the controversial al-Ḥallāj, whose influence is particularly apparent in al-Daylamī's treatise. The reports of Ibn Khafīf's having met al-Junayd, also a major source for the *ᶜAṭf,* would seem to be incorrect.[67] None of Ibn Khafīf's teachers

[59] Sobieroj, "Ibn Ḫafīf aš-Šīrāzī," p. 57, citing al-Maqqarī, *Azhār al-riyāḍ* (Cairo, 1358/1939), III, pp. 79–80. Cf. *Shadd al-izār,* pp. 41–42.

[60] MS, pp. 70, 88, 143.

[61] MS, pp. 296–97.

[62] Ibn Khafīf says that Abū Yaᶜqūb al-Aqṭaᶜ had a special affection for him and insisted that regardless where he might go during the day, he should spend the night with him (*Sīrat,* p. 74).

[63] See below, pp. lxi–lxii and nn. 227–33.

[64] Twice cited (MS, pp. 70, 87); see *Sīrat,* pp. 85–91, esp. p. 85. Sobieroj sees in Ruwaym rather than al-Ḥallāj the most significant spiritual master of Ibn Khafīf ("Ibn Ḫafīf aš-Šīrāzī," pp. 7, 46–48). Ibn Khafīf's first teacher in mysticism, Aḥmad b. Yaḥyā, was a great admirer of Ruwaym, valuing his statements on mysticism above those of Junayd. Ibn Khafīf shared Aḥmad b. Yaḥyā's high opinion of Ruwaym's statements on esoteric knowledge (ibid., p. 46, citing *Sīrat,* pp. 118, 134).

[65] Twice cited (MS, pp. 87, 238); see *Sīrat,* pp. 91–93.

[66] Cited three times (MS, pp. 38, 88, 142); see *Sīrat,* pp. 103–4.

[67] Schimmel (*Sīrat,* intro., p. 16) considers it unlikely that Ibn Khafīf actually met al-Junayd, despite reports to the effect that he did meet him (e. g., *Shadd al-izār,* p. 41) and is said to have argued with him—an apparent anachronism—about the merits of al-Ḥallāj (*Akhbār al-Ḥallāj* [1936], no. 61, Arabic, p. 92,

listed in the chapter on his sheikhs in Fārs is cited in the ᶜ*Aṭf.*

Ruwaym, Aḥmad b. ᶜAṭāʾ, and al-Junayd were held in particularly high esteem by Ibn Khafīf. According to al-Daylamī they were among the five spiritual masters who Ibn Khafīf recommended should be chosen as models. The other two were al-Junayd's teacher al-Ḥārith al-Muḥāsibī and ᶜAmr b. ᶜUthmān al-Makkī. These five combined canonical knowledge (ᶜ*ilm*) and esoteric truth (*ḥaqīqat*). Other teachers had at times uttered in moments of engulfment (*istighrāq*) things that were not in accordance with divine law (*shar*ᶜ) and that they regretted when they came back to themselves.[68] Of the five masters Ibn Khafīf singled out as models, it is al-Junayd and ᶜAmr b. ᶜUthmān al-Makkī who are of special importance in al-Daylamī's treatise on love.

The Teachings of Ibn Khafīf

The doctrines that pervade al-Daylamī's treatise on love may to a considerable degree reflect the views of Ibn Khafīf or developments of positions towards which he was tending. The text of the ᶜ*Aṭf* should of course be allowed to speak for itself, but in the virtual absence of external evidence concerning the author's own opinions, it is first to the teachings of Ibn Khafīf that one must turn to ascertain the dogmatic context within which al-Daylamī's work was produced. Sobieroj has made a thorough study of the sources we have for Ibn Khafīf's mystical doctrine and has likewise given a useful assessment of his attitude towards political authority and his stance on theological issues.[69] Schimmel, earlier, in the introduction to her edition of the *Sīrat,* pieced together an outline of Ibn Khafīf's doctrine and practice based on the two short works by him she edits in the appendix to the edition—his *Waṣīya* (Spiritual testament) and his *Mu*ᶜ*taqad* (Minor creed)[70]—as well as on a considerable number of reports gathered from other sources.[71] For the most part we rely here on

French, p. 99 and n. 2). Sobieroj likewise argues that Ibn Khafīf did not actually meet al-Junayd, the main evidence being a report according to which Ibn Khafīf asked Abū ʾl-Ḥasan ᶜAlī b. Bundār al-Ṣayrafī to precede him because he had met al-Junayd whereas Ibn Khafīf had not ("Ibn Ḫafīf aš-Šīrāzī," p. 43; al-Sulamī, *Ṭabaqāt al-ṣūfīya* [Pedersen], p. 535).

68 *Sīrat,* pp. 37–38; cf. *Shadd al-izār,* pp. 43–44. On Ibn Khafīf's direct or indirect dependence on these sheikhs, see Sobieroj, "Ibn Ḫafīf aš-Šīrāzī," pp. 42–49.

69 "Ibn Ḫafīf aš-Šīrāzī," pp. 214–64.

70 *Waṣīyat al-shaykh Ibn al-Khafīf* (*Sīrat,* pp. 274–83) and *Mu*ᶜ*taqad al-shaykh Ibn al-Khafīf* (*Sīrat,* pp. 284–308).

71 *Sīrat,* intro., pp. 25–46.

the studies of Sobieroj and Schimmel. We depend somewhat more on Schimmel's earlier work and the materials she cites, since this introduction was largely complete before Sobieroj's study became available to us. Sobieroj's most significant addition to Schimmel's material is his edition and translation of Ibn Khafīf's *Kitāb al-iqtiṣād,* but he has also found important citations of the mystic in other sources, in particular a long excerpt from his *Kitāb al-iᶜtiqād,* also referred to as *Kitāb al-muᶜtaqad al-kabīr* (Major creed), recorded by the Ḥanbalite Ibn Taymīya (d. 728/1328).[72]

Imamate. On the imamate Ibn Khafīf gives in his *Minor Creed* the standard Sunni position. One must believe that the best of mankind since the Prophet's death have been the first four caliphs, in order—Abū Bakr, then ᶜUmar, then ᶜUthmān, and then ᶜAlī.[73] However Ibn Khafīf seems to have retained remnants of pro-Alid sentiment similar to those we find in al-Daylamī's *ᶜAṭf.* In the *Sīrat* he relates the story of a dream a certain Muḥammad Isḥāq[74] had after the death of Aḥmad b. Ḥanbal. The man, having fallen asleep while worrying about a possible resurgence of heresy, beheld Ibn Ḥanbal strutting by in a pair of golden slippers. He asked the imam what God had done with him, and Ibn Ḥanbal answered that God had given him the golden slippers and a crown because he had held that the Koran was God's speech and that it was eternal (*qadīm*) and uncreated (*nā-āfarīda*). He added, however, that God had reprimanded him for relating traditions from a certain ᶜUthmān (apparently reflecting the name of Ḥarīz b. ᶜUthmān al-Ḥimṣī [d. 163/779–80] in an earlier version of the story).[75] When Ibn Ḥanbal had answered that this ᶜUthmān was a

---

[72] See n. 156.

[73] *Muᶜtaqad,* in *Sīrat,* p. 300. Cf., e.g., the creed of the strict Ḥanbalite contemporary of al-Daylamī known as Ibn Baṭṭa (*al-Sharḥ wa-l-ibāna* [ed. and trans. Henri Laoust], Arabic, pp. 61–62, French, pp. 113–16).

[74] See n. 76.

[75] Cf. al-Tanūkhī, *Nishwār al-muḥāḍara,* VIII, p. 109, where in a different, apparently earlier version of this story, the name Ḥarīz b. ᶜUthmān is corrupted to ᶜUthmān b. Jarīr. In this version it is Yazīd b. Hārūn (d. 206/821) rather than Aḥmad b. Ḥanbal who appears in the dream. Ibn ᶜAdī (277/890–365?/976) and Ibn Ḥajar relate an abbreviated version of the story about Yazīd b. Hārūn in their notices on Ḥarīz b. ᶜUthmān (Ibn ᶜAdī, *al-Kāmil fī ḍuᶜafāᵓ al-rijāl,* II, p. 857; Ibn Ḥajar, *Tahdhīb al-Tahdhīb,* II, p. 239). Ḥarīz was noted for his dislike of ᶜAlī. Aḥmad b. Ḥanbal is reported to have praised Ḥarīz and to have said that he was a reliable authority (*thiqa*) in *ḥadīth,* although he is likewise said to have taken exception to his attacks on ᶜAlī (*Kāmil,* II, p. 857; *Tahdhīb*, II, pp. 238–39). According to al-Khaṭīb al-Baghdādī, the story of Yazīd b. Hārūn's telling in

reliable authority in *ḥadīth,* God had said: "That he was, but he was an enemy of ᶜAlī b. Abī Ṭālib, upon whom be peace. Didst thou not know that any enemy of his is an enemy of mine?"[76]

Theology. In his *Spiritual Testament* Ibn Khafīf defines his conservative theological position by specifying its adversaries. His disciples are advised to avoid religious discussions with extreme free-willers (*qadarīya*), extreme predestinarians (*jabarīya, jabrīya*), Muᶜtazilites, and radical Shiites (*rāfiḍa*).[77] In his *Major Creed,* according to the text cited by Ibn Taymīya, he repeats conservative scripturalist doctrine in the traditional style: God is seated upon his throne, the Koran is his uncreated speech, believers will see him at the Resurrection, the acts of men are brought about by his omnipotence rather than their free will, all spirits

---

a dream that God had rebuked him for narrating tradition from Ḥarīz (the text has the graphically similar "Jarīr") was related *in the presence of* Aḥmad b. Ḥanbal (*Taʾrīkh Baghdād,* XIV, pp. 346–47; cf. Ibn Abī Yaᶜlā, *Ṭabaqāt al-Ḥanābila,* I, p. 167, which has "Ḥurayz"). Al-Tanūkhī's version is a combination of this and a subsequent story recounted by al-Khaṭīb. We are indebted to Wilferd Madelung for calling our attention to the identity of the "ᶜUthmān" referred to in al-Daylamī's version of the dream story and to the sources we have cited here. Sobieroj, using different sources, arrives at the same conclusion regarding the identity of the "ᶜUthmān" referred to in the *Sīrat* ("Ibn Ḫafīf aš-Šīrāzī," pp. 85–87).

[76] *Sīrat,* pp. 169–70; cf. Schimmel, intro., p. 26. The wording here seems too strong to be merely a reflection of the typical orthodox opposition to *wuqūf* (stopping after naming the first three caliphs and giving no opinion on ᶜAlī), although this may be the issue Ibn Khafīf was addressing. See Ibn Baṭṭa, *al-Sharḥ wa-l-ibāna,* French, p. 115, n. 2. The story is related to Ibn Khafīf by an Abū ʾl-Qāsim, presumably Abū ʾl-Qāsim al-Qaṣrī as suggested by Sobieroj ("Ibn Ḫafīf aš-Šīrāzī," pp. 85–87), about a Muḥammad Isḥāq Kh-z-y-m? Iskandarānī, whom Sobieroj identifies with Abū Bakr Muḥammad b. Isḥāq b. Khuzayma al-Sulamī al-Nīsābūrī, who died in 311/923–24 (ibid., pp. 86–87, citing Ibn al-Jawzī, *Manāqib Aḥmad b. Ḥanbal* [1349/1930], p. 439; cf. Sezgin, *GAS,* I, p. 601.) Cf. the report of a Muḥammad b. Isḥāq in the first *ṭabaqa* of Ḥanbalites, who related a vision of the Day of Resurrection in which he was asked by God what he believed about the Koran. "It is thy speech, O Lord of the Worlds," he had replied, citing Ibn Ḥanbal as his authority. (The report goes on to make the point that it is God himself—through Gabriel to the Prophet—who is the ultimate authority for the doctrine that the Koran is God's speech.) See *Ṭabaqāt al-Ḥanābila,* I, pp. 270–71. Al-Daylamī's story seems to combine elements of this story with that discussed in the preceding footnote.

[77] *Waṣīya,* in *Sīrat,* p. 279. The Arabic words are in the singular in the text.

are created beings.[78] Again the statements contained in his *Minor Creed* leave little doubt that what he is advocating is a moderate form of traditionalist Sunnism. But in this work, which conceivably dates from a later period than the *Major Creed,*[79] Ibn Khafīf's teaching is expressed in a language that reveals the influence of the speculative method of al-Ashᶜarī or early Ashᶜarism.[80] Muslim creeds like those of Ibn Khafīf were written in such a way as to exclude a patchwork of doctrines considered heretical by their authors. The creeds of Ibn Khafīf admit only those beliefs that are associated with the scripturalists, the *ahl al-sunna,* of whom the stricter Ḥanbalites are often considered paradigmatic.

But it was these very same beliefs that the theologian al-Ashᶜarī was attempting to defend. After his conversion from Muᶜtazilism, said to have taken place in 300/912–13, theology had become for al-Ashᶜarī a means of upholding the dogma of scripturalist Islam. It was thus not his doctrine as such, but his language and mode of argumentation, that led the militant Ḥanbalite al-Ḥasan b. ᶜAlī al-Barbahārī (d. 329/941) to condemn his teaching and to reject his *Kitāb al-ibāna,* which the theologian is said to have written to placate him.[81] Al-Ashᶜarī's reply to al-Barbahārī and his followers came in his *Risāla fī istiḥsān al-khawḍ fī ᶜilm al-kalām* (On the endorsement of engaging in speculative theology).[82] Postulating opponents who accepted the doctrine of the uncreated Koran, by whom he surely intended the Ḥanbalites, he argued that Aḥmad b. Ḥanbal and the early *ᶜulamāᵓ,* when they affirmed the doctrine of the uncreated Koran, were themselves making use of the methods of specu-

---

[78] Ibn Taymīya, *al-Fatwā al-Ḥamawīya al-kubrā,* pp. 45–46, 49. For a succinct review of the scripturalist doctrine that all spirits (*arwāḥ*) are created (as represented by ᶜAbd al-Qāhir al-Baghdādī and Ibn Qayyim al-Jawzīya), as well as some opposing views, cf. E. E. Calverley, *EI*², VII, p. 881a–82b, s.v. "Nafs."

[79] See pp. xlvii–xlviii and n. 159 below.

[80] Sobieroj points out not only that Ibn Khafīf taught al-Ashᶜarī's *Lumaᶜ* but also that he gave a personal welcome to the Ashᶜarite theologian al-Bāqillānī when he visited Shiraz in 370 or 371 (980–82) ("Ibn Ḫafīf aš-Šīrāzī," pp. 161–62). Sobieroj hesitates, however, to see in Ibn Khafīf a representative of an Ashᶜarite rationalism, in part because his documented contacts with Ḥanbalites and other scripturalists far outnumber his Ashᶜarite contacts and in part on the basis of his writings (ibid., pp. 214–18, esp. pp. 217–18).

[81] Ibn Abī Yaᶜlā, *Ṭabaqāt al-Ḥanābila,* II, p. 18. Cf. Michel Allard, *Le problème des attributs divins,* p. 52.

[82] Edited and translated by R. J. McCarthy in *The Theology of al-Ashᶜarī* (Beirut: Imprimerie Catholique, 1953), Arabic, pp. 87–97, English, pp. 119–34.

lative theology.[83] Al-Ashᶜarī, who had included in his *Maqālāt al-Islāmīyīn* a creed of Ḥanbalite type, to which he appended a statement that he subscribed to the beliefs set forth in it,[84] was attempting in his defense of theology to influence the form rather than the content of scripturalist teaching. Despite deep differences over method and terminology, and a correspondingly different range of concerns, the true doctrinal rift between Ḥanbalism and Ashᶜarism, which was never intended by al-Ashᶜarī himself, can hardly have developed before Ibn Khafīf and the theologian met. In situating Ibn Khafīf's *Minor Creed* in the context of the religious polemics of his age, therefore, the vocabulary and style of the creed and the nature of the concerns it reflects can be as important as the doctrines it asserts.

Ibn Khafīf's *Minor Creed,* while setting forth essentially the same articles of belief as the creeds of conservative Ḥanbalites like al-Barbahārī and Ibn Baṭṭa (d. 387/997), indeed at times using precisely the same traditional wording,[85] is none the less different in tone and terminology. (It also differs from his own *Major Creed* in these respects.) The Ḥanbalites would not have had much trouble with Ibn Khafīf's declaration in the *Minor Creed* that the believer is to accept all the divine attributes affirmed by the Koran, the sayings of the Prophet, and the consensus of believers without trying to interpret them.[86] But there is much in this creed that does not remind the reader of al-Barbahārī and Ibn Baṭṭa. Thus, when in the *Minor Creed* it is affirmed that God is *knowing,* this means, according to Ibn Khafīf, that he knows with an *attribute* (*ṣifa*) of knowledge. Likewise when God is said to be *mighty,* it means he is mighty by an *attribute* of might.[87] While the word *ṣifa* itself is used by

---

[83] Allard, *Attributs divins,* pp. 206–10, summarizing al-Ashᶜarī's arguments in McCarthy, *The Theology of al-Ashᶜarī,* Arabic, pp. 95–97, English, pp. 131–34.

[84] *Maqālāt* (ed. Ritter), I, pp. 290–97.

[85] For example the sentence *Al-īmān qawl wa-ᶜamal wa-nīya, yazīd wa-yanquṣ* (Faith consists in speech, deeds, and intentions; it increases and decreases). Cf. *Muᶜtaqad,* in *Sīrat,* p. 297; al-Barbahārī, *Sharḥ kitāb al-sunna,* extract in Ibn Abī Yaᶜlā, *Ṭabaqāt al-Ḥanābila,* II, p. 20; and al-Ashᶜarī, *Maqālāt,* I, p. 293. The words are based on a definition of faith given by Aḥmad b. Ḥanbal (Ibn Baṭṭa, *al-Sharḥ wa-l-ibāna,* p. 78, n. 1), which is in turn based on sayings attributed to the Prophet (cf. Wensinck, *Concordance,* I, p. 109b; al-Muttaqī al-Hindī, *Kanz al-ᶜummāl,* I, p. 9, *ḥadīth* no. 422; Zaghlūl, *Mawsūᶜat aṭrāf al-ḥadīth,* IV, p. 224a).

[86] *Muᶜtaqad,* in *Sīrat,* pp. 288–90.

[87] Ibid.

al-Barbahārī and Ibn Baṭṭa, they do not go into the relationship between descriptive verbs, participles, or adjectives and the names of God's attributes when listing examples of them. They content themselves instead with minimal statements or direct quotations from the Koran. Thus Ibn Baṭṭa writes, "God is living, speaking, hearing, seeing, 'he knows the secret and that which is yet more hidden,'[88] . . . he closes and opens [his hand],[89] he takes and gives, he is on his throne."[90]

Equally alien to the creeds of the early Ḥanbalites is Ibn Khafīf's preoccupation with a number of other theological subtleties. God is a thing, but he is not like other things. An attribute is not the same as the thing it qualifies, but rather something inherent in it. When God is said to have created Adam with his hand, the word *hand* is not a symbol for the power to create but refers to an attribute. God's descending to the heaven of this world is to be understood as an attribute rather than as movement.[91] In the Ashᶜarite defense of the "traditional" attributes of God, those affirmed by tradition rather than by reason, God's having a hand, or hands,[92] and his descent to this world are two of the attributes on which the argument focuses.[93] In a summary confession of faith like Ibn Khafīf's *Minor Creed* it is sufficient to point out that such anthropomorphic properties or acts are to be ascribed to God only as *attributes* (*ṣifāt*), any suggestion of a comparison (*tashbīh*) with creatures being excluded by the use of this carefully defined technical term. Al-Barbahārī, on the other hand, had asserted more bluntly that merely to discuss (*al-kalām fī*) the Lord is innovation and error, and that to ask *how* (*kayfa*) or *why* (*li-*

---

[88] Koran 20:7. Our translation, based on Arberry.

[89] Cf. Koran 2:245.

[90] *Al-Sharḥ wa-l-ibāna,* Arabic, p. 51, French, pp. 87–88. Cf. al-Barbahārī in Ibn Abī Yaᶜlā, *Ṭabaqāt al-Ḥanābila,* II, p. 19.

[91] *Muᶜtaqad,* in *Sīrat,* pp. 288–90.

[92] Cf., e.g., Koran 5:64.

[93] Allard, *Attributs divins,* passim, esp. pp. 255, 192 (citing al-Dārimī, *Kitāb al-radd ᶜalā l-ǧahmīya,* ed. Gösta Vitestam [Lund and Leiden: C. W. K. Gleerup and E. J. Brill, 1960], pp. 31–45, where *ḥadīths* on God's descent—not a Koranic doctrine—are collected). Cf. also on God's descent the *ḥadīth* in Ibn Māja, *Sunan, Iqāma,* no. 1389, and the traditions cited in Zaghlūl, *Mawsūᶜat aṭrāf al-ḥadīth,* III, p. 236. The problem of what to do with texts that suggest that God moves or occupies place is more commonly taken up in connection with the Koranic declarations that God seated himself upon the throne after completing his creation (7:54, 10:3, and other places), declarations for which the Muᶜtazilites suggested various allegorical interpretations. See, e.g., al-Ashᶜarī, *Maqālāt,* I, pp. 157, 210–15, esp. p. 215 on God's descent.

ma) with respect to the divine attributes is to doubt God himself.[94]

Another aspect in which Ibn Khafīf's *Minor Creed* differs from the creeds of the Ḥanbalites can be seen in the mystic's treatment of human accountability and the care he takes to stress that man's "acquisition" (*iktisāb*) of responsibility for his acts is God's creation (*khalq*), not man's. On the question of human responsibility, the mystic follows the fine line of Ashᶜarite acquisition (*kasb*) between the doctrines of free will and predestination. All human acts are willed by God. Sins, however, although willed by God (*bi-murādihi*), are not in accordance with his good pleasure (*riḍā*).[95] God being the creator of all acts, it is only the "acquisition" of them in the moral sense that belongs to man. But also this acquisition is God's creation, not man's.[96] Ibn Khafīf's apology here is meant to support rather than to assail the scripturalist-Ḥanbalite doctrine of the divine omnipotence (*qadar*), which allows little effective room for human will or creative power.[97] It is aimed against Muᶜtazilite notions of free will,[98] and in its insistence on God's being the "creator" of man's acquisition of moral responsibility for his acts it would seem to be directed at al-Jubbāʾī (d. 303/915–16) in particular.[99] But the concerns and the language of Ibn Khafīf are other than those of the strict Ḥanbalites, who are uninterested in the lexicographical details of how moral responsibility is acquired. When Ibn Baṭṭa, for example, speaks of "acquisition" or *kasb*, he is using the term in the everyday sense of "earning a living," in which meaning the word is also common in doctrinal literature.[100]

---

94 Ibn Abī Yaᶜlā, *Ṭabaqāt al-Ḥanābila,* II, p. 19. Cf. Laoust's comments in Ibn Baṭṭa, *al-Sharḥ wa-l-ibāna,* French, p. 87, n. 1.

95 *Muᶜtaqad,* in *Sīrat,* p. 290.

96 Ibid., p. 292. The corollary view that it is not reason but only divine law that determines which acts are good and which reprehensible is also affirmed in the *Muᶜtaqad* (ibid., p. 302).

97 Cf. Ibn Baṭṭa, *al-Sharḥ wa-l-ibāna,* Arabic, pp. 52–53, French, pp. 90–93, especially Laoust's notes.

98 On the Muᶜtazilite influence at the Buwayhid court in Shiraz, see Sobieroj, "Ibn Ḫafīf aš-Šīrāzī," pp. 173–74.

99 The majority of the Muᶜtazilites did not admit that man could properly be spoken of as "creating." On al-Jubbāʾī, see L. Gardet in *EI²,* II, pp. 569b–70b, s.v. "al-Djubbāʾī, Abū ᶜAlī Muḥammad b. ᶜAbd al-Wahhāb." For an example of al-Jubbāʾī's view of man as "creator," see al-Ashᶜarī, *Maqālāt,* I, p. 195.

100 *Al-Sharḥ wa-l-ibāna,* Arabic, p. 88, French, pp. 160–61. Al-Barbahārī's creed mentions acquisition (*iktisāb*) of intellect, the possibility of which it denies, saying that each person is born with that portion of intellect God has

Aspects of mystical doctrine. In his mystical doctrine Ibn Khafīf acknowledged the subordination of mysticism to revealed religion. This is inferred by his affirmation in the *Minor Creed* that the rank of prophet is higher than that of saint and that prophethood cannot be attained through deeds.[101] But submission to the revealed law must be balanced by a commitment to spiritual or esoteric reality. While Ibn Khafīf's Sufism places particular stress on asceticism, fasting, and frequent prayer, as Schimmel has pointed out,[102] the *Minor Creed* makes it clear that Sufism is attainable neither by works nor through exoteric knowledge. It is not the same as spiritual poverty or asceticism (*faqr*), nor is it to be equated with piety (*taqwā*). The world of the mystic is another. He "may be transported through the various states (*aḥwāl*) until he reaches a degree of spirituality that allows him to see the unknown, to cover great distances in a single step, to walk upon water, and to disappear from people's view."[103]

Along the path await perilous states such as spiritual intoxication (*sukr*), which may be tolerated in a novice (*murīd*) but is beneath the level of the spiritually advanced. Sobriety and clarity of mind (*ṣaḥw*) are to be preferred to intoxication.[104] Ecstasy (*wajd*) is a higher state than the intoxication of the novices. The true ecstatic is preserved from unbelief and depravity when he is in this state, though he may not always observe the obligations of the religious law (*wājibāt*). When he comes to himself, he will return to their observance, but if he remains in his ec-

---

granted him (Ibn Abī Yaᶜlā, *Ṭabaqāt al-Ḥanābila,* II, p. 26). The Ashᶜarite doctrine of acquisition belongs to an occasionalist system from which secondary causes have been banned in order to ensure the total liberty of God. This is precisely the aim of the scripturalist doctrine of God's omnipotence (*qadar*). There is no room in either system for the commonsensical notion of causality, which is accordingly denied in Ibn Khafīf's *Minor Creed.* Things do not act upon other things by their nature. Bread does not satisfy hunger, rather it is God who produces satisfaction in the eater when he eats. Similarly, whereas it is the killer who kills, death comes from God (*Muᶜtaqad,* in *Sīrat,* pp. 292–93). The theodicy of Ibn Khafīf's *Minor Creed* is similar. God saves or damns whom he will *for no cause,* yet no injustice may be attributed to him (ibid., p. 291). One must affirm, on the positive side, that it is only by God's grace and mercy, not by means of his own deeds, that a man can enter Paradise; but one may not say that God forces anyone to sin (ibid., p. 299).

[101] *Muᶜtaqad,* in *Sīrat,* p. 303. For a detailed analysis of Ibn Khafīf's mystical doctrine, see Sobieroj, "Ibn Ḫafīf aš-Šīrāzī," pp. 229–64.

[102] *Sīrat,* intro., pp. 34–36, 41–42; cf. Sobieroj, "Ibn Ḫafīf aš-Šīrāzī," pp. 252–54.

[103] *Muᶜtaqad,* in *Sīrat,* p. 304.

[104] Ibid., pp. 304–5. Cf. *Sīrat,* intro., p. 29 on *ḥuḍūr* and *ghayba.*

stasy, he is to be excused.[105]

Two methods adopted by a number of mystics for inducing ecstasy were listening to music—the "spiritual concert" (*samāᶜ*)—and gazing at a beautiful object (*naẓar*), on occasion among some controversial mystics a comely, still beardless youth. The two methods could in practice be combined into one by engaging a good-looking singer. Ibn Khafīf speaks out strongly against the spiritual concert in his *Major Creed,* and he censures gazing by implication in the same work when he affirms that God does not indwell in visible things. He likewise protests indignantly against an assertion he attributes to al-Ṭabarī to the effect that Sufis in general claim it is possible to see God in this world.[106] Even if one assumes that the *Major Creed* is an early work and represents a somewhat more conservative position than Ibn Khafīf held in his later years, there is nothing in the mystic's other extant writings to suggest that he substantially altered his view on these two questions.

Ibn Khafīf had been introduced to the spiritual concert in the circle of his first master, Aḥmad b. Yaḥyā, and had thus been aware of its dangers from his youth. He continued to be witness to the perils of the practice throughout his life. A friend of his with ecstatic tendencies, Abū Bakr Ushnānī, fell off a roof and was killed while in a state of ecstasy brought on by listening to a singer with a pretty face and an exceedingly beautiful voice. It is worth noting that Ibn Khafīf reportedly pretended not to know that the concert at which this happened was to take place and purposely stayed away.[107] Again, the premature death of his student al-Bayṭār, while recovering from an illness in 363/974, was apparently the result of a relapse brought on by the excitement he had experienced on hearing a singer.[108] Ibn Khafīf had presumably formed his opinion on the practice long before these casualties occurred.[109] The text of the *Minor Creed,* in any event, reflects an assessment of the spiritual concert that may well be

---

105 *Muᶜtaqad,* in *Sīrat,* p. 306.

106 Ibn Taymīya, *al-Fatwā al-Ḥamawīya al-kubrā,* pp. 49–50, 46–47.

107 *Sīrat,* pp. 157, 109, intro., p. 43. The addition cited by Schimmel to the effect that Ibn Khafīf later had the singer repeat the verses he had sung and himself went into a trance for (four) days and thus knew nothing of Ushnānī's burial is not from al-Daylamī's biography but is based on al-Anṣārī's *Ṭabaqāt al-ṣūfīya* and Jāmī's *Nafaḥāt al-uns,* which are later sources (*Sīrat,* p. 157n).

108 Junayd Shīrāzī, *Shadd al-izār,* p. 105.

109 One of Ibn Khafīf's teachers, Abū ᵓl-Ḥusayn al-Darrāj, died during a spiritual concert in 320/932, but this was most likely also after Ibn Khafīf had formed his opinion on the practice. See Sobieroj, "Ibn Ḫafīf aš-Šīrāzī," pp. 61, 153.

based on the author's experience. The practice is allowable for the spiritually advanced, but it is wrong for novices. Because of its many hazards, it should best be avoided altogether.[110]

Regarding Ibn Khafīf's opinion of the practice of gazing we are less well informed, but it is unlikely that he was more lenient towards it than towards the spiritual concert. He warns novices to avoid "looking at (*al-naẓar ilā*) those who deck themselves out, pretending to be dervishes and wearing patched robes, those beggars who refuse to work and make a profession of dancing and capering like catamites."[111] This warning, very likely, although not necessarily, reflects disapproval of most or all forms of ritual gazing and dancing. It is essentially the view expressed in the *Major Creed.* If any contradiction or paradox is to be found, it is not in the teaching of Ibn Khafīf, but in the extent to which the spiritual concert, dancing, and perhaps gazing seem to have gone on in circles fairly close to the spiritual master of Shiraz, and in the sophistication with which one of his disciples set forth a theory that may be related to the last of these practices.

That we do not know more about al-Daylamī's reaction to the recorded views of Ibn Khafīf on gazing is unfortunate, as chapter twenty of al-Daylamī's treatise on love, on the meaning of the word *shāhid* ("witness," contextually: "token of the divine beauty") constitutes one of the most important theoretical passages on the question of the contemplation of divine beauty through physical manifestation that have come down to us. Al-Daylamī does not explicitly link his thoughts in this chapter to the mystical practice of gazing, and it is possible that the primary reason he included the chapter in the *ᶜAṭf,* despite its coming near the end of the work, was to complement the theory of beauty he outlines in chapter three as an introduction to his observations on love. On the other hand,

---

[110] *Muᶜtaqad,* in *Sīrat,* p. 306. Cf. Sobieroj, "Ibn Ḫafīf aš-Šīrāzī," pp. 153–54, for a more detailed exposition of this view of Ibn Khafīf's on *samāᶜ*.

[111] *Kitāb al-iqtiṣād,* section 38, in Sobieroj, "Ibn Ḫafīf aš-Šīrāzī," Arabic, p. 32, German, p. 336. Our translation here is somewhat freer than Sobieroj's. A similar stricture against attending gatherings at which there is dancing is found in section 39, Arabic, p. 33, German, p. 338. Both passages are cited by Sobieroj in his discussion of *samāᶜ* (see preceding note). The various references recorded by Sobieroj in his discussion of Ibn Khafīf's teachers to associating with or looking at young boys and to seeing God in this life are not sufficient to give a complete picture of the mystic's opinion on gazing. In any event, they do not point in a different direction than the information cited here. Cf. "Ibn Ḫafīf aš-Šīrāzī," pp. 63 (Darrāj), 68 (Muʾammil), 71 (Hishām b. ᶜAbdān), and 90 (Abū ʾl-Adyān).

al-Daylamī's silence regarding the context of his remarks concerning the word *shāhid* may possibly be explained by the rigor of the attacks against mystical gazing. These often involved accusations of pederasty, suspicions of which the practice of gazing at beardless youths inevitably aroused.[112] It is difficult to escape the conclusion that al-Daylamī was aware of the relevance of his remarks to the practice, although it is unlikely that it was allowed in the immediate entourage of his master Ibn Khafīf. There can be no doubt, in any event, that al-Daylamī in principle approved the contemplation of beauty as a means to spiritual advancement. He makes this clear in chapter three of the *ᶜAṭf:*

> Since the lover, on the other hand, is a perceiver of beauty, [loving] according to the proper conditions of love as we have mentioned, namely the avoidance of vitiating accidents, he is also one who draws lessons from the evidence God has shown forth in this world. And one who draws such lessons is unanimously praised by the Book, the Sunna, and the consensus of the community. Let this be understood.[113]

According to both of Ibn Khafīf's creeds, and in agreement with the standard doctrine of the Ḥanbalite scripturalists and that of al-Ashᶜarī, believers will see God on the Day of Resurrection, but in this life the beatific vision does not occur.[114] While the *Major Creed* states that God cannot be seen with men's eyes in this world and that he does not indwell (*yaḥull*) in visible beings,[115] the *Minor Creed* stresses that nothing in the world of contingency can serve as a locus (*maḥall*) for God's indwelling. "He does not indwell (*lā ḥāll*) in things, nor do things indwell in him. He does not manifest himself in any thing, nor has he veiled himself in contingent being."[116] The reference, as Ibn Khafīf's use of the words *yaḥull, maḥall,* and *ḥāll* indicate, is to the doctrines that go

---

[112] See chapter twenty, n. 1.

[113] MS, pp. 27–28.

[114] *Muᶜtaqad,* in *Sīrat,* pp. 290, 303; see also *Sīrat,* intro., p. 28. Cf. Ibn Abī Yaᶜlā, *Ṭabaqāt al-Ḥanābila,* II, pp. 20, 23; Ibn Baṭṭa, *al-Sharḥ wa-l-ibāna,* Arabic, p. 51, French, pp. 89–90, 102, and nn.; and al-Ashᶜarī, *Maqālāt,* I, pp. 292–93. In this controversy the scripturalists based their position on Koran 75:22–23: "Upon that day faces shall be radiant, gazing upon their Lord." The Muᶜtazilites founded their argument on Koran 6:103: "The eyes attain him not, but he attains the eyes." Cf. Allard, *Attributs divins,* pp. 246–47, 264–65. Ibn Khafīf, in fact, uses the term *muḥāl* (impossible) of the beatific vision in this life (*Muᶜtaqad,* p. 303), but by this he presumably meant that it "never occurs" and that whoever lays claim to it is a liar, rather than that it is impossible for God to produce.

[115] Ibn Taymīya, *al-Fatwā al-Ḥamawīya al-kubrā,* p. 47.

[116] *Muᶜtaqad,* in *Sīrat,* pp. 286.

under the name *ḥulūl,* namely, the Christian doctrine of incarnation and the views of some Muslim mystics on divine indwelling or substantial union with God. Thus, although neither the *Minor Creed* nor the *Major Creed* takes up the question of gazing directly, neither leaves room for a theory of the practice that asserts the possibility of a substantial manifestation of the divine in the object of contemplation.

On the other hand, there is no reason to assume that Ibn Khafīf opposed the contemplation of the beautiful as a *reminder* of the divine. Schimmel mentions as evidence for the sheikh's view on looking or gazing his statement that the spirit takes pleasure in three things: a sweet smell, a beautiful voice, and looking (*naẓar*).[117] Alone this pronouncement may not be of much help, and in any case it cannot be taken to mean that Ibn Khafīf allowed looking at beloved persons other than those normally permitted (wives, concubines, immediate family). But we know that al-Daylamī himself made use of the same theme when describing the exclusive remembrance of the beloved that is a sign of man's love for God:

> Moreover, a lover does not perceive with his senses anything other than his beloved when he is together with him and unencumbered by division, for he himself has become his beloved in togetherness. Thus, if he sees something beautiful, it becomes one of the beloved's visible signs, if he hears something pleasant, it becomes a report about him, and if he smells something fragrant, it becomes a trace of him.[118]

Going further with the idea of the "trace" (*athar*) of the divine revealed in the beautiful, al-Daylamī, in his chapter on the meaning of the word *shāhid,* approaches the limits set by his master's creeds, but stays well within them. His boldest statements regarding the "tokens of divine beauty" are that "the beauty that a work acquires through the skill of its maker is *something from the artisan himself, . . .* something he has given it," and that "when you see in something a manifest beauty, this tells you . . . that it has been present at the scene of the universal beauty and has acquired from it a *clear trace."* [119]

The word *ḥulūl* was often used more or less synonymously with *ittiḥād,* the more specific term for mystical union.[120] What was meant by words like these and how they were to be used was a highly sensitive issue in mystical circles. One of the most damaging accusations against

---

[117] Cf. *Sīrat,* p. 214, intro., p. 31.

[118] MS, p. 207.

[119] MS, pp. 231, 233. Emphasis here ours.

[120] See L. Massignon/G. C. Anawati in *EI²,* III, pp. 570b–71b, s.v. "Ḥulūl."

al-Ḥallāj had been that he had claimed substantial union with the godhead. Ibn Khafīf insists on the absolute transcendence of God, and it is in this context that he denies the possibility of the divine inhabiting any created form. Textual evidence to suggest that it was he who influenced his disciple al-Daylamī to preserve and to some extent to incorporate the ideas of al-Ḥallāj on love, the *via unitiva,* is lacking. We have a report in which Ibn Khafīf is said to have defined another term for union, *wuṣla,* as "being joined together (*ittaṣala)* with the beloved to the exclusion of all else and forsaking everything but him."[121] But the noun *wuṣla* and the verb *ittaṣala* do not imply union of natures or indwelling. For the equivocal terms *ittaḥada* and *ittiḥād,* which can denote either of these two meanings or can simply mean the same as *wuṣla* and *ittaṣala,*[122] we know of no definition ascribed to Ibn Khafīf. In any event, the hypothesis that he might have given a favorable definition of *ittiḥād* is difficult to reconcile with the other texts we have from him. Al-Daylamī, notwithstanding the considerable influence of al-Ḥallāj on his thought, is presumably giving utterance to the view of Ibn Khafīf on union when he denounces in the *ᶜAṭf* those who express the culmination of mystical experience as an identity of natures.[123]

Views of Ibn Khafīf in the Sources

Despite his apparent sympathy for al-Ḥallāj, Ibn Khafīf is usually described in both primary and secondary sources as an orthodox mystic faithful to the revealed law.[124] The precepts set forth in his two creeds tally with this description, and while we have made only a cursory examination of the reports in the *Sīrat,* there is nothing in al-Daylamī's *ᶜAṭf al-alif* to suggest the image is false. For the record, however, it should be noted that there were some who did not share the general view of Ibn Khafīf as a staunch advocate of orthodox practice.

While the noted Ḥanbalite scholar Ibn Taymīya, as we have seen, elected to cite the mystic in support of his conservative views,[125] the ear-

---

[121] *Sīrat,* intro., p. 30, appendix, p. 273, citing al-Subkī (*Ṭabaqāt al-Shāfiᶜīya,* II, p. 154) and others.

[122] See R. Nicholson/G. C. Anawati in *EI²,* IV, pp. 282b–83b, s.v. "Ittiḥād."

[123] MS, p. 108: "This group says, 'We are God, and God is we.' But God is far too exalted and glorious for this to be the case." The concluding comment may be part of a longer quotation from Abū Saᶜīd b. al-Aᶜrābī, but al-Daylamī could have suppressed it had he wished.

[124] See, for example, the remarks by his elder contemporary Jaᶜfar al-Khuldī (ca. 252/866–348/959) (*Shadd al-izār,* p. 39); also Sezgin, *GAS,* I, p. 663.

[125] See pp. xxx–xxxi and n. 78 above.

lier Ḥanbalite Ibn al-Jawzī (510/1126–597/1200), who was the author of one of the major sources of biographical information on Muslim mystics, was among those who doubted Ibn Khafīf's orthodox credentials. "Ibn Khafīf is not a trustworthy narrator," he asserts, commenting in his *Talbīs Iblīs* on what he considers a suspect report that has Ibn Khafīf in its chain of narrators.[126] Further on in the same work he quotes a report from the judge Abū ᶜAlī al-Muḥassin b. ᶜAlī al-Tanūkhī (329/940–384/994) in which Ibn Khafīf is accused of sanctioning orgies among his followers.[127] The report, which Ibn al-Jawzī says is confirmed by an *isnād* going back to the judge through his son, is found in virtually identical form in al-Tanūkhī's *Nishwār al-muḥāḍara.*[128] The judge had it from a number of scholarly sources that in Shiraz the master of the Sufis was a shrewd and clever man known as Ibn Khafīf al-Baghdādī. His circle was attended by thousands, and he had enticed many into the Sufi sect. The following was told of him:

> A certain man among them, who was one of his companions, died, leaving behind him a wife who was also a Sufi. The Sufi women, of whom there were a great many, met together, and no one except them attended their funeral ceremony. When they had finished burying the man, Ibn Khafīf and the elite among his companions, who were many in number, came into the house and began to give their condolences to the woman after the manner of the Sufis. At length she said, "I am consoled." Ibn Khafīf then said to her, "Is there anyone else here?" "No one else," she answered. Whereupon he said, "Why should we burden our souls with the plague of sorrow and torment them with the pain of care? Why should we not mingle, so that lights may come together and spirits may be serene, so that [God's] recompense may occur and his blessings descend." [The narrator] continued: The women said, "If you wish." [The narrator] said: So the men mixed with the women the entire night and left just before dawn.

Al-Tanūkhī interpreted Ibn Khafīf's question "Is there anyone else here?" to mean: Is there anyone here who is not in agreement with our sect? The term "mingle" (*imtizāj*), which along with the word "lights" (*anwār*) is an obvious play on Sufi vocabulary, he took to denote copulation. "[God's] recompense" he understood as referring to surrogates for the women's departed or absent husbands.

Allegations of sexual immorality are a commonplace in the polemical literature against Sufism. Al-Tanūkhī, possibly with this fact in mind, states that he would not have related the report of such an enormity had

[126] *Talbīs Iblīs,* p. 334.

[127] Ibid., pp. 369–70.

[128] al-Tanūkhī, *Nishwār al-muḥāḍara,* III, pp. 228–29.

his informants not been people whose word in his opinion was beyond suspicion. (Since this remark is itself a commonplace, the judge's documentation is of course left open to the same suspicion as his charge.) Al-Tanūkhī adds that the incident mentioned in the report, as well as similar things, had become such common knowledge in Shiraz that the Buwayhid ruler, ᶜAḍud al-Dawla, had had a group of Ibn Khafīf's followers arrested and flogged, after which they had desisted.

Without trying to unravel truth from falsehood in al-Tanūkhī's accusation,[129] we can at least infer the likelihood of some troubles between Ibn Khafīf's followers in Shiraz and the authorities. Al-Tanūkhī, who was a contemporary of al-Daylamī, was well positioned to know what was happening in Fārs. He was close to ᶜAḍud al-Dawla (d. 372/983), who had inherited the rule of Fārs in 338/944 from his father Rukn al-Dawla (al-Ḥasan) and had also gained control of Iraq by 366/977. Although the relationship was not without turbulence, al-Tanūkhī seems to have spent much time in the company of the Buwayhid prince, and he served as a go-between between him and the caliph al-Ṭāᵓiᶜ in the matter of the latter's marriage with ᶜAḍud al-Dawla's daughter. This task involved a trip to Shiraz in 369/979, about two years before the death of Ibn Khafīf.[130] Sobieroj suggests that the troubles to which al-Tanūkhī refers between the Sufis of Shiraz and the authorities occurred in the context of the quelling of the unrest that took place in the city that year by the judge Bishr b. Ḥusayn.[131] It could be at this time that al-Tanūkhī heard the reports about Ibn Khafīf and his followers. But the report concerning the mystic's alleged immorality, which is based on second-hand information and suggests little personal knowledge of Ibn Khafīf ("I have been informed . . . that in Shiraz there is a man named Ibn Khafīf al-Baghdadī"), may conceivably have been recorded some years before al-Tanūkhī became involved with ᶜAḍud al-Dawla. In any event, al-Tanūkhī presumably heard it while he was still working on his *Nishwār al-muḥāḍara,* which is said to have been begun in 360 and completed twenty years later. No reason for personal enmity on the part of al-

[129] Sobieroj considers this report, which unquestionably presents a picture of Ibn Khafīf that is very different from that found in most other sources, to be a fabrication ("Ibn Ḫafīf aš-Šīrāzī," pp. 17–18, 160). While this assessment is almost certainly correct, it is at least conceivable that the story represents an exaggeration or embellishment rather than an outright fabrication.

[130] Cf. R. Paret in *EI¹*, VIII, pp. 655b–56a, s.v. "al-Tanūkhī," Brockelmann, *GAL,* I, pp. 161–62, *S,* I, pp. 252–53, and Yāqūt, *Muᶜjam al-udabāᵓ*, XVII, pp. 92–116. On ᶜAḍud al-Dawla, see H. Bowen in *EI²,* I, pp. 211b–12b, s.v.

[131] Sobieroj, "Ibn Ḫafīf aš-Šīrāzī," p. 160.

Tanūkhī against Ibn Khafīf has come to our attention, but the judge lived in an environment in which intrigue and personal rivalries were everyday fare. Moreover, his attack on the mystic, who was opposed to Muᶜtazilism, may be a reflection of his doctrinal leanings, which were presumably Muᶜtazilite, and at best skeptical towards Sufism.[132]

Followers

In the first generation of a teacher's disciples it is often difficult to determine what kind of contact and what degree of attachment or sympathy is to be associated with being numbered among his students. Thus Ibn Abī Yaᶜlā's inventory of the first generation of narrators from Aḥmad b. Ḥanbal includes not only the mystic al-Junayd, of whose master al-Ḥārith al-Muḥāsibī Ibn Ḥanbal had said, "Beware of al-Ḥārith, for he is the source of affliction,"[133] but also the imam Muḥammad b. Idrīs al-Shāfiᶜī.[134] No such exhaustive catalogue of those who heard Ibn Khafīf has come down to us, although much information is available in the *Sīrat* and later biographical works. As one might expect, the kind of relationship many who are named as his students actually had with him is unclear.

By far the most comprehensive treatment of the followers of Ibn Khafīf and those who narrated material from him is that given by Sobieroj in his "Ibn Ḫafīf aš-Šīrāzī und seine Schrift zur Novizenerziehung (Kitāb al-Iqtiṣād)."[135] Sobieroj, drawing on al-Daylamī's *Sīrat* and a wide range of other sources, has established a list of forty-eight persons who were in some way directly dependent on Ibn Khafīf. These he divides into two main groups: those who narrated material directly from Ibn Khafīf, but who cannot be considered his students, and his immediate disciples. The latter group he further divides into four sub-groups: (1) an outer circle, (2) an inner circle, (3) mystics who constituted a link

[132] Cf. ibid., p. 161, also p. 18. Muᶜtazilism was probably a family tradition. Ibn Khallikān mentions that al-Tanūkhī's father, Abū ᵓl-Qāsim ᶜAlī b. Muḥammad (d. 342/953), was a Muᶜtazilite (*Wafayāt al-aᶜyān,* III, pp. 48, 51). Cf. also al-Tanūkhī's poem, recorded by Ibn Khallikān, on how a certain sheikh had prayed for rain on a cloudy day and the skies had cleared before he finished praying (ibid., p. 302).

[133] Ibn al-Jawzī, *Talbīs Iblīs,* p. 167.

[134] Ibn Abī Yaᶜlā, *Ṭabaqāt al-Ḥanābila,* I, pp. 227–28, 280–84.

[135] "Ibn Ḫafīf aš-Šīrāzī," pp. 187–213. Unless otherwise noted, the material from the next paragraphs is from this source. Schimmel pointed earlier to some of the significant figures who derived material from Ibn Khafīf (*Sīrat,* intro., p. 22).

between Ibn Khafīf and Abū Isḥāq al-Kāzarūnī (d. 426/1034), and (4) others, the nature and extent of whose relationship to the master is difficult to determine. In addition, Sobieroj mentions a number of indirect disciples of the sheikh.

Those who narrated directly from Ibn Khafīf include the renowned Sufi authors Abū ᶜAbd al-Raḥmān al-Sulamī (d. 412/1021–22), who says of the reports he has from Ibn Khafīf in his *Ṭabaqāt al-ṣūfīya* that he received them all from the mystic himself with written permission to transmit them,[136] and Abū Nuᶜaym al-Iṣfahānī (336/948?–430/1038), compiler of the voluminous mystical biographical work *Ḥilyat al-awliyāʾ,*[137] who also had a written *ijāza* for the material he relates from Ibn Khafīf. In addition, the celebrated Ashᶜarite theologian al-Bāqillānī (d. 403/1013), who had come to Shiraz at the invitation of ᶜAḍud al-Dawla and met Ibn Khafīf in the period between 369/979–80 and 371/981–82, is cited as an authority for the story of Ibn Khafīf's meeting with al-Ashᶜarī.[138] The outer circle of the mystic's students included Abū Naṣr al-Sarrāj al-Ṭūsī (d. 378/988), author of the *Kitāb al-lumaᶜ,*[139] Ibn Bākūya (Bākawayh) (d. 428/1036–37), familiar to those interested in al-Ḥallāj for the material he related on him in his *Bidāyat ḥāl al-Ḥallāj,*[140] and Abū ʾl-Ḥasan ᶜAlī b. Bakrān al-Shīrāzī, the first narrator mentioned on the title page of al-Daylamī's *ᶜAṭf.*[141] The inner circle of disciples, that of Ibn Khafīf's personal servants (those given the name *khādim*), consisted of figures like Abū Aḥmad al-Kabīr (d. 377/987–88)

---

[136] *Ṭabaqāt al-ṣūfīya* (ed. Pedersen), p. 490.

[137] *Ḥilya,* X, p. 385.

[138] Sobieroj, "Ibn Ḫafīf aš-Šīrāzī," pp. 195–96. On al-Bāqillānī's visit to Shiraz in 370/980–81 or 371/982 and the personal welcome given him by Ibn Khafīf, see ibid., pp. 161–62. The visit occurred shortly before the death of Ibn Khafīf in 371 and that of ᶜAḍud al-Dawla about a year later. Cf. also Sezgin, *GAS,* I, p. 608.

[139] Al-Daylamī relates from Abū Naṣr al-Ṭūsī, apparently directly, the report of the death of Ibn Khafīf's son ᶜAbd al-Salām and a report in which al-Ṭūsī describes himself as present in the sheikh's circle or as being together with him (*Sīrat,* pp. 37–38, 204–5). We have in addition al-Daylamī's statement in the *Shadd al-izār* that he himself had been together with al-Ṭūsī (cf. n. 6 above; *Sīrat,* appendix, p. 222).

[140] On Ibn Bākūya, who is responsible for much information on the process against al-Ḥallāj, see *Shadd al-izār,* pp. 380–84 and 380, n. 3. Ibn Bākūya is also the authority for much of Ibn ᶜAsākir's material in his biographical notice on Ibn Khafīf. Cf. *Taʾrīkh madinat Dimashq,* XV, pp. 291–301.

[141] See below, pp. lxv–lxvi.

and Abū Aḥmad al-Ṣaghīr (d. 384/994 or 385/995).[142] Of the intermediaries between Ibn Khafīf and al-Kāzarūnī, the most significant seems to have been Abū ᶜAlī al-Ḥusayn b. Muḥammad al-Akkār (d. 391/1000–1), who is credited with having passed on the patched robe of Sufism from the great master in Shiraz to al-Kāzarūnī.[143]

Among the various other followers of Ibn Khafīf, Sobieroj numbers Muḥammad b. ᶜAbd al-Raḥmān al-Maqārīḍī (d. 411/1020–21), founder of a Sufi line in Shiraz that derived its authority from Ibn Khafīf, and al-Maqārīḍī's son ᶜAbd al-Salām (d. 424/1032–33). To this line belonged Abū Shujāᶜ Muḥammad b. Saᶜdān al-Maqārīḍī, the second transmitter named on the title page of the *ᶜAṭf.*[144] Also into this group fall two figures characterized by their broad education and their universal curiosity, Abū ᶜAbd Allāh al-Bayṭār[145] and our author ᶜAlī b. Muḥammad al-Daylamī. It may be surprising to find the student and biographer of Ibn Khafīf placed outside the inner circle of his followers. But since the reports on the last period of Ibn Khafīf's life are not related by al-Daylamī on his own authority, Sobieroj reasons that al-Daylamī may have left Ibn Khafīf before his death and collected the reports on his master's latter years on a return trip to Shiraz.[146] Al-Daylamī's statement that he observed Ibn Khafīf's "servant" Abū Aḥmad al-Kabīr for some twenty-five years—from about 352 to 377, when Abū Aḥmad died (some six years after Ibn Khafīf's demise), if the information on which our reckoning is based is correct[147]—would not seem to be consonant with the theory of a long absence from Shiraz on al-Daylamī's part in the latter part of Ibn Khafīf's life. But Sobieroj's argument, taken together with the suspicions he has raised regarding al-Daylamī's reliability in reporting his teacher's views on al-Ḥallāj,[148] make it difficult to conclude with any certainty that our author belonged to the inner circle of Ibn Khafīf's disciples.

Ibn Khafīf is often referred to by his later followers in Shiraz simply

---

142 Cf. pp. xii–xiv and nn. 6, 8 above.

143 See Maḥmūd b. ᶜUthmān. *Firdaws al-murshidīya* (ed. Fritz Meier), intro., pp. 18–19.

144 See below, pp. lxv–lxvi.

145 See above, p. xix–xx and n. 25.

146 "Ibn Ḫafīf aš-Šīrāzī," p. 209. An example of al-Daylamī's collecting reports about Ibn Khafīf after his death is the story he relates from an Aḥmad b. Muḥammad, whom he calls a trustworthy authority (*thiqa amīn*), of a dream in which the latter beheld the departed Ibn Khafīf (Ibn ᶜAsākir, *Taʾrīkh madinat Dimashq,* XV, p. 296.

147 See n. 6.

148 See n. 159.

as *al-shaykh al-kabīr,* a title that recognizes in him the greatest master of the Shiraz line. His first followers seem to have formed themselves into a group known to al-Hujwīrī (d. between 465/1072 and 469/1077) as the Khafīfīya.[149] The *ribāṭ* or hospice that Ibn Khafīf founded was still in existence, as Vadet has remarked, in the time of Ibn al-Jawzī (d. 597/1200), and it presumably remained active long thereafter.[150] However the Khafīfīya order was soon after its founding to be absorbed into a larger grouping. The militant Sufi Abū Isḥāq Ibrāhīm b. Shahriyār al-Kāzarūnī (352/963–426/1034), who had been initiated into Ibn Khafīf's path by al-Akkār, had begun his proselytizing and charitable activity in Kāzarūn, not far from Shiraz, already as much as half a century before al-Hujwīrī recorded his remarks on the Khafīfīya in the *Kashf al-maḥjūb,* a work written most likely during the last years of the author's life.[151] The order al-Kāzarūnī founded, which is said to have established sixty-five hospices outside Kāzarūn before his death, and which was to spread west to Anatolia and east as far as India and China, apparently absorbed Ibn Khafīf's following. The abstruse ecstatic Rūzbihān Baqlī of Shiraz (522/1128–606/1209), who is of special interest here because of the extensive use he made of al-Daylamī's *ᶜAṭf al-alif* in his own works, was initiated into Ibn Khafīf's line by the Kāzarūnī sheikh Sirāj al-Dīn Maḥmūd b. Khalīfa b. ᶜAbd al-Salām b. Aḥmad b. Sālbih (Sāliba) (d. 562/1166–67).[152] Rūzbihān is said to have established a branch of the Kāzarūnīya, the Rūzbihānīya, that lasted for a little over a hundred years in Fārs. The Shiite Safavids suppressed the central hospice of the Kāzarūnīya at the beginning of the tenth/sixteenth century, and during the course of the following century the order largely died out in Anatolia.[153] Ibn Khafīf is named as a pivotal figure in the chain of succession of the present-day Uwaysīya order in Iran. The *silsila,* through Najm al-Dīn Kubrā (d. 618/1221), includes also, along with other successors of Ibn

---

[149] al-Hujwīrī, *Kashf al-maḥjūb,* ed. Zhukovskii, pp. 317–23, esp. p. 317; trans. Nicholson, pp. 247–51, esp. p. 247.

[150] Cf. Vadet, *EI*², III, p. 823a, s.v. "Ibn Khafīf," citing *Shadd al-izār,* p. 58. The *ribāṭ* must have remained active at least until the death of Sheikh Muᶜīn al-Dīn ᶜAbd Allāh b. al-Junayd (d. 651/1254), who apparently spent the last fifty years of his life close by it (*Shadd al-izār,* pp. 58–59).

[151] See Hidayet Hosain/H. Massé in *EI*², III, p. 546a, s.v. "Hudjwīrī."

[152] *Shadd al-izār,* pp. 244, 299–300. The comments of Junayd Shīrāzī, the author of *Shadd al-izār,* on Rūzbihān's complicated style (ibid., p. 244) confirm the impressions of modern readers of the mystic's writings.

[153] H. Algar in *EI*², IV, pp. 851a–52a, s.v. "Kāzarūnī." See on the Rūzbihānīya, Ernst, *Rūzbihān Baqlī,* pp. 111–41.

Khafīf, al-Akkār, al-Kāzarūnī, Ibn Sālbih, and Rūzbihān.[154]

Ibn Khafīf's Works on Love

Ibn Khafīf's first book was a youthful work on the "dignity of poverty" (*Kitāb sharaf al-faqr*). It had aroused such great admiration at a gathering of Sufi sheikhs, as he himself later admitted, that they had entreated him to act as their leader in prayer.[155] According to the *Sīrat,* Ibn Khafīf's long works (*taṣānīf-i muṭavval*), of which this was one, numbered in all fifteen titles, while his short works or digests (*mukhtaṣarāt*) likewise numbered fifteen. The various tracts, or "questions" (*masāʾil*), he had authored could not be numbered.[156]

One of Ibn Khafīf's tracts, according to the *ᶜAṭf,* dealt with the use of the controversial term *ᶜishq* to refer to love between God and man. Al-Daylamī tells us in chapter two of his treatise that his teacher had at first been opposed to this use of the term, but that he had changed his mind after coming across a tract (*masʾala*) on the question by al-Junayd and had himself composed a *masʾala* supporting the usage.[157] In his *Major Creed* (*Kitāb al-iᶜtiqād*), if the text cited by Ibn Taymīya is authentic, Ibn Khafīf clearly rejects the use of the word *ᶜishq* with reference to

---

154 ᶜAnqā Shāh Maqṣūd, *Min al-fikr al-ṣūfī al-īrānī al-muᶜāṣir* (Arabic trans. al-Sibāᶜī and Shitā), pp. 11–15.

155 *Sīrat,* p. 21.

156 *Sīrat,* p. 213. Only fourteen works in each of the first two categories are actually named by al-Daylamī in the *Sīrat* (pp. 212–13). The shorter list in the *Shadd* adds two titles, a *Kitāb sharḥ al-faḍāʾil* (p. 42) and a *Kitāb al-manhaj fī ʾl-fiqh* (p. 43). Ibn Khafīf's *Waṣīya* and his *Muᶜtaqad (= al-Muᶜtaqad al-ṣaghīr),* as mentioned above, have both been edited by Schimmel in the appendix to her edition of the *Sīrat* (see n. 70). This appendix also includes many valuable quotations from or about Ibn Khafīf (ibid., pp. 220–73). The longest of his surviving works, his manual for novices entitled *Kitāb al-iqtiṣād,* has been edited and translated by Sobieroj in his "Ibn Ḫafīf aš-Šīrāzī und seine Schrift zur Novizenerziehung (Kitāb al-Iqtiṣād)," Arabic, pp. 1–46, German, pp. 276–357. Sobieroj (ibid., pp. 19, 266) has also pointed out an excerpt from Ibn Khafīf's *Kitāb al-muᶜtaqad al-kabīr* in Ibn Taymīya's *al-Fatwā al-Ḥamawīya al-kubrā* (Beirut; Dār al-Kutub al-ᶜIlmīya, ca. 1984), pp. 42–50, and his *al-Asmāʾ wa-l-ṣifāt* (ed. Muṣṭafā ᶜAbd al-Qādir ᶜAṭā [Beirut, 1408/1988]), pp. 56–66. Ibn Taymīya refers to this work as "a book by Ibn Khafīf that he named *Iᶜtiqād al-tawḥīd bi-ithbāt al-asmāʾ wa-l-ṣifāt"* (*al-Fatwā al-Ḥamawīya al-kubrā,* p. 42), by which he presumably intends Ibn Khafīf's *Kitāb al-iᶜtiqād* mentioned by al-Daylamī in the *Sīrat* (p. 212). Cf. also, on Ibn Khafīf's works, Sezgin, *GAS,* I, p. 664.

157 MS, pp. 9–10.

God. The usage, which is without linguistic or scriptural justification, represents pure "innovation and error." There is no need to go beyond God's own words in the Koran, which refer to his love as *maḥabba* (or, more precisely, by means of forms of the root *ḥ-b-b.*)[158] If both al-Daylamī's statement about his master's change of heart regarding the word *ᶜishq* and the text quoted by Ibn Taymīya are to be accepted as they stand, we must conclude that the *Major Creed* was written before Ibn Khafīf came across the tract by al-Junayd on *ᶜishq.*[159] The apparent absence of Ashᶜarite influences in the work, moreover, whereas they are hardly disguised in the *Minor Creed,* would seem to render the idea that the *Major Creed* is an early work plausible. More information is needed, however, before this hypothesis can be taken beyond the realm of conjecture.

From the list of Ibn Khafīf's works given by al-Daylamī in the *Sīrat*

---

[158] Ibn Taymīya, *al-Fatwā al-Ḥamawīya al-kubrā,* p. 47.

[159] Sobieroj suggests that it is possible to doubt the accuracy of al-Daylamī's account of Ibn Khafīf's change of heart regarding the use of the word *ᶜishq* in the sacred context. He mentions as reasons (1) that the discussions of *ᶜishq* he describes as occurring close to the circle of Ibn Khafīf seem to have bypassed Ibn Khafīf himself, (2) that any such change of heart, if it occurred at a relatively late date in Ibn Khafīf's life, is inconsistent with the view that he was converted to Ḥallājian doctrines (such as the permissibility of using the word *ᶜishq*) when he witnessed the miracles performed by al-Ḥallāj in prison (some sixty years before he himself died), (3) that Ibn Khafīf consistently uses *maḥabba* rather than *ᶜishq* to denote religious love in the quotes we have from him on the subject, and (4) that in the quotation from his *Kitāb al-iᶜtiqād* recorded by Ibn Taymīya Ibn Khafīf unquestionably censures the use of the word *ᶜishq* for sacred love ("Ibn Ḫafīf aš-Šīrāzī," pp. 7, 144–48). The *mas'ala* on *ᶜishq,* by this reasoning, may never have existed. Since al-Daylamī, when he speaks of his master's change of heart, acknowledges that Ibn Khafīf had previously opposed the use of *ᶜishq,* the third and fourth points raised by Sobieroj do not necessarily conflict with his assertion. Regarding the second point, the narratives we have used of Ibn Khafīf's visiting al-Ḥallāj in prison suggest an attempt on his part to be objective, rather than an uncritical acceptance of al-Ḥallāj's views (see below, p. lii). He need not have been converted to al-Ḥallāj's (or, more precisely, al-Junayd's) opinion on the use of *ᶜishq* at this time. On Sobieroj's first point, that the discussions of *ᶜishq* bypassed Ibn Khafīf, we do not have the necessary evidence to exclude the possibility he raises. But it does not seem improbable to us that al-Daylamī's information on the views of the Damascus school regarding *ᶜishq* (on this he quotes Ibn Khafīf directly in MS, p. 71), as well, perhaps, as much of his material on *ᶜishq* from al-Junayd, is taken from a *mas'ala* composed by Ibn Khafīf on the subject.

we learn that he also composed a *Kitāb al-maḥabba* (Book on love) and a *Kitāb al-wudd wa-l-ulfa* (Book on fondness and closeness), both of which are classified by al-Daylamī as "digests" (*mukhtaṣarāt*).[160] Neither of these titles would seem to refer to the tract on *ᶜishq,* which apparently was a separate work. On the other hand, the *Kitāb al-wudd wa-l-ulfa* may be identical with the *masᵓala* on *wudd,* which Abū Saᶜīd b. al-Aᶜrābī, one of al-Daylamī's most important sources in the *ᶜAṭf,* is reported to have showed great interest in when Ibn Khafīf visited him in Mecca.[161]

As can be seen from the texts collected by Schimmel, the quotations from Ibn Khafīf in the biographical literature provide little to compensate for the loss of his works on love.[162] Of greatest interest perhaps, after the passages cited by Ibn Taymīya, is Ibn Khafīf's report of a session when he was studying *fiqh* under the Shāfiᶜite jurist Ibn Surayj at which his teacher brought up the question of whether love for God and his Prophet is a religious obligation. Ibn Khafīf quotes the texts he adduced in answer to the jurist's question to prove that love is indeed an obligation.[163] The texts he cites are more or less the standard ones. What is significant is that Ibn Khafīf was making clear his stance on a controversial theological issue, since by asserting that love is an obligation he was likewise asserting that it is possible for men to love God.[164]

---

[160] *Sīrat,* p. 213. The first of these two works is missing from the list of Ibn Khafīf's writings given in the *Shadd* (pp. 42–43), while the second is misspelled as *Kitāb al-radd wa-l-ulfa.*

[161] See n. 228 below.

[162] *Sīrat,* intro., pp. 29–30.

[163] Ibid., appendix, p. 258, citing Maḥmūd b. Sulaymān al-Kaffāwī (d. 990/1582), *Katāᵓib aᶜlām al-akhyār* (İstanbul Üniversite Kütüphanesi 3216), fol. 111b, and al-Dhahabī, *Taᵓrīkh al-Islām* (Ayasofya 3008), III, fol. 114a. The texts cited by Ibn Khafīf are Koran 9:24: "Say: 'If your fathers, your sons, your brothers, your wives, your clan, your possessions that you have gained, commerce you fear may slacken, dwellings you love—if these are dearer to you than God and his Messenger, and to struggle in his way, then wait till God brings his command; God guides not the people of the ungodly'" (trans. Arberry), and the saying of the Prophet, "No one of you can be a believer until I am more beloved to him than himself, the members of his household, his property, his children, and all mankind." (Forms of this *ḥadīth,* with some variation in wording are to be found in a variety of sources, including al-Bukhārī and Muslim. See Zaghlūl, *Mawsūᶜat aṭrāf al-ḥadīth,* VII, p. 312.) Al-Daylamī cites the argument, without the *ḥadīth,* in chapters six (MS, p. 97) and fifteen (MS, p. 197) of the *ᶜAṭf.*

[164] Fundamental objections raised against the idea that men can love God in any true sense were (1) that love is based on a similarity between lover and beloved and (2) that love, being in the definition of many speculative theologians

The most important information we have on Ibn Khafīf's views on the subject of love are provided by al-Daylamī in the *ᶜAtf.* The mystic is first cited in the treatise in the passage mentioned above concerning the permissibility of using the word *ᶜishq* in speaking of love between God and man. Next he is quoted on the derivation of the word *ḥubb,* which he takes to be derived from God's attribute of love mentioned in the Koran,[165] and then on the lexicographic distinction between love (*maḥabba*) and bosom friendship (*khulla*).[166] Later he is cited in the chapter on the origin of love and eros (chapter five), first quoting the followers of the mystic ᶜAbd al-Wāḥid b. Zayd in Damascus to the effect that *ᶜishq* proceeds from *ḥubb,* and subsequently arguing that men's love (*maḥabba*) comes about without acquisition on their part through their hearts' being clothed with, or enveloped by, God's love.[167] On the essence of love, a subject on which mystics often tend to wax eloquent, two definitions that correspond to Ibn Khafīf's view of the origin of love are mentioned by al-Daylamī.[168] A few pages later the mystic's argument affirming that love is an obligation of faith is borrowed, although he is not mentioned as the source. The argument is used once more in chapter fifteen, which deals with the signs of man's love for God.[169] After this, Ibn Khafīf is quoted again in the last chapter of the *ᶜAtf* relating reports of the deaths of saintly persons and a story he had personally investigated of a pious shepherd boy who, while resting outdoors with a fever, had floated up and disappeared into the sky.[170]

---

equivalent to will, must have as its object a nonexistent or the continued existence of something that can cease to exist. The denial of the reality of man's love to God, originally a Jahmite position, received its classical formulation in the works of the celebrated Ashᶜarite theologian Imām al-Ḥaramayn al-Juwaynī (419/1028–478/1085). Statements by mystics that define love as conformity (*muwāfaqa*) or obedience (cf. the definitions attributed to al-Muḥāsibī [MS, p. 86] and to Abū ᵓl-ᶜAbbās b. ᶜAṭāᵓ [MS, pp. 87–88]) often reflect their hesitations on this issue. Cf. Bell, *Love Theory,* pp. 56–59, 109–10, 204–5.

[165] MS, p. 36; cf. Koran 5:24: "a people whom he loves (*yuḥibbuhum*)."

[166] MS, p. 38. On the relevance of this distinction in mystical thought, see MS, p, 38, n. 29.

[167] MS, pp. 71, 73.

[168] MS, p. 92.

[169] See n. 163.

[170] The first of these reports, which tells the story of the death of Shaᶜwāna al-Ubullīya (MS, pp. 289–91), is introduced thus: "I found the following in a book by Sheikh Abū ᶜAbd Allāh b. Khafīf, God's mercy be upon him, and in his own hand." Two more reports, that on the death of Abū Yaᶜqūb al-Aqṭaᶜ and the

Al-Daylamī acquired his material from Ibn Khafīf either directly as his student,[171] or from other immediate disciples who had been with the master longer,[172] or again from recent or original copies of works by him to which he had access.[173] The material must therefore be considered as reliable, but it may not represent very well the full range of Ibn Khafīf's thoughts on love because it was selected according to the requirements of al-Daylamī's own treatise. Until more evidence comes to light, however, we must be satisfied with the temporary conclusion that Ibn Khafīf's influence on al-Daylamī's treatment of love lies chiefly in the areas mentioned here. It was perhaps also Ibn Khafīf who first interested al-Daylamī in al-Ḥallāj and who was responsible for his cautious regard for him. There is, on the other hand, little to suggest that the wide rage of interests al-Daylamī shows in such areas as belles-lettres, poetry, philosophy, astrology, and medicine were inspired by Ibn Khafīf.

Al-Ḥallāj

We must leave unresolved here the complicated question of what it meant to be a Ḥallājian and to what extent the mystical doctrine al-Daylamī acquired from Ibn Khafīf may have been influenced by al-Ḥallāj.[174] We will also pass over the details of al-Ḥallāj's life, the peculiarities of his obscure teachings, his bold and unguarded statements, his

---

story of the shepherd boy, are also attributed to Ibn Khafīf by name (MS, pp. 296–99). Possibly all the material between MS, pp. 289 and 299 is from the same work by Ibn Khafīf.

[171] Explicit examples in the *Sīrat.* Cf., e.g., p. 10: "Abū ʾl-Ḥasan Daylamī related as follows: I heard from the Sheikh, relating from his father, that . . ."

[172] Explicit examples in the *Sīrat.* Cf., e.g., pp. 25–27.

[173] See n. 170.

[174] The question of whether and to what extent Ibn Khafīf may be called a Ḥallājian is the subject of a forthcoming study by Sobieroj. In the introduction to his "Ibn Ḫafīf aš-Šīrāzī" Sobieroj remarks that Ibn Khafīf seems to have "dissociated or clearly distanced himself from Ḥallāǧ—if he in fact ever was tied to Ḥallāǧ in the form of a special loyalty" (p. 7). Against the view put forward by Massignon that Ibn Khafīf remained a faithful follower of al-Ḥallāj, Sobieroj argues that it is equally plausible to conclude that Ibn Khafīf distanced himself from al-Ḥallāj after an initial enthusiasm (ibid., pp. 24, 50–54). He remarks further that al-Daylamī, in view of his own pro-Ḥallājian statements, cannot be totally relied on for an assessment of Ibn Khafīf's stance with regard to al-Ḥallāj. It is more appropriate, according to Sobieroj's argument, to reconstruct Ibn Khafīf's point of view on the basis of the opinions (mostly negative, often damning) expressed by the teachers he sought out and recognized as his authorities (ibid., pp. 50–54).

troubles with the authorities and with many of his fellow mystics, his trials for heresy, and his eventual execution in 309/922. These matters have all been the subject of considerable study.[175] It will be sufficient here to cite several reports that reflect the basic problems of the nature of Ibn Khafīf's relation to al-Ḥallāj. Since one of our sources for these reports is al-Daylamī himself, they must be considered as reasonably reliable.

First, it is clear that Ibn Khafīf did relate miracles he witnessed when he visited al-Ḥallāj in prison in Baghdad[176] (the mystic's predicting—or bringing about—the acquittal of his jail keeper, who had been accused of corruption, and his picking up with his hand a towel or cloth[177] that could not have been within his reach). However Ibn Khafīf was sufficiently objective to recognize that, whatever he himself may have thought of these wonders, it was feats of this sort that had led others to accuse al-Ḥallāj of sorcery.[178] We are also told by al-Daylamī that Ibn Khafīf, being asked about al-Ḥallāj, called him a "true monotheist" (*muwaḥḥid*). When the inquirer remarked that some people held al-Ḥallāj to be an unbeliever, Ibn Khafīf is said to have answered, "If what I have witnessed in him is not true monotheism, then who in this world *is* a true monotheist?"

On the other hand, when someone in the same gathering mentioned that al-Ḥallāj had spoken of the human and divine natures of God (*nāsūt* and *lāhūt*), Ibn Khafīf asked him if he had in mind the following verses, which were commonly attributed to al-Ḥallāj:

> Praise to him whose humanity has manifested
> the mystery of his radiant divinity!
> And who afterwards has appeared in his creation openly
> in the form of one "who eats and drinks."

When the inquirer answered that he did indeed have these verses in mind, Ibn Khafīf exclaimed, "May God's curse be upon the one who composed this and who has this belief, and upon anyone else who says

[175] See the sources cited in here and in the Bibliography under al-Ḥallāj and Louis Massignon.

[176] On the return journey from a pilgrimage in the period 308–309/920–21. See Sobieroj, "Ibn Ḫafīf aš-Šīrāzī," p. 108.

[177] Or "handkerchief" (*minshafa* in the Arabic; *dastārcha, sutra* in the Persian versions).

[178] *Sīrat,* pp. 93–97, esp. p. 97; Rūzbihān Baqlī, *Sharḥ-i shaṭḥīyāt,* pp. 47–49; Louis Massignon and Paul Kraus, *Akhbār al-Ḥallāj* (1936), Arabic, pp., 101–3, French, pp. 103–4.

or believes the like!"[179]

In a similar report, which could conceivably be construed as the record of an earlier occasion, it is not clear that Ibn Khafīf already knows of the verses before he is asked about them. After he has invoked God's curse on their author, he is told that the author is al-Ḥallāj. In his answer he expresses doubts about their ascription to him. "If this is his belief," he replies, "then he is an unbeliever, but they may be a fabrication."[180]

Al-Daylamī, for his part, does not seem to doubt that al-Ḥallāj spoke of a human as well as a divine nature in the godhead. In the *ᶜAtf* he names this as the point that distinguishes the doctrine of al-Ḥallāj from that of the other Sufi masters.

What distinguishes his doctrine is that in his spiritual allusions he calls eros one of the attributes of essence, absolutely and wherever it appears. The other teachers, for their part, allude to the uniting of lover and beloved when love comes to its extreme limit in the extinction of the totality of the lover in the beloved. They do not (like al-Ḥallāj) speak of the divine and human natures.[181]

The report from Ibn Khafīf mentioned above left the issue of whether or not al-Ḥallāj was to be considered an unbeliever unsettled. Those who, like al-Daylamī, believed that he indeed had attributed a human as well as a divine nature to God would be obliged to conclude, in accordance with Ibn Khafīf's condemnation as related in the report, that al-Ḥallāj was an unbeliever. It is clear from our text, however, that al-Daylamī did not draw this conclusion. The apparent ambiguity of Ibn Khafīf's attitude towards al-Ḥallāj and how his assessment of the mystic may have changed was to remain a puzzle.

We can see an example of how the later tradition dealt with the problem in Rūzbihān Baqlī's observations on the version of the report that he knew. Rūzbihān's goal was to counter the presumption of any real disagreement between Ibn Khafīf and al-Ḥallāj, while at the same time salvaging the verses ascribed to the latter. He achieved this by separating the report of Ibn Khafīf's endorsement of al-Ḥallāj from the report of his

---

[179] *Sīrat,* pp. 100–101. In translating the second hemistich of the first line we have followed the reading in al-Ḥallāj, *Le dîwân d'ál-Hallâj* (ed. and French trans. Louis Massignon [1955], p. 41), which has *sirra sanā* for *satra manā* (error for *sanā*) in the *Sīrat.*

[180] Ibn Bākūya relating in his *Bidāyat ḥāl al-Ḥallāj* (in Louis Massignon, *Quatre textes inédits relatifs à la biographie d'al Ḥosayn ibn Manṣoūr al Ḥallāj,* Paris: Librairie Paul Geuthner, 1914) from ᶜĪsā b. Yazūl al-Qazwīnī; cited by Schimmel, *Sīrat,* p. 101 n.

[181] MS, p. 91.

denunciation of the verses. Ibn Khafīf's comments on the poetry, he suggested, should be attributed either to his not knowing that al-Ḥallāj was their author or to his regard for the limited spiritual advancement of his audience.

> The master said [of these verses]: "May God curse whoever composed this, and whoever believes the like." Perhaps the master did not know that the one who composed the verses was Ḥusayn. He may have thought the author was an incarnationist (*ḥulūlī*), and this is why he invoked God's curse on him. For otherwise the master knew what he believed and what his doctrine was. He knew that he was the greatest monotheist of his time. Thus the master said, "Ḥusayn Manṣūr was a divine sage (*ᶜālim-i rabbānī*). He was executed in Baghdad at Bāb al-Ṭāq." Also ᶜAlī b. Muḥammad Daylamī, may God have mercy upon him, related that the master once was asked, "What is your opinion of Ḥusayn Manṣūr?" and he replied, "He was a Muslim." When the inquirers objected, "They accused him of unbelief," he said, "If what I have witnessed in him is not true monotheism, then there *is* no true monotheist in this world!"[182] Then again it is possible that the master knew of the weakness of the faith of the people in the gathering and took this into consideration, and that he said what he said because spiritual leaders are obliged to observe the outward form of [religious] knowledge. As for the spiritual reality to which the first of the two verses alludes (*ishārat-i īn bayt*), it is well known to the adepts of spiritual revelation and contemplation in the station of ambiguity (*iltibās*). It needs no further elucidation, because ample explanation has already been given in the passages on the laudable and the odious.[183]

The reservations his readers may have had about al-Ḥallāj's orthodoxy did not keep al-Daylamī from citing the mystic on crucial issues in his treatise on love. Al-Ḥallāj is first named together with other Sufis who permitted the use of the word *ᶜishq* to refer to love in the sacred con-

---

182 The wording of this report from al-Daylamī, although in Persian translation, is so close to that given above, that it may be surmised that Rūzbihān knew the rest of al-Daylamī's version.

183 Rūzbihān Baqlī, *Sharḥ-i shaṭḥīyāt,* pp. 432–33. Rūzbihān then proceeds to give a brief clarification of the meaning of the verse (pp. 433–34). "Laudable" and "odious" translate *mustaḥsanāt* and *mustaqbaḥāt*, respectively, which represent poles of alterity in this world—good and evil, virtue and vice, the beautiful and the ugly. In translating from al-Ḥallāj's *Ṭawāsīn,* Rūzbihān uses *mustaḥsanāt* and *mustaqbaḥāt* to render the etymologically related *maḥāsin* and *qabāʾiḥ*. Cf. *Sharḥ-i shaṭḥīyāt,* pp. 524, and al-Ḥallāj, *Kitāb al-ṭawāsīn* (ed. Paul Nwyia), VI, 18, p. 207. See also *Sharḥ-i shaṭḥīyāt,* pp. 222–23, on Abū ʾl-ᶜAbbās b. ᶜAṭāʾ, and other passages mentioned in the index of that work, s.vv. *mustaḥsanāt* and *mustaqbaḥāt.*

text.[184] Next al-Daylamī quotes an important and lengthy passage in which al-Ḥallāj accounts for the origin of eros perceived in this world in the primordial discourse within the unified divine essence that arose from God's contemplation of his attributes in preeternity. Through this discourse, reality, expressible in terms of the triad *agent* (active participle), *act* (verbal noun or infinitive), and *object of act* (passive participle), emerged into the realm of the knowable.[185] It is in this same passage that al-Ḥallāj speaks of a personification of the attribute of eros.

And God willed to see this attribute of eros alone, looking upon it and speaking to it. And he contemplated his preeternity and displayed a form that was his own form and his own essence. For when God contemplates a thing and manifests in it a form from himself, he displays that form, and he displays in that form knowledge, power, movement, will, and all his other attributes. Now when God had become thus manifest, he displayed a person who was himself, and he gazed on him for an age of his time.[186]

This passage was significant for the formulation of al-Daylamī's own account of the origin of love, which is given at the end of the same chapter, although the term used there is *maḥabba,* not *ᶜishq.*[187]

Al-Ḥallāj is cited again on the essence of eros, which in a complicated description he portrays as preeternal fire. In this same context al-Daylamī cites some verses by him on the eternal nature of eros. We shall return shortly to these, because they include the verse that seems to have inspired the title of al-Daylamī's treatise.[188] Later al-Daylamī relates a story explaining the circumstances in which al-Ḥallāj had composed two lines on obliteration. He had been told of the simultaneous death of two youths whose affection for each other he had been wont to observe in the mosque in Ahvaz.[189] Further on al-Daylamī reports a statement by al-Ḥallāj on the elimination of all conceivable relationships in the culmination of mystical longing and how this condition alternates with the awareness implicit in the state of longing.[190] Finally in the twenty-first chapter, "On the Extreme Limit of the Perfection of Love," al-Daylamī quotes some verses by al-Ḥallāj on union, pointing out that they consti-

---

[184] MS, p. 9.
[185] MS, pp. 51–56.
[186] MS, pp. 54–55.
[187] MS, pp. 74–81.
[188] MS, pp. 90–91.
[189] MS, pp. 141–42.
[190] MS, p. 179.

tute an example of his doctrine of essential union (*ittiḥād*).[191]

Al-Ḥallāj's Poem and the Title of al-Daylamī's Treatise

There seems to be no reason to question Massignon's suggestion that in choosing the title of his treatise al-Daylamī was thinking of the verses by al-Ḥallāj on the preeternal nature of eros that he cites in chapter six.[192] Further, he may have had in mind a work ascribed to al-Ḥallāj by al-Nadīm, a *Kitāb khazāʾin al-khayrāt,* known as *al-Alif al-maqṭūᶜ wa-l-alif al-maʾlūf* (The *alif* in isolation and the *alif* in union).[193] Letter symbolism in Islamic mysticism, and particularly the symbolism of the *alif* (A) and the *lām* (L) is a complicated subject, and the meaning ascribed to the various letters can vary considerably. Thus the *alif,* a vertical line (ا) that when used as a number means *one,* is generally taken to symbolize the divine unity. But it may be assigned other meanings. For example, because of its erect form it has on occasion been taken to symbolize Satan, since Satan, alone among the angels, refused out of pride to bow down to Adam.[194] There can be little doubt that *alif* in al-Daylamī's title is to be understood in the more usual sense as referring to God in his preeternal unity,[195] while *lām* probably represents contingent existence, or man. The title is almost certainly also a play on the saying ascribed to the Prophet that begins "The believer befriends and is befriended," *al-muʾmin ilf maʾlūf* in the form cited by al-Daylamī.[196] The words *ilf* and *alif,* when *hamza* and the vowels are not written, are homographs.

But the Ḥallājian verses quoted in the text are our surest clue to the meaning intended by al-Daylamī. We give here the relevant fourth and fifth verses:

---

[191] MS, p. 239.

[192] Massignon, "Interférences philosophiques et percées métaphysiques dans la mystique hallagienne: notion de 'l'essentiel désir,'" in Louis Massignon, *Opera minora,* II, p. 229. See MS, p. 90.

[193] Massignon mentioned this title in his list of the works of al-Ḥallāj and equated it with chapter eight of the mystic's *Ṭawāsīn* (*Passion* [1922], II, p. 819). Cf. al-Nadīm, *Fihrist,* ed. Flügel, p. 192.

[194] Cf. Schimmel, *Mystical Dimensions of Islam,* pp. 411–25, esp. pp. 417–18, and Massignon, *Essai* (1954), pp. 37, 98–101. See, e.g., Koran 2:34, on Satan's refusal to bow down to Adam.

[195] Cf. al-Ḥallāj, *Kitāb al-ṭawāsīn* (ed. Nwyia), *ṭāṣīn* VIII, p. 211, l. 1. For other examples of al-Ḥallāj's statements on the *alif* and the *lām-alif,* see *Akhbār al-Ḥallāj* (1936), no. 34, Arabic, p. 51, French, p. 79, and no. 64, Arabic, pp. 95–96, French, pp. 100–101.

[196] See MS, p. 115, and the note in our edition.

Lammā badā ᵓl-badᵓu abdā ᶜishqahū ṣifatan
fī-man badā, fa-talaᵓlā fīhi laᵓlāᵓū,
Wa-l-lāmu bi-l-alifi ᵓl-maᶜṭūfi muᵓtalifun,
kilāhumā wāḥidun fī ᵓl-sabqi maᶜnāᵓū.

When the beginning appeared, he displayed his eros as an attribute
in the one who appeared, and there shone in him a glistening light.
And the *lām* was in union with the conjoined *alif*:
the two in preeternity were one thing.

The second of these two verses contains not only the names of the two letters *alif* and *lām* but also both roots on which al-Daylamī plays in the title of his treatise, *ᶜ-ṭ-f* and *ᵓ-l-f.* The title has been understood and translated in different ways, and precisely because it plays on the various meanings implied by the roots *ᶜ-ṭ-f* and *ᵓ-l-f,* most of the translations that have been given of it can be justified. The basic meaning of *ᵓ-l-f* is "to keep to" or "to cleave to" (*alifa*), while that of *ᶜ-ṭ-f* is "to incline" or "to bend" (*ᶜaṭafa*).[197] Both roots can imply the joining together of two persons or things, and both can mean affection on the part of one for the other (cf. *allafa/alifa, ᶜaṭafa ᶜalā*). In the context with which we are concerned, moreover, some forms seem to be interchangeable with uncertain consequences for the meaning. Thus we have *al-alif al-maᵓlūf* in the title of al-Daylamī's treatise and *al-alif al-maᶜṭūf* in al-Ḥallāj's poem.

The last hemistich of the verses cited defines what is meant by the use of the participle *muᵓtalif* in al-Ḥallāj's poem, namely, to be "one thing." This would seem to reflect an intuitive sense that forms from the root *ᵓ-l-f* can be used to refer to an essential unity, while those from *ᶜ-ṭ-f* imply a relationship between two essentially different things. Al-Daylamī's title, then, may be suggesting two different kinds or degrees of union, while at the same time evoking the sense of fondness and inclination which the words also can mean.[198] The verbal noun *ᶜatf,* without the preposition *ᶜalā,* is defined by Rūzbihān Baqlī some two hundred years later as God's preserving one who desires him from stopping at anything beneath him.[199] Graphically, the joining of the *alif* to the *lām,* or its "inclination" towards it, would seem to refer to the combination of the two letters in the double letter *lām-alif.*[200] Since it was not possible to find a

---

197 Lane, s.vv.

198 The concept of a relationship of spiritual love between the letters *alif* and *lām* finds expression, for example, in the work of Ibn al-ᶜArabī (*Futūḥāt,* I, p. 259).

199 Rūzbihān Baqlī, *Mashrab al-arwāḥ,* pp. 104–5.

200 Massignon suggests the definite article *al-,* but the *alif* and the *lām* are not

solution that would accommodate all these nuances, we have chosen in rendering the words of the title page of the manuscript a translation that underscores certain of the different types of union the title implies but that has the admitted disadvantage of being at least as cryptic as al-Daylamī's original.[201] A play on syntactic as well as graphic conjunction, moreover, while not anachronous, may not have been intended by the author. Vadet's translation, which stresses the sense of inclination in the verb *ᶜaṭafa,* remains conceivably a more felicitous solution.[202]

Other Mystical Sources

In addition to Ibn Khafīf and al-Ḥallāj, al-Daylamī relied particularly heavily on two other mystics of the generation of al-Ḥallāj, ᶜAmr b. ᶜUthmān al-Makkī and Abū ᵓl-Qāsim al-Junayd, both of whom are among the five Sufi masters Ibn Khafīf ranked above all others. He also owes much to an elder contemporary of Ibn Khafīf, Abū Saᶜīd Aḥmad b. Muḥammad b. Ziyād al-Aᶜrābī, known as Ibn al-Aᶜrābī.

Abū ᶜAbd Allāh ᶜAmr b. ᶜUthmān al-Makkī (d. ca. 297/910, according to some 291 or 296) was a companion, among others, of al-Junayd and Abū Saᶜīd al-Kharrāz. He was the author of a number of works on mysticism, none of which is extant.[203] Al-Hujwīrī quotes from ᶜAmr a passage he says is from a *Book on Love* (*Kitāb-i maḥabbat*).[204] The quotations attributed to ᶜAmr in *Ḥilyat al-awliyā*ᵓ and *Ṭabaqāt al-ṣūfiya* reveal a concern for rendering as nearly as possible through highly eloquent speech the subtle emotions of the mystic. The passages bear on the subject of love at several points.[205]

Along with al-Junayd and the Ẓāhirite Muḥammad b. Dāwūd, ᶜAmr

---

joined graphically in this combination ("Interférences philosophiques," p. 229).

201 "Book of the Conjunction of the Cherished *Alif* with the Conjoined *Lām.*" See the title page of the manuscript in our translation.

202 Vadet translates "Livre de l'inclinaison de l'alif uni sur le lām incliné" (edition only, title page). Massignon translates "L'adjonction de l'Alif mis en composition au Lâm mis en adjonction," a title which he describes as "symbolically grammatical" ("Interférences philosophiques," p. 229). Schimmel renders the title as "The Book of the Inclination of the Tamed *alif* toward the Inclined *l*" (*Mystical Dimensions,* p. 418).

203 Sezgin, *GAS,* I, p. 650. For a list of works attributed to ᶜAmr and some surviving excerpts, see Sobieroj, "Ibn Ḫafīf aš-Šīrāzī," pp. 44–45.

204 al-Hujwīrī, *Kashf al-mahjūb,* ed. Zhukovskii, p. 399; trans. Nicholson, p. 309.

205 Cf. Abū Nuᶜaym, *Ḥilya,* X, pp. 291–96; al-Sulamī, *Ṭabaqāt al-ṣūfiya*, pp. 193–98.

condemned the controversial views of al-Ḥallāj. Considering his own evident preoccupation with elocution, the form his opposition to the mystic is reported to have taken is interesting. Al-Ḥallāj had visited him in Mecca, and ᶜAmr had asked him where he came from. Al-Ḥallāj's response had called into question his extrasensory powers and thus the authenticity of his spirituality. ᶜAmr, after long having harbored a grudge against al-Ḥallāj, finally accused him openly of claiming he could equal the eloquence of the Koran.[206]

ᶜAmr b. ᶜUthmān, although not without a certain amount of repetition, is cited at eight different places in our text. He is quoted regarding the etymology of the word love,[207] the definition of the emotion and its inception, God's creation of the gnostics to serve as signs of his love and his engendering love in their "hearts" before the creation of their bodies on the day of the *a-last* covenant,[208] the signs that constitute proof of love,[209] and the total annihilation of the lover's attributes when he reaches the final goal.[210] ᶜAmr is also the source of a lengthy passage containing two reports of dreams associated with the intervention of departed saints.[211]

Abū ᵓl-Qāsim al-Junayd (ca. 215/830–298/910), who is known in Sufi circles as "Lord of the Sect" (*Sayyid al-Ṭāᵓifa*), has been the subject of numerous studies.[212] At a tender age he became the disciple of the noted mystic Sarī al-Saqaṭī (d. 253/867), who was his maternal uncle. Later he also numbered among his teachers such figures as al-Ḥārith al-Muḥāsibī, who like al-Junayd was among the five masters Ibn Khafīf held in highest esteem, and the ecstatic Abū Yazīd al-Bisṭāmī. Along with his teacher al-Muḥāsibī, al-Junayd is considered one of the most important exponents of "the 'Sober' type of Ṣūfism."[213]

---

[206] *Akhbār al-Ḥallāj* (1936), no. 18, Arabic, p. 38, French, pp. 71–72. For a more detailed explanation, based on al-Anṣārī's *Ṭabaqāt al-ṣūfīya,* of ᶜAmr's enmity towards al-Ḥallāj, see Sobieroj, "Ibn Ḫafīf aš-Šīrāzī," p. 44.

[207] MS, p. 35.

[208] According to a view held by many mystics, the covenant mentioned in Koran 7:172–73, which was sealed with God's words "Am I not your Lord? (*a-lastu bi-rabbikum?*)" and men's answer "Yes," refers to a pact between God and the souls of men in their prior existence.

[209] MS, pp. 69–71, 71–73, 87, 178–79.

[210] MS, pp. 240–41.

[211] MS, pp. 291–97.

[212] Sezgin, *GAS,* I, pp. 647–50.

[213] A. J. Arberry, *EI²,* II, p. 600a–b, s.v. "al-Djunayd." See also Abū Nuᶜaym,

Many of al-Junayd's writings have come down to us, including a number of letters to various contemporaries. One of his most important contributions is his transmission of material from al-Ḥārith al-Muḥāsibī. His style is known for its difficulty and obscurity. Thanks primarily to the efforts of A. H. Abdel-Kader, quite a few of his surviving writings can be read in English translation.[214] Perhaps it was under the combined influence of al-Muḥāsibī, who was the author of a long passage on love (*maḥabba*) quoted in Abū Nuᶜaym's *Ḥilya,*[215] and of al-Bisṭāmī, who was counted among those who allowed the use of the controversial term *ᶜishq* (eros) in the sacred context,[216] that al-Junayd wrote the tract on *ᶜishq* that convinced Ibn Khafīf to accept the use of the word.[217]

The material from or about al-Junayd recorded in the *ᶜAtf* deals primarily with *ᶜishq* and may in part represent extracts from his tract on the subject. Al-Junayd is first named in connection with this tract.[218] Subsequently he is cited on the etymology of the word *ᶜishq*,[219] the progress of *maḥabba* to *ᶜishq*,[220] the definitions of *maḥabba* and *ᶜishq,*[221] and the deceptiveness of facial beauty.[222] A story is also told of his having sought out a man who had been coming to his circle regularly but who had began to stay away because he was ashamed at having been seduced by a beautiful face.[223] Following this story some verses by or related by al-Junayd are recorded that describe the total union of the spirits of lovers.[224] The mystic is likewise cited as the narrator of three lines of poetry

---

Ḥilya, X, pp. 255–87; al-Sulamī, *Ṭabaqāt* (ed. Pedersen), pp. 141–50; and Ibn al-Jawzī, *Ṣifat al-ṣafwa,* II, pp. 416–24. For the record we may recall here what we noted above, namely, that the champion of orthodoxy, Aḥmad b. Ḥanbal, is reported to have said: "Beware of al-Ḥārith [al-Muḥāsibī], for he is the source of affliction" (Ibn al-Jawzī, *Talbīs Iblīs,* p. 167).

214 Cf. A. H. Abdel-Kader, *The Life, Personality and Writings of al-Junayd,* E. J. W. Gibb Memorial, n.s., vol. 22, London: Luzac, 1976; and the articles by Abdel-Kader and Arberry cited by Sezgin (*GAS,* I, p. 648).

215 *Ḥilya,* X, p. 76ff. One of the two main transmitters is ᶜAmr b. ᶜUthmān al-Makkī.

216 MS, p. 9.

217 Cf. pp. xlvii–xlviii above.

218 MS, p. 9.

219 MS, p. 35

220 MS, pp. 65–66.

221 MS, p. 87.

222 MS, p. 141.

223 MS, pp. 139–40

224 MS, p. 140.

his uncle Sarī al-Saqaṭī had written down on the emaciation and skeletal appearance that identify true lovers.[225] Of greatest interest, however, is a long and rather obscure ode al-Daylamī records from al-Junayd on the progression of love to its culmination in the utter annihilation of the attributes of the lover.[226]

Abū Saᶜīd Aḥmad b. Muḥammad b. Ziyād al-Aᶜrābī, known as (Abū Saᶜīd) Ibn al-Aᶜrābī (246/860–341/952) represents a younger generation than ᶜAmr b. ᶜUthmān and al-Junayd, being only about twenty-two years older than Ibn Khafīf, if we have interpreted al-Daylamī's report on the latter's birth correctly. Of Basran origin, Abū Saᶜīd settled in Mecca and died there. He compiled works on *fiqh, ḥadīth,* biography, and, it is said, history, as well as on asceticism and mysticism.[227] As we have mentioned above, Abū Saᶜīd is not among the teachers Ibn Khafīf met in Mecca to whom separate sections are devoted in the *Sīrat,* but al-Daylamī does record that Ibn Khafīf encountered him in the holy city. Once while sitting in a gathering of Sufis at which Abū Saᶜīd happened to be present, Ibn Khafīf had found himself alone in protesting against the assertion that existence and non-existence are alike to the gnostic. He wished to make it clear that this assertion should be understood as applying only to the realm of mystical experience, not to the aspect of existence governed by religious law or *sharīᶜa.* When the others in the gathering pressed Ibn Khafīf to show indulgence, Abū Saᶜīd, apparently siding with Ibn Khafīf, intervened to ensure that he would be allowed to complete his argument.[228]

Abū Saᶜīd b. al-Aᶜrābī was one of al-Daylamī's most important sources on the theory of love. Chapter seven of the *ᶜAṭf* consists in its entirety of a summary of, or conceivably a long extract from, a work by him entitled *The Diversity of Opinions about Love (Kitāb ikhtilāf al-nās*

---

[225] MS, p. 178; cf. Dāwūd al-Anṭākī, *Tazyīn al-aswāq*, I, p. 29.

[226] MS, pp. 66–67. The poem is cited immediately after al-Junayd's comment on the origin of *ᶜishq* in the section of the *ᶜAṭf* that deals with the opinions of the Sufis on the origin of eros and love.

[227] Sezgin, *GAS,* I, pp. 660–61; al-Sulamī, *Ṭabaqāt,* pp. 443–48; Abū Nuᶜaym, *Ḥilya,* X, pp. 375–76; al-Dhahabī, *al-ᶜIbar fī khabar man ghabar,* II, p. 252.

[228] *Sīrat,* pp. 66–67. Another occasion on which Ibn Khafīf encountered Abū Saᶜīd in Mecca is recorded by Ibn ᶜAsākir. Abū Saᶜīd is reported to have showed particular interest in a *masʾala* on *wudd* (fondness, friendship) apparently authored by Ibn Khafīf. See *Taʾrīkh madīnat Dimashq,* XV, p. 298. Communication from Florian Sobieroj.

fī ʾl-maḥabba).[229] Perhaps this work is to be identified with the book on love (*Kitāb al-maḥabba*) ascribed to Abū Saᶜīd by Ibn Khayr al-Ishbīlī.[230] No work on love by Abū Saᶜīd is known to survive, and al-Daylamī's chapter seems to constitute our best record of his writing on the subject. The chapter in the *ᶜAṭf* consists of an exhaustive breakdown of the advocates of the various Islamic teachings on sacred love into forty-four distinct groups.[231] It covers non-conformist views, ranging from Ismaili doctrines to extreme mystical doctrines, as well as more conventional opinions.

Apart from the extensive passage contained in chapter seven, Abū Saᶜīd is cited at length in chapter four on the terms for the various stages of the evolution of passionate love (*ᶜishq*) and their definitions. The quotation is a superb example of the attempts of contemporary mystics to match as closely as possible the elusive degrees of emotional and religious experience with corresponding subtleties of language.[232] Near the middle of the *ᶜAṭf,* Abū Saᶜīd is cited once again explaining a statement attributed to Rābiᶜa al-ᶜAdawīya, who, when she was asked about her love for the Prophet, is said to have replied that love for the Creator had distracted her from love for the created.[233]

Among other mystics frequently cited by al-Daylamī are such earlier authorities as Abū Sulaymān al-Dārānī (d. 215/830–31), whose sayings are related by his companion and disciple Aḥmad b. Abī ʾl-Ḥawārī (d. 230/844–45), and Dhū ʾl-Nūn al-Miṣrī (d. 246/861). The sayings recorded from Abū Sulaymān dwell on the nature of selfless love and the insignificance for the true mystic of the pleasures and pains of both this world and the next.[234] The reports from Dhū ʾl-Nūn, which tend to be somewhat theoretical, concentrate mostly on terminology and the definition of mystical states, although some lines of his poetry are also

---

229 MS, pp. 98–109, esp. p. 99. The title is not mentioned in the notice on Abū Saᶜīd in Sezgin. See n. 227.

230 Ibn Khayr al-Ishbīlī, *Fahrasa,* p. 284.

231 In the text as it now stands one group may have fallen out, since al-Daylamī gives the total number of groups as forty-five at the end of the chapter (MS, p. 109).

232 MS, pp. 36–37. "All these stations and halts," remarks al-Daylamī of the stages of love enumerated by Abū Saᶜīd in this quotation, "are subsumed under the name *hawā* (passion, love, appetite), which applies to them all" (MS, p. 37).

233 MS, p. 152. An Abū Saᶜīd is also cited in MS, p. 70, but we have not been able to identify him.

234 Cf. MS, pp. 155–56, 173–74, 217–19, 239.

quoted.[235] Likewise frequent authorities are the ascetic Kufan traditionist Sufyān al-Thawrī (d. 95/713) and the mystic Sumnūn, a contemporary of al-Junayd, who was known as al-Muḥibb, "the Lover."

The list of mystics cited by al-Daylamī two or more times is long, but the quotations vary greatly in length. Some especially interesting authorities are cited only one or two times. Despite his master Ibn Khafīf's apparent opposition to Ibn Sālim and his school,[236] al-Daylamī quotes the teacher of the first Ibn Sālim, Sahl b. ᶜAbd Allāh al-Tustarī (203/818–283/896), on the creation of Adam out of the light of the primordial Muḥammad.[237] Sahl is cited once again on the definition of love, and a report is given regarding his death, according to which, just as ᶜUmar b. Wāṣil was about to wash his corpse, he had exclaimed "There is no god but God!"[238] In the final chapter of his treatise, towards the end, al-Daylamī twice cites the *mashyakha* of Aḥmad b. Manṣūr, the father of his acquaintance al-Bayṭār.[239] But the influence of al-Bayṭār's erudite father on al-Daylamī's method and thought may have been far greater than these two hagiographic reports suggest.

Non-Mystical Sources

The division into chapters followed by al-Daylamī in the *ᶜAṭf al-alif* is thematic, and especially in the earlier part of the book each chapter is subdivided so as to place together the opinions of particular groups whose views the author considers relevant to the subject of the chapter—the lexicographers, the belletrists, the Bedouin Arabs, the ancient Greek philosophers, the physicians, the astrologers, the speculative theologians, and the mystics. But while al-Daylamī often names the ultimate authority whom he is citing, he seldom identifies his immediate source. He introduces the section on the opinions of the astrologers in chapter five, for instance, as follows:

> I read in a book by a certain scholar that he had read in a book by Abū Maᶜshar, reporting from someone else, that this person had asked Ibn al-Ṭabarī about the nature and character of eros and that he had replied: . . .[240]

---

[235] Cf. MS, pp. 65, 86, 140, 208, 176–77.

[236] A "Refutation of Ibn Sālim" (*Kitāb al-radd ᶜalā Ibn Sālim*) is listed by al-Daylamī in the *Sīrat* among Ibn Khafīf's longer works (p. 212). Cf. references to the mystic's opposition to Ibn Sālim or his school in Schimmel, *Sīrat,* intro., p. 32, and Vadet, *EI²,* III, p. 823a–b (citing Massignon, *Essai,* p. 315).

[237] MS, pp. 67–68.

[238] MS, pp. 87, 291.

[239] MS, pp. 287, 299.

[240] MS, p. 56.

In the preceding section of the same chapter, he relates a statement on eros directly from a philosopher whom he had met:

> Once a certain philosopher was asked in my presence about the origin of eros. "The first to love with eros," he replied, "was the Creator. He loved himself with eros when there was nothing other than him. He appeared to himself through himself, in his beauty, his glory, and all his attributes. And thus he loved himself with eros."[241]

It has been speculated that the author of this near Ḥallājian statement was the philosopher Abū Ḥayyān al-Tawḥīdī.[242] But al-Daylamī's silence leaves us ignorant of the identity of a thinker who one suspects is the direct source of much of his philosophical material.

The statements on eros ascribed by al-Daylamī to the theologians, despite considerable variations in both wording and attribution, are so close to the statements given by the historian al-Masᶜūdī (d. 345/956) in an account of a symposium said to have been held by the vizier Yaḥyā b. Khālid (d. 190/805) that it is difficult to escape the conclusion that the author is using a version of al-Masᶜūdī's account or, more likely, has drawn on a common source. But again he leaves us in ignorance.[243]

Al-Daylamī makes a precious exception to his usual silence regarding his immediate authorities when he cites the history of al-Ṭabarī (d. 310/923) in the final chapter of his treatise, which deals with the deaths of "divine lovers," that is, prophets and saints.[244] This reference to al-Ṭabarī was of considerable use to us in the process of controlling uncertain readings in the manuscript. While variations in style and wording make it impossible to determine the precise extent of al-Daylamī's direct debt to the historian, it is unquestionably considerable throughout much of the lengthy last chapter of the *ᶜAtf.*

LATER REFLECTIONS

We have come across little information regarding the transmission and

---

241 MS, p. 56.

242 Cf. Massignon, "Interférences philosophiques," p. 230, n. 2.

243 See chapter five, n. 42.

244 Cf. MS, p. 272. Al-Ṭabarī is listed in the *Sīrat* (p. 209) as one of the authorities on *ḥadīth* al-Daylamī's teacher Ibn Khafīf heard in Baghdad. Ibn Khafīf was critical of an undifferentiated negative appraisal of Sufism given by al-Ṭabarī in his *Tabṣīr ulī ᵓl-nuhā,* an appraisal that tallies with other reports concerning the historian's attitude towards Sufi practice (Sobieroj, "Ibn Ḫafīf aš-Šīrāzī," pp. 37, 122–23).

influence of al-Daylamī's treatise on love other than the names of the transmitters given on the title page of the manuscript and the citations of the book in the works of Rūzbihān Baqlī. Much of the introduction to Vadet's French translation of the *ᶜAtf* is devoted to the transmission of the text, and Vadet's arguments have been examined in some detail by Sobieroj.[245] Subsequently Sobieroj has called our attention to the occurrence of the chain of transmission given on the title page of the *ᶜAtf* in several reports in Ibn ᶜAsākir's biographical notice on Ibn Khafīf in his history of Damascus.[246] Ibn ᶜAsākir's *isnāds* support the authenticity of the chain given in the *ᶜAtf* and confirm the identity of the first transmitter from al-Daylamī.

Named in the *ᶜAtf* as the first transmitter of the text is Abū ᵓl-Ḥasan b. Bakrān b. Faḍl. As is clear from Ibn ᶜAsākir's *isnāds,* Vadet was right in identifying this person with the Abū ᵓl-Ḥasan *ᶜAlī* b. Bakrān of Shiraz whom al-Hujwīrī describes as one of the major Sufis of Fārs.[247] Al-Hujwīrī states that he met this mystic and that he heard from him the story of how several of Ibn Khafīf's wives, once when talking among themselves, were amazed to discover that he had never sought to be intimate with any of them and how his favorite wife had confirmed that this was also the case with her.[248] We have found no dates for Abū ᵓl-Ḥasan ᶜAlī b. Bakrān, and al-Hujwīrī does not tell us when he met him. But if al-Hujwīrī, whose death Nicholson puts between 465 and 469 A.H., spent the last years of his life in Lahore,[249] then it may be assumed that he met Ibn Bakrān earlier, at some time during the period extending roughly from 415 to 450. That Ibn Bakrān should have been active in this period is most likely not inconsistent with his having been a disciple of al-Daylamī. Moreover, in Ibn ᶜAsākir's *isnāds* Ibn Bakrān cites al-Daylamī without an intermediary. There is thus little reason to doubt that his transmission of the text of the *ᶜAtf* from its author was direct.

From Abū ᵓl-Ḥasan b. Bakrān, according to the title page of the manu-

---

[245] Vadet, trans., intro., pp. 18–22; Sobieroj, "Ibn Ḫafīf aš-Šīrāzī," pp. 26–27.

[246] Ibn ᶜAsākir, *Taᵓrīkh madīnat Dimashq,* XV, pp. 296, 297, 298, 299, 300. Communication from Florian Sobieroj.

[247] Vadet, trans., intro., pp. 19–20. Ibn ᶜAsākir cites Ibn Bakrān twice in almost full form as Abū ᵓl-Ḥasan ᶜAlī b. Bakrān al-Ṣūfī (*Taᵓrīkh madīnat Dimashq,* XV, pp. 296, 299).

[248] al-Hujwīrī, *Kashf al-maḥjūb,* ed. Zhukovskii, pp. 215, 318–19; trans. Nicholson, pp. 172, 247–48.

[249] al-Hujwīrī, *Kashf al-maḥjūb,* trans. Nicholson, pp. x–xi; Hidayet Hosain/ H. Massé in *EI²,* III, p. 546a, s.v. "Hud̲j̲wīrī."

script, the *Kitāb ᶜaṭf al-alif* was transmitted by Abū Shujāᶜ Muḥammad b. Saᶜdān al-Maqārīḍī. Al-Maqārīḍī also follows Ibn Bakrān in the *isnāds* of Ibn ᶜAsākir's reports. We do not know the birth date of al-Maqārīḍī, but he is said by the authors of the *Shīrāznāma* and the *Shadd al-izār* to have died in 509/1115–16.[250] The time span is long, but assuming that both Ibn Bakrān and al-Maqārīḍī heard the *ᶜAṭf* and the reports quoted by Ibn ᶜAsākir at a relatively young age, the chain of direct transmission from al-Daylamī to al-Maqārīḍī is plausible.[251]

The biographical information on Ibn Khafīf that Ibn ᶜAsākir had from al-Daylamī through al-Maqārīḍī represents a second field in which al-Maqārīḍī was the intellectual heir of the author of the *ᶜAṭf.* He was not only a transmitter of al-Daylamī's treatise on love, he was also the author of a biographical work, a *mashyakha,* in which he included three generations or "classes" (*ṭabaqāt*) of the Sufi sheikhs of Fārs. Junayd Shīrāzī names al-Maqārīḍī along with al-Daylamī among the biographers of Shiraz in whose footsteps he says he is following in writing the *Shadd al-izār.*[252] Another work of which Junayd Shīrāzī made considerable use, the *Taᵓrīkh mashāyikh Fārs* (History of the sheikhs of Fārs) of Ṣāᵓin al-Dīn Ḥusayn b. Muḥammad (d. 664/1265–66), was patterned on the works of al-Daylamī and al-Maqārīḍī.[253]

The borrowings from the *ᶜAṭf* in Rūzbihān Baqlī's writings make it clear that Rūzbihān had access to al-Daylamī's work or to extensive extracts from it, although the text at Rūzbihān's disposal may have differed slightly from that of our manuscript.[254] Rūzbihān seldom acknowledges his debt to al-Daylamī. In his *Mashrab al-arwāḥ* (The drinking fountain of spirits) he cites al-Daylamī by name, quoting an abridged version,

---

[250] Zarkūb Shīrāzī, *Shīrāznāma,* p. 113; Junayd Shīrāzī, *Shadd al-izār,* p. 101.

[251] Al-Maqārīḍī must have lived a relatively long life. He is mentioned in the biography of Abū Isḥāq al-Kāzarūnī as having been a "pole" (*quṭb*) of the path for nearly fifty years. Cf. Maḥmūd b. ᶜUthmān, *Firdaws al-murshidīya fī asrār al-ṣamadīya* (*Die Vita des Scheich Abū Ishāq al-Kāzarūnī*), ed. Fritz Meier, p. 32; cited by Vadet, trans., intro., p. 18.

[252] See *Shadd al-izār,* pp. 4 and n. 2, 101.

[253] Ṣāᵓin al-Dīn was a Shāfiᶜite jurist and a follower of the orthodox mystic Shihāb al-Dīn ᶜUmar al-Suhrawardī (d. 632/1234) (ibid., p.177).

[254] See chapter five, nn. 7, 11, 12. Cf. Vadet's speculations on possible alternate routes of transmission of the text of the *ᶜAṭf* to Rūzbihān (trans., intro., pp. 18–22); see also Sobieroj, "Ibn Ḫafīf aš-Šīrāzī," p. 156, on the founding of the Maqārīḍī *ribāṭ.*

with slight variations in wording, of his definition of eros (*ᶜishq*) as "the boiling up of love" and "the loss of the lover's portion from everything except his beloved."[255] In the same context he cites four other statements about eros that are clearly borrowed from the *ᶜAṭf,* namely, the definitions of eros attributed to Abū Ḥafṣ al-Ḥaddād and al-Junayd, the second of two statements attributed to Heraclitus, and Ibn Khafīf's report concerning the progression of eros according to the mystics of Damascus. In each case the wording is either precisely the same or sufficiently close to indicate borrowing.[256]

Rūzbihān's borrowings in his *Kitāb-i ᶜabhar al-ᶜāshiqīn* (The jasmine of the adepts of love) are more extensive and reveal a considerable degree of indebtedness to the *ᶜAṭf.* Vadet has shown how Rūzbihān weaves his own additions into al-Daylamī's summary of the views on the permissibility of using the word *ᶜishq* in the sacred context.[257] He has also remarked the importance of the earlier sections of the *ᶜAṭf* for aspects of the structure of Rūzbihān's book on love and pointed out several other borrowings.[258] The titles of sections four and five of *ᶜAbhar al-ᶜāshiqīn,* which evoke the virtues of lovers who become close, of beauty, of the beautiful, of the perceiver of beauty, and of the one whose beauty is perceived, remind us of section titles in chapter three of the *ᶜAṭf.* The content of Rūzbihān's sections, however, while reflecting an awareness of the *ᶜAṭf,* is rather rhapsodic and differs considerably from al-Daylamī's treatment. Section six of *ᶜAbhar al-ᶜāshiqīn,* on "the nature and essence of human love," includes what is an obvious adaptation and abridgment of al-Daylamī's eleven stages of love. Even some of the poetic examples given in the *ᶜAṭf* for the various stages are repeated by Rūzbihān. These contain only minor variants, and none that would suggest that Rūzbihān was following a source other than al-Daylamī.[259] At the beginning of the

---

[255] *Mashrab al-arwāḥ,* p. 135; MS, p. 47.

[256] Cf. *Mashrab al-arwāḥ,* p. 135, and MS, pp. 25–26, 35, 49, and 71. A similar example is the definition of *ṣabāba* attributed to Abū Saᶜīd b. al-Aᶜrābī (*Mashrab,* p. 115; MS, p. 37).

[257] Vadet, trans., intro., pp. 13–14. Cf. Rūzbihān Baqlī, *Kitāb-i ᶜabhar al-ᶜāshiqīn,* pp. 9–10; MS, p. 9. Masataka Takeshita has subsequently investigated the relationship between the *ᶜAṭf* and Rūzbihān's *Kitāb-i ᶜabhar al-ᶜāshiqīn* in considerable detail. See n. 4 above.

[258] Vadet, trans., intro., pp. 13–15.

[259] Rūzbihān Baqlī, *Kitāb-i ᶜabhar al-ᶜāshiqīn,* pp. 40–42; MS, pp. 40–48. From Rūzbihān's clear dependence on al-Daylamī in this section it may be concluded that the word *istishhād* (*ᶜAbhar,* p. 41, l. 12) is to be read *istihtār,* as in the notes, and perhaps that *shaghaf* (ibid., l. 9) should be read *shaᶜaf.* Cf. MS,

following section of Rūzbihān's work we find a reflection of al-Daylamī's transmission of the teaching of al-Ḥallāj. Eros (*ᶜishq*) is proclaimed to be a divine attribute, and the function of the preeternal attribute is described in terms of the triad *agent, act,* and *object of act: ᶜāshiq, ᶜishq,* and *maᶜshūq.*[260]

In his *Sharḥ-i shaṭḥīyāt* (Commentary on the ecstatic utterances of the Sufis) Rūzbihān quotes a long passage by al-Ḥallāj on the origin of eros in God's self-love. Although he does not acknowledge his source, Rūzbihān apparently extracted the passage from al-Daylamī's *ᶜAṭf.*[261] Massignon reproduced and translated Rūzbihān's incomplete and somewhat altered Persian version of the passage in 1922 in his *Essai sur les origines du lexique technique de la mystique musulmane,* long before the edition of the *Sharḥ-i shaṭḥīyāt* appeared in 1981. In an article published in 1950 he also gave a translation of the passage as it appears in the *ᶜAṭf,* again while his source was still available only in manuscript form.[262] Rūzbihān's text has variants that could conceivably have their origin in an intermediary between al-Daylamī's work and his commentary or in a separate manuscript tradition of the *ᶜAṭf.* On the other hand, the changes may have been the work of Rūzbihān himself while copying or translating.[263]

Our information allows us to take the story of the influence of al-Daylamī's *ᶜAṭf* no further. But as Rūzbihān Baqlī's debt to al-Daylamī is so extensive, it is possible to hope that future research will extend the narrative. Rūzbihān is a difficult but original and inspired author, and he is a figure of some importance in the history of Persian mysticism. A great deal of attention has been devoted to him already,[264] but little to his

---

pp. 44–45. Carl W. Ernst has discussed al-Daylamī's stages of love and Rūzbihān's adaptation of them within a longer historical perspective ("The Stages of Love in Early Persian Sufism from Rābiᶜa to Rūzbihān," esp. pp. 444–45, 449–55).

[260] Rūzbihān Baqlī, *Kitāb-i ᶜabhar al-ᶜāshiqīn,* p. 44; cf. MS, p. 66, n. 61, and pp. 51, 11 and n. 1, 40–41 and n. 35, 74 (beginning of section six).

[261] *Sharḥ-i shaṭḥīyāt,* pp. 441–44; cf. MS, pp. 51–55.

[262] We have used later editions of both the *Essai* and the article. See Massignon, *Essai* (1954), pp. 424–26, and "Interférences philosophiques," pp. 232–34.

[263] Cf. MS p. 52, nn. 11, 12. We understand that an edition of the Arabic original of Rūzbihān's *Sharḥ-i shaṭḥīyāt,* his *Manṭiq al-asrār,* by Paul Ballanfat and Carl W. Ernst is forthcoming. The Persian version is Rūzbihān's own much amplified translation (cf. *Sharḥ-i shaṭḥīyāt,* intro., pp. 4–5, 33–34).

[264] In addition to the editions of Rūzbihān's works and the studies already

influence and to his following. When the spiritual heritage of Rūzbihān Baqlī has been more thoroughly investigated, perhaps new signs of al-Daylamī's significance for the history of the idea of love in Islamic mysticism will come to light.[265]

THE TRANSLATION

The present translation renders our edition of al-Daylamī's Arabic text. If there are occasional divergences, these are accidental and are most likely the result of our having changed our minds about how a given passage should be emended or translated during the various stages of our involvement with the work. The substantive footnotes that accompany the two versions are not identical. In particular, more attention is given in the edition to the identification of persons mentioned in the text and to technical observations regarding *ḥadiths* cited by the author. Our initial purpose was to provide an English translation of the Arabic text as established by Vadet. However, since the one manuscript of the work is replete with textual problems, only some of which could be solved by recourse to parallel texts, there were numerous passages that might be emended in more than one way, according to the judgment of the editor. Moreover, Vadet's Arabic text contains a relatively high number of misprints and inadvertent deletions that would have added to the difficulty of comparing our translation with his edition. We concluded that it would be useful to prepare a new edition that more nearly represented the text as we read it and understood it.

Our edition nevertheless owes much to Vadet's, both in a great many individual readings, and in the division into paragraphs, where we have in general, but not systematically, followed Vadet. To facilitate use of our work together with Vadet's, we have also followed him in referring to pages rather than folios of the manuscript. The draft of our translation was complete before the appearance of Vadet's French version, but we have since compared our renderings of problematic passages with his.

---

cited here, particular mention should be made of Nazif Hoca's edition of the mystic's *Kashf al-asrār* (1971), a forthcoming fuller edition of the same by Paul Ballanfat, French and English translations of the work by Paul Ballanfat (1996) and Carl W. Ernst (1997), and the doctoral dissertation by Alan Godlas ("The *ʿArāʾis al-bayān:* the Mystical Qur'anic Exegesis of Ruzbihan al-Baqli," University of California., Berkeley, 1991), as well as other important research on Rūzbihān's Koranic exegesis by the same author, including a forthcoming edition and translation of *ʿArāʾis al-bayān.* See the Bibliography and Ernst, *Rūzbihān Baqlī,* pp. 152, 154–55, 171.

[265] Cf. n. 4 above.

Translations of passages from the Koran are taken from A. J. Arberry's translation *The Koran Interpreted* unless otherwise noted. The references to verses, however, are to the widely accepted Egyptian standard edition of 1924, which was used by Muḥammad Fuʾād ᶜAbd al-Bāqī as the basis for his concordance (*al-Muᶜjam al-mufahras li-alfāẓ al-Qurʾān al-karīm*). Arberry uses Fluegel's numeration and does not distinguish clearly between the verses, since he numbers only every fifth verse. Capitalization has been changed to conform to our usage in the rest of our translation of al-Daylamī's treatise. In some cases we have altered Arberry's and others' translations of Koranic passages to suit the meaning understood by the author of the *ᶜAṭf* or the authorities he cites. Alterations are pointed out in the notes.

In sections of the text where the words *ḥubb* (or *maḥabba*) and *ᶜishq* occur together, and especially in more technical passages, we have rendered the former by *love* and the latter by *eros*. The result, admittedly, is not always felicitous. As on other linguistic matters, the Bedouin Arabs were often consulted about the passionate form of love known in Arabic as *ᶜishq*. The word *eros,* because of its Neoplatonic and modern psychoanalytic resonances, is not an entirely suitable translation of *ᶜishq* in this context.[266] We feel, however, that the advantages of rendering *hubb* and *ᶜishq* more or less consistently by two distinct words in English are such that the stylistic problems that result can be tolerated. Where we have wished to specify that verbal forms in the translation reflect forms of the Arabic verb *ᶜashiqa,* we have used expressions such as *to love with eros* or *to love passionately.*[267]

Brackets in the text mark additions made in our edition of the Arabic text, while parentheses denote additions made only in the translation. References to al-Daylamī's text in the notes are to page numbers of the manuscript, which are printed in the translation between brackets in boldface at the beginning of each page.

---

[266] Cf. MS, pp. 112–13, 128.

[267] Cf. MS, p. 128.

BOOK OF THE CONJUNCTION OF THE CHERISHED ALIF WITH THE CONJOINED LĀM

Work of the sheikh, imam, and gnostic Abū ʾl-Ḥasan ʿAlī b. Muḥammad al-Daylamī, may God have mercy on him, as related by the sheikh Abū ʾl-Ḥasan b. Bakrān b. Faḍl, from whom it was related by Abū Shujāʿ Muḥammad b. Saʿdān al-Maqārīḍī, may God Most High be pleased with him and grant him contentment. **[1]**

(AUTHOR'S PREFACE)

In the name of God, the Merciful and Compassionate
O Lord, grant ease and banish hardship![1]

Praise be to God, possessor of might, sublimity, light and splendor, of benefits and blessings, who lightened the darkness with the pearls of his light, clothed our inmost being with the radiance of his glory, and adorned our hearts with the resplendence of his beauty. There and at that time appeared the gleam of his lofty might, the splendor of his sublime glory, the radiance of his dazzling loveliness, and the brilliance of his effulgent beauty, and he aroused his lovers, drunk, inebriated, and delirious in him, enraptured, dallying, and flirtatious. And they rejoiced in him by him, and they gave praise to him through him, and they fled from him to him. And at that time he made them witnesses to himself,[2] guides to his servants, and succor to his lands, by the radiance of his glory, the splendor of his beauty, the signs of his favor, and the lights of his love that he had displayed in them. And the minds of men were baffled when they saw them, and their eyes were dazzled when their proofs appeared,

---

[1] Cf., e.g., Koran 2:185, "God desires ease for you, and desires not hardship for you." Trans. A. J. Arberry. As pointed out in the Introduction, we have used Arberry's translation *The Koran Interpreted* for a great many of the Koranic passages in the text and in our notes. Hereafter these will not as a rule be noted unless the translator's words have been altered to accord with the interpretation required by our text. Capitalization in this and other translations has been made to conform to the system followed here.

[2] "witnesses to himself": apparently an allusion to the *a-last* covenant mentioned in Koran 7:172, which is widely held by Muslim mystical and Neoplatonizing writers to refer to a covenant made between God and men's souls prior to the existence of their bodies.

and the animals were bewildered at the comeliness of their attributes.

And glory be to our glorious Lord, the Visible and the Invisible, who has no beginning and no end, so manifest as to make proof unnecessary and so hidden that no way to him can be found.[3] We ask thee, O God, **[2]** to make our hearts vessels of love for thee, our spirits seats of closeness to thee, our inner selves abodes of fear of thee, our minds agents of thy wisdom, and our limbs instruments of thy [might];[4] for we owe this to thee.

And we ask thee to bless our lord Muḥammad, the beloved, elect, and noble, who attained the goal, faithful through thick and thin, Muḥammad thy servant and prophet, the noblest emissary, the most truthful speaker, and the most successful intercessor, to bless his most excellent family, his righteous Companions, and his chaste wives, and to grant them all peace.

We began with the praise of the Lord because he is the master of our souls and the beloved of our hearts. Then we glorified him because he is our benefactor who bestows his favors upon us. And we concluded with the benediction of his prophet, may God bless him,[5] for by him he saved us from error and led us to the truth, and with the benediction of his good and upright family, our leaders,[6] his elect Companions, our examples, and his virtuous wives, our mothers, may God bless them.

Let us now mention our purpose in writing this book of ours and the goal of our undertaking. Love (*maḥabba*), we have observed, is the best known and most esteemed state (*ḥāl*) among **[3]** people, both the elite and the commonality, the ignorant and the learned, the noble and the ignoble, and the virtuous and the base. For this reason there has been widespread misunderstanding and misrepresentation concerning love, and it has come to seem iniquitous in the eyes of its own people, owing to the distortions, fabrications, and barefaced lies of these who trifle with

---

[3] "manifest" in his attributes, "hidden" in his essence.

[4] Reading *[qudra]tika;* perhaps, thy [will]: *[irāda]tika.*

[5] From this point on, in accordance with English usage, standard Arabic benedictions after the divine name and the name of the Prophet will not generally be translated. Where they may be of help to the reader, however, as when a particular nuance may be suggested, and after the names of figures mentioned less frequently in the work, they will be rendered.

[6] That al-Daylamī calls the family of the Prophet "our leaders," literally, "our imams," may suggest some inclination on his part towards Shiism or a Sufism imbued with Shiite principles, or it may reflect the dominance of Shiism in his day. His adherence to Sunnism, in any case, is clear from the text. Cf. MS, pp. 281–82, on the caliph ᶜUthmān, and chapter five, n. 53.

it and lay false claim to it. As a result, the truth about love is obscured by falsehoods, the good is hidden by the evil, and the real is lost in the metaphorical, so that it is impossible to distinguish one aspect of the matter from another.

Thus it occurred to us to gather the opinions of the eminent scholars, the wisdom of the sages, the pronouncements of the learned, the allusions of those who have drawn near to God, the utterances of the gnostics, and the intimations of the people of unification[7] about and concerning it, so that no ignorant fool, naive ascetic, or learned Salmānite[8] should look on one who has embraced love or is burdened and afflicted with it and rebuke him for it or ascribe his condition to an unbefitting licentiousness, depravity, or wanton abandon to the temptations of the soul,[9] putting him on an equal footing with the wicked and immoral, and further so that no one should look on those great and noble men among the prophets and those sent by God, the people of gnosis, and the pious, or those virtuous Muslims who have been afflicted with it and have divulged it **[4]** and not know to what to ascribe it or how to understand it or in what way he might [be delivered][10] from it and be secure from it.

Moreover, we have determined to set forth what is clearly evident on the subject and to lay bare what is obscure by mentioning love's reasons and causes, the derivation of its name and its definition, its origin and beginning, its essence and quiddity, its description, its effects, its signs

---

[7] A certain hierarchy is implied here, with the people of unification (*ahl al-tawḥīd*) representing the most advanced mystics.

[8] "Salmānite": possibly an adjective derived from the name of the Companion Salmān al-Fārisī, the first Persian convert to Islam. In this sense the word denotes a follower of one of a number of extreme Shiite sects that paid special reverence to him. Or conceivably the term may be used in the sense of "well-intentioned." The exact meaning of the word here is not clear, nor is there total agreement on the text (Ritter [Vadet, ed., xi] suggested *ᶜālmānī*). See, however, Louis Massignon, *Salmān Pāk and the Spiritual Beginnings of Iranian Islām,* esp. p. iv, summary of Shiite and Ismaili views of Salmān, and pp. 30–31, extract from Abū Ḥātim al-Rāzī's *Kitāb al-zīna* on extremist Shiite sects known as Salmānīya. Cf. also Massignon's article "Salmānīya" in *EI¹,* Supplement, p. 195a, and the article "Salmāniyya" by H. Halm in *EI²,* VIII, p. 998a.

[9] The soul is considered to be the seat of the passions, and striving against the soul (*jihād al-nafs*) is called the greater holy war (Ibn al-Jawzī, *Dhamm al-hawā,* pp. 36, 40). The Koran speaks of the soul as "inciting to evil" (12:53), and medieval Muslim scholars, after the ancients, ascribed the passions to the vegetable, appetitive soul (Ibn al-Jawzī, ibid., p. 296).

[10] Our conjecture for a lacuna in the manuscript. Hereafter such conjectures are generally marked only by brackets without being identified in the notes.

and symptoms, its praiseworthy and blameworthy kinds, that which is attributable to God and that which is attributable to man, the excellence of love in itself, those who have praised it and those who have censured it, and its divine and natural varieties, along with the brutish and the innate, the acquired and the bestowed. Furthermore we have furnished the discussion of each type with stories that indicate whether it is sound or corrupt, along with the remarks of the scholars concerning it and the verdicts of the jurists, theologians, mystics, and philosophers, so that whoever ponders our book will know all of these things and be able to discriminate between them, giving each opinion its due. We have divided the subjects into chapters and sections by the aid of God, who is the best helper, and I ask him to guide me and to grant me success.

Let us begin, then, by enumerating the chapters **[5]** and sections of the book, so that anyone who wishes to find them will know where they are in the book and have no difficulty in locating them.

CHAPTER ONE
ON THE CHAPTERS OF THE BOOK

The chapters of the book are twenty-four in number and include in all eighty-five sections.

Chapter one. Enumeration of the chapters of the book, as follows here.

Chapter two. May the word *ᶜishq* (eros) be applied to (love for) God [and from God]?

Chapter three. Preliminary considerations, comprising six sections: the excellence of beauty; [the excellence of the beautiful];[1] the excellence of that which is perceived to be beautiful; the excellence of love (*ḥubb*);[2] the excellence of the one who perceives beauty, namely the lover; the excellence of the beloved.

Chapter four. On the derivation of the word love, comprising three sections: the opinions of the belletrists; the opinions of the Sufis; our opinion.

Chapter five. On the origin and beginning of love, comprising six sections: [the opinions of the divine philosophers among the ancients]; **[6]** the opinions of the astrologers; the opinions of the physicians; the opinions of the theologians; the opinions of the Sufis; our opinion.

Chapter six. On the essence and quiddity of love, comprising five[3] sections: the opinions of the philosophers; the opinions of the theologians; the opinions of the Sufis; our opinion; [the kinds of love].

Chapter seven. On the diverse views people hold about love, comprising seven sections: those who hold that love is obedience; those who hold that love is fascination; those who hold that love is beholding; those who hold that love is will; those who hold that love is a natural disposition; [those who hold that love is knowledge]; those who hold that love is a commingling. These seven groups are divided within themselves into many others.

Chapter eight. On the description of eros and love,[4] comprising two

---

[1] Cf. MS, pp. 16–17. Some section headings have been inserted or rearranged to conform to the author's intention (MS, p. 5) and to the order in which they occur in the text. These are noted in our edition. See also n. 6 below.

[2] The text adds between this section and the next a section "on the opinions of theologians and scholars" (MS, pp. 25–27).

[3] MS: six.

[4] Where the words eros and love occur together, and generally elsewhere in

sections: the opinions of the belletrists; the opinions of the Bedouin Arabs.[5]

Chapter nine. On the description of praiseworthy love, comprising four sections: the opinions **[7]** of the jurists and the scholars; the opinions of the Bedouin Arabs; the opinions of the Sufis; our opinion.

Chapter ten. On those who have disparaged love [for some cause],[6] comprising three sections: those who disparaged love because their natures were not suited to it and out of ignorance of its essence; those who disparaged love because they were unable to bear it; those who disparaged it because their rank exceeded it.

Chapter eleven. On the effects of love and eros and their signs and symptoms, comprising three sections: the opinions of the philosophers; the opinions of the theologians; the opinions of the Bedouin Arabs.[7]

Chapter twelve. On the opinions of unimpeachable authorities (among divine lovers) concerning the signs of love and eros.

Chapter thirteen. On the classification of love according to our opinion.

Chapter fourteen. On the signs of God's love for man, comprising ten sections.[8]

Chapter fifteen. On the signs of man's love for God, comprising ten sections.[8]

Chapter sixteen. **[8]** On the signs of those who love one another in God, comprising ten sections.[8]

Chapter seventeen. On the love of the elite among believers, one section.

Chapter eighteen. On the love of the commonality of Muslims, one section.

---

the theoretical passages of the book, they render *ᶜishq* and *maḥabba* (or *ḥubb*) respectively.

[5] "Bedouin Arabs": *al-ᶜarab*. This is the usual sense in which the author uses the word, but at least one of the stories in a later section appears to occur in an urban context (MS, pp. 135–36).

[6] Cf. MS, p. 146. We have altered the order of the sections here to conform to the order in which they occur in chapter ten. However the order given in the manuscript is the same as that found in al-Daylamī's introduction to chapter ten.

[7] The author speaks of "lovers" (*ᶜushshāq*) rather than Bedouin Arabs in the actual title of the section (MS, p. 165), but the section deals strictly with Bedouin Arab lovers.

[8] This chapter is not divided into numbered sections. Ten "signs," unnumbered in the Arabic, are dealt with. These are given ordinal numbers in the text of the translation.

Chapter nineteen. On the love of all other animate beings,[9] one section.

Chapter twenty. On the meaning of the word *shāhid* (witness, token), one section.

Chapter twenty-one. On the definition of the perfection of love, comprising two sections: the opinions of the philosophers; the opinions of the Sufis.[10]

Chapter twenty-two. On those who died of love (*ᶜishq*), comprising two sections: the view of the philosophers; the declarations of lovers.

Chapter twenty-three. On those who killed themselves for love, one section.

Chapter twenty-four. On the death of divine lovers, who are divided into three groups, two being composed of prophets and one of saints.

This concludes the enumeration of the chapters and sections of the book.

---

[9] "animate beings": *kull dhī rūḥ.* The author means only animals. Cf. chapter nineteen and MS, p. 16.

[10] Chapter twenty-one in fact relates only the opinions of the Sufis. At the end of the chapter the author notes that what the philosophers have to say will be mentioned in the succeeding chapter (MS, p. 241). One opinion, attributed to Aristotle, is given there (MS, pp. 241–42).

CHAPTER TWO

MAY THE WORD *'ISHQ* BE APPLIED TO LOVE FOR GOD **[9]** AND FROM GOD?

Let us begin by discussing the permissibility of applying the word *ᶜishq* (eros) to love for and from God, first because the views of our teachers on the question differ and second in order that no one who hears us using this word in the appropriate contexts will find it unseemly and reject it because it is unfamiliar. Indeed our masters employed the term only in rare instances, or individually from time to time. Thus we have decided to mention the matter here, so that the reader will be informed before we use the word.

Our masters have held differing views on the subject. Some rejected the use of the word *ᶜishq* and some allowed it. Among the latter were the followers of ᶜAbd al-Wāḥid b. Zayd and the mystics of Damascus as a whole, together with their partisans in this opinion, whom we shall mention in the chapter on the diverse views people hold about love.[1] Also among those who allowed the usage were Abū Yazīd al-Bisṭāmī, Abū ʾl-Qāsim al-Junayd, al-Ḥusayn b. Manṣūr [al-Ḥallāj], and others. As for our teacher, Abū ᶜAbd Allāh b. Khafīf, may God have mercy on him, he was opposed to it for some time, until he came across a tract on *ᶜishq* by Abū ʾl-Qāsim al-Junayd in which he discussed its meaning, etymology, and essence. He then changed **[10]** his view, allowing the use of the term, and himself composed a tract on the issue.[2]

It has been related from the Prophet that he said: "God Most High says: 'If I know that [the heart of] my servant is overwhelmed by obsession with me, I cause him to desire to implore me and to confide in me. If the condition of a man is such, then he loves me (*ᶜashiqanī*) and I love him (*ᶜashiqtuhu*). And if the condition of a man is such, and he desires to

---

[1] The reference is to chapter seven, section three, where the followers of ᶜAbd al-Wāḥid b. Zayd are mentioned among those who hold that love consists in beholding (MS, p. 102). The Sufis of Damascus are cited in chapter five (MS, p. 71) as maintaining that beholding marks the passage from love to eros.

[2] Neither of the two tracts referred to here is mentioned by Sezgin. Ibn Khafīf, if an extract from his *Kitāb al-iᶜtiqād* (Major creed) cited by Ibn Taymīya is authentic, definitely rejected the use of the word *ᶜishq* with reference to God in that work. Cf. the Introduction, pp. xlvii–xlix and nn. 156, 158, and 159 there.

be forgetful of me, then I come between him and his forgetfulness. Such men are my saints (*awliyāʾī*) in truth. They are the true heroes.[3] They are those for the sake of whom, when I will[4] to punish the people of the earth, I set the punishment aside.'" Among the evidence proving that the Prophet said this, I mean the words "for the sake of whom, . . . I set the punishment aside," are God's words in the Koran to Muḥammad his beloved, "But God would never chastise them, with thee among them," to the end of the verse (8:33). It has been related that David, peace be upon him, was called the *ᶜashīq* (the beloved and/or lover) of God.

He (al-Daylamī)[5] said: In view of the above, I do not see how one can reject the usage, since *ᶜishq* is synonymous with the word *maḥabba* in the meaning "love." But *maḥabba* is more widely used and accepted and has unanimous approval. We prefer to use it when we speak of love, because a more usual **[11]** and unanimously approved usage is preferable to an exceptional and disputed one, although we do not reject the exceptional term, since the meaning of the two words is the same.

Therefore we will relate what people have said about the two just as they said it: if they used the word *ᶜishq,* so shall we, and if they used the word *ḥubb* (or *maḥabba*), we shall do likewise, (trusting in) God, the possessor of all power and might.

---

[3] "true heroes": *al-abṭāl.* Abū Nuᶜaym (*Ḥilya,* VI, p. 165) has the same.

[4] The Arabic verb *arāda/yurīdu* in the divine context is best rendered by *to will* (*wills*), rather than, for example, by *to desire* or *to purpose.* This translation makes clear the reference of the word to the totally free exercise of God's creative will (*irāda*), unfettered by want, lack, need, or purpose (*gharaḍ*). With the exception of the Muᶜtazilites on certain points, Muslim thinkers as a rule consider these to be impossible in a perfect being. See Bell, *Love Theory,* pp. 65–69. A. J. Arberry, in the translation of the Koran which we have regularly cited here (see author's preface, n. 1), renders the often recurring *arāda/yurīdu* by *to desire,* presumably because English style prefers it. Cf., e.g., his translation of Koran 36:82: "His command, when he desires a thing, is to say to it 'Be,' and it is," and 39:4: "Had God desired to take to him a son, . . ."

[5] Or conceivably Ibn Khafīf.

CHAPTER THREE
PRELIMINARY CONSIDERATIONS

At this point it will be useful to make some preliminary observations as an introduction to what we have to say and to the various opinions we shall set forth.

To begin with, the love with which lovers love one another is divided into five kinds, corresponding to five different kinds of men: divine (*ilāhī*) among (the most advanced mystics), the people of unification; intellectual (*ᶜaqlī*) among the gnostics; spiritual (*rūḥī*) among the elite; natural (*ṭabīᶜī*) among the commonality; and bestial (*bahīmī*) among the base. We mention these kinds of love first so that the intended meanings will present no difficulty to the reader when he comes across them in the appropriate contexts.

Considering the matter further, we find that all the causes of love and the reasons for it can be reduced to three.[1] The first is a thing (*maᶜnā*) that God displayed to (*abdā ilā*) this world and that he named beauty. He likewise displayed a person whom he endowed with this thing and called him beautiful. **[12]** Again, he willed to make manifest other things to set over against these things in order to reveal by means of juxtaposing them in pairs his design (*sirr*) in (creating) them. So he displayed a perceiver of the beautiful and set him over against the beautiful person. Thus he made manifest, by the perceiver's perception of the beautiful,[2] that thing we call love, and he endowed the perceiver with it, so that he became a lover. In this way love was set over against beauty, and the perceiver of the beautiful, [namely, the lover], over against the thing perceived to be beautiful, namely, the beloved.

These three constitute the sum total of love's causes. There are no others. Moreover, we find them all laudable according to both revealed law and reason. Hence those who scorn love and seek to discredit it have no valid objection; for any defect is accidental to it, and that which is sound and of enduring reality cannot be corrupted by an accidental defect. Let there be no misunderstanding. Having said this, we shall now

---

[1] Beauty, to which corresponds love; the beautiful person, to whom corresponds the beloved; and the perceiver of the beautiful, to whom corresponds the lover. Regarding such triads, see MS, p. 51, and chapter five, n. 61.

[2] "perception of the beautiful": *istiḥsān,* the first of the stages of love in many of the medieval Muslim hierarchies of love terminology. See Bell, *Love Theory in Later Ḥanbalite Islam,* pp. 157–58.

proceed to demonstrate in separate sections the excellence of each of the things we have mentioned, God willing.

Section One. On the Excellence of Beauty

God Most High, bestowing his favor on the one with whom he spoke, that is, Moses,[3] peace be upon him, said: "And I shed on thee love from me" (20:39). Qatāda held that the meaning of the word "love" here was comeliness in his eyes, that no one would see him without loving him. ᶜIkrima said that it was beauty or comeliness. Know also that Joseph, peace be upon him, **[13]** was endowed with half of all beauty. Whenever a woman saw him she would cover her face for fear of becoming infatuated with him. Indeed, God made Joseph's beauty one of his miracles.[4] He likewise bestowed on his chosen friend Adam, peace be upon him, an exquisite frame, and he said: "And he formed you (plural) and made your forms well" (40:64). It has been said that it is Adam who is intended here, and it has also been said that the meaning is: He shaped your image and did it well.

ᶜAbd Allāh b. Burayda related from his father that the Messenger of God said: "Three things increase the strength of one's vision: looking at greenery, looking at a beautiful face, and looking at running water." And ᶜĀʾisha, may God be pleased with her, related that the Messenger of God used to delight in greenery and in a beautiful face. She also related that the Messenger of God used to command the armies: "If you send a messenger, choose one with a beautiful face and a beautiful name." Again he said: "Take your needs to those with comely faces, for his beautiful countenance is the first benefit you receive from a man."[5]

Abū Bakr b. ᶜAbdān related to us from **[14]** al-Bāghandī from Abū Ṭāhir from Ibn Wahb from Ibn Lahīᶜa from ᶜUmāra b. Ghazīya from a man from Syria, who said:[6] "The Messenger of God used to loathe the cutting off of beautiful hair." And Abū Bakr al-Bāghandī related to us[7]

---

[3] Moses is known in Islamic tradition as "the one with whom God spoke" (*kalīm Allāh*) because of the experience on Mt. Sinai. Cf. Koran 4:164: "And unto Moses God spoke directly." See also chapter twenty-four, n. 30.

[4] Cf. Koran 12:30–31.

[5] On these and similar traditions, generally held to be spurious, see the notes to this passage in our edition and, e.g., Ibn al-Jawzī, *Kitāb al-mawḍūᶜāt,* I, pp. 159–65, and Ibn Qayyim al-Jawzīya, *Rawḍat al-muḥibbīn,* pp. 123–24.

[6] In this translation the various Arabic expressions used in relating a chain of transmission are rendered for the most part only by the word "from."

[7] There is an ellipsis or omission here. The text presumably means or should read, "And Abū Bakr (i.e., Ibn ᶜAbdān) [related to us from] al-Bāghandī, who

from Muḥammad b. ᶜAlī from Yaḥyā b. Bukayr from Ibn Lahīᶜa from ᶜUmāra from ᶜAbd al-Raḥmān b. al-Qāsim from his father, who said: "The Messenger of God said: 'Beautiful hair is a garment given by God. So let whoever has beautiful hair treat it with reverence.'"

The Messenger of God sought the hand of a woman of the tribe of Kalb, and he sent ᶜĀᵓisha to look at her. When she returned he said to her, "How did you find her?" "I saw nothing in her," she replied. "You saw something in her," he said. "You saw a mole on her cheek so beautiful that every single hair of yours quivered." "Nothing can be hidden from you," she answered.

A certain philosopher also said: "Beauty is the breaking forth of the light of the rational soul on the physical form."

ᶜAlī b. Muhammad (al-Daylamī) said:[8] (In addition to these proofs from authority) we have something to say about the substance of this matter. Know that God Most High, having willed to bring forth **[15]** to temporal existence a manifest form to bear witness to beauty and loveliness, displayed a witness in the manifest form of his chosen friend Adam. He created him with his hand and endowed him with attributes from his own beauty, loveliness, splendor, knowledge, power, volition, and will, and from his other attributes shared with men. Thus Adam was the noblest form and the mightiest witness God has shown forth in this world.[9]

---

related from. . . ." Al-Bāghandī, who like Ibn ᶜAbdān (Abū Bakr Aḥmad b. ᶜAbdān al-Shīrāzī) was also called Abū Bakr, died in 312 or 313/924–26 (al-Khaṭīb al-Baghdādī, *Taᵓrīkh Baghdād,* III, p. 213). Ibn ᶜAbdān was a recognized authority on al-Bāghandī's traditions (ibid., p. 212). Ibn Khafīf, al-Daylamī's teacher, heard traditions directly from al-Bāghandī (al-Daylamī, *Sīrat-i İbn al-Ḫafīf,* p. 209), but al-Daylamī himself could hardly have done so. Abū Bakr b. ᶜAbdān lived in Shiraz until 350/961, but he then moved to Ahvaz, where he died in 388/998 (al-Dhahabī, *al-ᶜIbar fī khabar man ghabar,* III, p. 38; Sobieroj, "Ibn Ḫafīf aš-Šīrāzī," p. 130). He thus left Shiraz shortly before al-Daylamī, according to our calculations, came into contact with Ibn Khafīf around 352 (see the Introduction, p. xii, and n. 6 there). Possibly al-Daylamī heard traditions from him in Ahvaz rather than in Shiraz. On al-Bāghandī (Ibn al-Bāghandī) see Sezgin, *GAS,* I, pp. 172–73.

[8] Cf. the same usage and the similar expression *qāla ṣāḥibu ᵓl-kitāb,* "the author of this book said," below, MS, pp. 18, 19, 28, 29, and passim. See also above, MS, p. 10.

[9] "Witness" and "manifest form" in this paragraph both translate the one Arabic word *shāhid.* The term is the subject of chapter twenty. There, as here, it is usually best rendered by "witness." Elsewhere, generally with a different plural, it often has the less technical sense of sign, as in the title of chapter fourteen,

The Messenger of God said: "God created Adam in his own image." Indeed, he gave him all created beauty and from him shed beauty upon his seed until the hour of resurrection, when beauty will return to its (original) place. And he created for him an abode close to himself and a place near to himself and called it the Garden of Paradise. And he bestowed upon it light from his own light and adorned it with his own beauty, so that it derived[10] light from his light, beauty from his beauty, loveliness from his loveliness, splendor from his splendor, and purity from his purity.

Thus the Prophet also said: "When God Most High created the Garden of Paradise, he planted its trees with his hand and caused its rivers to pour forth. Then he said to it: 'Be adorned with my beauty. For by my might and my glory, no miser shall dwell near me in thee.'" **[16]**

Then the Garden of Paradise shed its beauty on this world and on its various elements. So the beauty of all beautiful things in this abode is derived from these two witnesses (Adam and Paradise), one being animal, corporeal, and spiritual, and the other being inanimate and vegetable.[11] And that beauty has suffered change only as a result of its remoteness from its source. Let this be understood.

Among the proofs that beauty is the cause of love and that the place of beauty in God's design is made manifest by means of love is that the Prophet said: "I saw my Lord," that is, in a dream, "in the most beautiful form, and he said to me, 'Ask.' And I said to him, 'I ask of thee thy love and love for deeds that draw me near to thy love.'"[12] The report goes on. However our purpose here is not to relate the whole saying but only to mention one of the points it makes, namely, that because the manifestation occurred to the Prophet through the witness of beauty, he desired love for God, and he was unable to ask for anything other than love. So he asked first for love and its various kinds.

The above clearly indicates the excellence of beauty.

"On the Signs (*shawāhid*) of God's Love for Man." The word is used of God conceived of as manifest and present (see chapter sixteen, n. 1).

[10] The Arabic verb translated by "derived," *iqtabasa,* is transitive, meaning generally "to borrow" and being used more specifically of borrowing fire. But what the author intends is a totally passive reception of light, beauty, and the like. Further on he states, "The beautiful one does not acquire beauty. Rather God Most High chose beauty for him before creating him. . . . Hence there is no . . . acquisition (*kasb*)" (MS, p. 18).

[11] Vadet adds *maᶜdinī* (mineral).

[12] "thy love": *ḥubbaka, ḥubbika.* The subject and object of the verbal noun "love" are ambiguous in the Arabic as well as in the English.

Section Two. **[17]** *On the Excellence of the Beautiful*

The beautiful is that upon which this virtue, which is noble and praiseworthy according to reason and divine institution, has been bestowed. On this we may cite the saying of the Prophet related by ᶜĀᵓisha, Anas, Ibn Masᶜūd, Abū Hurayra, and a number of others: "Seek good from those with beautiful faces."[13] They related it with different wordings, but the meaning is the same. Again Anas b. Mālik related that the Messenger of God said: "He who has been blessed with beauty of countenance, beauty of character, a righteous wife, and a generous soul has been given the blessings of this world and the next."

Abū Hurayra related that the Messenger of God said: "God never endows a man with beauty of frame and character and then hellfire tastes him."[14] In another tradition it is said that God never endows a man with these qualities "but that he shrinks from letting hellfire taste his flesh."[15] According to Ibn ᶜAbbās, the Messenger of God said: "If God has endowed a man with a beautiful face **[18]** and placed him in a position that does not dishonor him, then he is among the chosen of God in his creation."[16]

God said (to Moses): "And I shed on thee love from me" (20:39); and it has been said that this means: I gave you bodily beauty. He also said, great is his praise: "We indeed created man in the fairest stature" (95:4). God swore by these things (that is, the fig, the olive, Mount Sinai, and "this land secure" mentioned at the beginning of the sura) that he created Adam, peace be upon him, and his seed with the best proportioned frame and the fairest countenance. It has been said that this refers to the prime of his youth, his sturdiness, and his strength, and that it means that Adam was the fairest, best proportioned, and best formed creature

---

[13] Ibn Qayyim al-Jawzīya, although he acknowledges that it is related with a chain of transmission, rejects this tradition (*Rawḍa,* pp. 123–24). The version he cites varies slightly in wording, having *min* rather than *ᶜinda* for *from* in the translation.

[14] The text has a masculine verb prefix for the usually feminine, sometimes masculine subject *al-nāru* (hellfire), which is carefully vowelled in the nominative. The gender of the verb suggests reading it in form IV: "and then (God) feeds him to hellfire." Some texts, like al-Haythamī's *Majmaᶜ al-zawāᵓid* (VIII, p. 21), have a masculine prefix as here, while others, for example al-Muttaqī al-Hindī's *Kanz al-ᶜummāl* (III, p. 18, *ḥadīth* 5237) have the feminine *tāᵓ* and vowel the text in such a way as to ensure that hellfire is taken as the subject.

[15] See preceding note.

[16] All three traditions in this paragraph are rejected by Ibn al-Jawzī. See the footnotes in our edition and Ibn al-Jawzī, *Mawḍūᶜāt,* I, pp. 160, 164.

that could be.

ᶜAlī b. Muḥammad, may God have mercy on him, said: Let us now consider the substance of the matter. A beautiful person has not *acquired* (*lam yaksib*) his beauty. Rather, God chose beauty for him before creating him, and likewise when he was inside the womb. Hence there is no (human) power (*qudra*) involved and no acquisition (*kasb*). It is therefore incumbent upon one who is beautiful to acknowledge this blessing and favor from God to him, so that he may give thanks to him for it. To acknowledge God's blessing is indeed to thank him for it. And when a beautiful person acknowledges these blessings and gives thanks for them, he merits an increase from God by his thanks, as God has said: "If you are thankful, surely I will increase you" (14:7). Thus a man merits love **[19]** by his perception of the blessing; and the increase that he merits because of his gratitude is God's love for him in response to his acknowledging the blessing. This love consists in obedience and conformity.[17] Other men, moreover, will come to love a man because of God's love for him. These are some of the virtues of the beautiful. Understand them well.

Section Three. On the Excellence of That Which Is Perceived to Be Beautiful

ᶜAlī b. Muḥammad, may God have mercy on him, said: Know that those things that we perceive to be beautiful have derived their beauty from the universal beauty, which is near to God. Moreover, beauty remains intense in things in proportion to their proximity to the universal (beauty) after proceeding forth; and it weakens and is diminished in proportion to their remoteness from it, even to the extent that hardly any beauty can be seen in them, so deeply it lies hidden. Only the gnostics can perceive it. But indeed both those things we perceive to be beautiful and those we do not, were they to be deprived of this quality for one instant, would perish without a trace and vanish altogether. The subtler and rarer a body, the clearer the manifestation of beauty in it, which shows, moreover, **[20]** that it is closer to the universal (beauty) and to its source. Because of its subtleness it is near, and because of its nearness it is subtle and receives beauty from its source.

---

[17] This is one of the most common Muslim definitions of man's love to God and might appear somewhat unusual as a description of God's love to man. However, according to a tradition related by al-Daylamī later in this same work (MS, p. 186), the Prophet was told by his uncle Abū Ṭālib, "Nephew, I see that your Lord whom you worship obeys you." "Uncle," he replied, "if you were to obey him, he would obey you too." See also MS, p. 108, on the sixth group.

Consider the eye. Since it is the subtlest of the bodily organs in the corporeal realm, it is the most receptive to beauty. The form of beauty is strongest, and the functions of the spirit are most apparent in the eye. The nearness of the eye to its source and to the universal (beauty) is shown by the fact that the Messenger of God, when he saw an early fruit, would kiss it and place it on his eye.[18] One day, also, he went out into the rain and took off his garment so that the rain would fall on him. When he was questioned about this, he said: "It has recently been with its Lord."

Similarly, since the intellect is the thing nearest to God, it is the most beautiful of all the things he has created. Hence he said to it when he created it, "Come forward," and it came forward. Then he said, "Turn around and go back," and it turned and went back. Then he said to it, "By my might and my glory, I have created no creature more beautiful than thee." This is because it received beauty from its source and from God Most High without any intermediary. What is perceived to be beautiful **[21]** is loved, and one does not oppose what one loves, but strives rather to be in conformity with it. It is because this is the case that God said (to the intellect): "In proportion to thee I take away and I give; thine is the [reward] and thine the punishment."[19] Such is the form of the beloved. Let this be understood.

If the case is as we have said, then the virtue of the one perceived to be beautiful is that he is an unimpeachable witness (*shāhid ᶜadl*) who testifies to the wisdom of his maker, a guide showing the way and pointing to the uniqueness of his creator, a noble intercessor who brings a man close to his beloved, and a truthful informant who tells him of the favor of his bosom friend. Take note.

Now let us proceed to the section on the effect of the thing perceived to be beautiful on the perceiver, that is, the effect of the beloved upon the lover, namely, love.

Section Four. On the Excellence of Love [and Eros]

God said (to Moses): "And I shed love on thee from me" (20:39). According to Mujāhid, "love" here means "affection (*mawadda*) in the hearts of believers."[20] In the same vein the Prophet said to ᶜAlī b. Abī

---

[18] For other versions of this tradition, see the note in our edition.

[19] This saying is not considered authentic by Ibn al-Jawzī (*Mawḍūᶜāt,* I, p. 175). Notwithstanding, he argues elsewhere that on the Day of Resurrection a man "will be rewarded only in proportion to his reason" (*Dhamm al-hawā,* pp. 5–6).

[20] This exegesis may have been understood by some as intended to avoid the

Ṭālib, may God be pleased with him and with his house: "Say, 'Lord, grant me affection in the breasts of believers, intimate friendship (*walīja*) and love in thy sight, **[22]** and a constant bond with thee.'" Then God revealed these words: "Surely those who believe and do deeds of righteousness—unto them the All-Merciful shall assign love (*wudd*)" (19:96). It has been said that this means love in the hearts of men.[21]

Among the virtues of love is that it is a sign of God's love for you. As the Prophet said: "Shall I tell you which of you is most loved by God?" "Yes," they replied. "The one who is most loved by other people," [he said].

Another of love's virtues is that it is a standard of measure between you and God. If you wish to know the extent of God's love for you, consider the extent of your love for God. For he loves you to the same extent that you love him.

Yet another of love's virtues was mentioned by Ṭāwūs, who said he had heard Ibn ᶜAbbās say: "Kinship can be denied, kindness can be forgotten, but nothing has ever been seen like the closeness of hearts to each other." Ibn Qudāma related that Ibn Munādhir composed concerning this remark the following lines:

> The closest kinship can be denied, and a kindness forgotten,
> but there is nothing like the closeness of two hearts.
> Passion draws this one and that one near,
> and there they are, one soul seeming to be two.

The author of this book said: I originally intended to devote to the excellence of love a separate chapter, but I found that the subject was in effect the same as that of the present chapter, **[23]** and that the two chapters were one. So I included the question in this chapter for the sake of brevity. Let us continue, then, by mentioning another of love's virtues, namely, that only by means of love can you hope to attain God's love for you, as God has said: "Say: 'If you love God, follow me, and God will love you'" (3:31). Thus it is your love for the Prophet that enables you to attain God's love for you.

---

suggestion that there is any real love on God's part for man. The view of the speculative theologians that God could have no anthropopathic attributes, and hence did not love, was followed by a number of mystics, including al-Qushayrī (*Risāla* [Cairo, 1912], p. 144) and al-Ghazālī (*Iḥyā*ʾ, XIV, pp. 95–99), but not by al-Daylamī.

[21] That Koran 19:96 was revealed after a like statement by the Prophet to ᶜAlī is related in al-Zamakhsharī, *Kashshāf,* II, p. 527. Cf. also al-Ṭabarī, *Jāmi*ᶜ *al-bayān* (al-Ḥalabī), XVI, p. 132, for similar commentary on this verse.

It has been related from the Prophet that he said: "Shall I tell you who among you is the most loved by God and the closest to me?" "Yes, O Messenger of God," they replied. "Those of you," he said, "who have the most beautiful character, who are easy to get along with, and who become close to others and to whom others become close."

Of Kaᶜb it is related that he said: "I find in the revealed books that there has been no love in anyone among men that did not have its beginning from God, who bestows it first upon the inhabitants of the heavens and then upon the people of earth." Then he recited this verse from the Koran: "Surely those who believe and do deeds of righteousness—unto them the All-Merciful shall assign love" (19:96). Thus among love's virtues is that only by means of it can you reach love (of any kind).[22]

It is related that an old woman used to go in to visit the Messenger of God and that he would draw her near to him.[23] **[24]** Once ᶜĀʾisha said to him, "I see that you draw this woman near to you and honor her." "She was a friend of Khadīja's," he replied, "and God loves [the preservation of] an old friendship." ᶜĀʾisha also recounted the following: "An old woman came to the Prophet, and he said to her, 'Who are you?' 'I am Jaththāma of Medina,' she answered. 'No,' he said, 'you are Ḥussāna of Medina.[24] How is Medina? How are you all? How have you been since we left?'[25] 'Very well,' she replied, 'may my father and my mother be your ransom.' When she left I remarked, 'O Messenger of God, you gave that old woman such a welcome!' 'She used to visit us in Khadīja's time,' he said, 'and loyalty to old friends is part of faith.'" Anas related: "Whenever a gift was brought to the Messenger of God, he would say,

---

22 This is the apparent sense of the text as it stands. Vadet (ed.) has "love [of God]." Kaᶜb was a Yemenite Jew said to have converted to Islam as early as 17/638. He is considered the oldest authority on Jewish traditions in Islam. Cf. M. Schmitz, *EI²*, IV, pp. 316b–17a, s.v. "Kaᶜb al-Aḥbār."

23 Or: "he would favor her." Cf. Lane, s.v. *q-r-b*.

24 A complimentary change of the woman's name. Jaththāma means, for example, "prone to crouching, unintelligent." Ḥussāna means "exceedingly beautiful."

25 The Prophet had relatively few occasions to ask such a question after he emigrated to Medina. Approximately the same narrative is found in Ibn Ḥajar's *Iṣāba,* where likewise the Prophet says, "How are you all? How have you been since we left?" But he does not ask about Medina. The Calcutta edition (V, p. 520), paralleling our text, calls the woman Jaththāma al-Madanīya (of Medina). However al-Bijāwī's edition (VII, pp. 580–81) has al-Muzanīya, as does Ibn al-Athīr, *Usd al-ghāba* (VII, pp. 47, 64). Since al-Madanīya seems to be a corruption of al-Muzanīya, the question may originally have been "How is Muzayna?"

'Take it to so-and-so, for she used to love Khadīja.'" Similarly, al-Awzāᶜī related from Yaḥyā, who said: "Solomon son of David said, 'Hold fast to your first beloved.'"

Likewise among love's virtues is that (God) called the most beloved of his creatures, Muḥammad, a "beloved" of God.[26]

Sumnūn[27] said: "Nothing can be expressed **[25]** except by means of something subtler than itself. But there is nothing subtler than love, so how can it be expressed?"

Also among love's virtues is that in the final abode near God every state—fear, hope, patient endurance, trust, submission, and the others—passes away with the vision, except love and a part of contentment (*riḍā*). This is because contentment has two aspects. One consists in renouncing all objections to affliction and to divine decrees, and this aspect, being of the same nature as patient endurance, passes away. The other aspect of contentment, the heart's rejoicing at the sight of all that comes to it from God (*al-wāridāt*), is of the same nature as love and does not pass away. The explanation of this is that all the other states have a cause or reason that ceases to exist in Paradise, and hence they too cease to exist. But the cause of love is the beholding of beauty and splendor, which ceases neither in this life nor the next.[28]

(Supplementary) Section. The Opinions of Theologians and Scholars on [Eros][29]

Abū Ḥafṣ al-Ḥaddād said: "The person possessed by eros has a luminous disposition, a shining nature, **[26]** and fragrant[30] traits. In the movements of his senses(?)[31] is evidence for the eyes."

---

[26] Perhaps the text originally read "the beloved of God" (*ḥabīb Allāh*) for *ḥabīban lillāh,* this being more usual. The term *ḥabīb* for the Prophet is not Koranic. For Ibn al-ᶜArabī's treatment of the epithet, see his commentary in his *Tarjumān al-ashwāq,* p. 44; R. A. Nicholson's translation of the same, p. 69; and Bell, *Love Theory,* pp. 161–62.

[27] The name is also vowelled Samnūn. See on the vowelling, al-Sulamī, *Ṭabaqāt al-ṣūfīya* (ed. Pedersen), p. 186, n. 1.

[28] This paragraph bears on the important question of whether love and longing cease with union, on which see Bell, *Love Theory,* pp. 168–70, 137–38.

[29] On the first two statements below and their occurrence in al-Masᶜūdī's *Murūj al-dhahab,* see chapter five, n. 42. The following three statements are not in the *Murūj.*

[30] Cf. Ibn Qayyim al-Jawzīya, *Rawḍa,* p. 174: "And they have said that eros . . . endows one with a pleasant fragrance."

[31] "his senses": *ḥissihi/ḥassihi* (al-Masᶜūdī, *Murūj,* IV, p. 374, has the same). The alternative *jasadihi* (his body) is perhaps too simple a solution. Ibn Qayyim

According to Ḥammād b. Abī Ḥanīfa: "Eros only afflicts the heart of a man marked by superior merit[32] and graceful form, and one afflicted with it is recognizable by his extreme tenderness."

A certain sage said: "Eros makes the coward courageous, the miser generous, and the numbskull clear-headed. It raises the resolve of the feeble. The might of kings is subjected to it, the strength of the brave is humbled before it, the will of the arrogant is obedient to it, every great obstacle is made easy before it, and every veiled thing is made manifest to it. It is the cause of refinement and the first gate at which men's minds are opened. By it schemes and ruses are invented, in it wandering cares subside, through it close companions are joined together, and in it contenders concur."[33]

[It has been said of eros]:[34] "It is a delightful comrade, a charming friend, a commanding companion, and a conquering king. Its paths are subtle, its ways lead in every direction,[35] and its laws are despotic. It possesses bodies and their spirits, hearts and their thoughts, eyes **[27]** and their glances, and minds and their opinions. It has been given the reins of their obedience and the halter of their actions."

A certain sage said: "Eros trains the soul and refines the character. To reveal it is natural, and to conceal it is an unnatural constraint. The mind is its chamberlain, and the limbs are its servant."

But descriptions of this kind are many, and place can be made for only a few of them here.

---

al-Jawzīya (*Rawḍa,* p. 176) has *nafsihi* (his soul).

[32] "superior merit": *al-barāᶜa.* Al-Masᶜūdī, *Murūj* (Meynard), VI, p. 374: *al-barᵓa* (innocence); *Murūj* (Pellat), IV, p. 240, n. 17, citing MS Mecca, 112 Taᵓrīkh: *al-barāᶜa,* as here. Cf. MS, pp. 163–64.

[33] Just about the same saying, ending differently, is ascribed to "one of the eloquent" in Ibn Qayyim al-Jawzīya, *Rawḍa,* p. 176; Maḥmūd b. Sulaymān b. Fahd al-Ḥalabī, *Manāzil al-aḥbāb,* MS Top Kapı, Ahmet III, 2471, fol. 15a; and Marᶜī b. Yūsuf al-Karmī, *Munyat al-muḥibbīn,* MS Dār al-Kutub, Adab 6252, fol. 11a.

[34] Maḥmūd b. Sulaymān b. Fahd al-Ḥalabī introduces the following saying with the words, "One of the sages was asked about eros and said: . . ." (*Manāzil al-aḥbāb,* fol. 12b). Jaᶜfar b. Aḥmad al-Sarrāj (*Maṣāriᶜ al-ᶜushshāq,* I, p. 11) and, following him, Ibn al-Jawzī (*Dhamm,* pp. 290–91) and Ibn Qayyim al-Jawzīya (*Rawḍa,* p. 139) ascribe the saying to the theologian Thumāma b. Ashras. But they do so in the context of a frame story in which, according to al-Daylamī, Thumāma said something quite different. Mughulṭāy (*al-Wāḍiḥ al-mubīn,* pp. 30–31) was aware of the two different versions of the story.

[35] "lead in every direction": *mutaḍādda.* Ibn Qayyim al-Jawzīya (*Rawḍa,* p. 139): *ghāmiḍa* (obscure).

Section Five. On the Excellence of the Lover, or the Perceiver of Beauty
It is the lover who is praised in the words of the Prophet: "There is no good in one who becomes close to no one and to whom no one is close." With these words the Prophet denied the existence of any good in a heart that grows fond of no one and a body of which no one is fond. The reason for this is that the causes of love are [many]: first, beauty of form; second, beauty of character; third, a pleasant wit; fourth, beneficence; fifth, an amiable nature; sixth, a cheerful spirit; and, seventh, a divine concord. If a soul scorns all these things, then there can be no good in it. It neither loves nor is loved, since it possesses none of the means and causes of love.

Since the lover, on the other hand, **[28]** is a perceiver of beauty, [loving] according to the proper conditions of love as we have mentioned, namely the avoidance of vitiating accidents,[36] he is also one who draws lessons from the evidence God has shown forth in this world. And one who draws such lessons is unanimously praised by the Book, the Sunna, and the consensus of the community. Let this be understood.

Section Six. On the Virtues of the Beloved
The beloved is the one on whom has been bestowed all (*sic*) the causes that arouse love in people that we mentioned when we explained the Prophet's words: "There is no good in one who becomes close to no one and to whom no one is close." If you find that a person is loved in the hearts of men, it is for one of these qualities we mentioned, or most of them, or all of them. In any event, it is evident that the beloved is possessed of praiseworthy attributes and a noble nature. Let there be no doubt about this.

The author of this book said: In view of the foregoing, it is no longer possible to censure any of the aspects of love except certain brutish practices that have no real connection with love according to the unanimous opinion of scholars, jurists, men of eloquence, rational thinkers, gnostics, theologians, and philosophers. Some scholars and mystics have indeed censured it (natural love) **[29]** and heaped scorn and blame upon it. But they did this only because they had risen above the level (of natural love) to a nobler and higher one. They scorned the first level only in comparison to the second, [not] because it is contemptible and blameworthy in itself. All of this, along with similar issues, will be explained in the appropriate passages below, God willing.

We mention natural love here first because it is from natural love that the adepts of the stations progress upwards to reach divine love. For we

---

[36] Cf. MS, p. 12, where the author states that any defect is accidental to love.

find that souls that are burdened with love but are not prepared to receive natural love cannot bear divine love. But if souls are prepared for love by possessing a subtle constitution, a pure essence, a tender nature, a generous disposition,[37] and a luminous spirit, they receive natural love and then rise above it, striving to attain their perfection, to arrive at their goal, and to ascend to their source. These souls struggle with the lovers to whom they belong, goading them on **[30]** until they raise them up to divine love step by step. Each time they come a step closer, their longing for the step above increases, and so they proceed until they reach the ultimate goal.

It was for this reason that the Messenger of God said: "The believer finds no repose short of meeting God." This is because everything finds its repose in its state of completion, and the completion of the believer consists in being joined (*ittiṣāl*) to his Lord. Take note.

In Mecca I heard one of our sheikhs relate the following: "Someone asked ᶜUmar b. ᶜAbd al-ᶜAzīz when he was caliph, 'Where is that comeliness, that fragrance,[38] and that manifest manliness you had before you assumed the caliphate?' 'My soul,' ᶜUmar replied, 'is a soul that tastes and yearns. Whenever it tastes one station, it yearns for the station above it. So when it attained the caliphate, the highest of stations, it yearned for that which is with God.'" This report shows that a noble soul that is marked by love, mixed with subtlety, kneaded with generosity, and sweetened with a spiritual[39] spirit does not rest until it reaches its goal and attains **[31]** its perfection.

The author of this book said: We have scattered throughout this book many subtle points and allusions that we need not enumerate here and that we have neither explained nor clarified but have left for those who come after us as an exercise for their minds and a test of their knowledge. So let whoever is searching for truth seek them out with all his ability, and he will gain mastery over them in accordance with his share of knowledge. Moreover, we have used expressions in this book that require explanation, but we have left them undefined for two reasons: first

---

[37] "a generous disposition": *aryaḥīyat al-nafs,* lit., "generosity of *soul,"* which would be inappropriate here.

[38] ᶜUmar b. ᶜAbd al-ᶜAzīz is reported to have used large amounts of perfume before he became caliph but to have given up perfume, as he did other luxuries, after he was invested with the office. Abū ᵓl-Faraj al-Iṣfahānī, *Kitāb al-aghānī* (Bulaq), VIII, p. 155.

[39] Or "luminous," reading *al-nūrānī* for *al-rūḥānī* (MS). Cf. sequence above (MS, p. 29): "a subtle constitution, . . . and a luminous spirit." Cf. also MS, p. 72.

for the sake of brevity, and second in the hope that after our time some-one may be given some understanding of them and undertake to elucidate them. May God grant us success in all our cndeavors.

Now we shall turn to the various opinions that have been expressed concerning eros and love. Let us begin with a chapter on the word love itself, its derivation, and its meanings.

CHAPTER FOUR

ON THE WORD LOVE, ITS DERIVATION, AND ITS MEANINGS

Section [One]. The Opinions of the Belletrists

A certain man of letters said: "Love (*ḥubb*) is a name for affection that is pure, **[32]** because the Bedouin Arabs call the purity and radiance of white teeth *ḥabāb*. Moreover, *ḥabāb* (froth, bubbles) is something that floats on water during a hard rain, and *ḥabāb* also means a pure white grain."

Another said: "Love (*ḥubb*) is taken from the word *ḥabāb,* because the *ḥabāb* (mass, bulk) of water is the greater part of it, and because the Bedouin Arabs also say 'Your *ḥabāb* is to do that,' meaning 'your *aim* is to do that,' where the initial *ḥ* is pronounced with a following *a.* So love seems to have been called *ḥubb* because it is the aim of the greater part of the concerns of the heart."

According to another: "The word is derived from persistence and perseverance without any interruption, since to describe a camel that kneels and does not rise we use the verb *aḥabba,* the verbal noun of which is *iḥbāb* and the active participle of which is *muḥibb*."[1] Thus, referring to the exegesis of the Koranic passage (in which Solomon says), "Lo, I have loved the love of good things (better than the remembrance of my Lord)" (38:52), Abū ᶜUbayda said: "The meaning is, 'I have clung to the world out of love for horses,[2] and so have neglected the time of prayer.'"

According to another of the belletrists: "Love (*ḥubb*) is derived from unrest (*qalaq*), because the Bedouin call an earring *ḥibb,* as the poet [al-

---

[1] For the reader unfamiliar with Arabic, the finite verb *aḥabba* and the active participle *muḥibb* are commonly used to mean "he loved" and "lover," respectively. Al-Daylamī's etymological concerns are typical of Arabic treatments of love. Ibn Qayyim al-Jawzīya, for example, cites this as well as several other derivations mentioned here (*Rawḍa,* pp. 15–16). Cf. also al-Qushayrī, *Risāla,* II, pp. 613–15.

[2] "out of love for horses": *li-ḥubbi ᵓl-khayl* (MS). Cf. Lisān, s.v. *ḥ-b-b.* Vadet: *ka-ḥubbi ᵓl-khayl.* "Good things" in the Koranic verse cited here is held by many commentators to mean "horses," and it is said that Solomon was distracted one day from performing the prayer by a review of some horses. See al-Zamakhsharī, *Kashshāf,* III, p. 373; al-Ṭabarī, *Jāmiᶜ al-bayān* (al-Ḥalabī), XXIII, pp. 154–56; and Ibn Kathīr, *Tafsīr,* VI, pp. 57–58.

Rā^cī][3] said:

> The tongue-flicking serpent spends the night as close to him
> as an earring (*ḥibb*) listening to the whispering of secrets.

The earring was called **[33]** *ḥibb* (earring, friend, loved one, love) either because it clings constantly to the ear or because of its unrest and agitation."

Another said: "It is derived from *ḥabb* (grain, grains). This is the collective of *ḥabba* (a single grain). The *ḥabba* (core, "bottom") of the heart is that by which the heart has its being, since it is to the heart what the heart is to the other members of the body.

Another said: "It is derived from *ḥibba,*[4] pronounced with *i* after the *ḥ*, which means the seeds of plants in the desert. Love was called *ḥubb* because it is the kernel of life, just as seeds (*ḥabb*) are the kernels of plants. Note that *ḥabb* and *ḥubb,* like the similarly vowelled words *ᶜamr* and *ᶜumr* (life) and *sadd* and *sudd* (barrier, dam), have the same meaning."

Another said: "It comes from *ḥubb,* which means the four wooden legs on which one rests the two-handled jug. Love was called *ḥubb* because the lover[5] bears on the part of his beloved every glory and humiliation, every deprival and bounty, not accepting for himself what his beloved is not pleased for him to have."

Another said : "It is taken from *ḥubb,* meaning a big jar, because it holds what is in it and is filled with it (*yastawfī minhu*) so that nothing more can enter it without something else leaving it in the same measure as that which **[34]** goes in. Hence it is said: 'Two loves cannot come together in one heart.' If [a person] executes in full (*istawfā*) the will of his beloved, he is called a lover." It is also said that the word is taken from *ḥubb al-māʾ* (the big water jar), because it stays firmly on the ground and remains fixed there.[6]

As to eros (*ᶜishq*), I heard Abū Bakr ᶜAbd al-Wāḥid b. Aḥmad al-Musharraf[7] relate from Abū [ʾl]-Qāsim al-Ṭayyib b. ᶜAlī al-Tamīmī[8] that

---

[3] As Vadet (ed., p. 17) has pointed out, these verses are found in *Tāj al-ᶜarūs,* s.v. *ḥ-b-b,* ascribed to al-Rāᶜī. They are also in the *Lisān,* s.v. *ḥ-b-b.*

[4] A plural or rather "quasi-plural" (collective) noun. Lane, s.v. *ḥ-b-b.*

[5] Cf. Ibn Qayyim al-Jawzīya, *Rawḍa,* p. 16, where "the lover" replaces an ambiguous pronoun in our text.

[6] Cf. on this and the preceding paragraph *Lisān,* s.v. *ḥ-b-b* ([Bulaq], I, p. 287).

[7] Uncertain. This name as given in the manuscript may be corrupt. Vadet (trans., p. 231) notes that there is a ᶜAbd al-Wāḥid b. Aḥmad mentioned in al-Dhahabī, *Mīzān al-iᶜtidāl,* II ([Cairo], 1325/1907–1908), p. 157. However in Ibn

Ibn al-Aᶜrābī said: "*ᶜAshaqa* means bindweed (*lablāb*), the collective term being *ᶜashaq,* whether it be green or yellow.[9] The lover is called *ᶜāshiq* after it because of his thinness and weakness."

Someone else[10] said: "*ᶜIshq* is the culmination of love, just as tender yearning (*ṣabāba*) is the culmination of longing (*shawq*), and mercy (*raᵓfa*) is the culmination of compassion (*raḥma*)." This thought has been summarized in a single verse:

> My compassion is mercy, my love is *ᶜishq,*
> and my longing is tender yearning I cannot bear.

Abū ᶜAmr al-Shaybānī said: "*ᶜAshaqa*[11] means a boulder that crashes down the side of a mountain and settles in a valley. Thus the lover is called *ᶜāshiq* because love settles in his heart and weighs heavily on it."

Al-Naḍr b. Shumayl said: "The sword is called **[35]** *ᶜashīq*,[12] and hence the lover is called *ᶜāshiq*; for love seems to act on him as though it were a sword." He also said: "The peaks of mountains are called *ᶜashaqāt,*[13] the singular being *ᶜashaqa*."

Ḥajar's *Lisān al-Mīzān* (IV, p. 79) the same man is called ᶜAbd al-Wāḥid b. Ḥumayd. Al-Bijāwī's edition of the *Mīzān* (II, p. 682) also has Ḥumayd (*ḥmd* in the manuscript). Sobieroj, in the examples he cites to establish the identity of an Abū ᵓl-Qāsim ᶜAbd al-Wāḥid b. Aḥmad al-Hāshimī, who would have belonged to the inner circle of Ibn Khafīf's students ("Ibn Ḫafīf aš-Šīrāzī," p. 206), cites two occurrences of the name ᶜAbd al-Wāḥid b. Aḥmad without *kunya* or *nisba,* the first of whom, according to al-Daylamī's *Sīrat* (p. 194), copied down and transmitted the works of Ibn Khafīf. Sobieroj mentions another occurrence of the name in his section on Abū ᵓl-Faraj ᶜAbd al-Wāḥid b. Bakr ("Ibn Ḫafīf aš-Šīrāzī," p. 188). Perhaps one or more of these occurrences should be identified with the ᶜAbd al-Wāḥid b. Aḥmad named here, who was evidently an authority from whom al-Daylamī received material directly.

[8] MS: Abū Qāsim b. al-Ṭabīb b. ᶜAlī al-Tamīmī. See, however, al-Khaṭīb, *Taᵓrīkh Baghdād,* IX, p. 363. Vadet (trans., p. 55) has Abū ᵓl-Qāsim b. Abī Ṭālib b. ᶜAlī al-Tamīmī.

[9] "*ᶜAshaqa* is a green tree that turns yellow when it is crushed (*tudaqq*), according to al-Zajjāj, who held that the word *ᶜāshiq* (lover) is derived from it." *Tāj al-ᶜarūs,* s.v. *ᶜ-sh-q*.

[10] Literally: "Someone other than these two."

[11] Vowelling uncertain in this meaning. The word is not in the *Lisān* or *Tāj al-ᶜarūs* in this sense.

[12] MS and our edition. Vadet (ed., p. 18) has *ᶜshq.* The word is not in the *Lisān* or *Tāj al-ᶜarūs* in this sense.

[13] Vowelling given in the manuscript is *ᶜashiqāt.* The word is not in either the *Lisān* or *Tāj al-ᶜarūs* in this sense. The word *ᶜashaq* with the same meaning

Section Two. The Opinions of the Sufi Masters
ᶜAmr b. ᶜUthmān said: "The word love (*maḥabba*) is construed in linguistic usage in accordance with the interpretation given to the word *ḥubb,* namely, that the application of the kohl stick to the eye is called *ḥubb,* and since the way attachment to the beloved enters the heart is similar to the way the kohl stick is applied to the eye, the same word is used of both."

According to Abū ᵓl-Qāsim al-Junayd b. Muḥammad: "*ᶜIshq* is taken from *ᶜashaq,* which is the peak and highest point of a mountain. Therefore love must be called *ᶜishq* when it waxes and rages, and rises until it reaches its highest point and attains the fullness of its being."

Another of the masters said that love is taken from clinging or keeping close to a thing, and he cited in this connection the words of the poet Abū Dhuᵓayb, describing a crouching lion when he spies his prey:

> Keeping fast to the ground (*muḥibb*) as though he were ill, but he
> only intends that the one he will assail not see him. **[36]**

Here the poet calls the way the lion keeps to the ground love (*maḥabba*).[14]

Our teacher, Abū ᶜAbd Allāh Muḥammad b. Khafīf, said: "It is probably taken from God's words 'a people whom he loves' (5:54). For he poured out his own love upon human hearts, and it took hold of them, and clothed them with a garment (attribute) of their beloved. Accordingly the word may rightly be used when speaking of the hearts of men, and the human attribute thus takes its name from the name and attribute of God."

Abū Saᶜīd Aḥmad b. Muḥammad b. Ziyād al-Aᶜrābī[15] stated the following: "This matter entails numerous steps, levels, meanings, and definitions. Each of its steps has a name, and each of its stations has a distinguishing sign. It begins with acquaintance, after which it goes on to contemplation, wonderment, ardor, anticipation, eagerness, attachment,[16] constant pursuit, closeness, fondness, love, infatuation, tender longing, abandon, obsession, eros, the pangs of love, enthrallment, distraction, and languishing away."

Now we shall relate how he explained and defined these terms.

(two paragraphs below) is unvowelled in the manuscript.

[14] Cf. MS, p. 32.

[15] On Abū Saᶜīd see the Introduction, pp. lxi–lxii.

[16] "Attachment" appears to be out of order here. It should perhaps be placed after "ardor," where it occurs in Abū Saᶜīd's explanation of these terms that follows.

Abū Saᶜīd said:[17] "Acquaintance (*taᶜarruf*) is the first perception by the soul of the object of conformity (*muwāfaqa*). Contemplation (*taʾammul*) is the mediation of the homeland between the soul and union (*muwāṣala*). Wonderment (*taᶜajjub*) is the soul's gaining **[37]** the object of request (*muṭālaba*). Ardor (*tawalluᶜ*) is the writhing of the soul at the overwhelming power of the urge (*munāzaᶜa*).[18] Attachment (*taᶜalluq*) is the submission of the heart to the soul in true participation (*mushāraka*). Anticipation (*tasharruf*) is the intense expectancy with which the soul awaits the time of pursuit (*mutābaᶜa*).[19] Eagerness (*taṭalluᶜ*) is the soul's impatience for the hour of welcome (*murāḥaba*).[20] Constant pursuit (*tatabbuᶜ*) is the soul's constantly requesting moments of candor and ease (*mubāsaṭa*). Closeness (*taʾalluf*) is the soul's resting secure beneath the wing of togetherness (*musākana*). Fondness (*wudd*) is indulgence unencumbered by the impediments of reckoning (*munāqaṣa*).[21] Love (*ḥubb*) is the soul's delighting in the sweetness of affectionate inclination (*ᶜāṭifa*).[22] Infatuation (*gharām*) is the liver's[23] hearing the call for the open declaration of love (*mujāhara*). Tender longing (*ṣabāba*) is the yearning of the spirit to inhale (*munāsama*) the fragrance (of the be-

---

[17] The translation of this passage from Abū Saᶜīd, as is the case with numerous other passages in al-Daylamī's treatise, is offered with appropriate humility. The words defined are generally familiar, but the words by which they are defined often are not. The word *murāḥaba,* for example, we have not found in the dictionaries, while in other cases no suitable meaning is given. Often more than one meaning would seem to be intended. Moreover, we cannot always be certain of the manuscript or of our own readings. The last word in all but one of the definitions is a verbal noun of the third form (*mufāᶜala*), the only exception being very likely a scribal error (see n. 22), while all the words defined, prior to *wudd,* are verbal nouns of the fifth form (*tafaᶜᶜul*). The repeated use of a given morphological pattern in the definitions suggests that we should not necessarily take the precise dictionary meaning in every case, but perhaps some other sense of the root. None the less, we have followed the dictionaries as closely as we could. The Arabic terms defined and the last word in each definition are given in the body of the translation to facilitate understanding and, where needed, criticism. For other lists of the stages of love, see Bell, *Love Theory,* pp. 155–62.

[18] Cf. Lane and *Tāj al-ᶜarūs,* s.v. *nāzaᶜa: nāzaᶜatnī nafsī ilā ḥubbihā* (My soul strove with me to incline me to love her [Lane's translation]).

[19] Or: compliance.

[20] Or: liberality; conceivably: *murājaᶜa,* "return."

[21] Possibly: insufficiency.

[22] Possibly a scribal error for *muᶜāṭafa,* which differs graphically only by the initial letter *mīm.*

[23] The liver is considered the seat of the passions.

loved's wafted breath). Abandon (*istihtār*) is favoring the place of abiding with the beloved (*muᶜākafa*). [Obsession (*kalaf*)][24] Eros (*ᶜishq*) is the granting of pure mingling (*mukhālaṭa*). The pangs of love (*shajan*) are the burning of the bowels at the limits of arrival (*mubālagha*).[25] Enthrallment (*tatayyum*) is the dissolution of the bonds of everyday existence by the successive recurrence of the assault (*munāzala*). Distraction (*tawalluh*) is to abandon seeking the conditions of vigilance (*murāqaba*). And languishing away (*tahāluk*)[26] is to relinquish the portion of life in face-to-face encounter (*muwājaha*)."

He (the author)[27] said: All these stations and halts are subsumed under the name *hawā* (passion, love, appetite), which applies to them all. **[38]** The meaning of *hawā* is that the soul has a predilection for a thing, as is shown by Abū ᵓl-ᶜAtāhiya's line:

If I had two hearts, I would live with one
and devote one to suffering in love (*hawā*) for you.

Hawā (here) is from the verb *hawā*, *yahwī,* meaning to fall(?).[28]

Someone once asked Abū ᶜAbd Allāh Muḥammad b. Khafīf about the difference between bosom friendship (*khulla*) and love (*maḥabba*),[29] and he answered: "Bosom friendship is from a thing's permeating (*takhallul*) another and mingling with it, as al-Shiblī[30] has said:

---

[24] "Obsession," although found in the original list, is not defined. One might conjecture the omission of a definition such as, "Obsession is continual service without opposition (*mumānaᶜa*)."

[25] Possibly: utmost endeavor.

[26] The word *tahāluk* can also refer to an enthusiastic passion, "dying for."

[27] Possibly Abū Saᶜīd. However we have assumed that the quotation from him ends with the preceding paragraph.

[28] "to fall": *waqaᶜta,* for *marra maᶜahu* (MS); conceivably "to cherish something": *wamiqahu* or *tawammaqahu.*

[29] This question is an important one for the Sufis and their scripturalist opponents. "The *khalīl* (bosom friend) of God" is an epithet of the prophets Abraham and Muḥammad. Many Sufis also call Muḥammad "the *ḥabīb* (beloved) of God." This may be understood to imply that the station of a mystical lover is higher than that of a prophet. The scripturalist Neo-Ḥanbalite Ibn Qayyim al-Jawzīya, who rejected this view, made his point by making *khulla* (bosom friendship), which is usually rather low in Muslim hierarchical arrangements of secular love terminology, the highest stage in his own ranking. See Bell, *Love Theory,* pp. 157–62, and chapter three above, n. 26.

[30] On the relation of al-Daylamī's teacher Ibn Khafīf to al-Shiblī, see Sobieroj, "Ibn Ḫafīf aš-Šīrāzī," pp. 53–54.

You have permeated (*takhallalta*) where my spirit courses,
and hence the bosom friend is called *khalīl*.
If I speak, you are what I say,
and if I remain silent, I am overcome with thirst.[31]

Love, on the other hand, is from tenacity and perseverance[32] in love, just as one describes a camel with the word *muḥibb,* when it kneels and does not rise."

The foregoing is sufficient for this book. If we were to go further into all the things these authorities have said about love, the book would become long indeed. So let what we have mentioned suffice. Next we will turn to the section on our own opinion on the meanings of the names of love and its degrees. **[39]**

Section Three. Our Opinion

Names are of three kinds: the [shared][33] names of God derived from his attributes, which inhere in his essence and with which he eternally has been qualified; the names of his exclusive acts, which are not shared; and the names of the acts of men, which come about by acquisition on their part.[34]

As for the shared names, such as knowing, powerful, loving, loved, willing, merciful, compassionate, and the like, these are derived from his attributes of knowledge, power, love, will, mercy, and compassion, which are preeternal, having always existed.

In the case of the names of his exclusive acts we know neither the why

[31] The first verse is found in Marʿī b. Yūsuf, *Munyat al-muḥibbīn* (MS Dār al-Kutub, Adab 6252), fol. 9a, ascribed to Rābiʿa. MS Dār al-Kutub, Ṭalʿat 4648, of the same work has both verses, with *kalīlā* where our manuscript has *ʿalīlā.* The translation of the second verse is uncertain. We have chosen to read *ghalīlā,* with Vadet and ʿAbd al-Raḥmān Badawī (*Shahīdat al-ʿishq al-ilāhī,* p. 120). Cf. the note in our edition and Dāwūd b. ʿUmar al-Anṭākī, *Tazyīn al-aswāq,* I, p. 19: "The words *barḥ* and *ghull* denote intense love, or *ghull* is from *ghalal,* with the meaning 'thirst.'" The unaltered text of the manuscript would possibly translate as "I fall ill," where we have "I am overcome with thirst."

[32] "perseverance": translating *muwāẓaba* (Vadet's suggestion, ed. p. 19, n. 6). In the Arabic text we have let stand the word *mufāwaḍa,* which is clear in the manuscript. But the term seems to make little sense here. See the footnote in our edition and MS, p. 32.

[33] See next paragraph.

[34] A reference to the concept of *kasb,* the "acquisition" by men of responsibility for their acts, which must be willed or created by God. On the teachings of Ibn Khafīf, see the Introduction. See also L. Gardet in *EI*², IV, pp. 692a–94a, s.v. "Kasb."

nor the wherefore, just as we do not know why a camel is called a camel, a horse a horse, a donkey a donkey, and so on with other things, such as a mountain or a desert.

The names of the acts of his creatures, that is, those acts that have come about by their acquiring them, are represented by words like *khayyāṭ* (tailor), said of someone who is good at **[40]** *khiyāṭa* (tailoring, sewing). Similarly, thread is called *khayṭ* because one sews (*yukhāṭ*) with it, and a garment is said to be *makhīṭ* (sewn) because the tailor has sewn it (*khāṭahu*). The same sort of relationship exists between *banā* (he built), *binā*ʾ (act of building), *mabnī* (built), and *bānī* (one who builds).[35] And it is likewise with all the arts that occur by men's acquisition. Whenever one thing is brought together with another, a third name is generated that is derived from the properties of the acts involved and is different from that [from which] they came about and from that from which they were formed.

Love, according to this approach, is taken from God's words "a people whom he loves " (5:54), with which he described himself. He went on to say, "and who love him" (5:54), describing the people. Thus love is called love (*maḥabba*) because that is what God called it, and because he described both himself and his friends[36] with it. This explanation is probable, but there are others that are possible.[37]

The author of this book said: Love has various names derived from its stages and degrees. The words may differ, but the meaning is one. As the stages become higher, their names change. In all there are ten stations (*maqāmāt*), ending in an eleventh, namely eros (*ʿishq*), which is their culmination. If love [passes][38] this station, **[41]** the name love (*maḥabba*) no longer applies to it, and another must be used.

The first station is closeness (*ulfa*). It is taken from the verb *allafa*, meaning "to gather together" or "to string," as in the expression "to

---

35 The manuscript has, with vowels, *banā* (spelled with *alif*), *bannā* (with *shadda*), *mubnī* (with *ḍamma*), and *bānī.* Our reading follows that of Vadet: *banā* (with *alif maqṣūra*), *binā*ʾ (apparently), *mabnī,* and *bānī,* which avoids the problem of two active participles but neglects the clear *shadda* on *bannā* in the text. Vadet's reading has the advantage of better paralleling the triad *muḥibb, maḥbūb, maḥabba* used by the author in speaking of God's self-love (MS, p. 74).

36 "friends": *awliyā*ʾ*,* in many contexts, "saints."

37 This is the opinion of al-Daylamī's teacher Ibn Khafīf. Cf. MS, p. 36.

38 We must supply "passes" and not "reaches" (*balagha*) as in Vadet, ed. p. 20. It is clear from MS, pp. 47–48 and 197, that *ʿishq* is still within the stages of *maḥabba.*

string (*allafa*) pearls," or "to compose," as in the expression "to compose (*allafa*) speech," that is, to place one word [after another], to join [one meaning] with another, [and] to place one section after another on a related topic. Closeness, then, according to this explanation, is taken from the proximity of one heart to another and the union of love with the heart.[39]

You may also say, "I am close to (*aliftu*) so-and-so," if your soul feels at ease with him and you prefer him to others. Again the meaning is as we have mentioned. It all goes back to one and the same meaning, namely, the close union (*iʾtilāf*) of hearts. Consider, for example, these verses of al-ᶜAbbās b. al-Aḥnaf:

> Those two close friends (*ilfayn*)! Like two branches withered by love.
> Their two spirits are one, and their two hearts are one.
> Distance brings them death from longing, when
> their abodes are far apart, and nearness gives them life.

If the affection increases somewhat, it is called delight (*uns*), which is to behold the beloved. It is taken from prolonged gazing[40] at the beloved and feeling comforted in his company. One says, "I delighted in so-and-so," meaning, "I felt comforted with him, **[42]** while beholding him." Thus the words of the poet:

> I delight in him and desire nothing else,
> for fear I should go astray and not behold him.

Moreover, God called the vision of Moses delight (*uns*) when he said (quoting Moses), "I perceive (*ānastu*) a fire" (20:10), that is, "I see it." He called it delight because Moses, in addition to seeing the fire, felt comforted by it and found relief from his troubled state. Thus God named this station delight for both reasons (both beholding and feeling comforted).

The next stage is fondness (*wudd, wadd*) or endearment (*mawadda*), which is to be joined together. The peg (*watad*) is called by this same name, that is *wadd,* because a rope is tied to it and joined to it, and the

---

[39] "the union of love with the heart": *ittiṣāl al-ḥubb bi-l-qalb.* Perhaps the text originally read *ittiṣāl al-qalb bi-l-qalb,* "the union of one heart with another," which seems more appropriate here.

[40] On the practice of some Sufis of prolonged gazing at objects of great beauty, particularly beardless youths, see H. Ritter, *Das Meer der Seele,* pp. 443–47 et passim, and Bell, *Love Theory,* pp. 139–44. See also the Introduction (pp. xxxvii–xxxix), on what has come down to us of Ibn Khafīf's teaching on the subject.

lover's love for his beloved and his constant remembrance (*dhikr*) of him is like a rope tied to a peg. Moreover, God said, "One of them would like to be allowed to live a thousand years" (2:96), where "would like" (*yawadd*) means "would love" (*yuḥibb*). Thus love was called *wudd* in this verse. Likewise, a peg is pounded into the wall and takes firm hold, and hence fondness is called *wadd,* because the firm hold of the remembrance of the beloved in the lover's heart is like the firm hold of the peg (*wadd*) in the wall. Majnūn spoke the following lines:

> I would like (*wadidtu*), by the House of God,[41] as long as I shall live,
> for her to be my portion in this world, and I hers. **[43]**
> If Laylā should requite someone for fondness (*mawadda*), let her requite me,
> and should she requite for kinship, let it be me, her kinsman.

The next stage is love (*maḥabba*). For[42] if the affection increases, it becomes real love (*maḥabba ḥaqīqīya*) as opposed to metaphorical (*majāzīya*). This is when the pleasures of the remembrance of the beloved take hold of the heart of the lover. As for the meaning and derivation of the term, they have already been mentioned at the beginning of the chapter. From this point begins the triumph of the power of love over the power of reason, and reason is assailed by temptation and base thoughts. On this consider the lines by Qābūs b. al-Ḥārith:

> Love leaves whoever loves crazed
> and bewildered, or puts a speedy end to him.
> The lightest love is heavy and burdensome:
> it weakens and fells the staunchest man.
> Whoever possesses strength, resolve,
> and courage, love is still braver than he.[43]

The next stage is bosom friendship (*khulla*). For if the affection increases again and surpasses the preceding station, it is called bosom friendship.[44] The word *khalīl* (bosom friend) in the Arabic language has

---

[41] The Kaaba in Mecca.

[42] The erroneous suggestion that al-Daylamī thinks of a progression from metaphorical to real love *within* the station of *maḥabba* and from bosom friendship to mystical poverty *within* the station of *khulla* (Bell, *Love Theory,* p. 160, table 5, A, stages 4 and 5) is based on a misreading of the Arabic conjunction *fa-* rendered here by *for* as consecutive rather than explanatory. It is perhaps a similar misunderstanding that led Vadet to substitute *ᶜishq* twice for *shaᶜaf* in the passage on "fascination" (ed., p. 22; corrected in trans., p. 61).

[43] Cf. MS, p. 150, where the second and third verses are given with slightly different wording.

[44] Al-Daylamī's placing *khulla* after *maḥabba* here accords with many

several meanings. It means companion, and it means friend. It is said that *khalīl* is derived from *khulla*, pronounced with *u*, which means friendship. **[44]** But *khalīl* may also mean needy, [being derived from *khalla* (poverty)], pronounced with *a*. Also, one says *khalaltu ʾl-shayʾ* to mean "I pierced something," and one uses the expression *takhallala ʾl-qawm* (he "permeated" the tribe) to mean "he came among the tribe." The noun *khalīl* conveys all of these senses, because it means friend, companion, and one in need of someone and of no one else, and because the remembrance of one's bosom friend permeates one's flesh and blood so that one can think of no one else. Hence the words of the poet:

Those bosom friends (*khillān*) with a single soul and spirit:
never through all time will they grow weary, as long as they are together.

The next stage is fascination (*shaᶜaf*). For if the affection increases still further, it becomes fascination. Fascination is intense and burning passion for the remembrance of the beloved. It also means captivation (*fitna*), as when one says, "He is fascinated with so-and-so," to describe someone who is deliriously carried away with the remembrance of another. Abū Dhuʾayb said:

The fierce hunting dogs have taken hold of (*shaᶜafa*) his heart,
and when he sees the break of day he is stricken with terror.[45]

In the same vein is Qays b. al-Mulawwaḥ's description of his burning passion for speaking of Laylā:

If I were to say, "I beg forgiveness of God," every time
I mention you, no sins would be charged against me. **[45]**

The next stage is heart-smiting love (*shaghaf*). One uses the verb *shaghafa* to mean "to smite in the pericardium (*shaghāf*)," just as one uses the verbs *kabada* and *baṭana* to mean "to smite in the liver (*kabid*)" and "to smite in the belly (*baṭn*)," respectively. *Shaghāf* means the sac that surrounds the heart, so it would seem that the verb *shaghafa* denotes a love that has reached the pericardium. But in fact it refers to love that has reached the heart itself and penetrated it. God said, "He smote her heart (*shaghafahā*) with love" (12:30), meaning, "He penetrated her heart with love." In this connection we may cite the following lines by Muzāḥim b. ᶜAmr:

---

medieval lists of the stages of love and does not seem to bear on the question mentioned in n. 29 above. See Bell, *Love Theory,* pp. 158–60.

[45] Cf. al-Sukkarī, *Sharḥ ashᶜār al-Hudhalīyīn,* II, pp. 26–27.

You cleft my heart and scattered in it (the seeds of) love
for you. The wounds were dressed and they closed.[46]
Your love penetrated where no wine has reached,
nor any sorrow, nor any joy.

The next stage is abandon (*istihtār*), which is incessant delirious raving and constant remembrance of the beloved, together with intense preoccupation with him and acute distraction by him from every thing and every one. The Prophet said on this matter: "Set out, for the solitarics have gone on ahead." When he was asked, "Who are they, O Messenger of God?" he replied, "Those who are wholly abandoned to the remembrance of God."[47] Majnūn said:

I sit in the assembly talking to them,
and I awake to find that woe has snatched me away. **[46]**
My thoughts carry my mind off towards you,
so that my companion tells me, "You are stark mad."

The stage that follows is delirium (*walah*), which is the mind's becoming distraught and confused as a result of intense sorrow. It is also a levity that comes over a person, either from intense sorrow or from rapture,[48] as we can see in a verse related from [al-Nābigha] al-Jaᶜdī, the poet:

I see myself in rapture after their departure,
a rapture like that of one delirious or demented.

Qays b. al-Mulawwaḥ alluded to this same idea:

If our owls[49] meet after our death,
when slabs have been set over our graves,
The owl of my grave, though I be a decayed cadaver,
will be gay (*yahushsh*) and rapturous at the cry of Laylā's owl.

The word *yahushsh* used here means to be lightsome at something and excited by it.

Then comes bewilderment (*hayamān*), which is the loss of solace and the power to endure because of the agonizing pain of the fires of love.

---

46 The *hamza* is elided in *līma* as well as in *iltāma* in the Arabic text.

47 On this tradition, and for another version, see the note in our edition.

48 "rapture": *ṭarab*. The Arabic word can signify being moved with grief as well as with joy. Rapture is too specific, but it fits in the context of this passage, which stresses the confused emotions of the distraught lover.

49 An owl, representing the soul, was believed by the Arabs to depart from the head of the deceased.

The word *hayamān* is derived from *huyām*, which is a disease afflicting camels in which they can never get enough to drink and finally die of thirst.[50] Hence Majnūn of the Banū ᶜĀmir said:

> I am sick with love, and the wandering disease (*huyām*) has struck me.
> Stay away from me so you will not catch what I have. **[47]**

And he also said:

> I am like the camel afflicted with the wandering disease. No water quenches her dryness (*ṣadā*), nor does her disease bring her death.

Ṣadā here means thirst (*ᶜaṭash*).

Then comes eros (*ᶜishq*), which is the boiling up of love until it pours out over the lover's outer and inner parts. Its derivation has been given earlier. Its meaning is the loss of the lover's portion from everything except his beloved (*maᶜshūq*), to the extent even that he becomes distracted by his beloved from his eros itself. Thus if you call out to him with any name other than that of his beloved, he will not understand, because of his lack of consciousness of himself or of anyone else but his beloved. Majnūn alluded to this when he said:

> When Laylā is named I regain my reason, and the fears
> of my heart return from a passion off on distant trails.
> I kept distant from Laylā, lest passion grip me fast.
> But in vain! I fell in love before I kept away.

This is the last of the stations of love. After this station, if the condition progresses **[48]** still further, it passes out of the bounds of love and becomes another condition. In this case, in the parlance of those who understand this matter, namely, the Sufis, it is called drunkenness (*sakra*) and vanquishment (*ghalaba*). This is to transcend love and eros in the vision of the object of love and eros, and to leave behind all things and their opposites.[51] Understand this well. Note also that within these stations we have mentioned there are many other names, which are derived from attributes that appear in lovers in particular moments and from alterations[52] that come over them in particular hours, both when they are

---

[50] Cf. Koran 56:55, in which those who err and deny the revealed message are promised a punishment in which they will lap up boiling water as though they were "thirsty camels" (*al-hīm*). The word *huyām* is also used to mean the malady or madness of love.

[51] Preoccupation with things and their opposites, that is, with the distinction between things, is incompatible with the undivided vision of this stage.

[52] "alterations": *talwīnāt.* Used as a technical term in Islamic mysticism. See,

present (in the state of awareness) and when they are absent (from it). But if we were to enumerate them, the book would become too lengthy. So now let us turn to the chapter on the origin and beginning of eros and love.

---

for example, al-Tahānawī, *Kashshāf iṣṭilāḥāt al-funūn,* III, p. 657. Moment (*waqt*) and hour (*sāᶜa*) are also mystical terms.

CHAPTER FIVE
ON THE ORIGIN AND BEGINNING OF LOVE AND EROS

Section One. The Opinions of the Divine Philosophers among the Ancients

Empedocles said: "The first things[1] that the first originator (*mubdiᶜ*) originated were love (*maḥabba*) and victory (*ghalaba*),[2] and out of[3] love and victory were originated **[49]** the simple spiritual substances, the simple material substances, and the compound corporeal substances."

Heraclitus of Ephesus said: "The very first thing among those things that first existed was an intellectual light that cannot be perceived by our intellects because our intellects were originated from[4] that intellectual light, which is truly God, glorious and sublime. The first things[1] that were originated and were the beginning of these worlds were love and strife (*munāzaᶜa*).[5] From[4] love came into being the upper worlds extending down to the sky, which is the sphere of the moon. What extends from the sphere of the moon down to this earth came into being from[4] strife." Heraclitus also used to say: "The creator (*al-bāriᵓ*), glorious and sublime, opens for those souls in every age a space so that they may see his pure light proceeding from his true essence. Then their eros and longing grow more intense, and so they remain forever."

The author of this book said: The statements of these two philosophers indicate that all the love that is in this world **[50]** is among the effects of that original love that was the first thing originated by[4] God. For from it emanated all that is contained in both the lower and upper worlds, [including] both divine and natural love.

By divine love I mean that which exists between God and man, and by natural love that which exists between human lovers, in all its varieties, and which is among the effects of that (original) love through the inter-

---

[1] The Arabic word is singular.

[2] The word *ghalaba* (victory) apparently reflects νῖκος, a later form of νίκη (victory), which at the time texts of this nature were rendered into Arabic, was indistinguishable in pronunciation from νεῖκος (strife). The same usage occurs in Abū Ḥayyān al-Tawḥīdī, *al-Muqābasāt,* pp. 282–83.

[3] *ᶜan.*

[4] *min.*

[5] Rendering, presumably, ἡ ἔρις.

mediary of the intellect, the soul, and the physical nature. Natural love, having thus fallen far away from God, has been changed and altered from love's original purity to that which you can observe. But divine love is pure, because it is received through the channel of the intellect (alone), and the intellect receives it from God directly, without any intermediary.

The opinions of these two philosophers, were it not for the mention of the first and second things originated[6] and the differences of terminology and expression, would be close to the doctrine of our teachers, may God have mercy on them.

Among our masters, the one whose opinion came close to that of the ancient philosophers **[51]** in the response he gave concerning the origin of eros was al-Ḥusayn b. Manṣūr, known as al-Ḥallāj, may God have mercy on him. We have not come across anyone among the Sufi masters who maintains the same position, but countless people among those who follow this path have adopted his view. We give his opinion on the matter here because of its similarity to that of the ancient sages.

Al-Ḥusayn b. Manṣūr said:[7] "God in his preeternity was conscious of

---

[6] "originated": *mubdaᶜ* (passive). It is tempting to read "the first and second originators," making the pair love and "victory," or strife, the second originator. But nowhere here is the verb *abdaᶜa* (to originate) used actively with love, victory, or strife as subject, whereas in the passage attributed to Empedocles passive forms of the verb are used first of love and victory and then of the remainder of originated existence. The verb is also used passively of love and strife in the passage attributed to Heraclitus. Al-Daylamī indeed uses the expression *mubdaᶜ mina ᵓl-Ḥaqq* in approximately the sense "originated *by* God," and the quotation from Heraclitus has the expression *ubdiᶜat min dhālika ᵓl-nūri ᵓl-ᶜaqlī,* which could perhaps be rendered "was created *by* that intellectual light." But when the passage attributed to Empedocles speaks of the origination of other things out of love and victory, the verb is used with the preposition *ᶜan,* not *min.* Massignon understood the reference to be to the first originator and the Intellect ("Interférences philosophiques et percées métaphysiques dans la mystique hallagienne: notion de 'l'essentiel désir,'" Louis Massignon, *Opera minora,* II, p. 231).

[7] The following passage has been translated by Massignon ("Interférences," pp. 232–34). Our version owes much to his but is nevertheless rather different. An incomplete Persian translation that does not always agree with our text is given by Rūzbihān Baqlī in his *Sharḥ-i shaṭḥīyāt* (ed. Henry Corbin, pp. 441–44; quoted by Massignon, before Rūzbihān's text was edited, in *Essai sur les origines du lexique technique de la mystique musulmane,* appendix, pp. 424–26). The Arabic original of Rūzbihān's text is contained in his *Manṭiq al-asrār,* of which the Persian *Sharḥ-i shaṭḥīyāt* is his own expanded translation (cf.

himself through himself, and there was no 'thing remembered'[8] until he displayed persons, forms, spirits, knowledge, and gnosis, and discourse came about in terms of possession, possessor, and possessed, and agent, act, and object of act became known. Thus in his preeternity he was contemplating himself through himself in his totality,[9] nothing having yet appeared.

"All the attributes that are known, including knowledge, power, love, eros, wisdom, majesty, beauty, glory, and all the others with which he is described, such as mercy, compassion, holiness, and spirits,[10] as well as the remaining attributes, are forms[11] within his essence that are his essence. **[52]**

Sharḥ-i shaṭḥīyāt, intro., pp. 4–5, 33–34). Copies of the corresponding pages from three manuscripts of *Manṭiq al-asrār* (Mashhad 156, Massignon, and Tashkent) were provided to us by Carl W. Ernst. See the Bibliography. An edition of the *Manṭiq al-asrār* by Paul Ballanfat and Carl W. Ernst is forthcoming (Ernst, *Rūzbihān Baqlī,* p. 155). The passage ascribed to al-Ḥallāj is a difficult one, and a number of our readings are tentative. The word rendered "conscious of" (*wājid*) at the beginning of the quotation, for example, is given as *wāḥid,* "one," both in our manuscript and by Rūzbihān (*Sharḥ-i shaṭḥīyāt,* pp. 441, 446, and all the manuscripts of the *Manṭiq al-asrār*). Moreover the assignment of the pronoun *hu* in MS, p. 53 (whether to God or to *ᶜishq*) is at times uncertain.

[8] Cf. Koran 76:1, "Has there come on man a while of time when he was not a thing remembered." Adapted from Arberry's translation.

[9] "in his totality": *fī ʾl-jamīᶜ*. The meaning is perhaps "in and through the totality of all his attributes." Cf. below in this passage. The Mashhad, Massignon, and Tashkent manuscripts of Rūzbihān's *Manṭiq al-asrār* all have *fī ʾl-jamᶜ,* "in union," which seems to fit better here. *Sharḥ-i shaṭḥīyāt* (p. 441) has *hamagī,* "the whole," which is not in conflict with our reading.

[10] "spirits": *arwāḥ,* both in the manuscript and Rūzbihān. Cf. *Sharḥ-i shaṭḥīyāt,* p. 441, and the author's commentary, pp. 446–47, as well as the Mashhad, Massignon, and Tashkent manuscripts of *Manṭiq al-asrār.* In the context of the divine attributes one would have expected a singular noun. The authority for al-Ḥallāj's reference to spirits as a divine attribute would seem to lie in such Koranic texts as 58:22, "He has strengthened them with a spirit from himself," and 4:171, "The Messiah, Jesus son of Mary, was only the messenger of God, and his Word that he committed to Mary, and a spirit from him" (trans. Arberry, capitalization altered). On al-Ḥallāj's controversial doctrine of the divine "spirit," see Massignon, *La passion d'al-Hosayn-ibn-Mansour al-Hallaj* (1922), II, pp. 661–64, and Massignon's edition of al-Ḥallāj's *Ṭawāsīn* (1913), pp. 131–37.

[11] "forms": *ṣūra;* singular in the manuscript, plural in Rūzbihān (all versions).

"And he contemplated, through the perfect totality of his attributes, the attribute of eros in himself, which is a form in his essence that is his essence. It was as when you approve of something in yourself and rejoice at something in yourself. He continued in this wise for a time of immeasurable duration. Indeed, were all the inhabitants of the heavens and the earth to try to calculate a single year of his years, by any human calculation, they would fail, for his years are preeternal moments, comprehended only by preeternity, incalculable by the calculations of temporal existence. If one were to seek to determine how long he remained contemplating this attribute, quality by quality, he would discover nothing knowable or unknowable. For it is one element among the visible signs of four hundred thousand times four hundred thousand plus another four hundred thousand [worlds], the last [of which][12] is this world in which the children of Adam appeared.

"Then he contemplated the quality of eros through all qualities, and he discoursed with himself about it with all discourse. Then he spoke[13] to it **[53]** with all speech; then he greeted it with the totality of greeting; then he deceived it with all deception; then he warred against it with all war; then he was kind to it with all kindness; and so on with other attributes too many to describe. For were all the people of the earth to write with all the trees of the earth and all the water of the sea, they could not record all he spoke and confided to it.[14] All this was from his essence, in his essence, and to his essence.

"Then he contemplated [it] through each [of] his qualities one [by one]. He contemplated it through love (*maḥabba*) alone. And from his contemplation of it came about speech and discourse like that explained in the preceding paragraph. Then he contemplated it through one of his attributes at a time, then through two attributes at a time, then through three attributes at a time, then through four attributes at a time, and so on until he had done so through the perfect totality of all his attributes together.

"Then he contemplated it through the attribute of eros itself according to the totality of this attribute. For eros has in its essence attributes that comprehend many qualities. Then he contemplated, through one of the attributes of eros, **[54]** another of its attributes, and there came about dis-

---

[12] Reading *ākhiruhā* (*Manṭiq al-asrār,* Mashhad, Massignon, and Tashkent manuscripts) for *ākhara* in the manuscript of the *ᶜAṭf.*

[13] Massignon ("Interférences," p. 233) and Vadet (trans., p. 66) translate "conversed" (*conversa*). We have chosen "spoke to it" to avoid the implication, not to be excluded, of reciprocity.

[14] Cf. Koran 31:27.

course and speech such as we have already mentioned. Thus he contemplated (all) the attributes of eros through (all) the attributes of eros. And he made in this manner manifold repetitions.

"Then he looked upon another of his attributes, and the course was the same with it. (And so he went on) until he had contemplated every attribute, and every attribute through every attribute, and all of his attributes through the perfect totality of his attributes, which is too long to be related here. Thus he continued for a duration beyond description, according to his preeternity, his perfect totality, his singleness, and his volition. Then he praised himself and glorified himself, and he praised his attributes and glorified his attributes,[15] and he praised his names and glorified his names and his holiness. In this wise he glorified his essence through his essence, and he glorified every attribute of his essence through his essence.

"And God willed to see[16] this attribute of eros alone, looking upon it and speaking to it. And he contemplated his preeternity and displayed a form that was his own form and his own essence. For when God contemplates a thing and manifests in it a form from himself, he displays that form,[17] **[55]** and he displays in that form knowledge, power, movement,[18] will, and all his other attributes. Now when God had thus become manifest, he displayed a person who was himself, and he gazed on him for an age of his time. Then he greeted him for an age of his time. Then he saluted him for an age of his time. Then he spoke to him; then he felicitated him; and then he rejoiced him with good news. And he continued in this wise until he had exhausted all that is known, and all that is not known, which is more.

"Then he praised him and glorified him. And then he made him his

---

15 "his attributes": *ṣifātihi,* plural in our edition but singular in the manuscript of the *ᶜAṭf* and all the manuscripts of *Manṭiq al-asrār*. Perhaps we should read, "he praised [his attributes through] his attribute," and similarly with the next phrase. This would parallel the last sentence of the paragraph. Rūzbihān (*Sharḥ-i shaṭḥīyāt,* p. 443) translates: *Āngah khvud-rā madḥ kard bi-nafs-i khvīsh. Āngah bi-ṣifat-i khvīsh ṣifāt-i khvīsh-rā thanā guft. Āngah bi-ism-i khvīsh asmāʾ-i khvīsh-rā thanā guft.*

16 "to see": *an yarā.* Rūzbihān (*Sharḥ-i shaṭḥīyāt,* p. 443): "to display" (*binamāyad,* rendering the graphically identical *yuriya,* although the Tashkent manuscript vowels *yarā*).

17 "that form": *al-ṣūra* (our edition and all the manuscripts of *Manṭiq al-asrār*), for *ṣūra* (MS). Rūzbihān (*Sharḥ-i shaṭḥīyāt,* p. 443) translates *ān ṣūrat.*

18 "movement": *al-ḥaraka.* MS and Rūzbihān (all versions) agree. Cf. also Massignon, "Interférences," p. 252, n. 1.

elect (by endowing him) with like attributes from his (attributes of) act as well as with those attributes he had (already) displayed in the quality of showing forth[19] this person who appeared out of his form. He[20] it is who is creator and sustainer, who creates and sustains, who is glorified and whose unity is proclaimed,[21] who displays attributes, acts, and forms, who substantiates substances and manifests wonders. And when God had gazed on him and possessed him,[22] he became manifest in him and manifest through him."

This is the opinion of al-Ḥusayn b. Manṣūr concerning the origin of eros and love. What distinguishes his view from that of the ancients is that they considered love to be originated, **[56]** while he held it to be inherent in the essence of God.

Once a certain philosopher[23] was asked in my presence about the origin of eros. "The first to love with eros," he replied, "was the Creator. He loved himself with eros when there was nothing other than him. He appeared to himself through himself, in his beauty, his glory, and all his attributes. And thus he loved himself with eros."

The preceding is all that we have come across of the teaching of those

---

19 "showing forth": *al-ẓuhūr bi-;* perhaps, "appearing in," as understood by Rūzbihān (*Sharḥ-i shaṭḥīyāt,* p. 444): *ẓuhūr dar.* The process of "showing forth" is apparently represented here as a "quality" (*maᶜnā*), or attribute.

20 MS and ed.: *huwa;* Mashhad, Massignon, and Tashkent manuscripts of *Manṭiq al-asrār: hiya,* which being feminine must be construed as referring to "his form (*ṣūratihi*). The pronoun in the Persian translation is, of course, genderless, and of no help.

21 The Arabic verbs here can be read either as active or as passive (*yusabbiḥu wa-yuhallilu* or *yusabbaḥu wa-yuhallalu*), either as "who glorifies and who proclaims the divine unity" or as "who is glorified and whose unity is proclaimed," although the context would seem to require the latter, despite its boldness, if the subject of this sentence is understood to refer to the person displayed rather than to God himself. Rūzbihān (*Sharḥ-i shaṭḥīyāt,* p. 444) translates in the active voice (*tasbīḥ va-tahlīl kard*), as do Massignon ("Interférences," p. 234) and Vadet (trans. p. 68). The Tashkent manuscript of *Manṭiq al-asrār* likewise vowels active.

22 Here we may read either "possessed him" (*malakahu*) or "his dominion" (*mulkihi*), the former perhaps relating to the mention of "possession, possessor, and possessed" at the beginning of the passage (MS, p. 51). Rūzbihān understands "possessed him," having *ū-rā dar mulk āvard* (*Sharḥ-i shaṭḥīyāt,* p. 444), while the Tashkent manuscript of *Manṭiq al-asrār* none the less vowels *mulk(i)h(i).*

23 Possibly Abū Ḥayyān al-Tawḥīdī. Cf. Massignon, "Interférences," p. 230, n. 2.

ancients who spoke of divine things. Now let us turn to the opinions of the second group of philosophers, namely, the astrologers, who affirmed that the natural world is a shadow of the spiritual world.

Section Two. The Opinions of the Astrologers on the Origin of Eros and the Conditions under Which It Is Generated[24]

I read in a book by a certain scholar that he had read in a book by Abū Maᶜshar,[25] reporting from someone else, that this person had asked Ibn al-Ṭabarī about the nature and character of eros and that he had replied: "Philosophers differ in their explanations of it and their statements about it.[26] From all their differences it is apparent **[57]** that neither has the cause of its occurrence been discovered nor is it known what it is. However Teukros related from Wāltus that Aratus the astronomer[27] told him that the stars that arouse eros are Saturn, Mercury, and Venus, all to-

---

[24] The translators wish to acknowledge their gratitude to Professors David Edwin Pingree, George Saliba, and David A. King for their assistance at various stages in the translation of this section. Professor Pingree kindly went over the preliminary draft and is responsible for a number of the suggestions contained in the notes.

[25] The passage in our text is apparently not contained in Shādhān b. Baḥr's *Mudhākarāt Abī Maᶜshar,* at least not in the manuscript at Professor Pingree's disposal. Other possible sources are Abū Maᶜshar's *Kitāb al-mudkhal al-kabīr* and his *Kitāb al-uṣūl,* also attributed to Abū ᵓl-ᶜAnbas al-Ṣaymarī (Cf. al-Nadīm, *Fihrist* [trans. Dodge], II, p. 658 and n. 96), but we have not consulted manuscripts of these works. In the non-astrological books where we have found the passage, it appears in two different versions with numerous variants. Cf. al-Masᶜūdī, *Murūj,* VI, pp. 382–84 (ed. Pellat, IV, pp. 243–44); Ibn Dāwūd, *Kitāb al-zahra,* p. 16; Ibn Abī Ḥajala, *Dīwān al-ṣabāba,* I, pp. 13–14; and Mughulṭāy, *al-Wāḍiḥ al-mubīn,* pp. 40–41.

[26] Possibly the quotation from Ibn al-Ṭabarī (on whom see Sezgin, *GAS,* VI, p. 137; VII, p. 130) ends here, but we think it includes the entire astrological section, which occurs as a unit in most of the other works in which we have found it.

[27] Teukros: reading with Vadet (ed., p. 28) Ṭīqrūs for Ṭīfūrus (MS). On Teukros, a Babylonian astrologer (presumably first century B. C. or A. D.), see Sezgin, *GAS,* VII, pp. 71–73, and IV, pp. 112–16. Wālṭus: probably Vettius Valens, the second century A.D. astrologer, who is often cited as Wālīs, Bālīs, or Fālīs (Sezgin, *GAS,* VII, pp. 38–41, and al-Nadīm, *Fihrist* [trans. Dodge), II, p. 641). Aratus: astronomer of the second half of the third century B.C., who is cited as Arāṭis or Arāṭīs in Abū Maᶜshar's *Kitāb al-mudkhal al-kabīr* (Franz Boll, *Sphaera,* pp. 492–93; Sezgin, *GAS,* VI, pp. 75–77; and n. 25 above, citing Mughulṭāy).

gether, when they share in the base-nativity.[28]

"Saturn disposes one to thought, hope, desire, bewilderment, grief, madness, and obsessional derangement.[29] Mercury arouses [and] disposes to poetry, eloquence in speech and written prose, and knowledge. Venus disposes to love, tenderness, and humidity, which causes one to incline towards lust and carnality.

"When the position of Mercury in the ecliptic is good, and it is in its exaltation or its house, in direct motion, and in a cardine, aspecting benefics,[30] the eloquence of the native[31] in poetry and composing prose flourishes. But when the condition and position of Mercury are bad, and it is [in] its dejection and in opposition to its house, being retrograde and aspecting a malefic, **[58]** or it is cadent, the eloquence of the native in poetry and composing prose is impaired, and his natural disposition[32] is weak. When the condition of Saturn is strong and its motion is direct, the native is able to carry out whatever he wishes in his affairs. However, he will be full of thought, hope, and desire. When Venus is strong, the native is tender and lovable, and hearts will incline to him.

"It is related that Ptolemy said:[33] 'Friendship and enmity are of three kinds. First there is the conformity of spirits, which is mutual eros between persons in which neither can avoid loving his companion. This conformity of spirits comes about when [the sun and the moon are in]

---

[28] "base-nativity": *aṣl al-mawlid,* geniture at the native's birth, to be compared with anniversary horoscopes.

[29] Cf. Ibn Qayyim al-Jawzīya, *Rawḍa,* p. 37: "Physicians are in unanimous agreement that it [eros] is an obsessional (*waswāsī*) disease, similar to melancholy, that a man brings on himself by having his thoughts set on delighting in certain forms and features."

[30] The benefics are normally Jupiter and Venus, and the malefics Saturn and Mars.

[31] "the native": *ṣāḥibuhu,* in the sense of the one "associated" with the dominant planet.

[32] "his natural disposition": *naḥīzatuhu.* Conceivably a scribal error, though from a text earlier than al-Daylamī's, for *maʿrifatuhu,* "his knowledge." Cf. the description of the influence of Mercury in the preceding paragraph in the text. Al-Masʿūdī (*Murūj* [Pellat], IV, p. 244) also has *naḥīzatuhu,* which supports its having been in the source used by al-Daylamī, although the edition of Barbier de Meynard and Pavet de Courteille and a manuscript consulted by Pellat have *maḥbūbatuhu,* "his beloved" (ed. Meynard, VI, p. 383; ed. Pellat, IV, p. 244, n. 9).

[33] This passage attributed to Ptolemy resembles *Tetrabiblos* 4.7, and may be from a commentary on pseudo-Ptolemy *Kitāb al-thamara* (*Centiloquium*) 33, perhaps Ibn al-Dāya's.

their two nativities together in a single house, or in trine, or in sextile. In this case the natives have a natural inclination to love (each other), especially if benefics aspect them in both nativities and malefics do not aspect them.

"'Then there is love based on utility. Two persons, in both of whose nativities it happens that the Lot of Fortune is in one and the same zodiacal sign, or in trine, **[59]** or in sextile, derive utility and happiness from the same thing, and each of them benefits from the other. This mutual benefit brings about love and affection.

"'Finally there is the effect of having an opposite (sun) zodiacal sign. When it happens that the ascendents of two (such) people are the same zodiacal sign and that benefics aspect it and it is free of malefics, these people will not remain in a single state, whether in love or in sorrow.'"[34]

This is what the astrologers have to say about eros and love. Now let us turn to the opinions of the natural philosophers.

Section Three. The Opinions of the Physicians on Eros and Love

In a book by one of the ancients[35] it is said that the students of Aristotle

---

[34] The text here has been emended on the basis of al-Masᶜūdī, *Murūj,* VI, p. 384 (ed. Pellat, IV, p. 245), which itself is not very reliable. The parallel passage in Ibn Dāwūd's *Zahra* (p. 16), instead of speaking of the identical zodiacal sign, mentions friendship and enmity based on sorrow or joy, thus corresponding more closely at this point to Ptolemy's text in *Tetrabiblos* 4.7, where the three causes of friendship and enmity are preference, need, and pleasure and pain. This type of love is not mentioned by Mughulṭāy or Ibn Abī Ḥajala (cited in n. 25). On the translation of *al-burj al-muḥādhī* as "an *opposite* zodiacal sign," see the standard dictionaries and, e.g., al-Tahānawī, *Kashshāf iṣṭilāḥāt al-funūn,* I, pp. 394–95, s.v. *muḥādhāh.*

[35] This section, with the exception of the last paragraph, has been translated into English and studied by Richard Walzer in "Aristotle, Galen, and Palladius on Love," in his *Greek into Arabic,* pp. 48–59. The essay was originally published in *Journal of the Royal Asiatic Society,* 1939, pp. 407–22. Our version owes much to his. Walzer suggests that the Aristotelian passage should most likely be assigned to a lost dialogue of Aristotle. As Biesterfeldt and Gutas have pointed out in a subsequent study ("The Malady of Love," *Journal of the American Oriental Society* 104 [1984], pp. 21–55), this and two further passages below, also purportedly from Aristotle and his students (MS, pp. 156–60, 241–42), apparently form a whole, according to their view a dramatized version of a Greek text in the genre of the Alexandrian *Problemata Physica.* (The last passage, it should be noted, is merely a repetition of part of the middle passage.) Biesterfeldt and Gutas edit the passages and also establish short, hybrid, and long versions of the text, referring to the sources we have used as well as to oth-

assembled before him one day and that he said to them: "As I was standing on a hill, I saw a young man standing on a rooftop and reciting a poem, the purport of which was this:

> Whoever dies of eros, let him indeed die thus,
> for there is no good in eros without death."[36]

Then his student Aysūs[37] said, "O philosopher, tell us of the essence **[60]** of eros, and of the [origin] from which it is generated." Aristotle replied: "Eros is a desire that is generated in the heart, and, once it is generated, it stirs and grows, and then it begins to develop. And as it develops, elements of covetousness are joined to it. The stronger it grows in the depths of the lover's heart, the more his excitement, persistence, desire, thought, and hopes increase. This leads him to covetousness and impels him to try to obtain (his beloved), thus bringing him finally to

---

ers. Al-Masᶜūdī includes a non-dramatized version in his long section on love in the *Murūj* (VI, pp. 377–79), ascribing it to "many natural philosophers and those physicians who have investigated the matter" or to "a certain physician," depending on the manuscript (p. 377 and n. 1). The translation given by Biesterfeldt and Gutas is of the combined dramatized and long versions and therefore does not always correspond to ours, which is limited to the dramatized version as given by al-Daylamī. It has none the less been of considerable use to us, particularly in chapter eleven.

[36] As Walzer has remarked, this verse is by an Arab poet and may have been substituted for a Greek original ("Aristotle, Galen, and Palladius on Love," p. 55, n. 6). It occurs in a love story told by al-Jāḥiẓ in al-Washshāᵓ, *al-Muwashshā* (p. 64; cited by Walzer, ibid., p. 49, n. 1) and Ibn Dāwūd, *Kitāb al-zahra* (p. 54), where it is a girl who recites the line and then throws herself into a cistern, and, among other sources in al-Qushayrī, *Risāla,* II, p. 621, there without a frame story. We hesitate to identify the Jāḥiẓ story related by Ibn Dāwūd and al-Washshāᵓ with the Aristotle frame story, as Biesterfeldt and Gutas do ("The Malady of Love," p. 49). Al-Daylamī has the Jāḥiẓ story later without the line of poetry we have here (MS, pp. 263–67), leaving the suicide of lovers from a height the only common element between the two.

[37] Vowelled thus in the manuscript. Walzer read this name as Issus (Ἴσος or Ἴσσος), which is extremely uncommon, as he pointed out. He based his reading on the assumption that there was "no reason to suppose that the name of the pupil (ᵓYSWS) is corrupt" ("Aristotle, Galen, and Palladius on Love," p. 54). However, while the manuscript indeed has at this point ᵓYSWS, it later gives the same name as ᵓSYWS (p. 157). Biesterfeldt and Gutas ("The Malady of Love," p. 52) have Zosimus, for their emendation RYSMWS in the text. Unable to determine the Greek original of the name, we have left both forms unchanged. Perhaps Hestiaeus or [Dion]ysios is intended. See chapter eleven, n. 4.

gnawing grief, constant sleeplessness, bewilderment, sorrows, and corruption of the mind."[38]

The author of this book said: This answer shows that the inquirer was a natural philosopher. For the answer was given on the inquirer's level, whereas Aristotle himself was a divine philosopher. But it is also possible that Aristotle held love (*maḥabba*) between two loving persons as well as eros (between them) to be generated by (their) physical natures and that he believed that these two affections have nothing to do with the world of the intellect and the soul.[39]

Palladius the physician was asked **[61]** about eros and he said: "Eros is a malady that is generated in the brain by the preoccupation of the mind, incessant reminding oneself of the beloved, and constant gazing at him."[40]

It is told of Galen that once he went into the presence of a sick man and, feeling his pulse, found it to be beating violently. While Galen was still holding his wrist, a woman came in to see the man and spoke to him. After she had gone, Galen said to the sick man, "Are you in love with that woman?" The man did not reply. When Galen was asked, "How did you know?" he answered, "Because his pulse beat violently when she spoke to him, and I knew that she had a place in his heart."[41]

The author of this book said: Although the statements of the philosophers of nature differ, the difference is merely one of expression. The

---

[38] Cf. a similar statement ascribed to Pythagoras, "the friend of Solomon, the prophet of God," in Dāwūd b. ʿUmar al-Anṭākī, *Tazyīn al-aswāq,* I, p. 17. See also, Walzer, "Aristotle, Galen, and Palladius on Love," p. 49, n. 2.

[39] Despite the Neoplatonic veil through which medieval Islam generally saw Aristotle, al-Daylamī has some sense, albeit uncertain, of the philosopher's true doctrine. Cf. Walzer, "Aristotle, Galen, and Palladius on Love," p. 56, citing on Aristotle's opinion regarding eros Eudemian Ethics 3.1.1229a and vii, esp. 12.1245a.

[40] On the possible channel of transmission of this quotation and the following anecdote about Galen, see Walzer, "Aristotle, Galen, and Palladius on Love," pp. 50–53. If the quotation from Palladius is genuine, it shows, as Walzer remarked (p. 53), that Palladius, since he held love to be generated in the brain, did not follow Plato's psychological doctrine. Dāwūd al-Anṭākī (*Tazyīn al-aswāq,* I, p. 17) cites al-Tamīmī's *Kitāb imtizāj al-nufūs* quoting Galen to the effect that love *is* the work of the soul.

[41] Galen himself relates something like this story, but without the obvious flaw that the sick man's pulse was beating violently before the woman came in (commentary on Hippocrates' *Prognostikon* 1.8.40–41, in *Corpus medicorum Graecorum* 5.9.2 [p. 218, 14]). Quoted in Walzer, "Aristotle, Galen, and Palladius on Love," p. 50.

meaning is the same and is summed up by what we have related here. They do not go beyond this limit, and there is nothing to be gained from providing further reports about them or from recounting their opinions at length. So now we will turn to **[62]** the views of the theologians on the matter.

Section Four. The Opinions of the Theologians on the Origin of Eros and Love and That from Which [They] Are Generated[42]

Ibrāhīm al-Naẓẓām said: "Eros is the fruit of similarity[43] and a sign of the mingling of two spirits. It belongs to the realm of delicateness, tenderness of nature, and purity of essence."

ᶜAlī b. Manṣūr said: "Eros comes from openness and homogeneity in constitution and temperament."

Abū ᵓl-Hudhayl said: "Eros is from liberality in a person's nature and openness in his disposition."

Muᶜammar[44] said: "Eros is the result of similarity, and it comes from natures being close together, spirits touching one another, hearts clinging to each other, and minds coming together."

Al-Naẓẓām al-Ṣaghīr[45] said: "Eros is subtler than wine. It is made of a

---

[42] The definitions of eros quoted below are given with frequent variations in wording by al-Masᶜūdī in an account of a fictitious or semihistorical symposium at which the Barmakid vizier Yaḥyā b. Khālid (d. 190/805) is said to have convened a number of the leading theologians of his day (*Murūj,* VI, pp. 368–76). The language is of considerable eloquence and is often difficult to render into English. Al-Daylamī generally breaks the statements up, placing the fragments in the chapters of his work to which they are relevant. Cf. MS, pp. 25–26, 85–86, 148, 162–64. Perhaps the *ᶜAṭf,* indirectly, as well as the *Murūj,* is drawing on al-Masᶜūdī's lost *Akhbār al-zamān,* in which the historian dealt with love at length (*Murūj,* VI, p. 386). However the textual variants are many, and the attributions very often different.

[43] See Bell, *Love Theory,* pp. 108–13, and ibid., chapter seven, n. 26.

[44] By Muᶜammar is most likely intended Muᶜammar b. ᶜAbbād, since in al-Masᶜūdī's *Murūj* (VI, p. 372) this statement is attributed to an early Muᶜtazilite named Muᶜtamir b. Sulaymān, which is apparently a corruption of Abū ᵓl-Muᶜtamir Muᶜammar b. ᶜAbbād al-Sulamī. See *Murūj* (Pellat), IV, p. 239, n. 6, and VII, pp. 691–92.

[45] The name occurs again below (MS, p. 163). We have not come across anyone known by this name. Moreover, the two statements attributed to al-Naẓẓām al-Ṣaghīr by al-Daylamī are both parts of a statement attributed to Ibrāhīm al-Naẓẓām in the *Murūj* (VI, pp. 371–72). Perhaps behind the word "al-Ṣaghīr" lies something like "al-Baṣrī" (Ibrāhīm b. Sayyār al-Naẓẓām [d. between 220/835 and 230/845] was from Basra), or even "ayyuhā ᵓl-wazīr."

substance that has been kneaded with sweetness and fermented in the vessel of seduction."

Abū Ḥafṣ al-Ḥaddād said: "Eros is the generation of reconciliation and the bonding of inhaling (the wafted breeze),[46] **[63]** as well as a sign of the refreshing breath of love and a witness to the spirit[47] of homogeneity."

Ḥammād b. Abī Ḥanīfa said: "Eros is only conceived out of the relationship of resemblance, and the one possessed with it is characterized by extreme tenderness."

Hishām b. al-Ḥakam said: "Eros arises from symmetry of physical and moral constitution, and from being alike in manner and similar in outward appearance."

Yaḥyā b. Aktham met one day with Thumāma b. Ashras before al-Maʾmūn.[48] Al-Maʾmūn asked Yaḥyā, "What is eros?" and Yaḥyā replied, "O Commander of the Faithful, thoughts that occur to the passionate lover for which he has a predilection and that engross him are called eros." But Thumāma said to him, "You should stick to legal issues like a request for advice from a man who divorces frequently, or the problem of a pilgrim in a state of ritual purity who has slain game. Questions like this are our affair." So al-Maʾmūn asked him, "[What do you say], Thumāma?" "O Commander of the Faithful," he responded, "when the essences of souls are mingled in the union of similarity and encounter the flash of a gleaming light by which the eyes of the intellect are illumined and at the radiance of which the natures [of living beings] quake, a particular light is generated from this in the soul and is joined to its essence, and this is called eros." (The one who narrated this report) said that al-Maʾmūn admired Thumāma's reply and said to Yaḥyā, "This is the right answer, **[64]** not the one you gave."

The author of this book said: This is the extent of what we have come across with regard to the replies of the theologians on the origin of love and eros. I have noticed, moreover, that their statements resemble each

---

46 Translating *Al-ᶜishq tawlīdu ʾl-musālama wa-ᶜaqdu ʾl-munāsama.* The word *munāsama* might possibly be translated as "intimate whispering" instead of "inhaling (the wafted breeze)." Al-Masᶜūdī (*Murūj,* VI, p. 374) has *walīdu ʾl-musāmaḥa wa-ᶜaqību ʾl-munāsaba,* or "the child of forbearance and the sequel of affinity."

47 "refreshing breath . . . spirit": *rawḥ . . . rūḥ.* The reverse is conceivable. Al-Masᶜūdī (*Murūj,* VI, p. 374) has *rūḥ . . . raḥim,* giving "a sign of the *spirit* of love and a witness to the *relationship* of homogeneity."

48 On this story, see chapter three, n. 34.

other closely in that the theologians base themselves on nothing beyond similarity of physical nature, mingling of spirits, and homogeneity of constitution. So now let us turn, God willing, to what the Sufis have said on the question.

Section Five. The Opinions of the Sufis on the Origin of Eros and Love and That from Which [They] Are Generated

I have observed that all their statements about love fall into three classes: first, love between [God and man, which is man's love for God and] God's love for man without any intermediary between them, this being the level of love attained by the people of unification and gnosis; second, love resulting from spirits knowing and conversing intimately with one another in the invisible world, which is the degree of the adepts of the mystical stations, who are the elite among believers; and, third, love among righteous believers and the commonality of the faithful, which results from a similarity of nature.

The replies they give do not go beyond these **[65]** three stages. If one of them who has attained gnosis is asked about love, he will reply according to the level of the inquirer and to the requirements of the conversation at that time and what occurs to him at the moment,[49] as well as according to that to which he has been drawn[50] and to the state in which he happens to be among the various states that befall them. If we have made ourselves clear, then let us now relate, God willing, what they have said about these things, adequately and sufficiently, and just as they themselves replied.

Dhū ᵓl-Nūn al-Miṣrī said: "The origin of love is closeness (*ulfa*),[51] and the origin of hatred is variance, while the origin of eros is gnosis, and the origin of closeness is conformity, and the origin of conformity is laying oneself open to one's close friend." When he was asked, "What is it to lay oneself open to one's close friend?" he replied, "To cease feeling estranged while maintaining awe during familiar association with him."

Al-Ḥārith al-Muḥāsibī said: "The beginning of love is when hearts remember the blessings of God, his benevolence, his kindness, his favors, and his grace."[52]

---

49 "level, time, moment": *maqām, ḥāl, waqt,* respectively, which are technical terms of mysticism, although apparently not meant to be understood strictly as such here.

50 "that to which he has been drawn": *mā ṭuliba bihi* (MS). Vadet: *mā ṭūliba bihi,* which is more common in this meaning.

51 Cf. MS, p. 41.

52 "his grace": *naᶜīmihi* (conjecture from the note in our edition) for *niᶜamihi*

From ᶜAlī b. Abī Ṭālib, may God be pleased with him,[53] it is related that he said: "Silence is a cause of love."[54] **[66]**

Abū ᵓl-Qāsim al-Junayd, [when asked about the origin of eros],[55] said: "Its beginning is love, which increases until it becomes eros." We have heard the following verses related from al-Junayd on the question of the beginning and the end of eros and love:[56]

My heart flew away in rapture to its beloved
  on a night when the stars clustered closely in the heaven.
Streaks of lightning flashed before it at the time of the visit,
  and it did not turn aside to knowledge or means.
(It flew) with a zeal that ranged unconfined[57] through the invisible realm,
  with no guide, it rises by that zeal to proximity.

(MS). The plural *niᶜam* occurs earlier in the sentence and is redundant here.

[53] The manuscript originally read after the name of ᶜAlī, "May God bless him and grant him peace," the formula used primarily, although not exclusively, after the names of prophets, and particularly after of that of the prophet Muḥammad. But this was changed by the scribe or someone else to "May God be pleased with him." The prophetic benediction occurs again, unchanged, when ᶜAlī is mentioned in MS, pp. 138 and 282 (see chapter twenty-four, n. 47), while the similar formula "upon whom be peace" is used for him in MS, p. 151. In MS, p. 282, "upon whom be peace" is used after the name of ᶜAlī's son al-Ḥasan. The first mention of ᶜAlī in the text (MS, p. 21) is followed by "May God be pleased with him and his house." These benedictions may point to Shiite leanings on the part of the author (or at least a copyist), although the author's basic commitment to Sunnism is made clear by the material he relates on the death of ᶜUthmān (MS, pp. 282–83).

[54] "a cause of love": *dāᶜiyatun ilā ᵓl-maḥabba.* The word *ilā* is inserted between the lines in the manuscript.

[55] Possibly some of the material from al-Junayd, here and elsewhere in the work, is from the mystic's tract on eros that came into the hands of al-Daylamī's teacher Ibn Khafīf. Cf. MS, pp. 9–10 and the Introduction, pp. xlvii–xlix.

[56] The following poem poses many problems regarding both the Arabic text itself and the correct rendering into English. It contains a number of Sufi technical terms or allusions to Sufi technical terms, such as the "streaks of lightning" (*lawāᵓiḥ*) in the second line (cf. al-Jurjānī, *Taᶜrīfāt,* p. 291). The "zeal" that is first mentioned in the third line may refer to the soul or to love itself, since al-Daylamī says the poem is about "the beginning and the end of eros and love."

[57] "ranged unconfined": *saraḥat . . . fa-ᵓnbasaṭat.* Perhaps the second verb should be rendered "and was filled with ease," or "and was filled with delight." *Basṭ,* from the same root, is a Sufi technical term.

And when its spirit hinted at union, that zeal[58] raced straight
to its beloved. It was drawn into the meadow of amplitude.
Any obstacle of the intellect to this is to be slain without retaliation,
for separation for that zeal is a care not yet vanished in the invisible.
Then, when it was joined to the beloved[59] and was united,
its tokens[60] were severed from the qualification of qualities.
Its one true qualification is that assigned by its qualifier,[61]
it was united in the upper world truly, beyond all doubt.
The intimation of God is something made true without cause;
it is a unity, dispersed only by perceptions in (the world of) works (?).
That zeal's tokens perished when God's token appeared,[62]
and it[63] has no return in the realm of etiquette.[64]
For God's token, in the brilliance of his manifestation,[65]
annihilated the signs of its existence, the scene of annihilation eternity.

---

58 The shift of main subject from "heart" to "zeal" is required by the succession of feminine pronouns.

59 "was joined to the beloved": *wuṣilat bi-l-ḥibb;* perhaps, "arrived by love" (*waṣalat bi-l-ḥubb*). Our translation fits better if the "zeal" is taken to refer to love itself, as al-Daylamī's remark on the poem might suggest.

60 "tokens": *shawāhid.* In al-Junayd's poem we have mostly rendered the recurrent term *shāhid* (singular of *shawāhid*) by "token," sensing this to be a reasonably adequate English equivalent in the context. The word, which is usually translated by "witness," refers here to a sign or token of the existence of a thing.

61 This line introduces the triad *agent* (active participle), *act* (verbal noun or infinitive), and *object of act* or *thing done* (passive participle), which according to the quotation from al-Ḥallāj above (MS, p. 51) proceeded from the unified divine essence. "Qualification" translates *nisba,* which is a verbal noun of the verb *nasaba* (to ascribe to, to assign to, to qualify with) and which at times, like the verbal nouns *waṣf, ṣifa,* and *naᶜt,* takes on the meaning of "quality" or "attribute" (cf. MS, pp. 234–35). "That assigned" (*mansūb*) and "qualifier" (*nāsib*) represent, respectively, the passive and active participles of *nasaba.*

62 "when God's token appeared": *fī badwi shāhidihi* (MS). The reading *fī badʾi shāhidihi* (Vadet), which gives "when God's token began," seems less likely.

63 "it": *hā* in *lahā*? for *lahu* (MS).

64 "realm of etiquette": *shāhid al-adab.* The meaning is apparently the contingent world of (mystical?) etiquette or discipline.

65 "his manifestation": *shāhidihi;* perhaps, "its appearance." Cf. the use of *shāhid* at the beginning of chapter sixteen (MS, p. 211 and n. 1), also MS. p. 15.

Its qualification became again known only by its knower,[66]
just as when he began it, when no beauty was in any rank-holder **[67]**
Among the angels, eternities being yet to come before their existence,
when there was no heaven, no earth, nor any green herb,
No stars, no sun, no moon,
no Paradise, no hell with its fire,
Nor was the reality of this sea yet forged,
manifest for a time with its clashing waves.
But he in whom all attributes have forever existed
in his knowledge was embracing (all) in himself and was concealed.
He was veiled in obscurity, minds conceiving with respect to him
at that time no manner, or time, or reckoning.

Sahl b. ᶜAbd Allāh said: "There are three seeds (*dharr*): a first, a second, and a third. The first is Muḥammad the Beloved (*al-ḥabīb*), for when God willed to create Muḥammad, he displayed from his own light a light [that] he spread through[67] the entire kingdom. And when it[68] came before (God's) majesty it prostrated itself, and God created from its prostration a column of dense light like a vessel of glass, the inside being visible from the outside and the outside being visible from the inside. In this column of light Muḥammad worshipped before the Lord of the Worlds a thousand thousand years with the primordial faith,[69] being in the revealed presence of the invisible within the invisible realm[70] a thousand thousand years before the beginning of creation. And God created Adam from the light of Muḥammad, **[68]** and then Muḥammad from the clay of Adam; and the clay he created from the column in which Muḥammad worshipped.

"The second seed is Adam, and the third is Adam's posterity descended from him. For Adam was created from the light of Muḥammad, and the chosen ones were created from [the light of] Adam, while the aspirants were created from the light of the chosen ones. God's proof is

---

[66] See n. 61.

[67] "[that] he spread through": *adāra[hu] fī* for *arāda* (MS). The emendations to this passage are based on Abū Ṭālib al-Makkī, *ᶜIlm al-qulūb,* pp. 93–94, and al-Tustarī, *Tafsīr al-Qurʾān al-ᶜaẓīm,* pp. 62–63, 145. On all these passages and the quotation in the following paragraph from Sahl, see Gerhard Böwering, *The Mystical Vision of Existence in Classical Islam,* pp. 149–57, 192–93.

[68] That is, the light of Muḥammad.

[69] "primordial faith": *ṭabāʾiᶜ al-īmān.*

[70] "being . . . realm": *bi-mukāshafati ʾl-ghaybi bi-l-ghayb;* possibly, "in the invisible's revelation of the invisible."

manifest against whoever sets up an equal to him, and his power is clear for whoever obeys him."[71] ᶜUmar b. Wāṣil said: "This view was advanced by Sahl alone. I do not know of anyone else [who] has mentioned it. But it is the truth, to which nothing need be added."

The author of this book said: According to this view, the love of everyone who loves must be from that same source, namely, the heart of Muḥammad, for his heart is the source (*maᶜdin*) of the essence of the profession of unity of those who profess the divine unity,[72] the bed in which is rooted the gnosis of the gnostics, and the spring from which flows the drink of the hearts of lovers. This is shown by Sahl's commentary on God's words (quoting Pharaoh): "I believe that there is no god but he in whom the Children of Israel believe" (10:90). Sahl [said]: "Pharaoh's belief did not avail him in any way, for God **[69]** had not established any favor for him in the core (*maᶜdin*) of the heart of his prophet Moses, may God bless him." These are obscure words in need of commentary and clarification, but this is not the place for it.

ᶜAmr b. ᶜUthmān al-Makkī, may God have mercy on him, said: "God created the people of gnosis (*ahl maᶜrifatihi*) to display his love and in order that they be signs of his love; and because they are the loved ones of God he has never ceased to remember them and to appear to them with love."[73]

When he was asked about the origin of love, he said: "It is that subtle thing that enters hearts and to which they become attached, in[74] the beloved, to whatever degree they become attached to it. Moreover love possesses qualities (*nisab*) that proceed from what it has wrought inside the heart. The first of its qualities that appear in the heart are three things, namely, continuous remembrance of the beloved, hoping to meet him, which is the same thing as longing [for him], and the lover's showing joy at his being mentioned. From the progression of these things in the heart come about effects that produce in the heart certain things,

---

[71] "for whoever obeys him": *ᶜalā man aṭāᶜahu.* This seems to be the translation that best reflects al-Tustarī's doctrine of men's recognition of the divine power on the day of the covenant. See al-Tustarī, *Tafsīr,* p. 61.

[72] The reference is to those mystics who have attained the highest stage. Cf. the similar classification above (MS, p. 11).

[73] "to appear to them with love": *wa-ilayhim bi-l-maḥabbati ẓāhiran;* possibly, "to show love to them." It may be that the ambiguity is intentional.

[74] "in": *min; bi-ḥaqq* ("with respect to") below (MS, p. 87), where the first part of this statement is quoted again. The end of the statement is also quoted again (MS, p. 179).

among which are mental unbalance and constant thoughts, in the course of which ensue[75] burning agony because of the absence of the beloved and pain at [the impossibility of] recovery through meeting him. If this is repeated continuously **[70]** in and upon the heart, the pain reaches the spirit and it becomes a compound malady, namely, eros."

Yaḥyā b. Muᶜādh said: "[Remembrance] comes continually and then goes on continuously, and then comes about love. [And] after love, the essential realities of love come to you."

Ruwaym b. Muḥammad,[76] when he was asked about love and its origin, said: "It comprehends many things, among which is a man's knowledge of God's favors to him and his good will towards him." It has also been said: "The hearts of the prophets were created with an innate disposition to love God, whereas other men (love him) for his favor which they see bestowed upon them."

[Abū(?)] ᵓl-Ḥasan al-Sīrawānī[77] related from Abū Saᶜīd that he said: "The key to Paradise is to acknowledge the blessings of God."

The following lines are attributed to Abū ᶜAlī al-Rūdhbārī:[78]

If, my beloved, we have been separated
by the calamities of time and misfortune,

---

75 "in the course of which ensue": *tajrī fīhā;* below (MS, p. 179): *yaḥduthu minhā,* "which produce" (literally, "from which are produced").

76 Abū Muḥammad Ruwaym b. Aḥmad was also known as Ruwaym b. Muḥammad, which is what he is called in our manuscript. See the note to the corresponding text in our edition.

77 Probably Abū ᵓl-Ḥasan ᶜAlī b. Jaᶜfar b. Dāwūd al-Sīrawānī, who was a disciple of, among others, al-Shiblī (d. 334/945) and al-Junayd (d. 298/910), and who is said to have lived to the age of one hundred and twenty-four lunar years (al-Khaṭīb al-Baghdādī, *Taᵓrīkh Baghdād,* XIV, p. 392, and Jāmī, *Nafaḥāt al-uns,* pp. 271–72, the *kunya* being given in the latter work as Abū ᵓl-Ḥusayn). He seems to have been important in passing on the Khafīfī tradition (cf. Sobieroj, "Ibn Ḫafīf aš-Šīrāzī," p. 113), and it is conceivable that he was the author of the anonymous mystical handbook *Adab al-mulūk* (cf. the edition by Bernd Radtke, intro., pp. 16–20). It is not impossible, but less likely, that his teacher, Abū ᵓl-Ḥasan (ᵓl-Ḥusayn?) ᶜAlī b. Muḥammad al-Sīrawānī, who lived in the latter half of the ninth century and the first half of the tenth, related this report from Abū Saᶜīd (246/860–341/952). Cf. *Adab al-mulūk,* intro., p. 18; Jāmī, *Nafaḥāt,* p. 288; and Junayd Shīrāzī, *Shadd al-izār,* p. 478 and nn. 4, 5, where the editor changes the *kunya* from Abū ᵓl-Ḥasan to Abū ᵓl-Ḥusayn to agree with Jāmī.

78 Al-Rūdhbārī died in 322/934. Reports on the relationship of al-Daylamī's teacher Ibn Khafīf to him are summarized by Sobieroj ("Ibn Ḫafīf aš-Šīrāzī, p. 59).

Yet, my close friend, your spirit and mine are joined together,
and we have met in the concealment of the invisible realm.
It does us no harm that fortune has divided us:
do we not have two spirits in close union?

Abū ᶜAbd Allāh al-Nibājī said: "Contentment is attained through entrustment of one's affairs to God, entrustment is attained through love, and love is attained through the heart's preoccupation **[71]** with remembering God's blessings."

We have heard the following lines ascribed to Sumnūn:

I love thee with a love for the old[79] that has past,
and a new love that has come to us since.
I see time diminish everything,
while my love for thee grows and increases.

Our teacher Abū ᶜAbd Allāh [b. Khafīf] related from the mystics of Damascus that they said: "Eros begins with love. After love comes beholding, and then eros."[80]

It is said that God said to Jeremiah the prophet, may God bless him and grant him peace: "O Jeremiah, before I created thee I made thee a prophet; before I shaped thee I made thee holy; and before I brought thee forth to the earth I purified thee and chose thee for a great matter."[81]

Shāh al-Kirmānī[82] said: "God has servants whom he loved in his prior knowledge with his will before he created their physical frames. He chose them in his knowledge for himself; he allotted them an abundance of his blessings in the garden of his holiness; and he guided them by his light." Al-Kirmānī then went on to give a complete description of these men. I have given this brief excerpt from his words to demonstrate

---

[79] "the old": *al-qadīm.* The Arabic word may also mean "preeternal," and thus the hemistich would seem to refer to the soul's original love for God before the creation of the world.

[80] Cf. MS, p. 103, on the fifth group of those who maintain that love is beholding.

[81] This resembles Jeremiah 1:5, "Before I formed thee in the belly I knew thee; and before thou camest forth out of the womb I sanctified thee, and I ordained thee a prophet unto the nations." Cf. al-Ṭabarī, *Tafsīr* (Maᶜārif), V, p. 448.

[82] Shāh b. Shujāᶜ, Abū ʾl-Fawāris (d. before 300/912–13), said to be of "royal lineage" (*min abnāʾ al-mulūk*) and a native of Merv. He was active in Kirmān, but visited Abū Ḥafṣ ᶜAmr b. Sālim al-Nīsābūrī (d. 264 or 266 or 270/883–84) in Nishapur. Al-Sulamī, *Ṭabaqāt al-ṣūfiya* (Pedersen), pp. 183–85, 105–6.

the point I am making.

ᶜAmr b. ᶜUthmān also said: **[72]** "God produced love in the hearts of the first class of gnostics by showing them the covenant (of lordship) he had assumed with regard to them[83] on the day he brought forth Adam's seed from his spine.[84] For he gazed on them with an eye of love for them, and he clothed their being on that day, both inwardly and outwardly, with that gaze, which indeed was love itself. Thus he produced love in their hearts when they came to know what he had done. For there appeared in the taste their hearts experienced two flashes. The first was from the beauty of the covenant with which he had befriended them, and they were delighted in him because of this and inclined to him in their love. The second flash was the light of the splendor of his gazing on them with love itself[85] and the brilliance of his favoring them thus that he caused to radiate in their hearts. In that splendor they were joined together, and in that brilliance they found delight. From this he produced in their hearts a sparkling spiritual delight[86] to accompany the sweetness that they had inhaled of the covenant he had befriended them with and had received from them.[87]

"All this distilled into their hearts in cool and refreshing showers, the first taste of the sweetness of which sank deeply **[73]** into their hearts. [Love] appeared through the conjunction of all this in their hearts, and thus their hearts came to love God,[88] and their spirits were aroused. They

---

83 "the covenant (of lordship) he had assumed with regard to them": *mā tawallāhu minhum.* Perhaps the text should read, *mā tawallā[hum bihi wa-mā wallāhu (tawallāhu?)] minhum.* Cf. MS (Arabic), this passage, below in two places. We have given what we believe to be the meaning required by the context, without however altering the problematic text.

84 The day of the *a-last* covenant between God and, according to the mystical view, the souls of men in their prior existence. Cf. Koran 7:172–73; MS, pp. 182–84; also Ritter, *Das Meer der Seele,* pp. 339–40, and Bell, *Love Theory,* pp. 114–15.

85 "love itself": *ᶜayn al-maḥabba;* perhaps, "the eye of love." Cf. the uses of *ᶜayn* earlier in this paragraph.

86 "delight": *rawḥ.* Massignon (*Essai* [1954], p. 40) understands *rūḥ* (spirit).

87 "had received from them": *wallāhu minhum.* Uncertain; cf. n. 83.

88 "came to love God": *ḥubbibat . . . ilā ᵓllāh,* if *ḥubbibat ilā* can be taken as equivalent to or a corruption of *taḥabbabat ilā* (cf. Lane and *Tāj al-ᶜarūs,* s.vv. *taḥabbaba, muḥabbab* and *mutaḥabbib*). On the other hand, the more usual meaning, "their hearts *were made lovable* to God," though seemingly out of place here, is in conformity with the divine saying, "My servant will not cease drawing near to me by supererogatory works until I love him" (MS, pp. 188,

longed bewilderedly for him in their fascination, and became restless for him in their obsession."

Such was the opinion of ᶜAmr concerning the love of the people of truth and how it originates. What we related from him previously was a reply he gave regarding love between human lovers,[89] which, indeed, is the source of divine love. For if a soul is not prepared to receive natural love, it will not receive the divine.[90]

Our teacher, Abū ᶜAbd Allāh b. Khafīf, was asked about the origin of love and he replied: "Out of God's [love] for his servants are generated effects that clothe their hearts and a covering that appears over their inmost beings, and they are qualified with these attributes even though they themselves did not acquire them." He also said: "Perhaps one should say that the effects of God's love illumined men's hearts and clothed them with a garb of light and a heavenly resplendence, and thus the beloved becomes distraught with love, because of God's love that has enveloped him."

This is the extent of what we have selected from all the sayings of our masters. Their statements, even though **[74]** they may differ, do not go beyond the limits of what has been mentioned here. Hence we have not needed to relate in full the replies of all of them on the matter.

Section Six. Our Opinion

The author of this book said:[91] As for the origin of love, it is that God has eternally been qualified with love, which is one of his attributes subsisting [in him]. In his preeternity he was contemplating himself through himself and for himself, just as he was conscious of himself through himself and for himself. And in like manner he loved himself through himself and for himself, and there (in preeternity) lover, beloved, and love were one thing without division, for he is pure unity, and in unity there is no multiplicity.

Then God brought forth from his preeternity, for each of his shared

---

198), and with al-Daylamī's statement, "And the increase he (a man) merits because of his gratitude is God's love for him" (MS, p. 19).

[89] The allusion is to the quotation in MS, p. 69.

[90] Cf. MS, p. 29.

[91] The following section, inspired to a great extent by the quotation from al-Ḥallāj above (MS, pp. 51–56), has previously been summarized by Massignon, who pointed out al-Daylamī's use of theologically more acceptable terms than those preferred by his predecessor: *maḥabba* (love) for *ᶜishq* (eros, passionate love), and *abraza* (brought forth) for *abdā* (displayed). "Interférences," pp. 234–36, esp. p. 235. Al-Daylamī is not consistent in this substitution, however. Cf. *ibdāʾ,* "being shown forth" (MS, p. 75), and *badat,* "appeared" (MS, p. 76).

names,[92] effects, which constituted temporal existence alongside the preeternal. From his love he brought forth love, from his compassion compassion, from his power power, and from his other attributes likewise their counterparts. We restrict our remarks here to love simply because it is the subject of our inquiry. With the other attributes **[75]** the case is similar to that of love.

Love, then, which was the first emergence that came forth from among the attributes, was a luminous entity that appeared out of preeternity into temporal existence, where it divided into three: lover, beloved, and love, although they were in their origin one.[93] Someone might object here, asking how the one could divide into three, and how the effect of the one could be three. Our reply is that love is three with respect to you, one with respect to itself. This is because our [main] purpose in such matters is to seek unity in everything, for unity is manifest in everything that can be perceived by the intellect, the imagination, and the senses. We will demonstrate this on the basis of the two firm foundations of proof that the gnostics do not doubt and to which one may turn in every difficulty, namely, letters and numbers.[94]

Let it be understood that love, before being shown forth out of pure oneness, was in union with it (*majmūᶜa*), having no form in the intellect or in knowledge. Thus there was no way to acquire knowledge about its nature. But since its emergence it has become possible to have knowledge of it, and we shall demonstrate this in both ways, that is, on the basis of both letters **[76]** and numbers.

With regard to letters it must be recognized that the origin of everything in existence, whether perceived by [the imagination], the intellect, or the senses, is the twenty-eight or the twenty-nine letters,[95] for they denote all things and are separate from[96] all things. Now the source of all letters is the *alif*, from which the others appeared. Moreover, the *alif* is an indication of the divine unity. It is a breath letter[97] that cannot be

---

[92] "shared names": those names (attributes) that God shares with men. Cf. above, MS, p. 39.

[93] Cf. n. 61 and MS, p. 51.

[94] On the letters of the alphabet, see Massignon, *Akhbār al-Ḥallāj, khabars* 32 and 64.

[95] Apparently the letters of the Arabic alphabet counted without or with the combination *lam-alif.* See Wright, I, 3, A.

[96] "are separate from": *bānat ᶜan* (MS). Possibly, "indicate clearly" (*abānat ᶜan*).

[97] "a breath letter": a long vowel or, more precisely, the length feature of a long vowel.

grasped[98] and that has no sensible form. Rather it is perceived in the first instance by the imagination

If you wish to bring forth the *alif* from the realm of the imaginable to that of the intelligible, you must give it a graphic likeness in temporal existence.[99] Thus you write the form of the *alif* standing alone, a self-subsistent form isolated from the other letters by distinct boundaries, namely, the beginning point, the prolongation into a line, and the lifting of the pen.[100] These three things give you the sense of one, and this is its shape: [ا].[101] It appears to you as a single self-subsistent form, denoting only itself and joined to nothing, whereas everything is joined to it.[102] It is an indication of the unity of God, **[77]** because it reflects his isolation, his self-subsistence, and the subsistence of all things in him.

Then if you wish to bring the *alif* from the realm of the intelligible into that of the knowable,[103] in order to have knowledge of the intellect's conception of this single, intelligible, and self-subsistent form, you join together three letters, which, being thus joined, guide you to knowledge of the essence of this one thing. These letters are those that spell out *alif*, namely, *alif*, *lām*, and *fā*ᵓ. And this is their shape: الف . Thus again in the third stage, that of knowledge, three things give you the meaning of one.

This is what we meant when we mentioned the division of the one into

---

98 "cannot be grasped": *lā yuḍbaṭ;* possibly, "takes neither vowels nor diacritical points." For the use Ibn al-ᶜArabī makes of the fact that the *alif* accepts no vowels, see al-*Futūḥāt al-Makkīya,* I, pp. 276–78.

99 "temporal existence": *al-ḥadath* (MS). Ritter (Vadet, ed., p. xii) suggested *al-khaṭṭ* (script).

100 "the beginning point, . . . the pen": *al-nuqṭa wa-l-madda wa-l-rafᶜ*. Vadet translates similarly (p. 80).

101 The separate form of *alif,* which is the first letter of the Arabic alphabet and has the numerical value of one. The manuscript, however, has a *madda,* apparently in place of the *alif,* perhaps as a result of a differing interpretation of the preceding description of the letter. Ritter (Vadet, ed., p. xii) suggested *alif* with *madda.*

102 This seems to be an allusion to the fact that *alif* is never joined to a following letter. But there are other letters that follow the same rule. Ibn al-ᶜArabī also refers to the rule: "The *alif* is a single essence, for no letter may be joined to it when it occurs at the beginning of a written word" (*al-Futūḥāt al-Makkīya,* I, p. 276).

103 The realm of the knowable would seem to have replaced that of the sensible here, since al-Daylamī has previously mentioned only the faculties of imagination, the intellect, and the senses (MS, p. 75). But the author specifically calls the knowable the third realm (this paragraph and MS, p. 79) and the sensible the fourth (MS, p. 80).

three and the fact that unity is manifest in three. For here you have gained knowledge of the one by means of three, and that which is one in its origin has become three in the derivative stages. That which is one is indeed three. But it is one with respect to itself and three with respect to you. Thus what is one in the realm of the imaginable is three in the realm of the intelligible, and [what is] one in the realm of the intelligible is three in the realm of the knowable. Let this be understood.

Now some have maintained **[78]** that love divided into two: lover and beloved, love not being distinct from them. But this is an error. Unity is more manifest in three than in two, since two is an equal sharing, whereas three is a singling out. Hence two is called an *even* number (*zawj,* "pair") and three is called *odd* (*fard,* "individual"). For this reason the Christians are closer to the true profession of the divine unity in their doctrine of the Trinity than are the Zoroastrians in their dualism. For the Christians claim that three is one without asserting any otherness, while the Zoroastrians assert otherness, opposition, and division. What we intend by these remarks is simply to demonstrate the truth of the affirmation of divine unity, nothing else. So let no one raise any objection.

Should you wish to ponder the unity of lover, beloved, and love in accordance with what we have set forth above, consider the (unvowelled) spelling of the letter *alif,* the shape of which is الف . If you take the different ways it may be read, you may say *alifa,* "he was close to," that is, "he loved," where the subject "he" refers to the lover. Then again you may say *ilf,* "close friend," which means the beloved. Lastly you may say *allafa,* "he joined them close together,"[104] which refers to the act of God between the lover and the beloved, namely, love. Thus the shape **[79]** of the *alif* in the realm of the knowable and the level of division, which is, as we have said, the third stage, has given you the meaning of lover, beloved, and love in a single form. In the realm of the intelligible it was likewise a single form that gave you the meaning of three. Let this be understood.

As regards numbers, we must recall that they are composed of three kinds: first the units, then the tens, and lastly the hundreds.[105] These

---

104 "he joined them close together": reading *allafa,* as in the manuscript, with *shadda* on the *lām.* Cf. Koran 8:63, and MS, p. 96 and n. 49 there.

105 In reckoning according to the numerical values of the letters of the Arabic alphabet, in which case the order is roughly that of the Hebrew and Greek alphabets, the first nine letters represent the numbers one through nine, the second nine letters ten through ninety, and the third nine letters one hundred through nine hundred. The last—twenty-eighth—letter represents one thousand, leaving no letters with which to extend this class.

three kinds of numbers give you the entire notion of counting, just as the starting point, the prolongation of the line, and the lifting of the pen gave you the notion of the *alif* [in the second stage], and the letters *alif*, *lām*, and *fā*ʾ gave you the notion of the *alif* in the third stage. The role of the units, then, is analogous to that of the starting point in writing, that of the tens to that of the prolongation of the line, and that of the hundreds to that of lifting the pen. These are analogous from beginning to end. Let this be understood.

If the number reaches one thousand, a repetition is involved. For the shape **[80]** of the thousand (*alf*) at the end in the case of numbers is the same as the shape of the *alif* at the beginning in the case of letters, and the meaning of each is the same, because the thousand[106] is one in its original form, one with regard to numbers, and one in reckoning by the letters of the alphabet. Now the meaning of this is that the thousand is one and the one is the thousand, in that you can reduce the end to the beginning and the beginning to the end. For it (the one) is the first and the last, the manifest and the concealed. It is the beginning of everything and the end of everything. Let this be understood.

Consider the shape of the thousand (*alf*) in the fourth degree, the realm of the sensible. With respect to numbers it is that you bend down the little finger of your left hand, which is precisely the same as the sign for one, except that you have moved it from one place to another.[107] In this same manner the one emerged from preeternity[108] into temporal existence and was divided. Then you moved it from the realm of the intelligible to that of the knowable, where it was divided again. Likewise in the case at hand the one has become a thousand in the realm of the sensible, **[81]** whereas in reality it is one.

On this matter some have said: "The one is the thousand,[109] [but the

---

106 "the thousand": conceivably, "the *alif.*"

107 That is, from the right hand, where the same sign means one, to the left. See the note at the corresponding place in our edition on *ḥisāb al-yad* (counting on the hands), and Ch. Pellat in *EI*², III, pp. 466a–68a, s.v. "Ḥisāb al-ʿaḳd." It is not certain that al-Daylamī is referring to only one counting system here and immediately above. In the first case he may be referring to Indian numbers, or possibly to the use of the forefinger to mean "one."

108 "preeternity": *al-azal* (Ritter's suggestion, Vadet, ed., p. xii). But *al-awwal* (the beginning) as in the manuscript and Vadet's text is possible. The emergence of the one from preeternity referred to here parallels that of the *alif* from the realm of the imaginable to that of the intelligible mentioned above (MS, p. 76).

109 "thousand": *alf;* conceivably the letter *alif,* as Vadet translates (p. 82), is

thousand][110] is other than the one, because the one did not emerge or divide. The thousand is other than the one because it did emerge and was divided. The one is the thousand without composition and without repetition. But the thousand is other than the one because it emerged into temporal existence and was divided in the realm of sense, only after which it became one in the intellect."

This is the sum of what we have to say on this subject. Let us go on, therefore, to the chapter on the essence and quiddity of love.

---

intended throughout this paragraph, although the references to repetition and to division in the realm of sense would seem to connect it to al-Daylamī's discussion of the thousand.

[110] Vadet's addition, vowelling unspecified (ed., p. 39).

CHAPTER SIX
ON THE ESSENCE AND QUIDDITY OF LOVE

Section One. The Opinions of the Philosophers

Plato said: "God Most High created all spirits together in the shape of a ball. Then he divided them amongst all creatures, placing them in the body of whomever he chose in his creation."[1] The author of this book, may God be pleased with him, said: According to this view, love must consist only in the mutual attraction **[82]** of certain souls to others.

Someone said: "God created the spirits of lovers originally as one spirit. He then split this spirit into two halves and placed each half in a different body. So when two persons happen to have the same original spirit, each half yearns for the other. Indeed, longing was given the name *shawq* because of the yearning of each half (*shiqq*) for the other."

Plato also said: "Love is possible in reality to God alone. Moreover, all things celestial and terrestrial move out of longing for their originator and mover, and for the universal love, which is towards God. Indeed, all the movements of the spheres are the result of their longing for their prime mover and first originator."[2]

Aristotle said: "A given nature is fond of its like."[3] Here he is referring to gold, for when copper[4] is mixed with it, its quality is improved, and it will not break if you strike it with a hammer. He also said: "A given nature loves its like." "Love" here **[83]** is the solidification[5] of the

---

[1] This and the following two sayings attributed to Plato have been translated by Franz Rosenthal in his article "On the Knowledge of Plato's Philosophy in the Islamic World," *Islamic Culture* 14 (1940), p. 420.

[2] Possibly only the first sentence of this paragraph is mcant to be attributed to Plato, the remainder in this case representing the author's commentary. The theory that the spheres move out of desire for their (unmoved) mover, which we have here in Neoplatonic garb, was set forth by Aristotle, not Plato. Cf. Aristotle *Metaphysics* 12.7; Plotinus *Enneads* 2.2.2.

[3] An alchemical axiom. It occurs also as "A given nature rejoices in its like (*Al-ṭabīʿa tafraḥu bi-l-ṭabīʿa*)," translating ἡ φύσις τῇ φύσει τέρπεται. See Manfred Ullmann, *EI*², V, p. 111b, s.v. "al-Kīmiyāʾ."

[4] "copper": *al-mis* (Persian). Cf. James W. Allan, *Persian Metal Technology 700–1300 AD,* p. 9, citing al-Hamdānī, *Kitāb al-jawharatayn,* ed. and German trans. C. Toll, fols. 28a, 71b–72a, on the gold, silver, and copper alloy used by jewelers, which "he says, can be stretched, is firm under the hammer and accepts solder, by virtue of the copper and the silver mixed with it."

[5] "solidification": *tajassud* (Vadet) for *taḥassud* (MS).

molten nature of the element[6] when something else that resembles it is mixed with it, as when gold is added to gold itself, or to some other body that is compatible with it in one element and incompatible with it in another. In the latter case composition is not impossible, but you need to make adjustments to compensate for the way you know one substance to be incompatible with the other.

When he says, "A given nature loves its like," he means that when brass[7] or copper is mixed with silver, they blend together, and the silver can then be worked suitably, without breaking or becoming brittle,[8] and it does not shatter into pieces when struck with a hammer. Rather, the more it is worked, the greater its malleability and the higher its quality.

The author of this book, may God be pleased with him, said: What I mean to accomplish by these two accounts is to point out something of interest on the subject of similarity and the conformity or divergence of natures. So ponder and reflect, and, God willing, you will understand it.

On this matter **[84]** one group has said: "The spirit is an entity that has been separated from the macrocosm and become attached to the microcosm and has been forced to dwell in the body. Each of the two seeks to escape from the other in order to return to its abode. But this is prevented by the physical nature. If, however, the physical nature is weakened by disease or some mishap, then each returns to its abode."

If this is the case, then the close union of two spirits must occur while both spirits are in their bodies. Indeed, love is simply the solace that a given kind of being finds in its like owing to its estrangement (from its abode) and the familiar ease the two sense with each other. Consider the example of the prisoner who discovers in prison someone of his own kind[9] and feels familiar and at ease with him.

Palladius said: "Eros is a malady that is generated in the brain by the preoccupation of the mind, incessant reminding oneself of the beloved, and constant gazing at him."[10]

---

[6] "the molten nature of the element": *ṭabīʿat al-juzʾ al-mudhawwaba* (MS, our edition); perhaps, "the nature of the molten element" (*ṭabīʿat al-juzʾ al-mudhawwab* [Vadet]).

[7] "brass": *shabah.* Cf. Allan, *Persian Metal Technology,* pp. 39–40.

[8] "becoming brittle": *yubūsa,* literally, "dryness"; in Aristotelian and subsequently medieval metallurgy the elementary quality associated with brittleness. Cf. Aristotle *De generatione et corruptione* 2.2.330a, and al-Hamdānī, *Kitāb al-jawharatayn,* pp. 154/55–156/57.

[9] "of his own kind": *min abnāʾ jinsihi;* conceivably, "of his own stock," but this is less suited to the context.

[10] The same statement is also ascribed to Palladius above (MS, pp. 60–61).

Another said: "Eros is a craving that occurs in the lover and a rejection that occurs on the part of the beloved. To the lover's initial craving is added avid desire because of the rejection that occurs **[85]** on the part of the beloved; and to the beloved's rejection is added aversion because of the avid desire that occurs in the lover. All of this leads to relentless insistence and agitation. If the lover persists in his insistent attitude, and the beloved persists in his aversion, death ensues. For this reason it has been said:

> The beginning of love is insistence;
> but when firmly entrenched it turns to gnawing distraction."[11]

Section Two. The Opinions of the Theologians on the Essence of Love[12]

ᶜAlī b. Manṣūr, when asked about eros, replied: "It is a malady delicate to the taste.[13] It mingles with the soul and permeates it, and it spreads through spirits and sinks into them."

When Abū Mālik al-Ḥaḍramī was asked about eros, he said: "It is a puff of magic,[14] and in its effect it is more insidious than wine."[15]

Abū ᵓl-Hudhayl said: "Eros is a draught from the infusion of death, a drink from the basins of bereavement."[16]

And Hishām b. al-Ḥakam said: "Eros is a trap that fate has set, in which it snares only people characterized by mutual sincerity and love. If the lover **[86]** becomes entangled in its net and caught between its teeth, little is the chance that he will escape safe and sound or free himself in short order."[17]

Section Three. Statements of the Sufis on the Essence of Love

Dhū ᵓl-Nūn said: "Love is fear of abandoning reverence while continuing to render service. It is to consider much on your part as little and

---

See chapter five, n. 40.

[11] It is not certain whether this verse belongs to the preceding quotation or is cited separately in support of it by the author.

[12] See chapter five, n. 42.

[13] "delicate (or perhaps, delightful) to the taste": *laṭīf al-madhāq*. One might think of translating "delightful to experience," but al-Masᶜūdī's longer version mentions "the one who drinks it" (*Murūj,* VI, p. 372).

[14] An allusion to a form of Arabian witchcraft in which women tied knots in a cord and then blew on them, perhaps also spitting on them. Cf. Koran 113:4, and Lane and Wehr, s.v. *n-f-th.*

[15] Cf. al-Masᶜūdī, *Murūj,* VI, p. 369.

[16] Cf. ibid., p. 370.

[17] Cf. ibid., pp. 370–71.

little on the part of your beloved as much."[18]

Bishr al-Ḥāfī[19] was asked about love and he said: "It is preference." "What is preference?" he was asked. "That you give preference to the beloved over what you love," he answered.

Al-Ḥārith al-Muḥāsibī, being asked about the essence of love, said: "It is for your heart to be in agreement with what your beloved wills." He[20] added: "This means that you are to be in conformity with your beloved, loving what he loves and hating what he hates."

Abū Yazīd (al-Bisṭāmī) answered an inquiry about love saying: "It is of four kinds: one from *him,* which is his grace; one from *you,* which is your obedience to him; one *for* him (*lahu*), which is your remembrance of him (*lahu*); **[87]** and one between the two of you, which is eros."

Abū ʾl-Qāsim al-Junayd was asked about eros and he replied: "Eros is the boiling up of love when it reaches its extreme limit."[21] He was also asked about love. "Love," he said, "is to rejoice in giving the beloved possession of one's soul."

ᶜAmr b. ᶜUthmān al-Makkī was asked [about love] and he said: "It is that subtle thing that enters hearts and to which they become attached, with respect to[22] the beloved, to whatever degree they become attached to it, whether high or low, firm or weak."[23]

Someone inquired of Abū ʾl-Ḥusayn al-Nūrī about love and he said: "Love is to love love and to disavow love."

Sahl b. ᶜAbd Allāh (al-Tustarī), being asked about love, said: "It is embracing obedience and abandoning need."[24]

Ruwaym b. Muḥammad[25] was asked about love and he said: "It is loyalty together with union, and service together with pursuit of

---

[18] Al-Qushayrī attributes this statement to Abū Yazīd al-Bisṭāmī (*Risāla,* II, p. 614).

[19] On Bishr al-Ḥāfī, see F. Meier, *EI²,* I, pp. 1244a–46b, s.v.

[20] "He": possibly the narrator or the author rather than al-Muḥāsibī himself.

[21] Cf. al-Daylamī's similar description of eros (MS, p. 47).

[22] See chapter five, n. 74.

[23] This quotation is given in more complete form above (MS, pp. 69–70), but referring to the "origin" (*aṣl*) of love rather than its essence and without the phrase "whether high or low, firm or weak."

[24] Cf. al-Hujwīrī, *Kashf al-maḥjūb,* ed. V. A. Zhukovskii, pp. 402–3 (trans. Nicholson, p. 311), and al-Qushayrī, *Risāla* (Cairo, 1966), p. 249. The first source replaces "abandoning need" in this statement by "avoiding acts of disobedience," while the second substitutes "abandoning disobedience."

[25] See chapter five, n. 76.

the source.[26]

Abū ᵓl-ᶜAbbās b. ᶜAṭāᵓ, when someone asked him about love, said: "It is conformity."[27] He also said: "It is jealousy[28] at **[88]** thc beloved's being mentioned once the lover is truly faithful (?)."[29]

Abū Bakr al-Shiblī was asked about love and he replied: "It is complete devotion to the beloved."

Abū ᶜAlī al-Rūdhbārī, being asked about love, replied: "Conformity." He also recited these verses:

Love for a beloved, O my God, will never be pure in me
until sincere deeds verify my words,
Until in heedless passion I prefer obedience in what he loves
to my desires, when fear and hope assail me.
I ask pardon of God for my love of this life, being not
taken up with him, while I still feel traces of love and dread.
And I seek refuge in him from bringing on myself
his abhorrence of me for what I have done or left undone.

The author of this book said: These, then, are their replies concerning universal love[30] and the outward signs of love. Their spiritual allusions to it and their most subtle statements regarding it are quite another matter. Altogether their answers do not go beyond three things: the original

---

[26] This statement, stressing deeds as well as the pursuit of the mystical goal of union, reveals concern over and opposition to the antinomian tendencies of some Sufis.

[27] "conformity": *muwāfaqa,* the least committing of the available terms implying some sort of affinity between man and God, and as such the term favored by the Ḥanbalite Ibn Taymīya to denote the affinity underlying sacred love. See Bell, *Love Theory,* pp. 76, 117–19, and 118, n. 83. Ibn ᶜAṭāᵓ heard a certain number of traditions in Ḥanbalite circles (al-Khaṭīb, *Taᵓrīkh Baghdād,* V, pp. 26–30; Ibn Kathīr, *al-Bidāya wa-al-nihāya,* XI, p. 144), but whether he had as much influence among the Ḥanbalites in Baghdad as Massignon suggests is not so readily discernible in the most obvious sources (cf. Massignon, *Passion* [1975], I, p. 71).

[28] The word rendered by "jealousy" (*al-ghayra;* Vadet: *al-ᶜizza*) is somewhat unclear in the film we have of the manuscript.

[29] "once the lover is truly faithful": *baᶜda ṣidqihi*? Cf. the remark ascribed by Abū Nuᶜaym to Ibn ᶜAṭāᵓ on acceptance of adversities with contentment as a sign of *ṣidq* (*Ḥilya,* X, p. 303).

[30] Since there are no preceding Sufi statements on "universal love" (*al-maḥabba al-kullīya*) in this chapter, al-Daylamī would seem to have at the back of his mind the statements attributed to Plato at the beginning of the chapter as well. By "universal love" he apparently means something like "love in general."

source of love; the derivative meaning of love; and the essence of love. All these referents are possible in the Arabic language and are legitimate in the opinion of those who study the uses of words. Thus the word "faith" (*īmān*) means in its *essence* **[89]** to believe. Its *derivative meaning* is the performance of prayer, which is also called faith, as in the Koranic verse, "But God would never leave your faith to waste" (2:143), where "faith" means "the prayer you previously performed in the direction of Jerusalem."[31] Likewise light, which is the *source* of faith from which faith comes, has been called faith. In the Koran we have, "Thou knewest not what the Book was, nor faith; but we made it a light, (whereby we guide whom we will of our servants)" (42:52). Here light, which is an act of God, is called faith. But faith is the act of the faithful; and, in its essence, faith is the act of belief. Thus when Abraham, peace be upon him, said, "Show me how thou wilt give life to the dead" (2:260), God answered him saying, "Why, dost thou not have faith?" (2:260),[32] that is, "dost thou not believe?" Nevertheless, we see that God (also) called the source of the human act of faith, (that is to say, light, which is his own act), [and its derivative referent], (namely, prayer), by the name faith.

Now let us come back to the subject and complete our review of what our teachers, may God have mercy on them, have said about the essence of love. The authority who spoke with great subtlety on the matter and set himself apart from his masters and his associates in what he maintained was al-Ḥusayn b. Manṣūr. The following is an account of his opinion on the essence of love. **[90]**

Al-Ḥusayn b. Manṣūr, known as al-Ḥallāj, said:[33] "Eros is fire, light, the first fire![34] In preeternity it was colored with every color and mani-

---

[31] Muslim prayer was directed towards Jerusalem before the Hijra, but the direction was changed, by revelation, to that of Mecca after the Prophet's flight from that city to Medina. Cf. Koran 2:125, 142.

[32] The Koranic quotation in not broken up in this manner in al-Daylamī's Arabic text.

[33] A somewhat different translation of this paragraph and the following verses, as well as of al-Daylamī's comments in the next two paragraphs and the two ensuing verses, can be found in Massignon, "Interférences," pp. 237–38, and again, slightly abbreviated at the end, in Massignon, *Passion* (1975), I, pp. 413–14.

[34] This renders the words of the manuscript read as *Al-ᶜishqu nārun, nūrun, awwalu nārin!* But we might understand as well, "Eros is fire, the light of the first fire!" reading, *Al-ᶜishqu nārun, nūru awwali nārin!* It is also conceivable to read with Massignon, "Eros is the fire of the light of the first fire" (see preced-

fest with every attribute. Its essence flamed through its own essence, and its attributes sparkled through its own attributes;[35] it was something truly realized, crossing the infinite distances from preeternity into the ages of ages. Its source is he-ness, and it emerges out of I-ness. What is hidden of what is manifest of its essence is the reality of existence, and what is manifest of what is hidden of its attributes is that form perfected through the concealment that proclaims universality in its perfection."

He also declaimed on this subject the following verses:[36]

Eros existed in the preeternity of preeternities, from all eternity,
in him, through him, from him; in it appears the manifestation of being.
Eros is no temporal being, for it is among the attributes
of one, the victims of (love for) whom still live.
His attributes are from and in himself, uncreated;
a created thing is something that originates from things.
When the beginning appeared, he displayed his eros as an attribute
in the one who appeared, and there shone in him a glistening light.
And the *lām* was in union with the conjoined *alif:*
the two in preeternity were one thing.[37]
But in dispersal they are two: if they should meet
in the realm of separation, they are slave and master. **[91]**
Such are the realities, the fire of longing blazes forth
out of reality, when the beloved's tribe departs or is far away.
Distraught with love, they were humbled and without strength,
for the mighty are humbled by longing.

The author of this book, may God have mercy on him, said: Al-Ḥusayn b. Manṣūr set himself apart by this opinion from the other Sufi masters. What distinguishes his doctrine is that in his spiritual allusions he calls eros one of the attributes of essence, absolutely and wherever it appears. The other teachers, for their part, allude to the uniting of lover and beloved when love comes to its extreme limit in the extinction of the totality of the lover in the beloved. They do not (like al-Ḥallāj) speak of the divine and human natures.[38]

---

ing note).

[35] "its own essence, . . . its own attributes": possibly, "his (God's) essence, . . . his attributes."

[36] In this poem the final phrases of verses 2, 6, and 7, and all of the last verse, represent characteristic motifs of Arabic love poetry. The assignment of the pronouns in the first verse is problematic. The rendering of the prepositions is less difficult, since in effect all possible relationships are implied.

[37] It is apparently this verse that inspired the title of al-Daylamī's treatise.

[38] Here al-Daylamī seems to attribute to al-Ḥallāj a doctrine emphatically re-

They also said that God's love for his loved ones is preeternal, but that their love for him is one of the effects of that love, not by commingling, but rather by the union of a man with God *as though* he were indeed God himself, owing to his annihilation in him, as the author of these lines[39] has said:

Thou hast made me pass away from myself in thee;
 I wonder at thee and at myself.
Thou hast made me stand in a station
 where I imagined that thou (art I), that I (am thou).

Such examples are too many to enumerate here, but we will mention [others] in the chapter **[92]** on the perfection and extreme limit of love.

Our teacher, Abū ᶜAbd Allāh Muḥammad b. Khafīf, may God have mercy on him, was asked about love and he replied: "It is an awareness of something from which there flows a breeze of refreshment that can be felt by men's spirits."[40] He also said: "Love is the manifestation that enfolds men's hearts of his kindnesses and the first signs of his favor, [and] it is to find delight in remembering the beloved."

Bundār b. al-Ḥusayn[41] was asked about love and said: "It is an army from the legions of God. One can neither perceive its extreme limit nor behold its depth. Yet it consumes its abode in flames and melts away the one who is afflicted with it. It joins the lover to his beloved, and as long as anything identifiable remains of the lover, he may be described with

---

jected by his teacher Ibn Khafīf. For the commonly cited example of al-Ḥallāj's speaking of the divine and human natures, see the poem alleged to be by him translated in the Introduction, p. lvii. Al-Daylamī records in his biography of Ibn Khafīf that, although his teacher called al-Ḥallāj a true monotheist, he condemned the lines in question and said that whoever had composed them was an unbeliever. See the sources cited in notes 179 and 180 in the Introduction.

[39] With a slight difference in wording, all but the first hemistich of the second line are ascribed to al-Ḥallāj in *Le dîwân d'âl-Hallâj* (ed. Massignon, p. 30).

[40] Or: "something that makes men's hearts feel its breeze of refreshment," reading with Vadet *yushᶜir* for *tashᶜur*.

[41] Originally from Shiraz, Bundār settled in Arrajān. He is said to have had discussions with al-Daylamī's teacher Ibn Khafīf on a number of issues. He died in 353/964–65 (or 357/968). See al-Sulamī, *Ṭabaqāt al-ṣūfiya* (ed. Pedersen), p. 491. Abū Nuᶜaym (*Ḥilya,* X, p. 384) calls him Bundār b. al-Ḥasan, but other authors, e.g., al-Qushayrī (*Risāla* [Cairo: Ṣubayḥ, 1966], p. 49), have al-Ḥusayn as here. He was a student of al-Ashᶜarī and may have been a teacher of Ibn Khafīf. Like Ibn Khafīf, he condemned al-Ḥallāj's verses on the divine and human natures (*lāhūt* and *nāsūt*) of God. See the long passage on him in Sobieroj, "Ibn Ḫafīf aš-Šīrāzī," pp. 78–82.

an attribute, but if his identity is obliterated by the force of love, then his only attribute is his drunkenness, his only strength is love, and the beloved is his, in his entirety, his might, and his act."[42]

It has also been said that God gave a revelation to David, saying: "O David, my love[43] is the guide to me."

These replies given by the Sufi masters are sufficient for the purposes of this book, **[93]** so let us proceed to the next section, in which we will put forward our own opinion.

Section Four. Our Opinion on the Essence and Quiddity of Love

Love in its essence is a luminous entity that appeared among the effects of the original love in the abode of the intellect.[44] The intellect conveyed it to a "spiritual" spirit, which received it. Then this spirit conveyed it to subtle bodies (that is, spirits), and they received it and were adorned with it. Then the spirits conveyed to bodies, together with love, the pleasure, tenderness, beauty, and kindness that they had found pleasing in their abode, and all of these things became ornaments of the lover and attributes of the beloved.

Someone might ask how love, at the time it came into contact with bodies, changed from its original clarity and purity so as to become sullied by the opposites of these, namely, turbidity and filth. To this we would reply that when it emerged from its noble abode and came into a vile abode, it changed in proportion to the change in its abode. Thus it emerged from preeternity into temporal existence, and its abode was the world of the intellect, **[94]** which is the purest of all possible worlds. Then the intellect conveyed it to the world of the spirit,[45] and it changed somewhat. After this, the world of the spirit shed it upon the world of physical nature, and it entered into composition and changed somewhat again. Then physical nature shed it upon compound, dark, dense bodies, and its clarity became mixed with their turbidity and its light entered into

---

[42] Both the text and the translation of this last sentence are uncertain. Cf. the notes in our edition and Vadet, ed., p. 45.

[43] "my love": *maḥabbatī.* The pronoun is ambiguous, denoting perhaps the subject or perhaps the object of love. The saying is quoted again below (MS, p. 185), where the context seems to support understanding God's love for men. There it is Gabriel, not David, who is addressed.

[44] By calling love in its essence one of the "effects" of the original love, al-Daylamī would seem to take issue with al-Ḥallāj, whom he has just described as maintaining that eros is "one of the attributes of essence, absolutely and wherever it appears" (MS, p. 91). Cf. also MS, p. 50.

[45] Cf. MS, p. 50, where al-Daylamī speaks of love as mediated by the intellect, the soul (*nafs*), and the physical nature.

composition with their darkness. Thus love became a third thing, which is neither pure light nor pure darkness. Similarly, when you mix honey with vinegar you produce a third thing, which is neither honey nor vinegar. Even though you still taste the sweetness of the honey, you will not miss in it the sourness of the vinegar.

It is the same when you take a lamp into a dark house. It shows you a third thing, which is neither pure light nor pure darkness. What you see, rather, is light compounded with darkness, for pure light dazzles one's vision, since vision is a part of the universal light. Indeed if a part is joined to the whole, it becomes united with it, and there remains only one thing. **[95]** Thus (in pure light) you would not sense that your total being was anything but light. It is to this that our teachers refer when they speak of the extinction of man in God and of the joining of the lover to the beloved.

Likewise when you come into absolute darkness you do not sense yourself, in your entirety, to be anything but darkness. This is why God compared unbelief to darkness, for the infidel does not sense his total being to be anything but unbelief. God said: "Layer upon layer of darkness. When he holds out his hand he scarce can see it. And he for whom God has not appointed light, for him there is no light" (24:40).[46] He said this because darkness has encompassed the unbeliever from every side, and he can hardly sense himself to be anything other than darkness, which indeed he is.

In like manner, when luminous love comes into dark bodies, it changes in proportion to the change in its abode and displays to you attributes that are different from each other and states that are opposite to each other. Examples are union and abandonment, nearness and distance, pleasure and aversion, and pain and comfort, which we will describe to you further on, God willing.[47]

Section Five. The Kinds of Love **[96]**

The author of this book said: People hold different views on the varieties of love, its essence, and its origin. Our teachers, may God multiply them, have said that love is divided into three classes: innate, acquired, and endowed.[48]

The explanation of this is as follows. Endowed love is of two kinds, and it is from God in its beginning. The first kind of endowed love is

---

[46] Pickthall's translation, altered.

[47] Cf. MS, p. 145.

[48] "innate, acquired, and endowed": *jibillī, muktasab,* and *mawhibī,* respectively.

found in the act of faith, of which it is one of the conditions, while the second is the love of those who have attained the goal among the gnostics. This kind of love has its origin from God, and it is for this reason that he said: "Hadst thou expended all that is in the earth, thou couldst not have brought their hearts together; but God brought their hearts together" (8:63).[49] It is likewise this love that the Prophet forbade men to think of as appropriate to any other than God; for he said: "If I were to choose a bosom friend (*khalīl*), I would chose Abū Bakr as a bosom friend." What he meant was that he had no choice or power to acquire this love.[50] For were it an acquired love, **[97]** he would have bestowed it on Abū Bakr.

The first endowed love is the one that is an obligation among the conditions of faith. We know it is an obligation because God has said: "Say, 'If your fathers, your sons, your brothers, your wives, your clan, your possessions that you have gained, commerce you fear may slacken, dwellings you love—if these are dearer to you than God and his Messenger, and to struggle in his way, then wait till God brings his command'" (9:24). Here he has warned men, when they neglect this (obligation of) love, to wait for a time and see.[51] This love is the love of the commonality of Muslims, while the other is the love of the gnostics who know him and of the adepts of love among the people of God.[52]

As for innate love, it is born from beholding God's favor and witnessing his grace, both the eternal and the temporal. To behold these blessings, by nature, produces love, as the Prophet has said: "Hearts have been created with an innate disposition to love whoever does good to them and to loathe whoever harms them." He also said: "Exchange gifts and you will love one another." This means: Be kind and devoted to one another **[98]** and God will bestow love on you. This love belongs both to those who pass through the mystical states and to those whose station is that of righteous deeds that draw one near to God.[53]

---

[49] The verb rendered "brought together" is *allafa.* Cf. MS, p. 78.

[50] Bosom friendship (*khulla*) is the special love God bestowed only on the prophets Abraham and Muḥammad. The version of the Prophet's saying we have cited in the footnote in our edition has "If I were to take a bosom friend other than my Lord . . ." See also chapter four, n. 29.

[51] This argument is borrowed from Ibn Khafīf. See the Introduction, p. xlix and n. 163. Al-Daylamī uses the argument again in chapter fifteen (MS, p. 197).

[52] "the people of God": *ahl al-ḥaqq taʿālā,* assuming *taʿālā* not to be a scribal addition.

[53] "those whose station . . . to God": *al-qāʾimīna maʿa wujūh al-qurubāt.* Translation uncertain.

As for acquired love, it is that which proceeds from acts of obedience, conformity in servitude, and compliance with the will of one's beloved in all circumstances. This is the love to which our teachers refer when they answer that love is obedience and conformity.[54] It is the state of beginners in love.

The author of this book, may God have mercy on him, said: All such stipulations and all such responses, according to which love consists in acts of obedience, toil, exertion, and the like, are answers in which our teachers have followed the customary usage of the learned[55] by distinguishing the canonical meaning of the word love from its linguistic meaning. Thus, for example, the word "faith," in its canonical sense, implies three things—words, deeds, and intentions, whereas in the linguistic sense it means "belief."[56] Similarly, the original love (to which the word love in its pure linguistic sense refers) is God's act in his creation exclusive of any human act, whereas the canonical meaning of love is conformity, obedience, and the like.

---

[54] Cf. MS, pp. 87–88.

[55] "the learned": *ahl al-maʿrifa;* possibly, "the gnostics."

[56] Cf. MS, pp. 88–89.

CHAPTER SEVEN

[99] ON THE DIVERSE VIEWS PEOPLE HOLD ABOUT LOVE

In his book entitled *The Diversity of Opinions about Love*[1] Abū Saᶜīd Aḥmad b. [Muḥammad b.] Ziyād al-Aᶜrābī related people's views without mentioning them by name. "People differ on the question of love," he said, "and they can be divided according to their views into seven groups: those who hold that love is obedience; those who hold that love is fascination; those who hold that love is beholding; those who hold that love is knowledge; [those who hold that love is a natural disposition]; those who hold that love is will; and those who hold that love is a commingling."[2]

Section One. Beginning of the Commentary on the Preceding Sentence

Those who hold that love is obedience are divided among themselves and form six groups.

First, there are those who say that love is obedience, toil, and exertion, basing their view on the Koranic text, "If you love God, follow me" (3:31). This group has its arguments and proofs.[3]

Second, there are those who hold that love is remembering God's favor, giving thanks to him for what he has done, and the soul's being pleased with all **[100]** the good and evil one may encounter.

Third, there are those who claim that love is to be grateful for and pleased with all that God causes to befall one or that he does with one.[4]

Fourth, there are those who hold that true love can be directed only to one person in the world, namely, the Disposer appointed by God, who is

---

[1] *Kitāb ikhtilāf al-nās fī ᵓl-maḥabba.* The title is not mentioned in the notice on Abū Saᶜīd in Sezgin (*GAS,* I , pp. 660–61). Perhaps this is the book by him on love (*Kitāb al-maḥabba*) mentioned by Ibn Khayr al-Ishbīlī (*Fahrasa,* p. 284). There is some apparently inconsistent language in this chapter, perhaps the result of its being an abbreviated version of Abū Saᶜīd's text.

[2] The order of the following discussion is not quite the same as that given here, the places of the proponents of knowledge and will being exchanged.

[3] Cf. Bell, *Love Theory,* pp. 115–17, on the *eros* and *nomos* motifs in Muslim discussions of love.

[4] Apparently the difference between this group and the preceding one is that a man must be not only pleased with but also grateful for the evil that befalls him.

his Proof among his creatures. He is always present on earth, and love in their view is to obey him. If he perishes, another like him takes his place.[5]

Fifth, there are those who claim that love means only to love the Prophet, God's "friends," and the "custodians." They deem God to be far too glorious for them to love him, since, as they say, love only occurs between those who are alike or similar.[6]

Sixth, there are those who hold that love is trust, contentment, and consolation[7] until the moment of arrival.

Section Two.

Those who hold that love is fascination (*shaᶜaf*) are divided into seven groups.

First, there are those who hold that love is fascination with God, joy, longing **[101]** to meet him, and exerting oneself in that which leads to beholding him.

Second, there are those who hold that love is to abandon the material preoccupations of the soul so that it no longer inclines towards anything other than remembrance of God and fascination with him and so that the soul's preoccupation with remembering God distracts it from the remembrance of the Prophet and from fascination itself.[8]

Third, there are those who hold that love is to love everything God has created because it is God who has created it, allowing, however, that some things are to be preferred to others because some of them resemble God's acts.

Fourth, there are those who hold that true love is to cause your soul to abide in the most intimate association and the closest proximity.

Fifth, there are those who hold that love is to restrain one's soul and to resist it, so that it will trust in its Lord, be fascinated with him, and be amorously inclined towards him.[9]

---

[5] This paragraph seems to describe an Ismaili or similar view on love. "Proof" translates *ḥujja,* while "Disposer" renders *mudabbir.*

[6] This argument, stressing the transcendence of God, apparently represents another Shiite position. The terms for "friends" (*awliyāᵓ,* sing. *walī,* which also means "saints") and for "custodians" (*awṣiyāᵓ,* sing *waṣī*) are both used in the sense of legal guardians.

[7] "consolation": *al-muwāsāh;* possibly, "charity, sharing one's worldly goods."

[8] "fascination itself": *al-shaᶜaf;* conceivably, "fascination [with him]," reading with Vadet, *al-shaᶜaf [bihi].*

[9] The soul is considered the seat of temptations. Cf. Koran 79:40–41, "And

Sixth, there are those who hold that love is to express one's contentment with the blessings God bestows by giving thanks to him. Giving thanks to him, in this view, is part of love for him, and love is fascination. Fascination, in turn, is nearness, and nearness **[102]** is arrival.

Seventh, there are those who hold that love is being pleased with what God does and with the situation in which he places one. To object by asking something of him, in their view, is unbelief.

Section Three.

Those who maintain that love is beholding comprise five groups.

First, there is a group of the followers of ᶜAbd al-Wāḥid b. Zayd, who hold that the beatific vision is proportional to one's love, just as ᶜAbd al-Wāḥid used to say that the vision is proportional to one's deeds.

Second, there are those who say that true love is admissible only to the Mahdi, whom they see and with whom they sit.

Third, there are those who hold that love is to gaze on the beloved in all things, seeing nothing without beholding the beloved in it. The vision of your beloved through the things about you is something you are aware of by your nature, for you come to know your beloved through your nature and your soul.

Fourth, there are those who hold that to love God is to endorse the statements of those who claim to behold him in the things about us. For if you endorse their claim, according to this view, God, who is the paragon of generosity, will show himself to you, because you have believed his saints (*awliyāʾ*).

Fifth, there are those who say that at the beginning of **[103]** love God arouses in your mind longing for the vision. Then he shows [himself] to you, and when you see him you love him, and then you are intimate with him. After this comes perplexity: love comes at one moment, intimacy at another, the vision at one moment, and deprivation at yet another. In this view, love is conditional on the vision.

Section Four.

Those who speak of will are divided into five groups.

First, there are those who claim that love is your will to love, for you cannot love without an act of your will. They follow this view, in accordance with their principles, in all cases.

[Second, there are those who claim that] love is that will [that is placed] in the mind at the moment when the heart is wholly devoted to

---

as for those who fear the time when they will stand before their Lord and restrain their souls from low desires, Paradise will be their retreat."

remembrance of God. In their opinion will is not an act of the human willer, but an act of God himself.

Third, there are those who hold that will is an act of the human willer and that it is an acquired act. This will is love, examples being your love for your manservant, your slave-girl, or your son.

Fourth, there are those who hold that love on the part of everyone who wills [is] one and the same as the love in which [all people] share. You are distinguished from the others only through knowledge, knowledge **[104]** being in their view something that is not acquired, whereas love is.

Fifth, there are those who hold that love is the triumph of the will in causing one to incline towards the beloved. This overwhelms all other things so that [everything passes away] and there remains only the beloved.

Section Five.

Those who maintain that love is a natural disposition are divided into seven[10] groups.

First, there are those who say that love is a natural disposition in every man, something always present in him, whether he is ignorant or wise. If God loves a man, he makes this natural disposition manifest in him.

Second, there are those who say that love is a natural disposition, [but] that it is you yourself who make love manifest, and that you will not make it manifest until you love God. Then, if it reaches perfection, it becomes equal on both sides, that is to say, that love on your part attains the same degree as God's love. They also say that God placed all things in the same rank. There is no distinction between any of them in their view.

Third, there are those who hold that if love is something you possess by nature, then all men share it with you, and you cannot surpass others by means of it. Preeminence in love consists in God's loving you **[105]** because of the sincerity of your love for him, so that you may act as God acts and have power to act like the power of God.

Fourth, there are those who hold that God loves all men. If we see in the visible world one person who surpasses another in love, this is because in the unseen reality the other has surpassed him in some other quality. For God is compassionate towards all men, and he provides for them all. We have never seen any wise being, this group says, who does not love his possessions.

---

[10] If the number of opinions given at the end of the chapter as forty-five (MS, p. 109) is correct, then an opinion has fallen out here. Only six are named in this section.

Fifth, there are those who hold that love is the abandonment of love and who change the names of realities to their opposites. These are the partisans of antithesis.[11] According to them there is no one who does not have love in his natural constitution, but if someone makes a claim to love, the opposite is said of him.[12]

Sixth, there are those who point to the fact that God is wise and all-knowing and who argue that no one has ever seen a wise or knowing being who squanders any of his wealth or possessions, or who has servants and does not have a chosen elite among them, or who does not choose as his beloved among that elite the wisest of them. Accordingly they affirm that God loves his creatures and that he has a chosen elite, who are all those who love **[106]** without exception, some of them, however, being superior in love to others.

Section Six.

Those who hold that love is knowledge comprise eight groups.

[First, there are those who hold that love is knowledge] because you do not love something until you know it. This group advocates the elimination of good works and the practice of licentious deeds.

Second, there are those who say that love comes after knowledge, because you may know a thing and yet not love it. If you come to know it, it is possible for you to love it, but you cannot love someone you do not know. In their view, love is God's revelation to you [and] (his granting you) knowledge.

Third, there are those who say that love ensues after you come to know God in his perfection, his majesty, and his power. In their view, your love is proportional to the amount of this knowledge you attain. If you have not attained such knowledge, then you are a lover who has failed to attain the reality of love.

Fourth, there are those who say that love is knowledge and that it comes about after knowledge is brought to its fullness. For you seek to know the beloved, [but] in your search to know him you [do not] love him. If, however, knowledge is perfected in you, you learn the realities of things and you attain love.

Fifth, there are those who say that to love God **[107]** is to gratify your soul [with that][13] which contains its ruin. In this way you approach God.

---

[11] "antithesis": *al-mughāyarāt* (plural).

[12] "the opposite is said of him": *ghāra hādhā ᶜalayhi;* text and translation uncertain. Possibly, *ᶜāda hādhā ᶜalayhi.*

[13] Vadet's suggestion (ed. p. 52) for a lacuna in the manuscript. But perhaps the original text gave the opposite meaning, for example, "that you gratify your

For he is the possessor of your soul, and if you enjoy his possessions, you will yearn for him.[14]

Sixth, there are those who claim that love is for you to give credence to the followers of all religions and not to embrace a particular faith, since the followers of all religions are seeking God. Consider what suits you, they say, and follow it, for whoever adopts anything whatsoever as his religion has hit the mark.

Seventh, there are those who hold that love is when you feel intimacy in one moment and desolation in another, when you know not in one moment and know in another, continuing in this fashion until you reach the reality of love and knowledge.

Eighth, there are those who hold that love for God has many aspects. Whoever presents any one of these aspects, therefore, is to be considered [among those who love him]. So the reality of love in each man, according to this view, is the knowledge and love to which his intellect leads him.

Section Seven.
Those who hold that love is a commingling are divided into [seven] groups.

First, there are those who hold that love is mingling, that is, that everything in you mingle **[108]** with everything in the beloved.

Second, there are those who hold that [love is that] you do not leave your beloved, nor he you, and that there be no empty space between you and him. This group says, "We are God, and God is we." But God is far too exalted and glorious for this to be the case.[15]

Third, there are those [who hold] that the one who loves God has never ceased to be with him, eternal, wise, and all-knowing, for such a one proceeds from his essence. They say that the Preeternal is alone in ordering the affairs of the heavens, and that they (his lovers) are alone in ordering the affairs of the earth.

Fourth, there are those who hold that love is God's mercy and compassion for his creatures, for his creatures are among his acts, and all his acts are goodness and compassion.[16] Divine justice, according to this

---

soul [while protecting it from that] which contains its ruin," supplying *wa-taḥmiyahā mimmā.*

[14] The text and translation of this sentence are uncertain. Our reading follows that of Vadet.

[15] To be included in this group is presumably al-Ḥallāj, whose claim to identity with God, despite al-Daylamī's respect for the mystic, is here repudiated.

[16] "compassion": *raḥma.* Perhaps the text originally read "wisdom" (*ḥikma*).

view, has no real meaning.[17]

Fifth, there are the manifestationists (*al-ẓuhūrīya*), who say that love is that which comes from God in the first instance. It is he who manifests his act in you, and your love will exist over against his love and your act over against his act, in accordance with God's words, "a people he loves and who love him" (5:54).

Sixth, there are those who say that your love for God is proportional to his love for you. If he loves you, then you will love him, and if he is obedient to you,[18] then you will be obedient to him.

Seventh, there are those who say that you will not possess pure love in its real meaning until you have the power to act just as God has the power to act. **[109]** They claim that this power is latent in every man. When you devote pure love to God, he will manifest it in you.

Here ends the chapter, which contains forty-five [opinions in seven] sections. Let us now turn to the description of love.

---

[17] As divine justice is conceived by the Muᶜtazilites.

[18] Cf. the *ḥadīth* on God's obedience to the Prophet below (MS, p. 186).

CHAPTER EIGHT
ON THE DESCRIPTION AND CHARACTER OF EROS[1]

Section One. The Opinions of the Belletrists

Al-Nāshiʾ[2] was asked to describe love and he said: "Love is divided into three parts: love for the soul, love for form, and love for movement. It is love for the soul that most completely comprehends the aspects of love and is the farthest removed from bother and weariness. Love for form is the sweetest to the senses and the most delectable to the sight. Love for movement is the most graceful to the glance and the most painful to the heart. However, love for form and love for movement are in most cases subordinate to love for the soul, even though they may at times occur independently. Thus one does not fall in love with a pictorial form, for there is no soul in it, nor any movement, **[110]** nor does one love lethargic[3] eyes, for there are no glances in them."

Al-Nuᶜmān b. al-Mundhir asked al-Zarqāʾ bint al-Khuss[4] about eros and she said: "It is of several varieties. One is madness, one is tenacity, and one is affectation. As for that which is affectation, it does not endure, and time effaces it in short order. It has no permanence, and affection for one loved in this way is not observed for long. As for that which is tenacity, in the beginning it is slight, but it becomes a mighty passion. When it gains a firm foothold, it grows as a fire grows when fed an abundance of firewood. As for that which is madness, it is a hidden malady and an oppressive burden that is relieved only by the expiration of one's appointed time."

---

[1] The title as given in MS, p. 6, is "On the description of eros and love."

[2] Presumably Abū ʾl-ᶜAbbās ᶜAbd Allāh b. Muḥammad, al-Nāshīʾ al-Akbar (d. 293/906), but possibly Abū ʾl-Ḥasan (ʾl-Ḥusayn) ᶜAlī b. ᶜAbd Allāh, al-Nāshiʾ al-Aṣghar (d. 365/975). Ibn Qayyim al-Jawzīya quotes some nice verses by the former (*Rawḍa,* pp. 76, 392) and points out that he followed the Muᶜtazilite al-ᶜAllāf in the view that every beloved must experience some inclination towards the one who loves him (ibid., p. 76).

[3] "lethargic": *musbita* (sleepy). The text at the beginning of MS p. 110 is apparently corrupt. Vadet reads *musabbiya/musbiya* (captivating?).

[4] MS: al-Warqāʾ bint al-Ḥasan. Pre-Islamic woman legendary for her eloquence, the nickname al-Zarqāʾ possibly resulting from confusion with Zarqāʾ al-Yamāma. See Ch. Pellat, *EI²,* III, pp. 454b–455a, s.v. "Hind bint al-Khuss," al-Ziriklī, *Aᶜlām,* IX, p. 103, s.v., and al-Jāḥiẓ, *al-Bayān wa-l-tabyīn,* I, pp. 312–13.

A certain man of letters described eros saying: "The way by which it comes in is hidden from the eye, and the way by which it proceeds lies veiled in the heart. The tongue cannot describe it, nor can eloquence portray it. It is something between magic and madness, obscure where it moves and hides."

Similarly, a Bedouin once described eros as follows: **[111]** "Too hidden to be seen, too glorious to be hidden. It lies concealed like fire in stone: if you strike the stone, it sparks; if you do not, the fire remains unseen."

In a work of belles-lettres I found that someone had described eros with these words: "Intellects are humbled before it, souls are obedient to it. The intellect is its prisoner, the regard is its messenger, the glance is its speech, and sighing is its silence. Its dwelling is inscrutable and its abode obscure. It is joined to the parts of one's heart and flows in one's movements. Its speech is expressed in distress, its allusions through breathing, and its gestures through crying aloud. Eros begins with escalation, stops at a peak, and falls back down in retreat to the utmost dissolution at the moment of weariness. Eros begins as love and then carries the lover along until it becomes eros itself. Moreover, a man may love someone who does not approach him in beauty or perfection. If he is asked for his reason, he can find none, except the saying, 'Love makes you blind and deaf.'"[5]

A certain physician said: "Eros is a malady **[112]** that afflicts the spirit and possesses the body by spreading from the spirit. This is because it is composed of both love and passion, which are the results of similarity and familiarity. It has an initial, medial, and final stage. At times the one afflicted with eros is said to be mad, though he may be the most rational of men, or he is said to be stricken with delirium, though he may be the most lucid of speakers. He burdens himself with every difficulty and plunges into every adversity until he obtains the goal of his quest and the object of his desire."

Manka the Indian was once asked to describe love and he said: "It is the brightener of intellects and the polisher of minds, as long as it is not excessive. If it exceeds its proper bounds, it becomes a deadly illness and a destructive disease. No expedients are useful against it and no judgments are effective. The treatment is more of the same."[6]

---

[5] The saying "Love makes you blind and deaf" is attributed to the Prophet. *Sunan Abī Dāwūd,* no. 5130.

[6] The same saying, in a somewhat longer version, according to Mughulṭāy (*al-Wāḍiḥ al-mubīn,* pp. 44–45), was ascribed to Manka (Indian scholar and translator favored by Hārūn al-Rashīd [Sezgin *GAS,* III, pp. 200–201]) by the

Section Two. The Opinions of the Bedouin Arabs

One of the Bedouin was asked about eros and he said: "Its path in the heart is more inscrutable than that of the spirit in the body. It has a greater hold over the soul than the soul (itself).[7] It is invisible and visible, subtle [and dense]. The tongue **[113]** cannot describe it. It is something between magic and madness, obscure in its movement and concealment." Then he said:

My two friends, speak as I do of passion (*hawā*), if you know it,
and if you do not, then ask me.
Was passion already in my heart? Or was it brought there
by the twinkling glances of girls?
Which one brought passion to the other?
Which began the thing you two describe?
You may say the heart began it, but not so,
or you may say the glance, but the cause was not two eyes.[8]
Rather it was two spirits, one meeting the other,
recognizing each other and joining in close union.[9]

A Bedouin was asked about eros and he said: "It is an oppressive king and a tyrannical ruler. Souls do its bidding and hearts obey it. Its dwell-

---

physician al-Tamīmī (d. late 4th/10th century) in his *Kitāb imtizāj al-arwāḥ (= al-nufūs?)*. Regarding the title of the lost work by al-Tamīmī it should be noted that Ibn Qayyim al-Jawzīya at one point mentions a *Kitāb imtizāj al-arwāḥ* by him (*Rawḍa,* p. 143) and at another a *Kitāb imtizāj al-nufūs* (ibid., p. 379). The latter title, apparently misplaced in Brockelmann under Ibn Juljul (*S,* I, p. 422), is not listed under either author by Sezgin (cf. *GAS,* III, pp. 309–10, 317–18).

[7] We hesitate to translate "has a greater hold over the soul (*nafs*) than the *breath* (*nafas*) has," or the other way round, partially because of a parallel text quoted by Ibn Qayyim al-Jawzīya (*Rawḍa,* p. 140), which reads, "has a greater hold over the soul than it itself has (*amlak bi-l-nafs min dhātihā*)."

[8] The upshot of these questions is whether it was the poet's *eye*, with which he saw the girl's glances, or his *heart* that brought on love. This is a traditional motif. There is a well-known story of a dispute between the eye and the heart over which is responsible for love. The liver, the seat of the passions, intervenes, saying that the two are like a cripple and a blind man who work together to steal fruit from a tree, the blind man carrying the cripple on his shoulders. Ibn Qayyim al-Jawzīya, *Rawḍa,* pp. 104–10.

[9] An allusion to the similarity, and prior existence, of lovers' souls, via the saying attributed to the Prophet, "Spirits are regimented battalions: those which know one another associate familiarly together, while those which do not know one another remain at variance." Trans. A. J. Arberry in his English version of Ibn Ḥazm's *Ṭawq al-ḥamāma,* p. 27. Cf. MS, pp. 220–22, 224.

ing is inscrutable and its abode obscure. It flows in one's movements and is joined to the heart. Indeed, I fear a sudden attack of fate may be brought on by passion, because of the violence of love."

Someone asked a Bedouin about judgment and passion, and he replied: "Passion is wakeful, whereas judgment sleeps. Therefore passion conquers **[114]** judgment."

A certain man of letters said [about passion]: "I came upon a Bedouin who was watering his camels. I sat down and spoke with him for a while and eventually brought up the subject of passion. But no sooner had I mentioned it than he fell into a swoon. When he recovered I asked him what was the matter, and he spoke the following verses:

> May God curse passion for the way it kills
> and the way it wreaks havoc in the livers of lovers.[10]
> Do not reproach me for my passion,
> for I see the strength of heroes come to naught in love."

Someone once said to a man of the Banū ᶜUdhra tribe,[11] "Why is it that your people dissolve in love just as salt dissolves in water?" "Because we see things you do not see," he replied, "and hear things you do not hear, and because we disobey those who censure and reproach us for love. By God, if you had in your heart any scars from love, you would elegize every lover, man or woman." Then he broke into verse:

> No one enslaved by love has ever described its pangs
> and been understood, except by another enslaved by love.

The author of this book said: We find the love with which human lovers love each other to have varying attributes, for there are both praiseworthy and reprehensible loves. It is our desire to distinguish the one from the other and to explain both cases. **[115]** Praiseworthy love is that which is untainted by the evils that may occur in it and corrupt it. It is that which has retained its original purity, its prior luminosity, and its preeternal spirituality. Reprehensible love, on the other hand, is that which has been polluted by the appetites of the bestial soul, that is, its sensual[12] delights, those appetites that are generated in the filth of the physical nature and that are reprehensible according to both reason and revelation. We shall begin by mentioning praiseworthy love, since this will allow us to dispense with mentioning that which is reprehensible.

---

[10] The liver is commonly considered the seat of the passions. Cf. n. 8.

[11] Arab tribe celebrated for its tradition of chaste, "courtly" love. *ᶜUdhra* means among other things "virginity" or "maidenhead."

[12] "sensual": *nafsānīya;* more precisely, "of the (appetitive) soul, appetitive."

CHAPTER NINE

ON PRAISEWORTHY LOVE

Jābir related that the Messenger of God said: "The believer befriends and is befriended, for there is no good in one who becomes close to no one and to whom no one is close, and the best of men is the one who is most helpful to others." But we have already dealt sufficiently with this subject in the section on the excellence of love,[1] so here we shall present accounts of some of the religious authorities and **[116]** imams who have gone before us.

We may begin with Abū Bakr b. Dāwūd because of the great quantity of material [he] has related about love.[2] It is related from Ibrāhīm b. Muḥammad b. ᶜArafa[3] that he said: "I visited Muḥammad b. Dāwūd while he was suffering from the illness from which he died, and I said to him, 'How do you feel?' 'The love of whom you know,' he said, 'has brought about what you see.' So I said to him, 'Why should you not enjoy him when it is within your power to do so?' But he replied, 'Enjoyment has two aspects. One is the permitted gaze, and the other is the for-

---

[1] Cf. MS, pp. 21–25. Part of the saying of the Prophet cited here occurs in the section on the excellence of the lover (MS, p. 27). On this *ḥadīth,* see the note in our edition.

[2] The near-Ḥallājian al-Daylamī cites as his first example the Ẓāhirite jurist Muḥammad b. Dāwūd (d. 297/909), who by a decision he rendered may have paved the way for the execution of al-Ḥallāj. See Massignon, *Passion* (1922), I, pp. 161–82, esp. p. 164, and Lois Giffen's reservation in her *Theory of Profane Love among the Arabs,* pp. 70–71, n. 8. Ibn Dāwūd was the son of the founder of the Ẓāhirite *madhhab* and the author of a celebrated book on profane love, the *Kitāb al-zahra* (see the Bibliography). Al-Daylamī can only approve of Ibn Dāwūd's amorous sentiments, but like many others he cites some of his most compromising, if most exquisite, verse. By ancient convention Ibn Dāwūd's passion for his friend Muḥammad b. Jāmiᶜ, for whom he wrote his work on love, ought to have waned when the youth began to grow a beard. The same story is related by al-Khaṭīb al-Baghdādī (*Taʾrīkh Baghdād,* V, p. 262), Ibn al-Jawzī (*Dhamm al-hawā,* pp. 120–21), and others. On the question whether it is permitted to look at one's beloved, see Ibn Qayyim al-Jawzīya, *Rawḍa,* pp. 111–36, Giffen, *Theory of Profane Love,* pp. 120–32, and Bell, *Love Theory,* pp. 19–29, 125–39.

[3] Known as Nifṭawayh (244/858–59 – 323/935), Ẓāhirite grammarian, lexicographer, and traditionist, a close friend of Ibn Dāwūd. See, e.g., al-Suyūṭī, *Bughyat al-wuᶜāh,* I, pp. 428–30.

bidden pleasure. As for the permitted gaze, it has brought about what you see. But as for the forbidden pleasure, I have been deterred from it by what my father reported to me, namely, that Suwayd b. Saᶜīd said that ᶜAlī b. Mushir related from Abū Yaḥyā al-Qattāt from Mujāhid from Ibn ᶜAbbās that the Prophet said: "He who falls in love, is chaste, conceals his passion, and dies, dies a martyr."'[4] Then he broke into verse:

Why do they blame the blackness in his cheeks,
when they do not blame the blossoms on their boughs?
If the flaw of his cheeks is the down of his beard,
then the flaw of his eyes is the fringe of his lashes." **[117]**

Section One. Sayings of the Followers and the Jurists and Religious Authorities Who Came after Them on the Description of Love and Lovers

Among the reports that have been handed down to us from the judge Aḥmad b. Muḥammad[5] is that a question in writing was referred to Saᶜīd b. al-Musayyab containing the following verses:[6]

O master of the Followers and the elect,
You have forgotten in the matter of love the Sura of the Cow.[7]
Be kind and gentle in your counsel to me,
may God boast of you to the most benevolent of the pious angels![8]

---

[4] This is a stronger version of the saying than is related in the same anecdote in *Taʾrīkh Baghdād* and *Dhamm al-hawā* (see preceding note), where the lover who dies "is forgiven by God and received into Paradise." But it is the version related by Ibn Dāwūd himself in his *Kitāb al-zahra* (p. 66). On the controversy over this tradition, see Giffen, *Theory of Profane Love,* pp. 99–115, and Bell, *Love Theory*, pp. 134–37.

[5] Perhaps to be identified with Abū ʾl-Ḥasan Aḥmad b. Muḥammad b. Ḥakīm al-Ḥakīmī (d. 345/956–57), who was for a time active as a Sufi, knew al-Junayd and Ibn Khafīf, and who in the thirties of the fourth century served as judge in Shiraz. Cf. Sobieroj, "Ibn Ḫafīf aš-Šīrāzī," pp. 92–93 and 176 (on the judges of Shiraz), and MS, p. 122 and n. 21 below.

[6] On this genre of verse *responsa* and for another translated example, see Bell, *Love Theory,* pp. 130–31. The point in many pieces seems to be to shock the reader by attributing to noted jurists an amazing degree of tenderness towards lovers. For other examples, see Ibn Qayyim al-Jawzīya, *Rawḍa,* pp. 112–16, and Mughulṭāy, *al-Wāḍiḥ al-mubīn,* pp. 70–75. Ibn Qayyim al-Jawzīya (*Rawḍa,* pp. 124–31) criticizes the purport or the attribution of the verses he relates.

[7] The reference seems to be to Koran 2:286: "Our Lord, do thou not burden us beyond what we have the strength to bear."

[8] Cf. Koran 80:13–16: "upon pages high-honoured, uplifted, purified, by the hands of scribes noble [*or* benevolent, generous] (*kirām*), pious (*barara*)." The

Has God forbidden kissing a succulent young thing,
an enticing and manifest beauty?

On the same sheet he responded:

O you who seek counsel regarding your hidden agony,
you must patiently endure, for you will surely praise the result.
Do not seek an excessive offense,
like the one whose flood exceeds his rain.[9]
Fear God and guard against his chastisement;
do not be like the transgressors and the wicked.
But kiss the mouth of that lover of yours
every day and night ten times.

He[10] also said that a question was once referred to Muḥammad b. Sīrīn containing these verses: **[118]**

O Ibn Sīrīn, advise me concerning my infatuation,
and by your counsel cure my malady.
I am bewildered by love. Were it not for hope, love had left me
bereft of heart, a companion of wandering camels.[11]
I am enraptured with one who has the most beautiful visage among men,
am I to be blamed for embracing him?

Ibn Sīrīn replied:

"scribes" mentioned here are generally considered to be the angels (or prophets) who transcribe holy books from the "tablet" (*al-lawḥ*) preserved in heaven or from revelation. Cf. al-Bayḍāwī, *Tafsīr* (ed. Fleischer), II, p. 387; al-Qushayrī, *Laṭāʾif al-ishārāt,* III, p. 689.

[9] Cf. the proverb *Sabaqa maṭarahu sayluhu* (His flood preceded his rain), said to be used of one who acts before he gives any warning (al-Maydānī, *Majmaᶜ al-amthāl,* II, p. 111) or of one on whose part evil precedes good (Abū Hilāl al-ᶜAskarī, *Jamharat al-amthāl,* I, p. 333).

[10] The pronoun "he" here, as well as in the introduction to most of the reports in this section, refers in principle to the preceding narrator. In this report and in the next three it refers to the judge Aḥmad b. Muḥammad, or conceivably to the one narrating from him. On MS, p. 121, it refers to Abū ʾl-ᶜAbbās Aḥmad b. Muḥammad (first mentioned on MS, p. 120), and it should also refer to him in the introductory sentences thereafter through MS, p. 124. In the report "to us" at the beginning of MS, p. 122, the first person pronoun would also seem to refer to Abū ʾl-ᶜAbbās Aḥmad b. Muḥammad. It is possible that a closer examination of the narrators involved would reveal problems with this scheme.

[11] "a companion of wandering camels": *ḥilfa ʾl-hawāmī,* i.e., an inhabitant of the wastelands.

Cure your soul with patient abstinence from that which
God has forbidden, and you will gain favor with the benevolent angels.[12]
Ask your lover to be with you always,
for in union with him is the cure of your disease.
To embrace in passion an intimate beloved
is better than a pilgrimage every year.
Doing what you have mentioned, you become nobler than one
who in his asceticism has reached the peak of Mount Lukām.[13]

He also said that a case expressed in the following verses was referred to al-Ḥasan al-Baṣrī:

O Ḥasan al-Baṣrī, man of understanding,
I long to see your face.
Tell me, my wise adviser,
whose counsel is never without proof,
Is it permissible to kiss one you love passionately,
a snatcher of hearts and a thief? **[119]**

To this he replied:

I say, as the All-Merciful is my witness,
I am not one to counsel gross sin.
If you long and lust after kissing
and crave amorous dalliance,
You will be deprived in Paradise of a houri,
rosy-cheeked and radiant.
So clad your heart in fear and piety and be submissive,
for in the fear of God lies your antidote.

Such a question, he said, was also referred to Ibn ᶜUlayya. The note contained these verses:

O Lamp of Islam, O Ibn ᶜUlayya,
love has left a burning in my heart.
I have long sorrowed and yearned for one
who a year ago captivated me with his coquettish gestures.
The sword of his languishing eyelids smote me,
and I felt I was caught in the fangs of a serpent.
His eyes have done to my heart
what al-Murtaḍā did to the House of Umayya.[14]

---

[12] See n. 8.

[13] Or Lukkām. Yāqūt notes that it is used in al-Mutanabbī's poetry with a single *kāf* (*Muᶜjam al-buldān,* IV, p. 364, s.v. "al-Lukkām").

[14] Al-Murtaḍā is a sobriquet of the first Abbasid caliph, Abū ᵓl-ᶜAbbās ᶜAbd Allāh b. Muḥammad, known as al-Saffāḥ, "the Generous" *or* "the Blood-

Ibn ᶜUlayya, he said, wrote at the bottom of the note:

> You who are afflicted with a thing and hope
> that the forbidden will be lawful with me,
> I am not of those who will waive the prohibition for you,
> for I will surely be called to answer for what I say.
> If you accept your passion with patient endurance and gratitude,
> you will be one with me and my followers and belong to my school. **[120]**
> If love beholds you following a proper course regarding it,
> you will always have the greatest freedom from it.
> The abominable acts you commit are not hidden
> from us, for we live in a small village.

In the circle of Mālik b. Anas, he said, a similar case was raised. The document contained these lines:

> O great jurist, may God confer honor on you,
> and provide you a flowery garden in Paradise,
> What do you find reprehensible in a lover's kissing
> the cheek of his beloved in Ramadan?

The jurist answered:

> We do not find this reprehensible for an old man, but
> we find reprehensible the rashness of youths.
> It is the same in law for [one enslaved by love] to kiss a beloved,
> whether in the months of fasting or the month of Shaᶜbān.[15]

Among the things that have been related to me from Abū ᵓl-ᶜAbbās Aḥmad b. Muḥammad b. Muḥammad b. Ṭalḥa b. Muḥammad is the following report, which has a chain of authorities going back to al-Rabīᶜ b. Sulaymān, who said: "A woman came to Muḥammad b. Idrīs al-Shāfiᶜī carrying a note and handed it to him. In it was this line:

> Ask the Meccan mufti: Is there any sin in exchanging visits
> and embracing one's heart's beloved?

At the bottom of the note al-Shāfiᶜī wrote: **[121]**

> God forbid that piety should be undone
> when two wounded livers cling one to the other."[16]

---

shedder," who relentlessly pursued the remnants of the Umayyad clan. His general ᶜAbd Allāh b. ᶜAlī (d. 147/764), who defeated Marwān II in the battle of the Zāb, is reported to have slaughtered eighty notables of the Umayyad house at a banquet to which he had invited them.

[15] Shaᶜbān apparently stands here for all the non-fasting months.

[16] Cf. Ibn Qayyim al-Jawzīya, *Rawḍa,* p. 112; Mughulṭāy, *al-Wāḍiḥ al-*

Also among the things that have been related from him is that he said he had heard Abū ʾl-ᶜAbbās b. Muḥammad al-Manṣūrī the jurist say: "A request for counsel containing the following line was referred to al-Shāfiᶜī:

> Ask the learned Meccan what
> kissing is lawful in Ramadan.

Al-Shāfiᶜī replied:

> The Meccan says to you: If your wife,
> seven times, but a girlfriend eight.[17]

But the note was returned to him with another verse:

> How and why could that be, may my charms be your ransom,
> and may the Lord receive you in the Delight of Gardens.[18]

To this the jurist answered:

> Because kinfolk may have many opportunities,
> But this one receives enjoyment only for a time."[19]

He also related from al-Rabīᶜ b. Sulaymān that he said: "We were sitting in the assembly of [Abū] ᶜAbd Allāh Muḥammad b. Idrīs al-Ṣhāfiᶜī, when someone handed him a note with the following:

> May God grant pardon to one who aids by prayer
> two bosom friends who were ever bound by affection
> Until a maligner of passion maligned
> one to the other and they withdrew from their bond.

---

mubīn, p. 70; al-Mubarrad, *Kāmil,* I, p. 290; Abū Nuᶜaym, *Ḥilya,* IX, pp. 150–51; and al-Subkī, *Ṭabaqāt al-Shāfiᶜīya al-kubrā,* I, pp. 303–4.

[17] Cf. Ibn Qayyim al-Jawzīya, *Rawḍa,* p. 113, and Mughulṭāy, *al-Wāḍiḥ al-mubīn,* p. 72, both citing al-Mubarrad (= *Kāmil,* I, p. 286), who heard these verses, perhaps in a slightly different form, as well as those cited just above, from Abū ʾl-ᶜĀliya (d. 240/854). The narrator named here has the same *kunya* (Abū ʾl-ᶜAbbās) as Muḥammad b. Yazīd al-Mubarrad.

[18] "the Delight of Gardens": *naᶜīma jinānī,* but without final *yāʾ*. The manuscript has the *yāʾ* written out, which would make the hemistich read "and may the Lord grant you the Delights of *my* Gardens." A pun of such nature on a Koranic expression would be inconsistent with the overall tone of the material al-Daylamī relates. Cf. e.g., Koran 5:65, 10:9, and 22:56.

[19] Both the text and the translation are uncertain. The word translated as "enjoyment," *mutᶜa,* can mean a separation gift to a divorced wife or a temporary marriage.

On reading this, al-Shāfiᶜī stretched out his **[122]** hand and prayed for the author of the note."

(Again he said:) "It has also been related to us that al-Shāfiᶜī composed these verses:[20]

> They say, 'Do not look, for looking brings affliction.'
> On the contrary! Everyone with two eyes must look.
> The meeting of eyes is no cause for suspicion,
> when hearts are chaste."

He also stated that he had received a report from the judge Aḥmad b. Muḥammad, Abū ᵓl-Ḥasan al-Ḥakīmī(?),[21] who said: "An old woman came to Abū Khalīfa al-Faḍl b. al-Ḥubāb, the judge of Basra,[22] bearing with her a sealed note that contained the following verses:

> Say to the sage Abū Khalīfa:
> What was the opinion of Abū Ḥanīfa?
> What does he say to a soft-fleshed girl
> the blaze of whose forehead (?) is lofty in beauty[23]
> Who desires the ornament of mankind,
> chastely and without sin?

Abū Khalīfa read the lines and said to his scribe, 'Write this:

> To the maiden of consummate refinement:
> The state of passion is a noble condition.
> If you are sincere in the thing
> you have disclosed without fear,
> This is bliss, martyrdom,
> and honor,[24] my gracious child.' **[123]**

The old woman said to him, 'Sign below in your own hand.' So he wrote:

> This is surely allowed.
> So says Abū Khalīfa."

---

[20] The following verses are also ascribed to al-Shāfiᶜī elsewhere. Cf., e.g., Ibn Qayyim al-Jawzīya, *Rawḍa,* p. 112.

[21] The manuscript has what appears to be al-ᶜAnbasī. Our suggestion is based on Junayd Shīrāzī, *Shadd al-izār,* p. 40, n. 4, and al-Samᶜānī, *Ansāb,* IV, p. 188. Cf. MS, p. 117 and n. 5 above.

[22] A source of Ibn Khafīf. Cf. Sobieroj, "Ibn Ḫafīf aš-Šīrāzī," p. 37.

[23] Text uncertain. Cf. our edition and Yāqūt, *Muᶜjam al-udabāᵓ,* s.v. "al-Faḍl b. al-Ḥubāb."

[24] "bliss, martyrdom, and honor": probably an allusion to the saying of the Prophet that promises a martyr's reward to the one who dies of love (cf. MS, p. 116 and n. 4 there).

Again he said that he had heard Abū ᶜĪsā al-Anmāṭī say: "When Muḥammad b. Dāwūd began to hold audiences, while he was still a youth,[25] the poet Ibn al-Rūmī wrote to him:

O Ibn Dāwūd, O jurist of Iraq,
    Advise us concerning the eyes that slay.
Is retaliation due for murder?
    Or in passion is the blood of lovers lawful for them?

Ibn Dāwūd gave his answer in his assembly, but in such a way that no one else at the time was aware of it.

I have the answer to the questions of lovers,
    so hear it from one with anguished entrails, one sick with longing.
When you asked about passion, you filled me with yearning,
    and I shed tears that would not cease.
You are mistaken in your question itself,
    you who feel some compassion.
Agony is nothing, if not betrayal and separation,
    and the burning of entrails without any flame."

He also said that he had heard from Abū ᶜAmr ᶜUthmān b. Muḥammad al-ᶜUthmānī, who had heard it from **[124]** Abū [Aḥmad][26] ᶜAbd Allāh b. ᶜAdī, the custodian of tradition, that Manṣūr b. Ismāᶜīl the jurist recited these verses of his own:

Sir, I seek from you redress of a wrong.
    Consult in the matter Ibn Abī Khaythama.
For he relates from his grandfather,
    who said al-Ḍaḥḥāk related from ᶜIkrima,
From Ibn ᶜAbbās, then from the Chosen One,
    our Prophet who was sent with mercy,
That for a bosom friend to spurn his friend
    More than three days, our Lord has forbidden it.[27]

---

[25] Ibn Dāwūd became head of the Ẓāhirite school of jurisprudence at the age of sixteen upon the death of his father, the founder of the school, in 270/884 in Baghdad. See, e.g., Sezgin, *GAS,* I, p. 521.

[26] Addition from Vadet, trans., p. 108, n. 1. Abū Aḥmad ᶜAbd Allāh b. ᶜAdī, known as Ibn al-Qaṭṭān (277/890–365?/976), was a *ḥadīth* scholar from Jurjān, whose work on the criticism of narrators, *al-Kāmil*, was of great importance for later scholars, notably Ibn Ḥajar. Cf. Sezgin, *GAS,* I, pp. 198–99, and, e.g., al-Dhahabī, *Tadhkirat al-ḥuffāẓ* (Hyderabad, 1970), III, pp. 940–42.

[27] Cf. the tradition, "It is forbidden for a Muslim to abandon his brother for more than three days. . . ." Al-Nawawī, *Riyāḍ al-ṣāliḥīn,* p. 385.

For a month now you have forsaken us.
Is this not a sin against us? Be gentle then.

Others, he said, had furnished him with additional reports. Thus Muḥammad b. Nuṣayr al-ᶜAṭṭār said: "I attended the assembly of Abū ᶜUmar the judge[28] when both Abū ᵓl-ᶜAbbās b. Surayj[29] and Ibn Dāwūd were present. The two men engaged in a controversy over a question concerning the annulment of marriage. Ibn Dāwūd was clearly besting Ibn Surayj, who hoped to cut him short. So Ibn Surayj said to him, 'Abū Bakr, stick to your book *Kitāb al-zahra.*'[30] 'What can you possibly say about *Kitāb al-zahra?*' Ibn Dāwūd replied. **[125]** 'In it I composed a work the like of which has never been written before and will never be written again. I am the one who says:

---

[28] The manuscript has Abū ᶜAmr. Presumably intended is the judge Abū ᶜUmar Muḥammad b. Yūsuf b. Yaᶜqūb b. Ismāᶜīl (d. 320/932), as specified by al-Subkī (*Ṭabaqāt al-Shāfiᶜīya,* III, p. 26), but conceivably his father Yūsuf b. Yaᶜqūb (d. 297; cf. al-Samᶜānī, *Ansāb,* VIII, pp. 298–99). Abū ᶜUmar Muḥammad followed his father, who followed his paternal cousin Abū Isḥāq Ismāᶜīl b. Isḥāq b. Ismāᶜīl, the celebrated Mālikī jurist (d. 282/895), in a career as caliphally appointed *qāḍī* in Baghdad, and was subsequently followed by his own son. Born in 243, he was appointed *qāḍī* already in his father's lifetime under al-Muᶜtaḍid (d. 289/902). He was known for the debates he sponsored and, among other things, for being the first of the jurists gathered by the vizier Ḥāmid b. al-ᶜAbbās to authorize the death penalty for al-Ḥallāj. Cf. biographical notices on him in, e.g., Ibn Farḥūn, *al-Dībāj al-mudhhab,* II, pp. 181–83, and al-Dhahabī, *al-ᶜIbar fī khabar man ghabar,* II, pp. 183–84. Ibn Khallikān (*Wafayāt al-aᶜyān,* ed. M. M. ᶜAbd al-Ḥamīd, III, pp. 390–91) and al-Ḥuṣrī (*Zahr al-ādāb,* ed. al-Bijāwī, II, pp. 728–29; ed. M. M. ᶜAbd al-Ḥamīd, III, pp. 783–84) place this particular altercation between Ibn Dāwūd and Ibn Surayj in the *majlis* of the vizier ᶜAlī b. ᶜĪsā b. Dāwūd b. al-Jarrāḥ (245/859–334/946). The references to him as vizier, at least, are anachronistic, since Ibn Surayj (d. 306) and Ibn Dāwūd (d. 297) had both passed away before ᶜAlī b. ᶜĪsā's first term as vizier. However ᶜAlī b. ᶜĪsā had been in high administrative posts since 278/892. See H. Bowen, *EI²,* I, p. 386b, s.v. "ᶜAlī b. ᶜĪsā."

[29] Preeminent Shāfiᶜite jurist (d. 306/918–19 in Baghdad), a student of al-Muḥāsibī and al-Junayd, judge in Shiraz from 296 or 297 to 301 and teacher of Ibn Khafīf in law. See the Introduction, pp. xxv–xxvi.

[30] Ibn Dāwūd wrote his *Kitāb al-zahra* in his youth for his beloved, Muḥammad b. Jāmiᶜ al-Ṣaydalānī. His father, who died when Ibn Dāwūd was sixteen (see n. 25), reviewed it and presumably approved of it. See Ibn al-Jawzī, *al-Muntaẓam fī taᵓrīkh al-mulūk wa-l-umam,* VI, p. 94.

I promenade my eye in the gardens of charms
and forbid my soul to partake of the forbidden.
My eyes speak what is hidden in my mind,
which, if my glances did not steal its thoughts, would speak aloud.
I find passion to be claimed by all,
but I find no true, incontestable love.'[31]

Ibn Surayj replied, 'And it is I who say:

That fair one who cooed honey in his tones,
with whom I passed the night, denying him the pleasures of sleep,
Craving the beauty and variety of his words,
and glancing continually at his cheeks,
Until, when the bright gleam of morning appeared,
he went away with the seal his Lord gave him and his innocence.'[32]

To this Ibn Dāwūd said 'Judge, you have confessed to passing the night, but you need two unimpeachable witnesses to prove your innocence.' Then the two men embraced and parted."

It has been related from ᶜUbayd Allāh b. ᶜAbd Allāh b. Samura al-Baghawī that he heard from Abū ᶜAbd Allāh Aḥmad b. Sulaymān **[126]** al-Ṭūsī, having read the report aloud in al-Ṭūsī's presence, that he heard from Abū ᶜAbd Allāh al-Zubayr b. Bakkār the judge, that he heard from Ibrāhīm b. Mundhir from Maᶜn b. ᶜĪsā, who said: "Ibn Sarḥūn[33] al-Sulamī came to Mālik b. Anas while I was in his presence and said to him, 'O Abū ᶜAbd Allāh, I have composed some lines of poetry in which I mention you, and I would like you to allow me to say them freely.' 'You are free to mention me as you please,' Mālik replied. But his face changed, for he thought he had been lampooned. 'I wanted you to hear them,' said Ibn Sarḥūn. 'Recite them,' Mālik answered. So he recited these lines:

---

[31] Cf. the piece with the same first line ascribed to Abū ᶜAlī al-Rūdhbārī, as well as to Ibn Dāwūd's friend Nifṭawayh, quoted and translated in Bell, *Love Theory,* chapter two, n. 50. Al-Daylamī takes note of the attribution of the third line to al-Rūdhbārī but insists that it is by Ibn Dāwūd (MS, p. 143).

[32] On both of these poems, cf. al-Ḥuṣrī, *Zahr al-ādāb* (ed. al-Bijāwī), II, pp. 728–29. The last line of Ibn Surayj's piece seems to indicate that the masculine pronouns in the poem refer to a female, which is common in Arabic poetry.

[33] Al-Sarrāj (*Maṣāriᶜ,* II, p. 185; also Maṭbaᶜat al-Saᶜāda edition [Cairo, 1335/1907], p. 336) has Ibn Sarḥūn. Our manuscript can be read Ibn Sarḥūn or Ibn Sarḥūf. Dāwūd al-Anṭākī (*Tazyīn al-aswāq,* I, p. 8) has Ibn Saḥnūn, which is adopted by Vadet.

Ask Mālik the mufti about amorous dalliance and youthful passion,
and the love of comely, pleasing ladies who hate their husbands.
He will tell you that I have hit the mark,
for indeed I dispel my soul's cares with such things as these.
For is the lover who conceals his love and passion to be punished
for sin, or one dying of love when he embraces?"

"When Mālik heard this," Maᶜn concluded, "his anxiety was relieved and he laughed."

It is said that Yaḥyā **[127]** b. Aktham went early one morning to see the caliph al-Maᵓmūn, and al-Maᵓmūn said to him, "Why has the judge some so early?" "An extraordinary thing occurred last night," he replied, "and I was eager to tell you of it." "What was it?" the caliph asked. "In my neighborhood," Yaḥyā answered, "a young man received a visit from a youthful friend, and he asked him to spend the night with him. But the youth swore he would stay only until the call to the last night prayer. The young man, being greatly distressed, took a piece of paper and wrote to the imam of the mosque:

Say to the one who calls to prayer, 'Delay a while.
We have always fulfilled the duty of prayer.
It is nothing if you delay a while,
rather you will rewarded by God for your good deed.
You will respect the obligations of manly conduct towards us,
and you will avoid being thought a disagreeable man.'

"When the imam read the note, he cried, 'I bind myself to divorce thrice[34] if I give the call to prayer tonight or pray in this mosque,' and then he went off. Some of us said, 'How long shall we wait?' But others complained, 'How long? It is already the middle of the night.' This went on until we finally stood up and prayed on our own." Al-Maᵓmūn laughed, the report continues, and said, "I must see the imam, the young man, and the youth." When they were brought into his presence, he ordered that the imam be given **[128]** five hundred dinars and said to him, "Keep to your manly conduct." To the young man he awarded the position of a scribe in the chancellery, and he assigned the youth to him. In addition he gave him ten thousand dirhams.

The author of this book said: These are the opinions on the description of love and lovers and of eros and those it afflicts[35] that have been given by the jurists and learned men among the Followers, the imams of the

[34] "to divorce thrice": i.e., definitively, with no possibility of retraction.

[35] The distinction between love (*ḥubb*) and eros (*ᶜishq*) has not been observed in the translation of non-technical reports like those in this chapter.

Muslims, and the devoted and pious. Let us turn now to the section on some of the sayings of the Bedouin Arabs on eros and love and how they are to be described.

Section Two. What the Bedouin Arabs Say about Eros

Ibn Sīrīn related the following: "They used to love passionately and meet together without giving any cause for suspicion. The man would sit with the woman, talk to her, and keep company with her, without carnal commerce occurring between them."

A lover from the Banū ᶜUdhra tribe was once asked, "Why has passionate love, among all the tribes of the Arabs, taken such a hold on your people, to the extent even that most of you die of love?" **[129]** "Because our women are the most beautiful of Arab women," he replied, "and our men the most chaste of Arab men."

Likewise it is related that Qays b. al-Mulawwaḥ, Majnūn (the Madman), once went in to visit Laylā. One of the young men of the tribe saw him and went to tell her father. Her father was exceedingly angry and beat both Laylā and her mother. When Qays returned, Laylā told him what had happened. On hearing the story, he wept so profusely that he almost perished. Then he went off, without going inside to visit her, and composed these verses:

> I have visited you long and often, Mother of ᶜAmr,
> and people have never heard anything shameful about us.
> Yet when time brought abandonment,
> and the rope was cut and severed in two,
> I became to those around you a stranger.
> But I will offer no apologies for my love for you.

It is related from Abū ᵓl-Ḥakam al-Madanī that his father said to him: "I went in to visit the caliph [ᶜAbd] al-Malik b. Marwān and seated myself. While I was there, Kuthayyir, the lover of ᶜAzza, came in. He was a poet who would only recite his poetry when comfortably seated. 'Recite your poetry about ᶜAzza,' ᶜAbd al-Mālik said to him. 'Let me recite rather the poems in which I praise you,' he replied. **[130]** 'I ask you in the name of Abū Turāb,'[36] the caliph cried, 'let me hear your poetry on ᶜAzza!' 'You have asked me in the name of one very great,' the poet answered, and tears welling in his eyes he began to recite to him. 'How strong your love for ᶜAzza is!' the caliph exclaimed, 'Have you ever seen anyone whose love is stronger than yours?' 'I will tell you, O

---

[36] Abū Turāb: ᶜAlī, the Prophet's son-in-law and fourth caliph. Kuthayyir was a Shiite.

Commander of the Faithful,' he replied.

"'Once I set out wandering, full of longing to mention the name of ᶜAzza. At the time ᶜAzza's people were in a pasturage of theirs near our tribal territory. As I was making my way, I came upon a man who had set up some snares while he was grazing his camels far from his kin. Going up to him I asked, "Is there any food for a guest?" "I am a good distance away from my tribe," he said, "and I have set up snares. So bear with me a while, and I will drive the gazelles to you. If something falls into my snares, we will eat it together, for I have not eaten a thing for three days now." Whereupon he set to driving the gazelles.

"'Into his snare there fell a long-necked, fair-coated gazelle, and he rushed towards her. I followed close behind him and listened. He released her from her fetters, and while I looked on, he wiped off the dust she had gotten on her and kissed her, sipping her saliva. Then he let her go and set the snare again. When he came over to me, **[131]** I said, "What was that? Have you ever heard of anyone doing what you just did? Here we are both complaining of hunger. God gives us relief and provides for us, and you deprive us of our food." "Alas," he said, "I looked at her, at the base and the full length of her fine neck, and found that she resembled the one I love. So I released her for the sake of the one I love. Have you ever seen anyone who would eat what looks like his beloved?" As the gazelle was going off, he spoke these lines:

> O image of Laylā, do not be afraid,
> for today, wild beast that you are, I am your friend.
> I say this, having freed her from her bonds,
> Is it not for Laylā's sake, if you wish to give thanks, you are free?

"'Then he said to me, "Stay, and if we catch anything we will eat it." By now I was suffering the most intense hunger, so I stayed with him, hoping that his own hunger would keep him from doing what he had done again. When another gazelle fell into his snare, he ran over to it and once more let it go. Then he walked over to me, exclaiming as he came:

> O image of Laylā, if only you would tarry a while,
> perhaps my heart would recover from its grief.
> If you resemble her, and yet do not return
> safely, I am not tender and compassionate towards Laylā in this life. **[132]**

"Alas," I said, "you are tormented by hunger, and yet you do this!" "By God, I am totally overcome by hunger," he replied, "and I can bear it no more. I will drive the gazelles to you, and if we catch something, we will satisfy our needs."

"'Another gazelle was snared, and we both ran over to her. But he got to her ahead of me and released her. So she too went off. I left her alone and sprang upon him. Whereupon he broke into verse:

Today I see in the features of your gazelle
the likeness of Laylā, so release her.

"'I went off and left him, since it was obvious that he was crazed with love. But I passed by some gazelles grazing, and I wanted to make a try for them, hoping that if I showed them to him he would drive them. Then if one of them chanced to fall into the snare, he would recognize it as my game and would eat and let me eat with him. So I went back and said to him, "Do you see those gazelles grazing peacefully over there?" "Yes," he answered, "I have been seeing them in that same place for several days now, but I have not disturbed them because they are in a forbidden pasture." "What forbidden pasture?" I asked. "I saw Laylā in the middle of that meadow," he said, "grazing happily, frolicking, and enjoying its tender herbs and flowers. **[133]** So I composed these lines:

I saw gazelles grazing in the middle of a flowery meadow,
and I saw Laylā there crushing blossoms.
O gazelle, eat your fill with delight, and do not fear,
for though you fear, I am ever the protector of you all."

"'Then he went off and left me,' Kuthayyir concluded, 'And this, O Commander of the Faithful, was the most passionate lover I have ever seen.' 'Who was it, then?' the caliph asked. 'The Madman, Qays b. al-Mulawwaḥ,' the poet answered."

It is said that Jamīl [b. ᶜAbd Allāh] b. Maᶜmar al-ᶜUdhrī met Kuthayyir,[37] the lover of ᶜAzza, one day and asked him, "Where have you been?" "I have been with Buthayna's paternal uncle," he replied. To this Jamīl said, "Do you desire reward in heaven?" "What do you mean?" Kuthayyir asked. "I want you to go back and arrange a meeting with her for me," Jamīl said. "Do you two have any signal?" Kuthayyir responded. "Yes," he answered, "The last day we met was in the Valley of the Doum Palms. There were girls with her washing clothes." So Kuthayyir turned back and went again to Buthayna's uncle.

"What has brought you back, Abū Ṣakhr?" her uncle inquired of him. "Some verses I composed about ᶜAzza," the poet replied, "that I wanted **[134]** to let you hear." "Let me hear them," her uncle said. So Kuthayyir recited these lines:

---

[37] Kuthayyir was Jamīl's narrator.

I said to her:[38] O ᶜAzza, I am sending my companion,
though our abodes are distant, and the messenger's charge
Is that you fix a rendezvous between you and me,
and command what I should do.
Do you not remember our meeting the day we were together
at the bottom of the Valley of the Doum Palms, when clothes were washed?

From within the tent, the narrative continues, Buthayna cried out, "Get away! Get away!" "What has frightened you, girl?" her uncle asked. "A dog that came here from near the hill of such and such a tribe," she said. Then Kuthayyir went back to Jamīl and said to him, "She has promised to meet you tonight near the hill of such and such a tribe."

The author of this book said: This story reveals the cleverness of lovers as well as the excellence of love itself because it inspires in them such cleverness and ruses.

It is said that Zuhayr b. Mujāhir al-Tamīmī related from his uncle that he said: "I went once to visit al-Sāᵓib b. al-Mukhtār al-Makhzūmī and found him like a worn-out water skin, owing to a malady from which he was suffering. 'What is wrong with him?' I asked his family. 'A little love has taken hold in his heart,' they said, **[135]** 'and has brought him to what you see.' So I began to exhort him with reproofs and admonitions, and he wept, tears flowing profusely from his eyes. Then he broke into verse:

I will never desire to be free of passion,
though I should possess everything in East or West.
This is my prayer day and night,
and this will be my reply when my Lord questions me."

Ghawrak[39] the Madman was once asked, "O Abū ᶜAbd Allāh, when were you afflicted with this passionate love?" "A long time ago," he said, "but I used to keep it concealed. Then when it overpowered me, I revealed it." On saying this, he broke into verse:

I concealed my madness as long as it was in my body alone,
but when it ripened in my body, love made it public,
And left it to waste my sound body away.
And when it had wasted my body, my heart yielded to it.

---

[38] "to her": *lahā* for *lahū,* "to him" (MS). Reading with the manuscript we might translate, "I told him (the messenger) to say."

[39] The name is not clear in the manuscript. Al-Sarrāj (*Maṣāriᶜ,* II, p. 25) has Ghawrak, while Dāwūd al-Anṭākī (*Tazyīn al-aswāq,* I, p. 134) has al-Fuwayrik. The verses following, except the last, are among a number of reports about Ghawrak in al-Nīsābūrī, *ᶜUqalāᵓ al-majānīn,* pp. 114–15.

My body and my heart belong to madness and passion:
one is plunder for the former, the other for the latter.
So I said to it: Fear no physician,
for since the death of al-Maʾmūn,[40] medicine is dead.

It is related from Qays b. Sulaymān that he said: "I saw ʿAlī b. Muḥammad al-Hāshimī standing on a bridge, bewildered and distraught with love. So I said to him, 'Tell me, my dear friend, **[136]** your story with your beloved.' 'Brother,' he answered, 'my beloved is this illness from which there is no recovery, or, should it choose, it can become a recovery with no illness. It is closer to me than my own entrails, but is a more distant quest than a star in the horizon of the sky.' 'What if you sought consolation in something else, my brother?' I asked him. 'How could I do that, my brother?' he said, 'Passion is far too precious for that. Moreover, it is despotic in its ways. Hearts do its bidding and souls obey it. The intellect is its prisoner, the spirit is its plunder, and souls are its prey.'[41] Then he turned away weeping and said:

My heart embraces his heart when we meet,
and we consummate the desires of passion with our eyes.
With longing, languishing looks we complain
of pains and sorrow abiding in our breasts."

From Abū Muṣʿab al-Madanī it is related that he said: "I went in to visit al-Rabīʿ b. ʿUbayd and found him talking to himself and saying:

If love were to hack me into pieces,
I would not say it had wronged me.
I was free of care for a time,
and then I became an emblem of love.
I concealed it for a time,
but now what was hidden is revealed.

'How are you?' I asked him. 'One night comes and another goes,' he answered, 'while I sit here waiting for **[137]** death.' 'May God judge between you and the one who has wronged you,' I said. 'Easy,' he replied, 'for, by God, I wish no evil to befall him in this world or the next.' Then he began to heave such sighs that I felt pity for him and shed a tear. Shortly afterwards he became totally bereft of reason, and I left him."

Section Three. The Opinions of the Sufis on the Description of Love

The author of this book said: I find that our teachers, may God have

---

[40] Al-Maʾmūn: Vadet proposed in a note (ed. p. 67, n. 2) *al-māḍūn* (the ancients). The line is not in the parallel texts cited in the preceding note.

[41] Cf. MS, pp. 111, 113, and 162.

mercy on them, have given two different kinds of replies concerning love, one concerning natural love and another concerning divine love, because in their view there exist both natural and divine loves. Let us begin by considering what they say about praiseworthy natural love, since this is the subject of the chapter. We will relate what they say about divine love later. The reason for proceeding in this fashion is that we ascend from natural love to the divine, for if the lover's soul is not prepared to receive natural love, it will not be suited for divine love. Hence if God wills to bring a man to the station of lovers and to raise him to the attribute of spiritual men, he prepares him for these things by giving him a refined constitution **[138]** and a delicate nature, and by disposing his spirit to love him.[42] Then a man can receive love when it falls to his lot. This should be borne in mind.

In this connection it is related that Joseph said one day to Zulaykhā, "Where is that fascination (*shaᶜaf*)[43] and that emotion you used to feel? I no longer see it in you." "I tasted love for God," she replied, "and love for you departed from my heart."

The first thing we shall relate of what our teachers have said is the story of a certain ascetic who fell in love with a slave-girl belonging to ᶜAlī b. Abī Ṭālib, may God bless him.[44] Whenever this slave-girl passed by the ascetic he would say, "By God, I love you!" After he had done this many times, the girl said to ᶜAlī, "O Commander of the Faithful, sometimes I pass by a recluse in such and such a place, and when he sees me he says, 'By God, I love you!'" "If he says it again," the Commander of the Faithful answered her, "tell him, 'I love you too. What is your wish?'" So she passed by him as she had done before, and when he spoke to [her] in the same manner as [he had previously], she said, "And I love you too, by God. What is your wish?" "I wish to endure it patiently," he said, "for God says, 'Surely the patient will be paid their wages in full **[139]** without reckoning'" (39:10). When she went back to the Commander of the Faithful, [she said], "I spoke to him as you commanded me." "What did he say?" [he asked]. "He said, 'I wish to endure it patiently, for God says, "Surely the patient will be paid their wages in

---

42 The pronoun "him," although in the Arabic, may be out of place here.

43 Considering the words of Koran 12:30, "He smote her heart (*shaghafahā*) with love," which is cited by the author above (MS, p. 45), one would like to read, with Vadet, *shaghaf,* "heart-smiting love," which differs only by a dot from *shaᶜaf.* But the MS has this report twice (here and MS, p. 151) with *shaᶜaf.* There is moreover a reading of the Koranic text with *shaᶜafahā* (see, e.g., Ibn Qayyim al Jawzīya, *Rawḍa,* p. 23; Lane, s.v. *sh-ᶜ-f*).

44 See chapter five, n. 53.

full without reckoning,'"" she replied. "Go!" the caliph said, "You are free without price for the sake of God." Then he summoned the ascetic and married her to him.

It is told of Abū ʾl-Qāsim al-Junayd that he began to miss the presence of a certain man who previously had been coming to visit him regularly. When the man had been absent for a long time, al-Junayd said to his companions, "Come let us see whether this is love or vengeance." So they went to the door of the man's home and asked permission to enter. Having obtained consent, they went in and found [the man. The sheikh asked him, "Why have you kept away] from us?" "Because I am ashamed to see you, Master," he answered. "Where is your friend?" al-Junayd asked. "Here he is," he said, calling him. Now the one who came in was as beautiful as a full moon when it is rising. Al-Junayd looked at him and said, "It is love." After speaking to him for a while, he stood up to leave and went out with his companions. When they had left the house, the narrator said, one of them inquired of al-Junayd, "We heard you say before you came here, 'Come let us see whether this is **[140]** love or vengeance.' Just now you said, 'It is love.' Tell us the meaning of what you said." "If God afflicts a man with a beautiful face," he replied, "it is love, but if he tries him with an ugly face, it is vengeance."

The following verses have also been related to us from al-Junayd:

Some folk have spoken, but I have not spoken,
  asking about affliction, but I have not asked.
Yet my spirit is the spirit of the one I love:
  our spirits are one spirit with no separation.

It is said that a youth with a beautiful face came to Bishr b. al-Ḥārith al Ḥāfī and said to him, "I wish to be your companion and to become righteous." "Before you become righteous," Bishr remarked, "you will corrupt many righteous men."

Dhū ʾl-Nūn was asked about the gnostic's state of intimacy, and he said: "He delights in every comely face, every fair form, and every pleasing fragrance." **[141]**

Al-Junayd said: "We lack in these days three things that we shall scarcely find before death: a beautiful face together with respectability, fair speech together with piety,[45] and good friendship together with loyalty."

Al-Nūrī said: "The first affliction with which God tries a man in this world is separation from his loved ones."

---

[45] "piety": *diyāna;* unlikely here in the sense of "loyalty" or "fidelity," since this quality is mentioned next.

And Bishr b. al-Ḥārith said: "I read in a certain book that among the words revealed by God are the following: 'One thing with which I punish my servants is to afflict them with separation from their loved ones.'"

I heard Abū ᶜAbd Allāh al-Ḥusayn b. Muḥammad al-Hāshimī say in Ahvaz(?):[46] "When al-Ḥusayn b. Manṣūr (al-Ḥallāj) would go into the mosque in Ahvaz he used to see two youths who were in love with each other sitting together by a column. He was in the habit of looking at them, but one day he found they were gone. After many days had passed he asked about them and was told that they had both died at the same time. He lowered his head for a while thinking and then recited these verses:

The beloved was united for his lover.
The cherished one was divided for his admirer.[47] **[142]**
These two like souls shared in a single state,
they were obliterated in the world that obliterates.

From Abū Bakr al-Shiblī the following lines have been recited to us:

Do not be taken up today with thoughts of love,
for passionate love is a kind of affliction.
In days gone by passion was good,
noble men loving noble men.
But as for our lovers of today, their souls
desire transgressions and immorality.
So should you encounter some wasted lover,
give him, for me, three good slaps.

It is reported that Marwān b. ᶜAbd al-Malik b. Marwān[48] said: "ᶜAzza, the beloved of Kuthayyir, went in to visit Umm al-Banīn, the sister of ᶜUmar b. ᶜAbd al-ᶜAzīz. Umm al-Banīn, who was a pious and godly woman, said to her, 'Tell me about Kuthayyir's line,

Every debtor has paid his debts in full,
but ᶜAzza's creditor is put off and distressed.

What was the debt he speaks of?' 'I had promised him a kiss,' ᶜAzza answered, 'but I held it back.'" Marwān continued: "To this Umm al-Banīn said, 'Discharge the debt to him, and let the guilt fall on me.'" It is

---

[46] reading *bi-l-Ahwāz* (Vadet's suggestion) for *bihā* in the manuscript.

[47] Cf. MS, p. 205.

[48] Ibn al-Jawzī (*Dhamm al-hawā,* p. 225) has Marwān b. Muḥammad. Approximately the same story is related by al-Sarrāj (*Maṣāriᶜ,* II, p. 84) about ᶜAzza and Sukayna bint al-Ḥusayn b. ᶜAlī.

said that Umm al-Banīn freed forty slaves for what she had said **[143]** and that when she remembered it she would exclaim, "Would that I had kept quiet and said nothing!"

It is also reported that one day the caliph ᶜAbd al-Malik b. Marwān looked at ᶜAzza and remarked, "What does Kuthayyir find so beautiful in you, that he should love you with such excessive passion?" "O Commander of the Faithful," she replied, "he has seen me with eyes that are not in your head." "True," he said.

We have heard the following lines ascribed to Abū ᶜAlī al-Rūdhbārī:

> I find passion to be claimed by all,
> but I find no true, incontestable love.

But this line is by Ibn Dāwūd, as has been mentioned above.[49] Perhaps he (Abū ᶜAlī) recited it as evidence to illustrate a point he was making. Here, however, are some verses that are indeed by Abū ᶜAlī:

> Have the perils of love made you forswear amorous dalliance,
> when you suffer the tender longings of one ailing, enslaved by love?
> May you find comfort in the crazed lover's plaint over his love,
> and in the quelling of yearning concealed in a heart. **[144]**
> May God preserve whoever preserves affection and love,
> and gives thanks for this bond to the most generous benefactor,[50]
> Whoever finds complaint in compliant submission sweet,
> and sweet the tear of a longing lover, or the agony of one infatuated.
> He is distracted with love for one who offers him illness and emaciation,
> and the fire of longing that blazes in passion.
> The eyes of the women who censured him weep for him, and wrapped
> in sorrow are the women who censured him, after their smiles.
> His languishing[51] is an eternal burning thirst, and his tears
> flow in streams like pearls on a string.
> He yearns with tender longing to be near his beloved,
> whose soft flank sears his heart with desire.

The author of this book said: Reports like these are numerous. Let us now proceed to the section on our own opinion.

Section Four. Our Opinion

It will be recalled that love's light is mixed with darkness, its clarity with turbidity, and its sweetness **[145]** with bitterness, as we stated above in

49 MS, p. 125.

50 Text and translation of this hemistich uncertain.

51 "His languishing": *wanāhu* for *danāhu* (MS). Vadet: *ḍanāhu* (His feebleness). Conceivably: *ranāhu* (His spellbound gaze).

the appropriate place.[52] (Of the first four of these contraries), luminosity has produced pleasure, and darkness has produced distress; clarity has produced sweetness, and turbidity has produced bitterness. From these have been generated states that are different from each other and antithetical, and thus it happens that the states of lovers may differ and that the things they experience may be opposites. Examples are love and hate, nearness and distance, abandonment and union, going away and drawing near, cruelty and loyalty, harshness and tenderness, hardship and ease, misery and relief, chastisement and mercy, pain and comfort, contentment and displeasure, patient endurance and anxious care, pardon and punishment, despair and desire, fear and hope, humble submission and obstinacy, and sickness and health. The end of all this is death, and here ends the section.

Now let us turn to what has been said by people regarding love [that is reprehensible] for some cause—not in it (but in themselves)—for that which we have related above concerning praiseworthy love allows us to dispense with mentioning reprehensible love. **[146]** There is nothing to be gained from saying more about it than we already have.[53]

[52] MS, pp. 94–95. This is the section announced at the end of MS, p. 95.

[53] Cf. MS, pp. 114–15.

CHAPTER TEN
ON THOSE WHO DISPARAGED LOVE FOR SOME CAUSE

Those who disparaged love for some cause (in themselves) are divided into three groups. One is comprised of those who censured it because their rank exceeded it. Such persons, having risen from natural to spiritual love, perceived natural love from the perspective of their exalted rank. They despised it in comparison with that which they had attained and disparaged it accordingly. For natural love, even though it is noble in itself, is vile in comparison with spiritual love, because the highest degree of the perfection of natural love is the first stage of spiritual love. The perfection of the former, let it be understood, is merely a part of the latter.[1] Similarly, one who has ascended from spiritual to divine love will think little of the spiritual in comparison with the divine.

The second group comprises those who were unable to bear love's burdens and afflictions and were vexed by its injustice and tyranny **[147]** and its abasement and humiliation.

The third group includes those who disparaged love out of ignorance of its source or because their natures were not suited to receive it. We will relate a selection of reports about each of the three groups.

Section One. The Opinion of the Physicians

Those who disparaged love out of lack of knowledge [of its source and because their natures were ill-suited] to receive it include some who are described as scholars, and not only uninformed ascetics who never concerned themselves with knowledge. Thus it is related of Fūrus the physician[2] that he said: "How little passionate love (*ᶜishq*) there is in the land

[1] In this sentence the author uses *hādhihi* to mean "the former" and *dhālika* (possibly it should be *tilka* here) to mean "the latter," which is the opposite of current usage. Cf. also MS, p. 151 (Arabic text), the author's comments on the report concerning Joseph and Zulaykhā.

[2] Fūrus the physician: The name occurs again below (MS, p. 161). Perhaps intended is Rufus of Ephesus (d. ca. 200 A. D.), who lived in Egypt and at Rome and is considered the most important physician of the imperial period after Galen (Sezgin, *GAS,* III, pp. 64–68). Another possibility is Paul of Aegina, cited as Fūlus or Būlus in Arabic texts, who lived in Alexandria just before Islam (Sezgin, ibid. p. 168). Yet another is Ghūrus, who is said to have been a well-known physician (Ibn Abī Uṣaybiᶜa, *ᶜUyūn al-anbāʾ,* I, p. 22). Vadet, who mentions all the above possibilities (trans., p. 219), considers Porphyry (Furfū-

of the Greeks. This is because most of them are preoccupied with medicine and philosophy and do not concern themselves with foul things, nor do they desire them." The author of this book said: If the one who said this had known that love does not come about as the result of human desires or wishes, he would have refrained from censuring it.

It is said that a certain physician was asked about eros and that he replied: "Eros comes **[148]** from retarded understanding, for I have never seen a lover who was not weak of mind."

The author of this book said: The Greeks seldom experienced eros and love because most of them had risen to the level of divine things and were preoccupied with these to the exclusion of love. But as for the natural philosopher, he has no excuse for censuring love, since his concerns do not extend beyond the world of nature. For him to censure it is impossible.

Section Two. On Those Who Disparaged Love Because They Were Unable to Bear It

This is a group whose portion in love was nothing but abandonment, distance, separation, turning away, cruelty, banishment, humiliation, and hardship. They disparaged love because of these things, not for itself. Thus a certain man of letters said that Abū Ḥafṣ al-Ḥaddād was asked about eros and replied: "God has not willed to honor any man whom he has tried with this affliction."

A Bedouin Arab, being asked about love and passion, said: "Passion (*hawā*) is disgrace (*hawān*) with a mistake in the letters of its name. But only one who has been brought to tears by the sight of halting places and abandoned campsites will understand what I say." Then he recited this verse: **[149]**

> The *nūn* of disgrace (*hawān*) has been stolen from passion (*hawā*):
> for every victim of passion is a victim of disgrace.[3]

Another Bedouin, when he was asked about passionate love, recited these verses:

> Would that passion had never been created for those it afflicts,
> or rather, that my heart had never become attached to passion.

---

riyūs), who is mentioned by Ibn Abī Uṣaybiʿa as a physician (*ʿUyūn al-anbāʾ*, I, pp. 35, 36), to be more probable. Other, remote, possibilities are Fūrnūs and Fūrlus, said by Ibn Abī Uṣaybiʿa to have been students of Plato in medicine (ibid., p. 23). A Fūrus is cited in Abū Sulaymān al-Manṭiqī al-Sijistānī, *Ṣiwān al-ḥikma,* p. 234.

[3] Cf. the very similar verses exploiting the same play on words in Ibn al-Jawzī, *Dhamm al-hawā,* p. 33 (translated in Bell, *Love Theory,* p. 17).

The one to whose heart passion has attached itself
is like one hanging in the middle of the sky, suspended there.
He cannot come down because of his miserable state,
but every care rises to him.
Passion (*hawā*) is disgrace (*hawān*) itself:
no one has known the taste of humiliation who has not loved.

A Bedouin woman who had studied the literary arts was once asked about passion and she replied: "May passion not be allowed to enjoy its dominion or its power, and may God prevent its hand from attaining any desire. For never is it just in any decree, nor does it respond to any reproach, nor is it restrained by any blame, nor is it susceptible to any description. It spares no person of intelligence or understanding or reason. Were passion to be given power and mankind to obey it, it would turn things back on their heels[4] and refuse the ideas of those who are wise." Then she recited: **[150]**

Passion or love, my friends, is not such
as to be humbled by an eloquent tongue and described.
But it is a thing that God has decreed
is death itself. Indeed it is harsher than death.
Its beginning is heedlessness, its middle is violent grief,
and its end is longing that deals wrong and ruin,
And alarm, sleeplessness, care, and sorrow,
and suffering upon suffering, increasing and multiplying.[5]

Another Bedouin was asked about passion and replied: "God deafen the ears of passion and blind its eyes, for it is hardly just in its decrees or fair to the one afflicted with it. Nor does passion come about by debate or deliberation. Rather it has certain of the characteristics of love, and the affection one experiences is proportional to the conformity one discovers between oneself and one's companion. If the accord in natures is great, the malady of passionate love takes firm root. Then the affliction becomes grievous and devices against it are few." When he had said this, he recited these lines:

The beginning of love is violent and burdensome:
it weakens and fells the strongest man.
Whoever possesses firmness and resolve in passion,
along with courage, love is still braver than he.[6] **[151]**

---

4 "back on their heels": Cf. Koran 3:149.

5 Cf. al-Ḥuṣrī, *Zahr al-ādāb,* III, p. 780; Mughulṭāy, *al-Wāḍiḥ al-mubīn,* p. 50; and Ibn Qayyim al-Jawzīya, *Rawḍa,* pp. 186–87.

6 Cf. the almost identical verses above (MS, p. 43), ascribed to Qābūs b.

Section Three. On Those Who Disparaged Love Because They Had Risen above It

ᶜAlī b. Abī Ṭālib, peace be upon him, was asked about passionate love and he said: "God punishes hearts that have been unmindful of him with love for each other."

It is related that Joseph, peace be upon him, said to Zulaykhā after he married her, "Where is that fascination (*shaᶜaf*) you used to feel before?" and she replied, "When I tasted love for God, love for you left me." The author of this book said: It was not that love left her. Rather she rose to a higher stage. She despised the former in comparison with the latter and became distracted from the former by the latter.[7]

It is related that Rābiᶜa (al-ᶜAdawīya) looked at Rabāḥ al-Qaysī as he was hugging and kissing a young girl of his household. She said to him, "Do you love her, Rabāḥ?" "Yes," he replied. Then she exclaimed, "I did not think that you had in your heart any empty place for the love of another than him!" On hearing this, the narrator said, Rabāḥ cried out and fainted. When he regained consciousness, he wiped the sweat from his face and said, "Because of compassion from him, compassion he has made to dwell **[152]** in the hearts of men."[8]

ᶜAbbās b. al-Walīd al-Mashriqī[9] related the following: "Someone said to Rābiᶜa, 'Tell me of your love for the Prophet.' 'I love him,' she replied, 'but love for the Creator has distracted me from love for the created.'" Abū Saᶜīd b. al-Aᶜrābī said: "What she meant was this: I love the Messenger of God with faith, belief, and conviction, because he is the Messenger of God and because God loves him and has commanded us to love him. But my love for God demands preoccupation with constant remembrance of God, intimate conversing with him, and constant delight in the sweetness of his speech and in his looking into men's hearts, while still remembering his blessings."

The words of the Prophet, "If I were to choose a bosom friend, I would choose Abū Bakr as a bosom friend," belong to the same category. The meaning is this: If I had not risen above this degree, and if I

---

al-Ḥārith.

[7] Cf. MS, pp. 137–38.

[8] "compassion": *raḥma,* very close to "tenderness" here. Al-Sarrāj, *Maṣāriᶜ* (Constantinople), p. 181, has "compassion for children" (*lil-aṭfāl*).

[9] The *nisba* may also be read al-Mushriqī and al-Mishraqī. Al-Dhahabī (*Mīzān al-iᶜtidāl,* II, p. 386) and Ibn Ḥajar (*Tahdhīb al-Tahdhīb,* V, p. 131) mention an al-ᶜAbbās b. al-Walīd al-Dimashqī, who is said to have died in 248 A.H.

were to choose by my own choice[10] a bosom friend, I would choose Abū Bakr. However I have gone beyond this degree to that which is above it, for I have come to love God.

It is said that when Moses returned from his intimate conversing with God he could not hear what anyone said except from close at hand. He withdrew for a time from **[153]** his family and his dwelling and betook himself to a shelter made of palm branches far removed from other people.

ᶜAbd Allāh b. Qays related this: "Harim b. Ḥayyān met Uways and said to him, 'Peace be upon you, Uways b. ᶜĀmir.' 'And upon you, Harim b. Ḥayyān,' he replied. 'For my part,' Harim said, 'I knew you by your description. How did you know me?' 'My spirit knew your spirit,' Uways answered, 'for the spirits of believers sniff each other as horses sniff each other, and those that recognize each other associate familiarly together, while those that do not remain at variance.'[11] 'Truly I love you in God,' Harim exclaimed. Whereupon Uways replied, 'I did not think that one could love any other than God.' 'I wish to be your intimate friend,' said Harim. 'I did not think that one could be the intimate friend of any other than God,' Uways responded. 'Advise me,' implored Harim. 'Take to the shores,' Uways replied, meaning the seacoast. 'But where shall I find means of subsistence?' Harim protested. 'Alas,' Uways cried, 'Doubts have assailed you regarding this counsel. Is it with your body that you will draw near to God, that you should question him about your sustenance?'"[12]

Someone said to Ḥudhayfa (b. al-Yamān), "O Abū ᶜAbd Allāh, do you not pray to God?" "How beautiful I find prayer," he replied. "And do you not ask for Paradise?" the person inquired. "It never enters **[154]** my mind," he answered.

From Ibn Abī ᵓl-Ḥawārī it is related that he said that Muᶜādh the brother of Maḥmūd had told him the following: "I came to my father in the afternoon and found him sitting by the pulpit. He said to me, 'It would seem that you have come with the sole desire of making me glad.' 'Yes,' I replied. 'Get up and go,' he said, 'for my gladness is not in you, but in another.'"

---

[10] "by my own choice": Cf. al-Daylamī's interpretation of this tradition above (MS, pp. 96–97).

[11] The last two clauses are a partial quotation of a well-known saying of the Prophet. The *ḥadīth* is cited by the author in chapter seventeen (MS, p. 221). Cf. chapter eight, n. 9.

[12] The same story with some variants occurs in Abū Nuᶜaym, *Ḥilya,* X, p. 20.

From Ḍamra b. Ḥabīb it is related that Abū Rayḥāna, having returned home to his wife after an absence, took his supper and went out to the mosque to pray the night prayer. When he came back to his house, he began to pray again, beginning his Koran recitation in each *rakᶜa* with a chapter and reciting it to the end. In this manner he continued until the break of day. When he heard the muezzin, he put on his clothes to go out once more to the mosque. But his wife complained, "Abū Rayḥāna, you were off on your raid for some time. Now you have returned, but I have had no lot or portion from you." "On the contrary," he said, "you had your lot (in my heart), but I was distracted from you." "Abū Rayḥāna," she asked, "what was it that distracted you from me?" "My heart was constantly engrossed," he answered, "with the garments, the wives, and the blessings of Paradise that God has described (in his Book), and you did not come to my mind **[155]** until daybreak."

Among the reports that have been handed down to us is that someone told the caliph ᶜUthmān b. ᶜAffān, may God be pleased with him, about ᶜĀmir b. ᶜAbd al-Qays and described him to him. ᶜUthmān wrote to Muᶜāwiya commanding him to fetch ᶜĀmir and to honor him. So Muᶜāwiya had him brought to Damascus and prepared for him a fine house, a table, a slave-girl, furnishings, and whatever he might need. But ᶜĀmir would go out into the desert and come back late in the evening with a piece of bread that he had dipped in his leather drinking vessel. This he would eat, although the table would already be spread and the slave-girl would be sitting there decked out in her finery. When he went into his house, he would say "God is great!" and start to pray, and he would not stop before morning, when he would head back to the desert. [After] this had gone on for some time, Muᶜāwiya wrote to ᶜUthmān and informed him of the matter. But ᶜUthmān wrote back to him saying, "Let him be."

Such men scorn every state and every elevated station in comparison with that which they have reached, although they know the reward and nearness to God that result from these things according to the sacred law. Similarly they scorn every love and every close relationship in comparison with love for God.[13]

Aḥmad b. Abī ᵓl-Ḥawārī related the following: "I heard Abū Sulaymān al-Dārānī **[156]** say: 'Aḥmad, they have served God with their hearts. Aḥmad, in God's creation there is a people who are unconcerned

---

[13] It is conceivable that this paragraph belongs to the quote from ᶜUthmān. A similar report is related of ᶜĀmir in Abū Nuᶜaym, *Ḥilya,* II, p. 90, but is given as having taken place during the caliphate of Muᶜāwiya.

with Paradise and its blessings because they are distracted by him.'[14] Abū Sulaymān also said: 'If God were to disparage Paradise itself, they would not long for it. So how should they love this world, when he has bidden them abstain from it?'" Aḥmad continued: "I related this remark to Sulaymān (his son), who said, 'If he were to disparage Paradise to them?' 'That is what he said,' I replied. 'By God,' he said, 'he has given them every reason to long for it, and yet they have not.'"[15]

From Ḥudhayfa it is related that he said: "I came to Raqqa seeking Abū Aḥmad al-Raqqī, and I saw one of his sons come up to him. Abū Aḥmad stroked his son's head, and I said to him, 'Do you love him?' 'I do not love anything alongside God,'[16] he replied,' but I feel compassion for him.'"

The author of this book said: If we were to continue with reports like these, we could cite a great many. But what we have given is adequate and sufficient.

---

[14] This report contains elements of two different reports related in Abū Nu^caym, *Ḥilya,* IX, pp. 262 and 276.

[15] Cf. ibid., p. 273.

[16] On the opposing Muslim views on love for objects other than God, see Bell, *Love Theory,* pp. 85–88.

[CHAPTER ELEVEN]
ON THE EFFECTS OF LOVE [AND EROS] AND THEIR SIGNS AND SYMPTOMS

Section One. The Opinions of the Philosophers

Aristotle[1] was asked about the cause of the corruption of the mind that results from passionate love (eros), and he said: "Its cause is dryness of the brain in consequence of the departure of the lifeblood,[2] disconsolateness,[3] **[157]** and bewilderment." Thereupon Kībās[4] said to him, "O phi-

---

[1] This passage continues the pseudo-Aristotelian dialogue begun in chapter five (MS, pp. 59–60). We are indebted in several places to the translation given by Biesterfeldt and Gutas in "The Malady of Love," pp. 41–44. As we have pointed out above (chapter five, n. 35), their translation is of the combined dramatized and long versions of the dialogue and therefore does not always correspond to ours.

[2] "lifeblood": *nafs* (soul), reflecting the belief that the soul courses through the body with the blood or is identical to it (not an Aristotelian notion). "Blood" or "lifeblood" is one of the meanings of *nafs* attested in Arabic dictionaries (Lane, s.v.). Cf. also Aristotle *De anima* 1.2.405b, describing the opinion of Critias that the soul is blood; Genesis 9:4, "But flesh with the life thereof (*bənafsho*), which is the blood thereof, shall ye not eat"; and Virgil Aeneid 9.349, "He vomits up his crimson soul" (all cited by Lane). In a parallel to our passage further on, al-Masᶜūdī substitutes *dam,* the usual word for blood, for *nafs* (see n. 6). Biesterfeldt and Gutas read *nafas* (p. 29) and translate "breathlessness" for *dhahāb al-nafas* ("The Malady of Love," p. 42 and n. 38, where they maintain that *li-dhahāb al-nafas,* "*on account of* breathlessness" in our text should be read without *li-,* "on account of," if the student's following question regarding the dryness of the brain is to make sense).

[3] The Meccan manuscript of part three of al-Masᶜūdī's *Murūj al-dhahab* (ed. Pellat, IV, p. 242, n. 5) has "loss of nourishment" (*faqd al-ghidhāᵓ*), which graphically is quite close to our text (*faqd al-ᶜazāᵓ*).

[4] The name is given in MS, p. 159, as Kīnās. We have not been able to ascertain the Greek originals of the names in the next few paragraphs. Walzer ("Aristotle, Galen, and Palladius on Love," p. 57) suggests that the fragment of this passage quoted above (MS, pp. 59–60) belongs to Aristotle's largely lost dialogue *On Love* (Ἐρωτικός). The questioners on this assumption would have to be actual students or acquaintances of Aristotle. The only place we have found anything resembling the names mentioned here in a single passage is in Diogenes Laertius' list of the students of Plato (3.46): *Kīnās:* Timolaus of Cyzicus ([Kyzi]kēnós); *Isiyūs:* Hestiaeus of Perinthus; *Jarsiyūs:* Corsicus of

losopher, explain to us the cause of the brain's becoming dry, which you have said is the cause of the corruption of the mind." To this he replied: "Persistent desire causes the blood to burn, and when the blood burns it is transformed into black bile. When the black bile increases, it causes obsessive thought. Now when thought dwells on things that cannot be obtained, heat flares up and the yellow bile is inflamed. When the yellow

---

Scepsus; *Ghāmidmūn:* Chamaeleon (cited as a source, not a student). Even considering the corruptions of Greek names one finds in Arabic texts (cf. Walzer, "New Light on the Arabic Translations of Aristotle." p. 74), these identifications are rather farfetched. While it is possible, or probable, that the names are the fancy of an Arab interpolater, presumably some Greek original lies behind them, or behind most of them.

Biesterfeldt and Gutas ("The Malady of Love," p. 52) maintain there can be little doubt about two of their identifications: "^{c}Āmdmwn [Ghāmidmūn] . . . is certainly Agathodaimon, while Kīnās/Kībās . . . is Chymes, the 'heros eponymos' of alchemy." (Cf. Sezgin, *GAS,* IV, pp. 47–48, and pp. 54–55, 62, 92, respectively.) Agathodaemon (Aghāthūdīmūn, Aghādhimūn, etc.), suggested previously by Vadet (trans., p. 129), was thought of as "a prophet of the Greeks and Egyptians" and either teacher or student of Hermes (Ibn Abī Uṣaybi^{c}a, *^{c}Uyūn al-anbāʾ,* I, p. 16; Sezgin, *GAS,* IV, pp. 47–48). For Isiyūs/Aysūs, Biesterfeldt and Gutas suggest Zosimus (for an emended RYSMWS) (cf. *GAS,* IV, pp. 73–77), or perhaps Apollonius, "(<B>lynyws), as in the Leiden MS of the Long Version" (cf. *GAS,* IV, pp. 77–91); for Jarsiyūs, they suggest Chrysippus (cf. *GAS,* IV, p. 299, citing Kraus suggesting Chrysippus for Khurūsbus; their text, p. 33, "Ḥrsbws"), or a doublet for Isiyūs. These suggestions, for the most part, have the advantage of reflecting names that were fairly widely known to the medieval Islamic scientific world. But they represent only a few of the possibilities.

Other possibilities, some anachronistic, are: for *Kīnās* (or *Kībās*): Cebes, a disciple of Socrates (Vadet, trans., p. 129, n. l; Diog. Laert. 2.125; Lucien Leclerc, *Histoire de la médicine arabe,* I, pp. 201–3), Kīnās, used as a pseudonym by an Arab astrological writer (Sezgin, *GAS,* VII, p. 66), Clinias (Diog. Laert. 9.40), Cynax (attested in W. Pape and G. Benseler, *Wörterbuch der griechischen Eigennamen*), or *kynes*, acc. *kynas*, "dogs," a nickname for Cynics; for *Isiyūs* (or *Aysūs,* as in MS, p. 59): Issus (Walzer, "Aristotle," p. 54), [Dion]ysius (Diog. Laert. 3.61), [Theophrastus Er]esius, Aristotle's most distinguished disciple, Isaios, mentioned by Demetrius of Phalerum (Fritz Wehrli, *Die Schule des Aristoteles,* [IV], pp. 44, 89), or Isios, "man of Isis" (attested in Pape and Benseler); for *Jarsiyūs:* Gessius (Jāsiyūs), one of the editors of Galen's writings (Ibn Abī Uṣaybi^{c}a, *^{c}Uyūn al-anbāʾ,* I, pp. 99, 103, 104; Sezgin, *GAS,* III, pp. 160–61), Gorgias (Diog. Laert. 8.58), or Gergithios, mentioned by Aristotle's putative student Clearchus (Wehrli, *Die Schule des Aristoteles,* [III], pp. 13–14, 52–53). *Wa-ʾllāhu a^{c}lam.*

bile burns, it becomes turbid and is corrupted, and having thus been corrupted it tends towards black bile and supplements it, and consequently the black bile boils up."[5]

Isiyūs said to him, "Tell us the cause of the bewilderment of the mind that results from passionate love." To this he replied: "It is the nature of black bile to corrupt thought, and when thought is corrupted, the humors fall into disorder because of the corruption that has come about. When the corruption becomes strong, bewilderment sets in. At this point occur deficiency of mind and hope for what cannot be. Now if the deficiency of mind reaches its extreme limit as a result of the dryness of the brain, it causes **[158]** madness, which, if it becomes firmly established, drives the person to kill himself. Or perhaps he may suddenly die, because of accumulated grief, prolonged brooding, and his estrangement from other people."

Jarsiyūs said to him, "O philosopher, tell us what causes the lover to fall into a swoon when he looks at his beloved." To this he replied: "The reason for this is the intense joy of the spirit. By this we mean that when the lover looks at his beloved suddenly, his spirit becomes agitated inside him for joy. As a result, his spirit flees and disappears for twenty-four hours, and it is when his spirit disappears that he faints. He may even be taken for dead and be buried alive. Or perhaps when he looks at his beloved he may heave a deep sigh, and his lifeblood[6] may become throttled inside his pericardium. When the blood is throttled[7] within the pericardium, the heart closes over it **[159]** and does not open until the one afflicted dies. Or perhaps thought and passionate love may wear him down and he may imagine that were he to see his beloved he would be relieved. But when he sees his beloved suddenly, his soul departs."

Kīnās then said, "O teacher, would you tell us of the cause of the pal-

---

[5] "it tends towards (*mālat ilā*) black bile and supplements it, and consequently the black bile boils up (*tafūr*)": Biesterfeldt and Gutas (p. 31), incorporating elements of their "long version," have "it mixes with (*takhtaliṭu bi-*) the black bile, becoming its fuel, and the black bile thus gains in strength (*taqwā*)." Additions in parentheses ours.

[6] See n. 2. Al-Masᶜūdī (*Murūj,* VI, p. 378) has the usual word for blood (*dam*) here. Biesterfeldt and Gutas (p. 35) note this variant but prefer *nafas/nafs* in the text, apparently because al-Masᶜūdī is the only witness to this seemingly interpretive reading.

[7] "is throttled": *ikhtanaqat* for *ikhtafat* (disappears) as in the manuscript here. The manuscript as this point, however, is not far in word, shape, and meaning from al-Masᶜūdī, *Murūj,* VI, p. 379, which has *yakhfā* (disappears) where we have *takhtaniqu* (may become throttled).

lor in the lover's face when he looks at his beloved." To this he replied: "The cause of this is that when the lover looks at his beloved, or hears him mentioned, his soul quakes and his blood flees. When his blood flees, his color changes, and when his color changes, it causes him to become pale."

Then Ghāmidmūn said to him, "Tell us why the lover's color is pale when he looks at his beloved, whereas there is a red flush in the color of the beloved, although both share the same agitation of heart." To this he replied: "The reason for this is that together with the blood there is fright(?) and together with fright there is anxiety.[8] **[160]** But blood cannot abide in a place where fear has taken hold. Rather it flees from it, and when the blood flees, the color changes and becomes pale. Or again, if the lover looks at his beloved suddenly, his heart may begin to throb violently and burn with heat, after which it will cool down. Now when the heart cools down, the lover's color changes to pallor. But once he no longer sees his beloved, the blood returns to its place, and his face regains its flush. As for the blood's appearing in the face of the beloved, this is the result of shyness and shame.[9] Some obstacle to the blood's movement intervenes in his pericardium, and heat rises from there to his head, rarefying and clarifying the blood."[10]

So (Ghāmidmūn) said to him, "Tell us why the blood appears in the face and not in the rest of the body." To this he replied: "This happens because when the blood is contending with the heat that has set in and the latter is struggling with the blood, the blood rises and seeks to escape, continuing up until it reaches the brainpan, but this obstacle prevents it from passing out of the body. So it sinks down again, turning

---

[8] The word for "fright" (*fazaᶜ*), which is repeated, should perhaps in the first instance be read *faraḥ,* or "joy." Moreover, the word for "anxiety" (*jazaᶜ*) rhymes with the word for fright (*fazaᶜ*), suggesting that the last clause, which is not essential to the point made in the passage, may have been added by a translator or emended from the graphically similar word for "sorrow" (*ḥuzn*) by a scribe or an embellisher. There are problems with the text here. Cf. Biesterfeldt and Gutas, p. 38.

[9] Biesterfeldt and Gutas, following their long version, take "shame" as the subject of the following sentence (p. 44, n. 54).

[10] This discussion of the lover's pallor is reduced to one sentence in al-Masᶜūdī (*Murūj,* VI, p. 379). There is no mention of the beloved's blushing. Biesterfeldt and Gutas (pp. 43–44) have "yellow" where we have "pale" or "pallor" for *aṣfar* and related forms. But their combined translation contains a range of colors (red, green, black, ruddy, yellow, pink). "Pale," the normal translation with respect to a face, is appropriate for our text as it stands.

back towards the face, and the cheeks become flushed." **[161]**

Hippocrates was asked about eros and he said: "The lover's eyes are sunken, his eyelids are heavy, and his color is pale. He does not show the usual signs when palpated. His pulse is an intense throbbing that does not exhibit the natural dilation of the pulse. Its beat is unrestrained and differs from the [natural] rhythm, being quite distinct from the normal pulse and irregular, especially when the lover thinks of his beloved. His pulse may even cease suddenly, or perhaps his artery will stop beating while his heart still throbs, or his heart may stop beating while the throbbing continues in his artery."

Fūrus the physician[11] was asked about eros and he said: "The lover's neck is a block for the swords of desire, his heart is a mark for the lances of ardor, his eye a target for the arrows of pursuit, his mind a bed for the torrents of hope, and his breast a halting place for the steed of passion."

Section Two. The Opinions of the Theologians **[162]** *on the Effects of Eros and its Signs*[12]

Al-Naẓẓām was asked about the effects of eros and he said: "There is nothing that dulls its sharpness and nothing that protects against its sting. As it increases, the body diminishes."

Abū Mālik [al-Ḥaḍramī] said: "Eros sinks into the heart as water shed by rain clouds sinks into sand. It is a despotic king to whom intellects are obedient and judgments are submissive. Everything novel or antique is dispensable for its sake."[13]

Abū ᵓl-Hudhayl said: "Eros vanquishes the mind, sets a seal upon the heart, grazes in the body, and waters in the liver. The one afflicted with it is assailed by erratic suspicions and capricious illusions. Nothing he has in hand is trouble free, and nothing promised to him is secure."

Muᶜammar b. [ᶜAbbād][14] said: "The bonds of the prisoner of eros are tightly tied. Seldom is the one felled by it revived, and no blood money is paid for the one it kills. His joy is never complete because he must anticipate separation at the time of meeting and must watch for slanderers **[163]** at the time of agreement."

Al-Naẓẓām al-Ṣaghīr[15] said: "Eros is subtler than wine,[16] and if it be-

---

[11] See chapter ten, n. 2.

[12] See chapter five, n. 42.

[13] Reading with additions from al-Masᶜūdī, *Murūj,* VI, p. 369, n. 2, we would have "Everything novel or antique is beneath it [and] allowable [to it]."

[14] Vadet's addition. See chapter five, n. 44.

[15] See chapter five, n. 45.

[16] Cf. MS, p. 62, for the sentence that originally followed here. Al-Masᶜūdī

comes excessive it turns into a deadly madness [and] an incurable corruption. Remedies cannot hope to cure it. It comes on like an abundant cloud that rains over hearts and stirs up obsession (*kulaf*). Its victim is in constant fear, anxious of soul, on the point of chronic illness,[17] and constantly engaged in thought. When night comes upon him he is sleepless, and when day shows itself he is distraught. His fast is tribulation, and the breaking of his fast is complaint."

Abū Ḥafṣ al-Ḥaddād said: "Eros is a subtle [malady] that flows through the frame like wine. The person possessed by it has a luminous disposition, a shining nature, and fragrant traits. In the movement of his senses is evidence for the eyes.[18] God has not willed to exalt any man whom he has tried with this affliction."[19]

Ḥammād b. Abī Ḥanīfa said: "The contagion of eros may be spread merely by hearing of it, [before ever seeing its effects], and it only afflicts the heart of a man marked by superior merit **[164]** and graceful form."[20]

ᶜAlī b. ᶜUbayda [said] : "Eros is a banishment of slumber and an invitation to subjection. The one it afflicts is humbler than the sheep called *naqad,*[21] though he may possess the strength of a lion. He delights at every promise and rejoices at every desire. He feeds on hopes and allays his hunger with desires. The least thing he offers his beloved is to be killed in defense of him, or to be taken captive."

Hishām b. al-Ḥakam said: "Eros is a trap that fate has set with great cunning and in which it snares only people characterized by mutual sincerity in love. If the lover becomes entangled in its net and caught between its teeth, [little is the chance] that he will escape safe and sound or free himself in short order. It ties in knots the eloquent tongue and leaves the king a slave and the master a servant."[22]

This is similar to what the philosophers affirm when they say: "Every

---

(*Murūj,* VI, p. 371) adds: "It is sweet to the one who partakes of it as long as it is moderate."

17 "on the point of chronic illness": *mushārif li-l-zaman* (MS: *al-marmaq*). The reading is Vadet's, based on al-Masᶜūdī, *Murūj,* VI, p. 373.

18 Cf. MS, p. 25.

19 Cf. MS, p. 148.

20 Cf. MS, p. 26. The translation of the addition in brackets is uncertain.

21 *naqad:* a kind of sheep with ugly faces, or a kind with short legs and ugly faces, or a small kind, or simply lambs. One says, "More abject than the sheep called *naqad.*" Lane, s.v., and al-Maydānī, *Majmaᶜ al-amthāl,* I, p. 19.

22 Cf. MS, pp. 85–86, where the same statement, without the last sentence, is cited.

member of [the body has its own disease, and every disease has its own][23] remedy that goes to the affected part, except the disease of eros. For it makes its nest next to the heart, and drinks from the streams **[165]** of the liver. It takes hold of the lead ropes of the ribs, and seizes the reins of the limbs. Then it becomes generalized and bursts into flame, it flares up and burns, and flames and rages. It leaves physicians helpless and puts sorcerers to shame. It slashes open the snares of ruses, blocks [the paths][23] of remedies, and seizes the routes by which potions rise. It is God who protects one from it by his grace and restrains one from it by his acts."

He[24] said: "Salm[25] wrote down this report, and Jaᶜfar[25] pondered it and remarked: 'These are the utterances of intellects dictated by spirits as a lesson to those who possess subtle intellects [and] minds. Analogy indicates the truth of this, and souls confirm it by proofs from spiritual geometry derived from the dispositions of the heavenly persons and their spherical movements. This effect in the things that they cause comes about by the gracious wisdom of God, the originator of the marvels of creation and the god of all.'"

Section Three. What Lovers Have Said about the Signs of Love **[166]**

It is said that a Bedouin Arab fell desperately in love and was asked, "How are you getting on with this passion of yours?" Breaking into verse, he replied:

In my heart is something I cannot describe
except to say it was not there but is now acute.
The days pass on, dragging their hems, and pass away,
but they do not cause it to pass away: it is ever renewed.

---

23 Addition from Vadet.

24 "He": prima facie, but not necessarily, al-Daylamī, or the narrator of the preceding report. The commentary does not fit very well and seems to be from a new report.

25 Possibly the poet Salm al-Khāsir (d. 186/802). If this Salm, who was known for his praise of the Barmakids, is meant, then Hārūn al-Rashīd's vizier Jaᶜfar b. Yaḥyā b. Khālid al-Barmakī may be intended by Jaᶜfar. That al-Masᶜūdī's setting for the remarks on love in this section is a symposium held by this Jaᶜfar's father, the Barmakid vizier Yaḥyā b. Khālid (d. 190/805), enhances somewhat the likelihood of these identifications. Cf. chapter five, n. 42. Other possibilities might be Salm b. ᶜAbd Allāh al-Ṣūfī al-Shīrāzī, through whose son Zakarīyā, Ibn Khafīf related a report that reached al-Daylamī concerning Salm's vision of al-Khaḍir (Vadet, trans., p. 7, citing Junayd Shīrāzī, *Shadd al-izār,* p. 132), or Salm al-Ḥarrānī (?), mentioned in Abū Ḥayyān al-Tawḥīdī, *Risāla fī ᶜilm al-kitāba* (in *Thalāth rasāʾil*), p. 44.

Another Bedouin was asked about passionate love and said: "The call to passion does not neglect the one who answers it, nor does [the one] who answers it forget what calls him. Passion's call is heard in a generous heart, even if the one who hears it is not [possessed of a keen mind]."[26]

It is said that when Laylā saw that Qays, that is, Majnūn (the Madman), was continually visiting her, she said to herself: "Qays would not always be visiting me and neglecting the others whom he used to visit and converse with without some reason. By God, I will see whether he has the same feeling for me that I have for him, or whether he comes merely because he is delighted by the conversation like the others." **[167]** One day, the report continues, he came to see her when the young men of the tribe had come together to visit her. But she ignored him and turned her attention to the others. When Qays saw this, it was more than he could bear, and it showed in his face. Suddenly he broke into verse:

> Others have long asked me to be their intercessor,
> but who will intercede for me this morning with Laylā?

On hearing this she turned her face towards him and exclaimed:

> Each of us feigns loathing for the other in front of people,
> but each of us has a firm place in the heart of the other.

When Qays heard this he fainted. Laylā started to shake him. Those who were there with her shook him as well, but he did not recover. So those who were there with her, and Laylā herself, took him for dead. The visitors then left him, for fear people would say they had killed him. After they had left, Laylā sat by his head trying to speak to him, but he gave no answer. Eventually she lost all hope that he might still be alive. But when the day was over he recovered as though he had been resurrected from the grave. **[168]**

Opening his eyes, he saw her sitting by his head weeping, and he began to weep with her. Whereupon she said to him, "My beloved, my hope, and my desire, what was it that came over you earlier in the day, and why are you weeping?" "As for my weeping, O my hope," he answered, "I saw you weeping, and I wept because you were weeping. As for what has afflicted me, by the one whom I ask never to deprive me of gazing at you, it came about only because you ignored me and gave your attention to the others." Then he spoke

---

[26] "[possessed of a keen mind]": text uncertain. We have followed Vadet's reading.

these verses:

> I love you with such love that if your love for me is the same
> you will be stricken with madness out of love for me.
> Love subtly pervades my entrails. By day it is
> shedding of tears, and by night it is moaning.

To this Laylā replied: "O my beloved, by the one whom I ask to let me enjoy gazing at you forever, whatever love you have for me, mine for you must be greater, and whatever feeling you have for me, it must be less than mine for you. I swear before God I shall never sit with any man other than you until I taste death, unless I am forced to do so **[169]** by some matter that cannot be avoided."

From that time on a firm bond existed between them. He parted from her suffering as no one ever had before and exclaiming:

> It seems to me that my passion for her will leave me in a land
> where I cannot find my way, deprived of possessions and kin,
> Without anyone to whom I can entrust my last will and testament,
> without any heir except my mount and my saddle.
> My love for her has effaced all love for those who came before her,
> and she has alighted in a spot where no one has ever alighted before.

It is said that one of his friends in the tribe came to him after he became delirious and that when Qays saw him he went at him with a stone in his hand. His friend related the rest of the story as follows: "I sat down, unafraid and unintimidated by what he had done. Seeing me thus, he remained where he was, playing with the dust. Then I recited these two lines by him that he had recited to me previously:

> Though my abode is distant from Laylā, perhaps
> we may yet enjoy some blessing when our abodes are near.
> Laylā, my soul is notched with longing for you,
> and my heart is cleft with feeling for you.

"When he heard these lines he wept so bitterly that it made me weep as well. **[170]** I said to him, 'Alas, my brother, have you no fear of God when it comes to your own life? By God, I fear you may encounter your death in this burning passion of yours.' 'What should I do, my brother,' he asked, 'for, by God, I know no cure for my affliction?' 'Go back to the tribe and stay with them as before,' I said. 'By God, my brother, I cannot bear to look at anyone, nor will my heart obey me if I try,' he replied. So I said to him, 'Recite for me what you have composed about her,' and he began to recite:

> Who will aid a soul whose innermost garment is love for Laylā,
> whose partner, after its friends are gone, is inundation?

In this soul is an attachment, the love of Laylā, that is increased
by the passing of the nights, the long ones and the short ones."

By this he meant that his love for her had inundated him and distracted him from his friends.

It is said that Nawfal b. Musāḥiq, who was of the tribe of the [Banū] ᶜĀmir b. Luᵓayy, came upon him and found him naked and playing with the dust. So he said to his servant, "Bring a robe and throw [it] over him." But he replied, "This is Qays b. al-Mulawwaḥ, who is mad with love and who, by God, never wears a robe." Nawfal spoke to him, the report continues, and Qays gave him an answer **[171]** that had nothing to do with what he had said. "If you wish him to come to his senses and answer you properly," (the servant)[27] said, "then mention Laylā to him." So Nawfal asked him, "Qays, do you love Laylā?" "Yes," the poet replied. "Tell me your story with her," Nawfal said. Whereupon Qays recited these lines:

I have been distracted from understanding any speech except
that which comes from you,[28] for love for you is my distraction.
The one who speaks to me with nonsense[29] thinks
that I have understood, but my mind is with you.

At this, according to the narrator, Nawfal said, "Has love brought you to what I see?" "Yes," Qays replied, "and it will end in something much worse than this."

ᶜAlī b. Muḥammad [al-Daylamī] said: "This is the description of the uppermost limits of the signs of human love. To the sayings of divine lovers [we will devote a special chapter, because these sayings deal with something that far surpasses] the circumstances of the men mentioned here. In it we will present a few reports about divine lovers, and then we

---

[27] This is how our text must be understood. Cf., however, Abū ᵓl-Faraj al-Iṣfahānī, *Kitāb al-aghānī* (Bulaq), I, p. 173, where it is clear that Nawfal did not recognize Qays when he saw him and that it was one of Qays's own tribesmen, not Nawfal's servant, who identified him.

[28] "comes from you": *minki* (MS). Ibn al-Jawzī, *Dhamm al-hawā,* p. 351, and Abū ᵓl-Faraj al-Iṣfahānī, *Aghānī* (Bulaq), I, p. 181, have *fīki,* "is about you," which better suits the context here, but *Aghānī,* II, p. 7, has *minki* like our text, and the variant fits the frame story there.

[29] "nonsense": *al-hujr* (Vadet's reading). It is also possible to read *al-hajw* (mockery, disparagement). There are several versions of this hemistich, but the others we have found do not help us with this one. See preceding note and Dāwūd al-Anṭākī, *Tazyīn al-aswāq,* I, p. 80.

will turn to the chapters on the signs of God's love for man, man's love for God, and the love of those who love one another in God.[30]

[30] Al-Daylamī neglects to mention here the chapter on the classification of love, which immediately follows the next chapter.

CHAPTER TWELVE

ON THE SIGNS OF LOVE, INCLUDING THE SAYINGS OF UNIMPEACHABLE SPIRITUAL AUTHORITIES AMONG THE MYSTICS [172] AND THE RIGHTEOUS

Sufyān b. ᶜUyayna said: "When God had brought Joseph and his family together again and had bestowed upon him the fullness of his favor, Joseph longed for God and said: 'O my Lord, thou hast given me to rule, (and thou hast taught me the interpretation of tales. O thou, the originator of the heavens and earth, thou art my friend[1] in this world and the next. O receive me to thee in true submission, and join me with the righteous)'" (12:101). Likewise Ṣāliḥ b. Ḥassān[2] said: "When death came to Ḥudhayfa, he said, 'This is my last hour in this world. O my God, thou knowest that I love thee. Grant me the blessing of meeting thee.' And then he died."

It is related from Ḥumayd b. ᶜAbd al-Raḥmān al-Ḥimyarī that a man called Ḥumama,[3] who was among the Companions of the Messenger of God, came to Isfahan during the caliphate of ᶜUmar, may God pleased with him, and said: "O my God, Ḥumama claims that the object of his love is to meet thee. If Ḥumama is truthful in his claim, then determine his lot in accordance with his truthfulness, but if he is false, then determine his lot in accordance with his falseness. O my God, do not send Ḥumama back from this journey of his." Then, according to Ḥumayd, Ḥumama was stricken with an ailment in his belly and died in Isfahan. Abū Mūsā arose[4] and said: "O people, by God, **[173]** neither among the things we have heard from your Prophet nor among the things that have come to our knowledge otherwise have we heard anything but that Ḥumama died a martyr."

---

[1] "friend": *walī.* Arberry, whose translation this otherwise is, has "Protector." We have substituted the word that gives the sense apparently understood here by al-Daylamī.

[2] Cf. al-Dhahabī, *Mīzān al-iᶜtidāl,* II, pp. 291–92.

[3] Mālik b. Saᶜd b. ᶜAdī (cf. al-Ṭabarī, *Taʾrīkh,* VI, p. 617, and, e.g., Ibn al-Athīr, *Usd al-ghāba,* II, pp. 57–59.

[4] Vadet (ed.) adds here *khaṭīban,* "to preach, to speak"; trans.: "en public."

From Jābir we have this report: "I heard Yazīd [b.] Marthad[5] say: 'By God, were I made to choose between living in this world a hundred years, worshipping God and not disobeying him for a single moment, and death, I would choose death.' 'Why?' I asked him. 'Out of longing for God, his Prophet, and his righteous servants,' he replied."

Aḥmad [b. Abī ᵓl-Ḥawārī] related the following: "I heard Abū Sulaymān (al-Dārānī) say: 'A wise man would find no joy in this world, though the world were licit for him from the time it was created until the time it passes away, and though he were to lead a life of ease in it and not be held answerable on the Day of Resurrection, if he were to be veiled from God for a single moment. What then shall we say of a man who is veiled from him all the days of this world and the next?' Then he fell into a swoon." This report pertains to the sphere of longing.

Aḥmad b. Abī ᵓl-Ḥawārī also related that he heard Abū Sulaymān say that he heard Ṣāliḥ b. ᶜAbd al-Jalīl say: "Those who obey God have carried off **[174]** the pleasure of life in this world and the next. God will say to them on the Day of Resurrection: 'You found contentment in me rather than in my creatures, so you will receive from me, today in my presence, my munificence and my free gift; and you gave preference to me over your own appetites, so indulge them today in my presence. For, by my might, I created Paradise for your sake alone.'"

It is related that Jeremiah the prophet, peace be upon him, said: "O my Lord, who among thy servants are the most beloved to thee?" God answered: "Those who most often remember me, who so wholly abandon themselves to remembrance of me that they no longer think of created beings, who beguile themselves neither with delusions of permanence nor with desire for the world. If some worldly sustenance comes their way, they pay no heed to it, and if the world turns away from them, they rejoice. These are the ones upon whom I bestow my love and to whom I give far beyond what they seek."

It is related from al-Ḥasan, the companion of Fuḍayl b. ᶜIyāḍ, that he said:[6] "I went in to visit Fuḍayl and found him weeping. [So I asked him, 'Why are you weeping],[7] Abū ᶜAlī?' To my query he replied, **[175]**

---

[5] Vadet's reading; MS: Yazīd Murīd. Cf. Abū Nuᶜaym, *Ḥilya*, V, pp. 164–66. Conceivably the Yazīd b. Yazīd mentioned in ibid., X, p. 152, the Follower Yazīd b. Yazīd mentioned in Ibn Saᶜd, *Ṭabaqāt* (ed. Sachau), VII, pt. 2, p. 170, or the Companion Yazīd b. Zayd mentioned in Ibn Ḥajar, *Iṣāba,* VI, p. 657.

[6] A similar but longer report, beginning almost identically and containing many of the same phrases, is found in Abū Nuᶜaym's *Ḥilya* (X, pp. 16–17) related by Aḥmad b. Abī ᵓl-Ḥawārī and ascribed to Abū Sulaymān al-Dārānī.

[7] Vadet's addition, from *Ḥilya,* loc. cit.

'Poor Ḥasan! When night falls and eyes take their rest, when darkness obscures the vision, the people of love (*mawadda*) stand on their feet and make their legs their bed. Their tears flow down their cheeks and can be heard falling on their feet. The Glorious One looks down upon them and boasts of them to the cherubim who bear his throne, calling out: "Precious to me are those who take pleasure in my speech and who delight in remembering me. I watch them in their retreat, hear them weeping, and see them groaning. Why dost thou not say to them, O Gabriel, 'Why this weeping I hear from you? Has anyone ever told you that a beloved friend can torment his loved ones?' How can it be fitting for me to torment folk whom I find, even over their slightest transgressions, imploring my good pleasure. In my own name I have sworn that when they come to me [on the Day of] Resurrection, my gift to them will be that I unveil my face so that they may gaze on it, while I gaze on them."'"

In a certain report the following is related: "He is a liar who claims to love me **[176]** but who, when night comes upon him, falls asleep and forgets me. Does not every lover love to meet his beloved? I look down from above on my loved ones. When night comes upon them, I remove their vision to their hearts and make myself appear in their eyes. They speak to me while beholding me, and they ask of me in my presence. Nothing is more fitting than that I should refresh their bodies on the Day of Resurrection. When others are grieved and distressed, they will be sitting on seats of light beneath my throne."

Aḥmad [b. Abī ʾl-Ḥawārī] related the following: "I heard Muʾmina bint Bahlūl say: 'Do not punish me and cause me to be without thee at the same time. For how lonely is the hour in which thou art not remembered.'"

Muḥammad b. Qatan said: "I heard Fuḍayl b. ʿIyāḍ say as he was prostrating himself: 'By thy might and glory, shouldst thou burn me with fire, my love for thee will not leave my heart. How can I forget what thou hast done with me?'"

To Dhū ʾl-Nūn [al-Miṣrī][8] are attributed the following verses:

Tears wrote on his cheek a line,
  read even by one who does not read well. **[177]**
The lover's death from pain of longing
  and fear of separation is not without excuse.
He vied with patience, then patience sought aid from him,
  and he cried out to patience, Have patience!

---

[8] The verses are included in Kāmil Muṣṭafā al-Shaybī's *Dīwān Abī Bakr al-Shiblī* (p. 104). Of the sources cited there, only al-Kāshānī (*Miṣbāḥ al-hidāya*) attributes the verses to al-Shiblī.

Al-Ḥārith al-Muḥāsibī was asked, "What is it that rules the hearts of lovers of God in their comportment with God?" "That nothing other than God be given preference over God," he replied. He was also asked, "How may one describe the lover's comportment with God during the night?" To this he replied, "His intimate conversing with God is constant, his remembrance of him is sweet, his watch is enduring, and his vigil is unending."

Yaḥyā b. Muᶜādh said: "Whoever claims to be a lover is still seeking love, for when he loves, he will be silent." He also said: "He is a liar who claims to be a lover but in whom you do not find these three things: fear, modesty, and constant abstinence from his appetites."

Sahl b. ᶜAbbād said: "Whoever loves money loves not religion, whoever loves this world loves not the next, and whoever loves Paradise **[178]** loves not the Lord."

We have heard the following verses attributed to Sumnūn:

> I have never found among men a lover
> who, deprived of his passion, did not grieve.
> But I, O Lord, see deprivation as a gift,
> confident that the right choice is being made [by thee] for me.
> I have little patience for what patience demands.
> I swear by my love for thee, I shall never ask for patience.

Al-Junayd said: "Sarī al-Saqaṭī gave me a written note and said, 'Memorize this.'[9] It contained these verses:

> When I complained of love, she said, You are lying to me.
> Why do I see your limbs clothed with flesh?
> For love is not real until your skin clings to your entrails,
> and you wither away and can no longer answer one who calls,
> And you waste away until passion has left of you nothing
> but a weeping eyeball whispering secrets of love."

ᶜAmr b. ᶜUthmān said: "The proof of love **[179]** in the heart is the lover's yearning for the beloved to such an extent that he finds no rest without him." He also said: "From the progression of longing and yearning for the beloved come about effects that produce in the heart certain things, among which are mental unbalance and constant thoughts,

---

[9] "Memorize this": *iḥfaẓ hādhihi;* MS: *iḥfaẓ bi-hādhihi.* Possibly, "Hold on to this." The story and verse, with slight variation, are also in al-Qushayrī, *Risāla* (Cairo: Dār al-Kutub al-Ḥadītha, [1966]), II, p. 619. According to al-Junayd, al-Saqaṭī often used to recite the lines in question (al-Sarrāj al-Ṭūsī, *Lumaᶜ,* p. 251.).

which produce burning agony because of the absence of the beloved and pain at the impossibility of recovery through meeting him."[10]

Al-Ḥusayn b. Manṣūr said: "The longing that grows in lovers' hearts takes possession of them because of the beloved's majesty and beauty. Thus they set out,[11] and come finally to[12] beholding his being. Nothing remains for them but him. And if [any of them] is in accord with his will, for him, from him, with him, by him, to him, in him, on him, him,[13] himself, then he himself will be the one who longs for them, until the veils and covers come over them again, and they recover and begin to long for him once more. Nothing more need be said on the matter."

The author of this book said: If we were to narrate all [we] have come across **[180]** of what they have said about love's signs, the book would become much too long and, we fear, tedious. What we have mentioned, God willing, should be sufficient. So let us turn now to the chapter[s] in which we set forth our own opinion regarding the signs of love.

---

[10] Cf. MS, p. 69, where this sentence, with minor variants, occurs as part of a more complete statement.

[11] "they set out": *yasdūna* (MS); perhaps *yashtaddūna* (Vadet), roughly, "their affection becomes more intense."

[12] "come finally to": *yantahūna fī* (MS); perhaps, *yatīhūna fī* (Vadet), which gives "become lost in."

[13] A string of Arabic prepositions and a particle allowing a suffixed pronoun to stand alone, each followed by the pronoun *hu* (him). It is doubtful whether a precise sense can be assigned to them, the intent being apparently to indicate all possible relationships.

CHAPTER THIRTEEN
ON THE CLASSIFICATION OF LOVE ACCORDING TO OUR OPINION[1]

The author of this book said: Love, in our opinion, is of six kinds. The first is God's love towards men. The others are the love of men for God, the love of those who love one another in God, the love of the elite among believers, the love of the commonality of Muslims, and the love of all other animate beings.[2]

Regarding God's love towards men there are differences of opinion. Some say that God's love for a man consists in his granting him success in all his affairs. Others hold that God's love for a man is his guiding him to him, so that to say that God loves every believer and every Muslim means only that he has guided every believer and every Muslim to belief and to Islam.[3] **[181]** Still others maintain that his love for men is like men's love for him and like your love for yourself,[4] for you are his property, and a wise being loves his property. Moreover, your love for him is like his love for you, because your love for him proceeds from his love. It is also said that his love for you is like his love for himself, because man is his act, but his acts are his attributes, and he loves his attributes. Indeed God loves all his creation in its various degrees.

The preferred opinion on this question is that God's love for men has no image in the souls of men, since it is one of his attributes, subsisting in him eternally, and his attributes have no image in our intellects, just as his essence has no image in our intellects. For our intellects are originated in time, and the originated cannot form any image of the Originator or of the mode of his acts. Rather God's love for his loved ones (*awliyā*ʾ) is known by its signs, which are certain characteristics we shall discuss later in the appropriate chapter.[5]

As for man's love for God, **[182]** it is God's act in the heart of man.

---

[1] This chapter serves as an introduction to the following six chapters, the subjects of which are enumerated in the first paragraph.

[2] See chapter one, n. 9.

[3] For a discussion of similar arguments intended to purge the divine attribute of love of anthropopathic associations, see Bell, *Love Theory,* pp. 55–60.

[4] "your love for yourself": One might have expected here "your love for your property" (*li-milkika* for *li-nafsika*), but there is no graphic evidence in the manuscript to support this suggestion.

[5] The following chapter (fourteen).

But there are differences of opinion regarding it. Some say that it is an attribute of man, since he is a lover and hence possesses the attribute of love. Others, a branch of the Sufis, say that it is an attribute of the beloved.

Another group defines man's love for God as nothing more than his obedience to him and his giving preference to him over everything he loves, by which they mean that love for God consists in giving up what one loves out of desire for God's reward, or simply in obedience to his command. In their opinion real love on the part of man for God is impossible and unattainable. God is far above this, they contend, for love can only come about after beholding him and comprehending the reality (*maᶜānī*) of his attributes which cause love. But it is impossible to behold him or to comprehend his attributes.

Others explain (the origin of man's love for God) as follows: When God spoke to men while they were still seed **[183]** and received the Covenant from them with these words: "And when thy Lord took from the children of Adam, from their loins, their seed, and made them testify touching themselves, 'Am I not your Lord?' they said, 'Yes . . .'" (7:172), and so on to the end of the verse, men heard his speech and saw him, and he caused them to experience the pleasure of that vision and the sweetness of that speech. The pleasure and sweetness they experienced in what they heard and saw, moreover, remained in them, and when God created them in the second existence and spoke to them of servanthood,[6] that pleasure was stirred up from within their spirits and produced love in them. And they were bewildered with love as a result of it.[7]

If someone were to object that love appears in some people but not in others, we[8] would reply that (when the Covenant was made) some men answered willingly and some unwillingly. As for those who answered unwillingly, their unwillingness remained in them and became manifest in them in the second existence. As for those who answered willingly, their love varies in accordance with their rank with respect to God, the purity and sweetness of their constitution, the coarseness **[184]** and deli-

---

[6] "servanthood": the response to God's lordship, affirmed in the Covenant.

[7] "were bewildered with love as a result of it": *hāmū bihā ḥubban* (MS); perhaps, "were bewildered with love for him," reading *bihi* for *bihā.*

[8] Al-Daylamī is still relating the position of those who hold that it is possible for men to know and love God because of his having revealed himself to their souls on the Day of the Covenant. It is difficult to know whether the "we" in "we would reply" (*qulnā*) refers to al-Daylamī himself or was already present in a text he is citing. His "own" position, in any case, he takes up in the next paragraph.

cateness of the nature of their souls, and the degree of annihilation attained by those who have trained themselves for love by abandoning their appetites and by enduring the hardships they encounter in it.

Our own opinion on this matter is that [man's love for God is of two kinds]: love that has come about as the result of a cause and love that has come about with no cause. That which has come about as the result of a cause, moreover, is divided into three further kinds. The first is that which has come about as the result of beholding beauty, the second is that which has come about as the result of beholding God's favor in preeternity, and the third is that which has come about [as the result of beholding God's favor in this world. As for that which has come about][9] with no cause, it is seen in the love of the prophets, because they were created with an innate disposition to love God. It is also seen in the love of the people of unification, because their spirits, being pure and free from the bondage of the impediments that might have veiled them from God, have gone back to their original abode and their source, drawing the people of unification with them, by force and by longing, to their beloved. This love has signs that we shall mention in the appropriate chapter, God willing.[10]

The signs of the loves of the elite and the commonality **[185]** we have already dealt with.[11] [As for] the love of every animate being, we shall describe it to you further on, God willing.[12]

[9] Conjecture for a considerable lacuna in the manuscript.

[10] Chapter fifteen, and perhaps chapter sixteen as well, which otherwise is not mentioned here.

[11] The author is apparently referring to chapters eleven and twelve, but possibly to other sections of the book as well. A chapter on each of these two subjects follows below (chapters seventeen and eighteen), but both are quite short.

[12] Chapter nineteen.

CHAPTER FOURTEEN

ON THE SIGNS OF GOD'S LOVE FOR MAN

The first of these signs is that you love him as he loves you. The second is that he cause you to be loved by your brethren. The third is that he grant you success in your affairs. The fourth is that he take upon himself the burden of your service. The fifth is that he give you only what you need. The sixth is that he multiply your affliction. The seventh is that he conceal you and not reveal you. The eighth is that he straiten you and not be indulgent towards you. The ninth is that he embellish your virtues. And the tenth is that he cause this world to be loathsome in your sight.

As to the first sign, that you love him as he loves you, this means that when God clothes a man with the light of his love he removes him from a human attribute to a divine attribute and subsumes his human quality in his own divine quality so that the man is joined in union with him. Then there is no longer any distinction between the beloved and his lover, **[186]** nor is there any division, since the lover has been annihilated in him. Let this be understood. It is this love about which God said to Gabriel, peace be upon him, "O Gabriel, my love is the guide to me."[1]

It is related that the Messenger of God went in to visit his paternal uncle Abū Ṭālib when the latter was ill and that Abū Ṭālib said to him, "Pray for me to your Lord whom you worship so that he may heal me." So the Messenger of God prayed for him, and he recovered immediately. Then Abū Ṭālib said to him, "Nephew, I see that your Lord whom you worship obeys you." "Uncle," he replied, "if you were to obey him, he would obey you too." And ʿĀʾisha, may God be pleased with her, said to the Messenger of God: "I see that your Lord hastens to fulfill your wishes." A certain wise man also said: "If you desire to know your portion with God, then consider the portion of God in your heart."

As to the second sign, that he cause you to be loved by your brethren, the reason is that when God's love abides in a place **[187]** it imparts gracefulness to that place and clothes it with attributes from its own comeliness, beauty, and splendor, and these draw hearts to it by their gracefulness. Hearts love it for its beauty, eyes gaze at it for its comeliness, and souls are in awe of it for its glory. This is why the Prophet said: "The best of the servants of God are those who, when we behold them, stir us to remember God." The reason for this is the breaking forth of the

---

[1] The same words are spoken by God to David above (MS, p. 92).

light [of that] with which God has clothed them, which draws everyone who looks on them to God.

It is said that when Moses, peace be upon him, returned from his intimate conversing with God, whoever looked at him died. So he veiled his face for forty days, which was the time he had remained on Mount Sinai in intimate conversation.[2] Hence God said: "And I loaded on thee love from me" (20:39), and "Surely those who believe and do deeds of righteousness—unto them the All-Merciful shall assign love" (19:96).[3]

As to the third sign, that he grant a man success in all his affairs, the reason is that the beloved is someone desired,[4] and the one who desires someone assumes responsibility for the one he desires. Also, **[188]** one provides one's beloved with a life of ease, and to provide someone with a life of ease is to protect him. Moreover, a lover wishes for his beloved whatever is good and pleasant, because he has assumed guardianship over him. How happy, then, is the state of one whose guardian is God.

Thus the Prophet has said: "When God loves a man, he lessens his greed, purifies his garment,[5] and causes him to be loved by other men." The Prophet also said, relating the words of God: "My servant will not cease [drawing near to me by supererogatory works][6] until I love him. And when I love him, I will be his heart with which he understands, his hand with which he grasps, his eye with which he sees, and his ear with which he hears, and I will be a helping hand and support for him." When a man reaches this state, he will be provided with an excuse for his falling short, as God has said: "And we made covenant with Adam before, but he forgot, and we found in him no constancy" (20:115).[7] He will also be pardoned before he is blamed, as God has said: "God pardon thee! Why gavest thou them leave?" (9:43), and he will be praised for what he has not done, as God has also said: "And (he) fastened to them **[189]** the word of godfearing, to which they have better right and are worthy of"

---

[2] Cf. Koran 7:142; Exodus 34:28–33.

[3] The author makes the point here that what shone so brightly in Moses' face that no one could behold it was the light of God's love.

[4] "someone desired": *murād.* The Arabic word as used here is free of the creaturely connotations of its English counterpart.

[5] "garment": meaning here "heart," "conduct," or "reputation." Cf. Koran 74:4, and Lane, s.v. *thawb.*

[6] This addition is from the standard version of the tradition. The saying is related again below (MS, p. 198), however, without the words "by supererogatory works."

[7] The excuse, if it needs pointing out, is that Adam forgot. Cf. MS, pp. 215–16.

(48:26).[8] Consider, too, the following line of poetry:

Whoever is not worthy of union,
all his good works are sins.

As to the fourth sign, that he take upon himself the burden of one's service, this is because when a lover passes away in his beloved, he no longer possesses any self (*nafs*) or selfhood (*nufūsīya*)[9] with which to experience the burden of service. Also, one who is loved is sought after, and one who is sought after is desired, and one who is desired is supported and preserved from toil. Moreover, a lover is a seeker, and one who seeks is one who desires, and it is the one who desires who bears the fatigue. For this reason Muḥammad was taken up to his Lord without fatigue, whereas Moses swooned, fell to the ground, and repented. Muḥammad was desired, whereas Moses was one who desired. Muḥammad did not ask, whereas Moses asked, and the tongue is the source of every calamity.[10] Thus the Prophet said to ᶜAbd al-Raḥmān b. Samura: "ᶜAbd al-Raḥmān, do not ask for authority, for if you are given it without asking, you will be assisted in it, whereas if you are given it in response to your request, you will be left on your own."

Ayyūb al-Sakhtiyānī[11] used to say: "O my God, if thou hast **[190]** ever permitted anyone to perform the prayer in his grave, then permit me. On this matter the gypsum miners[12] used to say, "When we would pass by his tomb just before dawn, we could hear his recitations from his grave." This was because he found pleasure in service and ease in worship. It is

---

[8] The allusion is apparently to God's praising the Muslims in the context of his own act of confirming their faith. The verse was revealed in connection with the Ḥudaybiya truce. See W. Montgomery Watt, *EI²*, III, p. 539a–b, s.v. "al-Ḥudaybiya."

[9] Perhaps this term is used to avoid the negative connotations of the alternative derivation *nafsānīya,* "selfishness, sensuality."

[10] Moses spoke to God and asked him to show him his face. When God revealed himself (to the mountain, causing it to crumble), Moses fell down senseless and on awaking repented (Koran 7:143; cf. Exodus 33:18, 20). The author illustrates the risk involved in this request by citing a proverbial saying attributed to Abū Bakr. Cf. al-Maydānī, *Majmaᶜ al-amthāl,* I, pp. 26–27.

[11] Cf. MS, p. 287, where the same story is related of Thābit al-Bunānī, of whom it is also related in Abū Nuᶜaym, *Ḥilya,* II, pp. 319, 322. On the vowelling of the *nisba* Sakhtiyānī, see, e.g., Lane, s.v. *sikhtiyān/sakhtiyān,* and al-Suyūṭī, *Lubb al-lubāb,* s.v. "al-Sikhtiyānī."

[12] "gypsum miners": *aṣḥāb al-jiṣṣ,* "the gypsum men"; possibly "plasterers" who worked in the cemetery. See the corresponding note in our edition.

said that when ᶜĀmir b. ᶜAbd al-Qays was about to die, he wept. On being asked, "Why are you weeping?" he said, "I am weeping for the thirst of the midday heat and for the winter night vigils." All of this was because God had lifted from them the burden of service and made them experience pleasure in its stead.

As to the fifth sign, that he give you only what you need, this is because he knows that worldly goods are harmful to you, and he keeps you from excessive indulgence in them in order to protect you. Thus it is out of care for you that he gives you only what you need. Similarly, "one does not give water to a person who is ill,"[13] for a person who is ill should abstain from too much water, since he knows it will harm him. Also, a lover loves for his beloved what he loves for himself. But God, since the time he created this world, has never looked at it, because he loathes it. The Prophet **[191]** said: "If the world were worth a gnat's[14] wing in God's sight, he would have given none of it to any unbeliever."

As to the sixth sign, that he multiply one's affliction and tribulation, this is so that one will not seek comfort in the world, for God watches over his beloved jealously, and so that one will continue to seek help from him against the world and will avidly desire to depart from it and proceed to him. On this point the Prophet said: "This world is a prison for the believer and Paradise for the unbeliever." For the believer desires to be joined with God, but the world confines him, and one who is confined is a prisoner.

The Prophet also said: "When God loves a man, he visits affliction on him, and when he loves him with exceeding love, he makes him his possession." When he was asked, "What is the meaning of 'he makes him his possession?'" he said: "He causes his wife and children to pass away and makes him devote himself exclusively to worship of him." It has also been reported that God said: "Whoever seeks me I kill, whoever loves me I visit with affliction, and whoever flees from me I burn." Similarly, the Prophet said: "We prophets bear the greatest **[192]** affliction of all men. Then come the righteous, and then all other good men according to their rank. When a man's piety is great, his affliction will be great, and when his piety is small, his affliction will be small."

As to the seventh sign, that he conceal a man from his creatures, this is because other men, were they to know the degree of God's love for him, would worship him. But God guards his beloved far too jealously to divulge him to others, and he is far too kind to him to afflict him with their

---

[13] Part of a *ḥadīth.* See Zaghlūl, *Mawsūᶜat aṭrāf al-ḥadīth,* I, pp. 221–22, and, e.g., al-Muttaqī al-Hindī, *Kanz al-ᶜummāl,* III, p. 183, *ḥadith* 6068.

[14] "gnat": *baᶜūḍa.* The word may also mean "mosquito."

esteem.[15] The Prophet said: "God loves those who are pious and remain unperceived, who when they are absent are not missed and who when they are present are not noticed. Their hearts are lamps in the darkness. Were one of them to entreat God with an oath, God would grant his plea." Another version of the saying has the following: "Were God to divide his love (for one of them) among all the people of the earth, it would be sufficient for them."[16] The lamps in their hearts, it should be understood, are the light of love.

As to the eighth sign, that he straiten a man and not be indulgent towards him, this is because contrariness on the part of a beloved at the scene (*mashhad*) of proximity is more difficult to bear than on the part of a stranger in the state (*ḥāl*) of distance. Thus Adam was expelled **[193]** from the Garden for a mere slip on his part, the kind we commit daily over and over without being called to account.

It is reported that Abraham, the Friend of God, was thinking one night about what had happened to Adam, God's blessings be on both of them, and said: "O my Lord, thou createdst Adam with thy hand, breathedst thy spirit into him, and marriedst him to Eve, thy handmaiden. But with one slip on his part thou hast busied the mouths of mankind until the Day of Resurrection: 'And Adam disobeyed his Lord, and so he erred'" (20:121). Then these words were revealed to Abraham: "O Abraham, be not beguiled because thou art my friend. Be watchful of thy heart and guard it. Make rounds around thy heart as one who fears a surprise attack by night and is afraid of sudden death. Take care lest I should look down upon thy heart and find in it something other than me, and so fill it with shame and fire, and then call out against thee: 'This is Abraham, my friend, whom I have chosen among men and have singled out for close friendship with me. But he has preferred to follow his own desires rather than to obey me.' (Take care) lest I should (find thee thus and) then command thee to be cast into the fire of hell."

[Also], the meaning of God's words, "And Dhū ᵓl-Nūn,[17] when he went away enraged **[194]** and thought we would not straiten him (*lan naqdira ᶜalayhi*)" (21:87), is that Dhū ᵓl-Nūn thought that God would not "bring him into straits" (*lā nuḍayyiqa ᶜalayhi*) for such slight disobe-

---

[15] "with their esteem": *bi-qabūlihim lahu* for *bi-qawlihim lahu* (MS), "with their saying to him," which, if correct, points to a lacuna in the manuscript. Our reading, while admittedly conjectural, requires few graphic changes and fits the context.

[16] Text and translation of this variant uncertain.

[17] Dhū ᵓl-Nūn: "the Man of the Fish," Jonah.

dience or punish him for it.[18] A similar usage is found in God's words, "And whoever has his sustenance straitened to him (*man qudira ᶜalayhi rizquhu*), let him expend from that which God has given him" (65:7), where the expression *qudira ᶜalā* means "to be straitened to someone."[19]

As to the ninth sign, that he embellish a man's virtues, this is because he bestows on him robes of honor[20] from his love and virtues from his virtues. Thus he clothes him with light from his light, beauty from his beauty, splendor from his splendor, generosity from his generosity, forbearance from his forbearance, benignity from his benignity, munificence from his munificence, and so on from the rest of his attributes. In this manner a man receives the virtues of God.

When God said to his Prophet, "And surely thou hast sublime virtues" (68:4), it was because he had received the virtues that characterize God. Moreover, the Prophet said: "God has three hundred and sixty virtues. Whoever receives just one of them will enter Paradise." What will be the case then with one who receives most or all of them? The Prophet likewise said: **[195]** "The most beloved of you to God is the one who has the noblest virtues." He said this because it is in proportion to his love for a man that God bestows virtues on him and marks him.

As to the tenth sign, that he cause this world to be loathsome in one's sight, this is because the world is distant from God, and a lover does not love that which removes him from his beloved. Moreover, this world is loathsome to God himself, and the beloved must be in conformity with his lover and loathe it because he loathes it. Thus it has been said: "The true meaning of love is that you love what your lover loves and loathe what he loathes."

In a certain report it is related that God says: "Those who trust in me are deserving of the perfection of my love. But my love has no markers along the way, [no end], and no term. Whenever I cause them to experience one marker, I raise another marker before them of which they have never conceived. They are the ones who look on the world as I look on it. . . ." Let the reader recall for himself the rest of

---

[18] The meaning is not, in other words, that he thought God would not "have power over him," the more usual meaning of the expression *qadara ᶜalā* used here.

[19] Cf. Lane, s.v. *qadara.*

[20] "robes of honor": *khilaᶜ*. We would expect "love" (*ḥubb*) here, considering the parallels in the rest of the paragraph.

this report.[21]

Having examined the various signs of God's love **[196]** for man, let us now turn to the signs of [man's] love for God.

[21] The report is repeated with an omission but otherwise in fuller form below (MS, p. 238).

CHAPTER FIFTEEN

ON THE EXPLANATION OF THE SIGNS OF MAN'S LOVE FOR GOD

The first of these is that you give preference to him over all the other things you love. The second is that you obey him both in your outward behavior and in your inward dispositions. The third is that you be in conformity with him in all your affairs. The fourth is that you love his loved ones (*awliyāʾ*)[1] with all your heart for his sake. The fifth is that you choose meeting him over your own survival. The sixth is that you despise all else in comparison with your love (for him). The seventh is that you rejoice in the remembrance of his blessings and favors to you. The eighth is that you wholly abandon yourself to remembering him in all your moments. The ninth is that you find delight in his signs in the world around you. The tenth is that you annihilate[2] every lot that comes to you other than from him. The author of this book said: After this stage a man enters the state of annihilation **[197]** and drunkenness. Thus if he surpasses this stage,[3] a word other than love must be used to describe his condition.

As to the first sign, that you give preference to him over all the other things you love, it must be recalled that love begins with a preference for your beloved and a selection of him that comes about in your innermost heart. Hence you give preference to him over every other beloved. This is why the spiritual masters have replied when asked about it: "Love is giving preference." Moreover, this kind of love is an obligation (of faith), for God has said: "Say: 'If your fathers, your sons, your brothers, your wives, your clan, your possessions that you have gained, commerce you fear may slacken, dwellings you love—if these are dearer to you than God and his Messenger, and to struggle in his way, then wait . . .'" (9:24). In this verse he has warned men who neglect this obligation to wait for a time and see.[4]

As to the second sign, that you obey him both in your outward behavior and in your inward dispositions, we say that outward obedience is

---

[1] The word *awliyāʾ* (sing. *walī*) covers "saints" as well as "friends." Both connotations are relevant here.

[2] See n. 24.

[3] That is, when he leaves behind both love and eros. Cf. MS, pp. 47–48.

[4] This argument, which the author has used above (MS, p. 97), is borrowed from his teacher Ibn Khafīf. See the Introduction pp. xlix and n. 163.

service, whereas inward obedience is humility before him, because obedience comprises both humility and compliance. Also, one who is in need entreats, and one who entreats **[198]** bears the humility of the request in order to obtain his desire from the one he is entreating. On this point the Prophet related that God said: "[My servant] will not cease drawing near to me and seeking my favor [by supererogatory works] until I love him."[5] Similarly it has been said: "Love is obedience." And obedience, let it be noted, is the state of aspirants (*al-murīdīn*) among the votaries of the mystical states.

As to the third sign, that you be in conformity with him in all your affairs, [this means for you to conform to him] to the degree that, with him, you no longer have any choice, any will, or any preference of your own. Rather you will what he wills, you love what he loves, and you hate what he hates. On this a poet has said:

If you leave Nejd, I will leave Nejd and everyone there,
but if you dwell in Nejd, how dear Nejd will be to me.

The Messenger of God, may God bless him and his house, when Ka^{c}b b. ^{c}Ujra said to him, "I love you," answered: "Prepare for yourself armor against affliction," or in another version, "armor against poverty." Both versions mean the same, that is, as the Prophet said: "We prophets bear the greatest affliction of all men,"[6] or, as he also said: "I have chosen poverty," the point being that Ka^{c}b, if he was speaking the truth, should prepare himself to be in accord with him in both of these two states, **[199]** namely, poverty and affliction.

As to the fourth sign, that you love his loved ones for his sake, this comes about because love is conformity. Thus when you know that your beloved loves something, you will be in accord with him in what he loves. Hence Layth b. Abī Sulaym said: "The believer is a beloved of God. Whoever is generous to him is in fact being generous to his Lord."[7] Likewise it is related from ^{c}Awwām b. Ḥawshab that he said: "I met Qatāda, and I was pleased by his appearance. So I said to him, 'I love you,' and he replied, 'You love your Lord!'" Finally, it should be mentioned that a "friend" (*walī*) shares with you in the object of your concern, and sharing in a thing, by nature, causes love.

As to the fifth sign, that you choose meeting him over your own sur-

---

[5] For the remainder of this tradition see MS, p. 188.

[6] Cf. MS, pp. 191–92.

[7] Reading *yukrimu* for *yukrimuhu* (MS and Vadet). The latter is possible and would give something like, "Whoever is generous to him will receive the generosity of his Lord." Cf., however, the report immediately following.

vival, this results from the fact that a lover loves to remain near his beloved. But nearness is the result of meeting, and meeting comes about in annihilation. Once the lover learns this, he will prefer annihilation in proximity to his beloved to survival at a distance. For annihilation in proximity is union, whereas survival at a distance is separation. Moreover, when the lover realizes that his annihilation **[200]** lies in his survival and his survival in his annihilation, he will choose annihilation over survival. Indeed, it is related that Moses, peace be upon him, said, "O my Lord, show me, that I may behold thee,"[8] and that God replied, "Moses, when any creature sees me, he dies." But Moses said, "O my Lord, I would rather see thee and die than not see thee and live."

ᶜĀʾisha, may God be pleased with her, related the following: "The Messenger of God fainted while his head was in my lap. So I began to stroke his head and to pray for his recovery. But when he came to his senses he said: 'Not thus. Rather I ask God for the highest and most blessed company, together with Gabriel, Michael, and Isrāfīl.'"[9] Also, Jābir (b. ᶜAbd Allāh al-Anṣārī) related that the Messenger of God, may God bless him and his house, said: "God gave a certain man the choice between living in this world eating whatever he liked, and meeting his Lord. This man chose to meet his Lord." Hearing this, Abū Bakr wept and said: "May we ransom you with our fathers and ourselves," **[201]** and so on to the end of the report.[10] Likewise, Abū Hurayra al-Madanī[11] said: "When Ḥudhayfa was about to die, he cried: 'Squeeze and tighten as hard as you can, O Death!' My heart will still love you out of hope for a life of ease after you. You are a friend in need! May one who regrets (this life) never prosper!"

Among the most amazing things we have heard on this subject are two reports that are not entirely relevant to our present discussion. Nevertheless we have chosen to relate them here because of the noble message they convey.

In the histories it is related that the delegation of the tribe of ᶜĀd, when it came to Mecca to pray for water for the tribe, was headed by

---

[8] This sentence is apparently not intended as a quotation of the words of Koran 7:143, to which it is identical except for the addition of the vocative particle *yā,* but as part of a separate narrative. God's reply in the Koran is different.

[9] The same report, with variants, is given below (MS, p. 280).

[10] The same report is given below with an addition from another tradition (MS, pp. 279–80).

[11] The *nisba* al-Madanī is clear in the manuscript. Abū Hurayra is usually known by the *nisbas* al-Dawsī and al-Yamānī. Cf. Ibn Ḥajar, *Tahdhīb al-Tahdhīb,* XII, p. 262.

three men who were leaders and overseers: Qayl b. ᶜAtar, Luqmān b. ᶜĀd, and Marthad b. Saᶜd. When [God] destroyed ᶜĀd and its people, and the news reached the delegation, a cloud came over them and a voice called to them from it, "I shall give you whatever you wish, so choose for yourselves anything, save eternal life." Whereupon Marthad said, "O Lord, grant me kindness and truthfulness." Luqmān **[202]** b. ᶜĀd, for his part, said, "Give me long life, and God gave him the life of seventy vultures, the life of each vulture being eighty years. But when Qayl b. ᶜAtar was told, "Choose for yourself as your comrades have done," he said, "I choose to be stricken with that which befell my people." "It was death," the voice replied. "I do not care," he said, "There is no reason for me to live when they are dead." Then he perished as had the tribe of ᶜĀd.[12]

It is also related that Thābit b. Qays b. al-Shammās, on the day of the battle against the Banū Qurayẓa, came across al-Zubayr b. Bāṭā al-Quraẓī, an old man who had been taken captive and had been brought forth to be beheaded.[13] Now al-Zubayr had been merciful to Thābit on the day of the Battle of Buᶜāth. He had taken him, cut his forelock, and let him go. Thābit said to him, "Do you know who I am, [Abū] ᶜAbd al-Raḥmān?" "Can a man like me fail to know someone like you?" he replied. "I want to repay your kindness to me," said Thābit. "One generous man **[203]** will always repay another," al-Zubayr answered.

Then Thābit went to the Messenger of God and said, "O Messenger of God, al-Zubayr was merciful to me, and I owe him a favor which I should like to repay. Give me the authority to let him live." "You have it," the Prophet replied. Thābit came back to al-Zubayr and said to him, "The Messenger of God has given me authority to spare your life, and you shall live." But he answered, "An old man deprived of wife and children? What does he have to live for?" So Thābit returned to the Messenger of God and said, "O Messenger of God, allow me to spare his wife and his children." "They are in your hands," he replied. Then Thābit came back to al-Zubayr and said, "The Messenger of God has allowed me to spare your wife and your two children. They are yours." But al-Zubayr answered, "A family in Hejaz with no animals or possessions? How can they survive?"

So Thābit went back to the Messenger of God again and said, "O

---

[12] Cf. Koran 69:6–7. Possibly the meaning is that Qayl died in precisely the same manner as ᶜĀd had perished. Cf. the longer and somewhat different version of this story in al-Ṭabarī, *Taᵓrīkh,* I, pp. 219–24. On Luqmān, see B. Heller/N. A. Stillman, *EI*², V, pp. 811a–13b, s.v. "Luḳmān."

[13] This story is also found in al-Ṭabarī, *Taᵓrīkh,* II, pp. 589–90.

Messenger of God, his property." "It is in your hands," he replied. Thereupon Thābit returned to al-Zubayr and said, "The Messenger of God has allowed me to spare your property. It is yours." But the old man answered him, "Thābit, what happened to the lord of townsmen and desert folk, Ḥuyayy b. Akhṭab?" "He was killed," he replied. Then al-Zubayr asked, "What became of that man whose face shone like a Chinese mirror **[204]** in which the girls of the tribe could look at themselves, Kaᶜb b. Asad?" "He was killed," he replied. "What became of our leader when we attacked and our defender when we wheeled about to return to the charge, ᶜAzzāl b. Shamwīl?" the old man asked. "He was killed," Thābit replied. "And what of the two companies of men?" al-Zubayr asked, meaning the Banū Kaᶜb b. Qurayẓa and the Banū ᶜAmr b. Qurayẓa. "They were killed," Thābit answered. Then the old man said to him, "So now I ask you, by the favor for which you are indebted to me, to join me to my people. For, by God, life no longer means anything to me without them, and I cannot bear to be away from them, not even the time it takes to dump a bucket of water from the well,[14] so much I desire to meet my friends." So Thābit had him brought forth, and he was beheaded.

As to the sixth sign, that a man despise all else in comparison with love for him, this comes about because the most important thing to a lover is his love for his beloved. Nothing is sweeter or more delightful to him than this. For this reason the Prophet used to say: "I am the lord of the children of Adam, but I take no pride in it. Adam and those after him are gathered beneath my banner, but I take no pride in it. . . ." And so on to the end of the report. After each of these things[15] he would say **[205]** "but I take no pride in it," because he despised all these honors in comparison with the honor of the love he enjoyed with God. Similarly, Mumshādh al-Dīnawarī[16] said: "Paradise has been offered to me for fifty

---

[14] "the time it takes . . .": *qablata dalwin naḍaḥa.* Cf. al-Ṭabarī, ibid., p. 590, and *Lisān,* s.v. *q-b-l,* esp. s.v. *qābil.* The manuscript has *fa-qtulnī wa-law bi-ṣafḥin,* which resembles our reading graphically and seems to be a corruption of it. Reading with the manuscript we would have an independent sentence: "So kill me, though it be with the broad edge of a sword, so that I may meet my friends."

[15] "After each of these things": *kulla dhālika.* Cf. the use of the same expression later in the text (MS, p. 283, Arabic text).

[16] Mystic (d. 299/911–12). The father of Abū Nuᶜaym met him. Cf. *Ḥilya,* X, p. 533; al-Sulamī, *Ṭabaqāt al-ṣūfiya,* pp. 318–20. On the origin and pronunciation of the name Mumshādh, Mimshādh, or Mamshādh, see Fritz Meier, *Abū Saᶜīd-i Abū l-Ḫayr,* p. 322 and n. 22.

years now, but I pay no heed to it."

As to the seventh sign, that a man rejoice in the remembrance of his blessings and favors to him, this happens because the lover consoles himself with remembrance when his desire is intense but no way to reach his goal can be found. But those who have reached the goal view this sign differently, saying that when the lover's heart is confined to the vision of its beloved, it is joined with him in union and is distracted from experiencing any pleasure in him, because in him it has passed away from pleasure. But when the heart hears another person mention him, this distracts it from union with him and brings about division from (and consequently awareness of) the beloved.[17] Then it experiences pleasure and enjoyment again, because these occur in the state of division.

As an example of this sign we have the report in which the Prophet said to Ubayy b. Kaᶜb, "Recite to me from the Koran." "How should I recite it to you, when it was revealed to you?" Ubayy replied. "I wish to hear it from someone else," the Prophet answered. **[206]** "So I recited to him the Sura of the Women," said Ubayy, "and when I reached God's words, 'How then shall it be, when we bring forward from every nation a witness, and bring thee to witness against those?' (4:41) I looked at the Messenger of God and saw that his eyes were filled with tears."[18]

It is also related that Abraham, the Friend of God, was sitting once on top of a mountain watching his sheep graze. Below him were four hundred flocks of sheep, each with a shepherd and a dog with a golden collar. The angels, said the narrator, protested, asking, "Why, O Lord, hast thou taken Abraham as thy friend, when he possesses all these worldly goods?" But God said to Gabriel, the report continues, "Go to him, stand, and mention me." So Gabriel went to him in the form of a man, stood behind him, and said, "O Most Holy One!" Abraham turned around and exclaimed to him, "Say it again, my friend, and I will give you a flock of sheep—dog, sheep, shepherd, and all." So Gabriel said it again, [and Abraham continued to reply], "Say it again, and you shall have another," until Gabriel had said it four hundred times **[207]** and Abraham had given him all his flocks. Then Abraham said, "Say it again, and make me your slave and sell me." Whereupon, the report concludes, Gabriel said to him, "It is indeed fitting [that you] should have been chosen as a friend.

As to the eighth sign, that you wholly abandon yourself to remembering him at all times, this comes about because one who loves something

---

[17] Cf. the verses by al-Ḥallāj in MS, pp. 141–42.

[18] In almost all accounts the tradition goes back to Ibn Masᶜūd, not Ubayy. Cf. Bell, "'Say It Again and Make Me Your Slave,'" pp. 198–99.

constantly remembers it. Moreover, a lover does not perceive with his senses anything other than his beloved when he is together with him and unencumbered by division, for he himself has become his beloved in togetherness. Thus, if he sees something beautiful, it becomes one of the beloved's visible signs, if he hears something pleasant, it becomes a report about him, and if he smells something fragrant, it becomes a trace of him.[19] Similarly, when he hears, he hears him, when he sees, he sees him, and when he speaks, he speaks him. For this reason Majnūn of the Banū ᶜĀmir never came to his senses except when Laylā was mentioned. When he was called by his own name, he never understood. So when they wished him to hear, they would mention Laylā to him.

It is also related that Rāfiᶜ,[20] the client of the Messenger of God, said: "I passed by the Messenger of God once when I was carrying a big basket with a roasted lamb in it, **[208]** and he said to me, 'Rāfiᶜ, what is that you have?' 'A roasted sheep,' I replied. 'Put it down and give me a front leg,' he said." Rāfiᶜ continued: "So I gave one to him and he ate it. Then he said, 'Give me the other front leg.' So I gave it to him and he ate it. Then he said, 'Give me the other front leg,' and I protested, 'Does a sheep have more than two front legs?' But he said to me, 'If you had said nothing, you would have found it.'" Consider the meaning of this report, how the Prophet used to take things from the invisible world, where nothing familiar applies. Then consider his words to Rāfiᶜ, "If you had said nothing, you would have found it." For by these words he was drawing Rāfiᶜ to his own state, saying in effect: "If you had not returned to the realm of the familiar, and had been in conformity with me, you would have found it; and if you had given to me from the realm from which I was asking, you would have found that the sheep had many front legs." He meant that what is in that realm lies beyond the limits of the things with which men are familiar.

As to the ninth sign, that his signs delight you, this happens because a lover, when his beloved is absent from him and he is overcome by longing, finds comfort in the signs and tokens of his beloved, since these signs are an indication of him. Hence [Dhū] ʾl-Nūn said: **[209]** "The gnostic, when he reaches the ultimate degree of knowledge, finds delight

[19] Cf. a statement by Ibn Khafīf to the effect that the spirit takes pleasure in three things: a sweet smell, a beautiful voice, and looking or gazing (*naẓar*). See al-Daylamī, *Sīrat,* p. 214, and Schimmel's introduction, p. 31.

[20] Versions of the following report are generally related from *Abū* Rāfiᶜ, who was a "client of the Messenger of God." See, e.g., al-Haythamī, *Majmaᶜ al-zawāʾid,* VIII, pp. 311–12, and other sources cited in Zaghlūl, *Mawsūᶜat aṭrāf al-ḥadīth,* X, p. 7. On Abū Rāfiᶜ, see al-Ṭabarī, *Taʾrīkh,* III, p. 170.

in every comely face and every lovely sound."[21] Similarly, it is related that the Messenger of God was pleased by beautiful faces, running water, and greenery.[22] Anas, moreover, related the following: "It began to rain while we were together with the Messenger of God, and he went out and removed his garment from his head so that the rain would fall on him. 'O Messenger of God,' I asked, 'why have you done this?' 'It has recently been with its Lord,' he replied."[23]

As to the tenth sign, that you annihilate[24] every lot except that which comes to you from him, this happens because your union with him distracts you from everything it is possible to behold other than him, and there remains for you no portion in anything except through him. Thus with him you no longer possess either act or omission, presence or absence, survival or annihilation, appetite or will, knowledge (*ᶜilm*) or ignorance (*jahl*), or recognition (*maᶜrifa*) or lack of recognition (*nakira*). Hence Majnūn of the Banū ᶜĀmir said:

> I need only see her suddenly,
> and I am bewildered, unable to know (*ᶜurf*) or not know (*nukr*) (her). **[210]**

He also said, when his portion from her[25] had passed away:

> I swear with an oath, I do not know
> whether my love for Laylā is diminishing or increasing.

The latter[26] verse by him contains a denial of knowledge and ignorance, while the former denies recognition and lack of recognition.[27]

---

21 Cf. Dhū ʾl-Nūn's similar statement above (MS, p. 140).

22 Cf. MS, p. 13.

23 Cf. MS, p. 20.

24 The text may be read *an tufniya* (that you annihilate), *an yufniya* (that he annihilate), or *an yafnā* (that . . . be annihilated), since the prefix letter of the verb is undotted in the manuscript. We have read *tufniya* and altered a following third person pronoun to agree with the remainder of the passage and the parallel clause in the introduction to the chapter (MS, p. 196). One might argue for *yafnā* here, and perhaps there too, particularly in view of the passivity of the lover in this stage.

25 Perhaps a reference to Majnūn's passing to a higher kind of love, unless we are to read "when his portion [except] from her had passed away," supplying *illā*.

26 "The latter, the former": *hādhā, dhālika,* respectively. Not in accordance with the author's uncommon usage in two places above (MS, pp. 146, 151), but apparently required by the context.

27 English cannot do justice to the distinction between the Arabic words *ᶜilm* and *maᶜrifa,* which corresponds roughly to the distinction between *savoir* and

Here ends the explanation of the characteristics we mentioned above. Now we shall turn to the signs of the love of those who love (one another) in God.

---

connaître in French. Perhaps "awareness and unawareness" would fit as well as "recognition and lack of recognition."

CHAPTER SIXTEEN

ON THE SIGNS [OF THE LOVE] OF THOSE WHO LOVE ONE ANOTHER IN GOD

The author of this book, may God be pleased with him, said: Those who love one another in God are those adepts of the stations who have risen above natural love to spiritual love. Their spirits are alike in some feature, and they delight in one another because of this similarity as long as they remain in the state of division. Moreover, these persons, having turned towards their origin and concurred in rising towards the beloved, inhale the breeze that wafts from him and seek to be joined with him, **[211]** until, when they have become joined, they are united and brought together with him. Thus they rise beyond this rank to that above it, in which both their love for him and their love for one another in him perish.

Let it be understood that those who love one another in God do so by the spirit of God, which is one manifestation among his signs. Now a lover finds comfort in the signs of his beloved as long as he is not united with the manifestation.[1] But when he is joined to the manifestation, he is distracted by it from the (other) signs. There is never any hostility whatsoever between the adepts of this station.

It is related from Ibn Masᶜūd of the Prophet that he said: "Those who love one another in God are set upon a column of ruby and look out over the inhabitants of Paradise. When one of them looks down, his beauty illumines the houses of those who dwell there, just as the light of the sun illumines the houses of those who dwell in this world, and the people of Paradise say: 'Let us go out and look at those who love in God.' Then they go out and look, and they see written on their foreheads: 'These are those who love one another in God.'"

The signs of love in God **[212]** are ten in number. The first is that both parties seek no other end from their love than God. The second is that they aid each other in obedience to God. The third is that each seek God's pardon for the sins of the other. The fourth is that each offer excuses for the shortcomings of the other. The fifth is that each seek to im-

---

[1] "the manifestation": *al-shāhid,* which may be used of God described as appearing and present for the mystic. Cf. al-Tahānawī, *Kashshāf iṣṭilāḥāt al-ᶜulūm,* I, p. 738. The word used for "signs" here is the same (*shawāhid,* sing. *shāhid*).

prove those of the other's actions he finds to be wayward. The sixth is that each be unconscious of doing the other a favor when he is kind to him. The seventh is that each freely repay what he owes the other but not ask of the other what the other owes him. The eighth is that each despise what is much on his part and deem much what is little on the part of the other. The ninth is that each be gladdened by what gladdens the other and distressed by what distresses him. The tenth is that each act in the matter of the other's property as the other would himself.

As to the first sign, that both parties seek no other end from their love than God, this means that they should seek from it neither worldly goods nor status, nor anything else. Thus it is related from the Messenger of God that he said: "A man set out to visit one of his brethren in God in another village. But God sent an angel to stop him on the way. 'Where are you going?' the angel said. 'I am going to visit a brother of mine **[213]** in this village,' the man replied. Then the angel asked, 'Do you owe him any wealth from which you are seeking to make a profit for you both?' 'No,' he answered, 'it is just that I love him in God.' To this the angel said, 'I am a messenger to you, to tell you that God loves you just as you love your brother [in him].'"[2]

It is related from ᶜAbd Allāh b. ᶜAbbās that he[3] said: "He who loves in God and hates in God, befriends in God and is hostile in God, receives thereby the friendship of God, and a man will not taste the savor of faith until he is like this." Then he recited: "Thou shalt not find any people who believe in God and the Last Day who are loving to anyone who opposes God and his Messenger, not though they were their fathers, (or their sons, or their brothers, or their clan)" (58:22). It is also reported from Kaᶜb that he[4] said: "Whoever performs the prayer, pays the alms tax, and hears and obeys has reached the half-way mark of faith, but whoever loves in God, hates in God, and gives in God has reached the perfection of faith."

As to the second sign, that they aid each other in [obedience to] God, this is in accordance with God's command, **[214]** "Help one another to

---

[2] The same tradition, although varying slightly, is related from Muslim by Ibn Qayyim al-Jawzīya (*Rawḍa,* p. 410).

[3] This tradition and the following are introduced in a way that does not make it clear, in the context, whether the words are ascribed to Ibn ᶜAbbās and Kaᶜb respectively or to the Prophet. Both, however, are very close to sayings commonly attributed to the Prophet. Cf., with regard to the first tradition, Abū Nuᶜaym, *Ḥilya,* I, p. 312, and al-Haythamī, *Majmaᶜ al-zawāʾid,* I, p. 90.

[4] See n. 3. This saying, with slight variation, is related from Kaᶜb in Abū Nuᶜaym, *Ḥilya,* VI, p. 31. Cf. Zaghlūl, *Mawsūᶜat aṭrāf al-ḥadīth,* VIII, p. 31.

piety and godfearing; do not help one another to sin and enmity" (5:2). Similarly, Luqmān said to his son: "My son, when you come upon folk, shoot at them with the arrow of salutation. If they shuffle their arrows in the quiver of remembrance of God, shuffle your arrow along with them.[5] If they do not, then pass them by and go on to other folk."[6]

Yūsuf b. Asbāṭ related that he heard Sufyān say: "If you love a man in God who innovates in Islam and you do not hate him for it, then you do not truly love him in God." Also, Abū Ḥamza al-Nīsābūrī was asked who are to be called brethren in God, and he said: "Those who strive to obey God, who aid one another in carrying out God's command, though their abodes and they themselves may be far apart." The narrator added: "So I related what he had said to Abū Sulaymān,[7] and he replied: 'They may do all these [things] and still not be brethren until they pay visits to one another and are generous to one another.'"

As to the third sign, that each seek God's pardon for the other when he sins, God commanded **[215]** this to his Prophet, since the Prophet loved in God those who believed and was merciful and compassionate towards them.[8] God said: "Know thou therefore that there is no god but God, and ask forgiveness for thy sin, and for the believers, men and women" (47:19). This verse contains an important point that the reader should understand, namely, that God was in effect saying to the Prophet: "Know that I am a god who has sole possession of his creatures, and if you have reached this state in your belief in divine unity, then seek pardon for your sin to confirm your servanthood, and seek pardon for the believers because you know that my decrees apply to them."

The brothers of Joseph, moreover, said to their father Jacob: "Ask forgiveness of our crimes for us; for certainly we have been sinful" (12:97). They said this because they were too ashamed before God presumptuously to make this request of him themselves, after having committed

---

5 The expression alludes to the game of hazard called *maysir,* or to divination by means of arrows. Both practices (*maysir* is generally understood to cover all gambling) are forbidden by the Koran. Cf. Koran 3:3, 90; 2:219; al-Ṭabarī, *Tafsīr* (Maᶜārif), IX, pp. 510–15, IV, pp. 321–25; and Lane, s.vv. *ajāla* and *maysir.*

6 The Koran relates other advice given by Luqmān to his son (31:13, 16–19).

7 Presumably not Abū Sulaymān al-Dārānī, who died in 830 A.D., while Abū Ḥamza al-Nīsābūrī (= al-Khurāsānī) died about 902 A.D. Perhaps the ninth-century Shiite traditionist Abū Sulaymān Dāwūd b. Abī Zayd of Nishapur is intended. Cf. Al-Nadīm, *Fihrist* (trans. Dodge), I, pp. 488–89; II, p. 979.

8 The Prophet is called "merciful and compassionate" towards believers in Koran 9:128.

such a flagrant offense. So they approached him through the one whom they had betrayed and sinned against, hoping thereby to make a more efficacious confession of their offense and to make pardon more likely.

As to the fourth sign, that each offer excuses for the shortcomings of the other, it will be recalled that God **[216]** offered an excuse for the shortcoming of his chosen friend[9] Adam when he said: "And we made covenant with Adam before, but he forgot, and we found in him no constancy" (20:115).[10] Likewise it has been related from Abū Qilāba that he said: "If you hear that your brother has said or done something and you are angry at him for it, try with all your might to find an excuse for him; [and if you can find no excuse], then say to yourself, 'Perhaps his excuse is something of which I have no knowledge.'" A certain sage also said: "Do not take anyone as a brother until you know his affairs from beginning to end. But when you find your experience with him pleasant, and you are content with his companionship, then make him your bosom friend, always dismissing any slips and comforting and aiding him in difficulty."

As to the fifth sign, that each seek to improve what is wayward in the other, we have the following statement from al-Ḥasan b. Abī ᵓl-Ḥasan (al-Baṣrī): "The believer is the other half of his fellow believer. He experiences his needs, his maladies, and his troubles. He is sad when he is sad and happy when he is happy. He is his brother's mirror. If he sees in him something he dislikes, he guides him aright and sets him straight. He is his companion in secret and in public. **[217]** Something of your bosom friend will reflect on you. And something will reflect on you from the way the one you love is mentioned. So choose well your brethren, your friends, and the assemblies in which you sit."

Similarly ᶜAbd Allāh b. Jaᶜfar[11] said: "If you must love men, then choose one who if you keep company with him adorns you, who if you disclose something to him[12] preserves you, who if he promises you something does not deny you, who even if he mentions no promise[13] does not forsake you, who if he sees a gap fills it, who if he sees some-

---

[9] Cf. Koran 3:33.

[10] See MS, p. 188 and n. 7 there.

[11] Perhaps ᶜAbd Allāh b. Jaᶜfar al-Arzakānī (d. 311/923–24), a teacher of Ibn Khafīf's in *ḥadīth* in Shiraz. Cf. Sobieroj, "Ibn Ḫafīf aš-Šīrāzī," p. 33.

[12] "disclose something to him": *kashafta lahu* (Vadet) for *kafafta lahu* (MS). Vadet (trans., p. 162) has apparently opted for *takaffafta lahu (tu lui tends la main).*

[13] Subject uncertain. Possibly, "who when you say nothing to him," as in Vadet, trans., p. 162. But this involves repetition of the phrase *sakatta lahu.*

thing good in you counts it, who when you have not asked him offers to you without your asking, and who when you ask him gives to you."

As to the sixth sign, that each see it as a favor to himself when he does the other a kindness, Yūsuf b. Asbāṭ has related the following: "Sufyān al-Thawrī said to me, 'Never thank anyone unless he understands the meaning of thanks.' 'What is that, Abū ᶜAbd Allāh?' I asked. 'It is when I do you a favor and am happier because of it and more abashed than you are. Otherwise you should not thank a man.'"

Aḥmad b. Abī ᵓl-Ḥawārī said that he heard Abū Sulaymān **[218]** say: "I set out on one of my journeys having been provided by my wife[14] with two small sacks, one filled with lumps of sugar and one with almonds. As soon as my companion and I were up in the camel litter, I opened the two sacks and began to put lumps of sugar into his mouth, and an almond along with each lump. As he was eating I said to him, 'You are the one who is eating, but I have a sweet taste in my heart from your chewing.' 'Abū Sulaymān,' he said, 'if that is the way it is, then, by God, there is no one on the face of the earth dearer to me than you.'"

As to the seventh sign, that each give to the other but not ask of the other what the other owes him, it is related from one of the companions of Abū Sulaymān that he once said to Abū Sulaymān while they were sitting together, "I have been looking for a brother in God for the past thirty years and have yet to find one." To this Abū Sulaymān replied, "Perhaps you have been looking for a brother who will be kind to you. If you seek someone to whom you can be kind, you will find many." Also, Abū Aḥmad al-Qalānisī said: "The principle on which we act is never to ask others to meet their obligations towards us and never to diminish **[219]** any obligation of ours towards others."

As to the eighth sign, that each deem much what is little on the part of the other and deem too little what is much on his own part, it has been related from Ibn ᶜAbbās that he said: "There are three kinds of men I shall never be able to repay, and a fourth whom only God can ever repay for me. The three I can never repay are a man who makes room for me in his sitting room, a man who gives me water when I am thirsty, and a man whose feet are covered with dust from frequenting my door. The fourth, whom only God can repay for me, is a man who is in need and spends the whole night awake unable to forget his need and who then at the end of the night, when morning comes, sees me as the answer to his need. Such a man only God can repay. Moreover, I would be ashamed before any man who visited me three times, if no trace of my kindness could be

---

14 "my wife": *ahlī;* possibly, "my family."

seen in him."

As to the ninth sign, that each be gladdened by [what gladdens the other] and distressed by what distresses him, the Prophet said: "Believers in their affection, love, and compassion for one another are like the members of a man's body. If the head complains, the other members are likewise afflicted **[220]** with fever and sleeplessness."

As to the tenth sign, that each act in the matter of the other's property as the other would himself, it is related that the Messenger of God united his Companions in brotherhood and that among them he united in brotherhood ᶜAbd al-Raḥmān [b. ᶜAwf] and Saᶜd b. al-Rabīᶜ. Now Saᶜd said to ᶜAbd al-Raḥmān, "I have some herds of which one half will be yours. I also have two wives. Choose one of them, and I will divorce her. When she becomes lawful, you will marry her."[15] "May God prosper you in your wives and your herds," replied ᶜAbd al-Raḥmān, "Show me the way to the market."

There are many similar tales and reports, but those we have mentioned here should suffice.

---

[15] A divorced wife, before she can remarry, must wait an appointed period (*ᶜidda*) of three menstruations (three months if she does not menstruate) or, if she is pregnant, until she gives birth. See Koran 2:228; 65:4.

CHAPTER SEVENTEEN

ON THE LOVE OF THE ELITE AMONG BELIEVERS

ᶜAlī b. Muḥammad (al-Daylamī) said: The elite among believers are a group below those who love one another in God. Their love results from their spirits recognizing one another when they meet in the spiritual world. They associate familiarly together when they know one another, and they remain at variance when they do not. This makes the rank of the elite one step lower than that of those who love one another in God and two steps lower than the first rank. It is their great distance from **[221]** the beloved that causes them (at times) not to know one another, and it is because they fall short of perfection[1] that opposition occurs between them. The spirits of the elite strive to draw them up to the rank of those who love one another in God, whereas the spirits of those who love one another in God seek to come together with the beloved. The essence of the love of the elite is a spiritual cheer that comes into their hearts when they remember their beloved. On this love it has been related from the Messenger of God that he said: "Spirits are regimented battalions: those which know one another associate familiarly together, while those which do not know one another remain at variance."[2]

It is related from ᶜIkrima from al-Ḥārith b. ᶜUmayra that he said: "I met Salmān and he said to me, 'How are you, Ḥārith b. ᶜUmayra?' 'How are you, Salmān?' I answered. 'How did you know me?' he asked. 'My spirit knew your spirit,' I replied. Then he said, 'I heard the Messenger of God say: "Spirits are regimented battalions: those which know one another associate familiarly together, while those which do not know one another remain at variance."'"

The following verses have been related to us from al-Raqāshī: **[222]**

> He had to love you with all his heart;
> So our masters and forefathers have informed us.
> In their view hearts are not free to choose,
> but acknowledge authority over earthly passions to God.

---

[1] Text and translation of this phrase uncertain. See the notes in our edition.

[2] Arberry's translation. See chapter eight, n. 9. The tradition is often related from Abū Hurayra, Ibn Masᶜūd, or ᶜĀʾisha (cf. MS, p. 224). The authorities and circumstances mentioned in the following paragraph are found, for example, in al-Haythamī, *Majmaᶜ al-zawāʾid,* VIII, p. 88, X, p. 273, and Abū Nuᶜaym, *Ḥilya,* II, p. 198.

So those that know one another associate familiarly,
while those that do not remain at variance.

It is related from Harim b. Ḥayyān that he said: "When I met Uways al-Qaranī,[3] I greeted him, and he returned my greeting. Then I said to him, 'God prolong your life,' and stretched out my hand to take his. But he refused to give me his hand and said, 'God prolong your life!' I could not hold back my tears because of my love for him and the pity I felt for him, having seen the state he was in. I wept and he wept with me. Then he said, 'May God have mercy on you, Harim b. Ḥayyān! How are you, my brother? Who showed you the way to me?' 'God the Mighty and Glorious,' I answered. **[223]** 'God? There is no god but God!' he exclaimed, '"Glory be to our Lord! Our Lord's promise is performed"' (17:108). 'How did you know my name and the name of my father,' I asked, 'for, by God, I have never seen you before today?' To this he replied, '"I was told of it by the All-Knowing, the All-Aware" (66:3). My spirit knew your spirit when my soul spoke to your soul. For spirits have souls like the souls of living beings, and believers know one another and love one another by the spirit of God, even if they have never met before. They love one another even if their abodes are distant and their camps are far apart.'" Let the reader recall the remainder of this story.

The author of this book said: We have already mentioned the signs of the love of the elite,[4] so there is no need to relate them at greater length here.

---

[3] Cf. the story of Harim's meeting with Uways related above (MS, p. 153); also below (MS, pp. 286–87).

[4] In chapter twelve. See also the end of chapter thirteen, MS, pp. 184–85, and n. 11 there.

CHAPTER EIGHTEEN

ON THE LOVE OF THE COMMONALITY OF MUSLIMS

The commonality are a group whose rank is below that of spiritual lovers. Their love is the result of similarity of nature and conformity of character. **[224]** The essence of their love is the inclination of the heart towards a thing and its delighting in it. Of this type of love the Prophet said: "A man will follow the religion of his bosom friend, so take care whom you befriend." Also, it is related [from] ᶜAmra that she said: "There was in Mecca a woman buffoon who went to Medina and stayed with another woman like her. The news reached ᶜĀᵓisha and she said, 'I heard the Messenger of God say: "Spirits are regimented battalions: those which know one another associate familiarly together, while those which do not know one another remain at variance."'"[1] And a certain poet said:

> Ask not about a man, but look at his comrade,
> for every man's example is his comrade.

Similarly, ᶜAbd Allāh [b. Masᶜūd][2] said: "A man [who believes] will enter the mosque when there are a hundred men in it, but only one believer, and he will go and sit by his side, while a hypocrite will enter the mosque when there are a hundred men in it, but only one hypocrite, and he will go and sit by his side."

Of the poetry one hears sung, consider this verse: **[225]**

> Do not deprive my soul, when you are its beloved,
> for every man yearns for the one he is like.

We have mentioned the signs of this love above,[3] but we may recall here that al-Kindī said: "Blood relationship is a transitory accident, but brotherhood based on similarity is an enduring substance."

---

[1] A. J. Arberry's translation. See chapter eight, n. 9.

[2] Cf. al-Ghazālī, *Iḥyāᵓ ᶜulūm al-dīn* (al-Maktaba al-Tijārīya al-Kubrā), II, p. 262 and n. 1. (The notes on al-Ghazālī's traditions by ᶜAbd al-Raḥīm b. al-Ḥusayn al-ᶜIrāqī have the separate title *al-Mughnī.*) Vadet (trans., p. 166) adds here "b. Sahl," but gives no source for the addition.

[3] In chapter eleven. See also the end of chapter thirteen, MS, pp. 184–85, and n. 11.

CHAPTER NINETEEN

ON THE LOVE OF ALL OTHER ANIMATE BEINGS

The author of this book said: The love of the other animals is a closeness of natures and the inclination of like to like, as is seen in the close companionship of livestock, wild animals, and birds. Thus one hears a camel grumble and utter cries of longing when he must leave his companions in the herd, or a horse neigh when he must leave his close companion whom he is accustomed to be with at the manger. The same is the case with other livestock and beasts of burden. **[226]** As for the closeness of dogs to their masters, it is so well known we hardly need mention it. Indeed Buzurjmihr said: "I have learned from everything a moral lesson, even from the dog, the crow, and the cat." When he was asked, "What have you learned from the dog?" he replied: "His closeness to his masters."

It is related that Solomon the son of David, peace be upon him,[1] was sitting in his assembly hall when he saw two sparrows. One of them said to the other, "Will you be contrary with me? Even if you were to order me to pick up Solomon's assembly hall with my beak, I would obey you and do it." Solomon laughed and, calling to them, said to the male, "Are you the one who said such and such?"[2] "Yes, O Prophet of God," he replied. "What brought you to say such a thing?" Solomon asked. "O Prophet of God," the sparrow answered, "a lover is not to be blamed."

I heard one of our teachers say: "I was out in the desert, and I saw a camel that had twisted his head to the right and would not turn it **[227]** in any other direction. So I asked the camel driver, 'What is the matter with this camel that he keeps his head turned to the right?' 'I had him tied in line with a female,' he answered, 'but then [a man came] and untied her and went off with her to the right. The camel turned his head after her, and he has kept it turned in that same direction ever since.'"

We have seen similar things ourselves. Once when I was in the Sacred Mosque in Mecca I saw a female pigeon walking around a male, flapping her wings and lowering her head for him. But he paid no attention to her. After things had gone on like this between them for a long while,

---

[1] "upon him": so in the manuscript, not "upon the two of them" as would be expected.

[2] Solomon had been taught the speech of birds. See Koran 27:16.

another male pigeon came and made advances to her, strutting around her in a circle trying to seduce her. But she refused him. Indeed, although he continued to circle around her for a long while trying to seduce her, she still refused him. Now when the first male pigeon perceived her behavior, he came and offered himself to her. But now that he had come to her, she refused him too. He did his utmost, but she rebuffed him and flew off, and he flew off after her. I do not know **[228]** what became of them. But I was amazed by the fact that she offered herself to him and to no other pigeon, and that she humbled herself before him but disdained the other male. Moreover, I was amazed at the first male. When he saw that another had offered himself to her, while she still inclined to him, he returned to her, seeking to possess her. But when he came back to her, she turned on him and refused him. I have never seen two animals more like human beings.

Another time, when I was out in the desert with the pilgrims, I saw a camel aroused by lust that would neither eat nor drink and that kept wandering up and down the dunes until he died. [So I asked about him, and a man said, "He was my camel],[3] and he was my favorite. So I bought him a she-camel and tied her in the same place as him and made her kneel down beside him. [But she died.][3] Then he became so aroused I was completely unable to cope with him, and he remained in the same state until he died."

Moreover, I have heard a number of people report that when a camel has mated too often and refuses to cover females, a beautiful woman should be decked out **[229]** in fine clothes for him, or a beardless youth with a comely face brought to him. When he sees the person, he will begin mating again.

Here is something else we were witness to. A group including ᶜAlī al-Aḥwal and Abū Ṭāhir b. al-Qazzāz went one day to the Elephant House at Bāb al-Salā[ma].[4] They stayed there for some time in front of the ele-

---

[3] Conjecture for a lacuna in the manuscript.

[4] Bāb al-Salā[ma], for Bāb al-Salā in the manuscript. Vadet emends to Bāb al-Salā[m]. The events seem to have taken place in Baghdad. The city, according to al-Ṭabarī (*Taʾrīkh,* IX, p. 315), had in 252/866–67 a Bāb al-Salāma, and it also had an "Elephant House" or Dār al-Fīl. The latter, in the reign of al-Ṭāʾiᶜ (363/974–381/991), which corresponds roughly to the period of al-Daylamī's literary activity, was opposite one of the gates of the Dār al-Khilāfa (Bāb al-Khāṣṣa) near Bāb Kalwādhā (Yāqūt, *Muᶜjam al-buldān,* I, p. 444). (The name Bāb Kalwādhā, it may be noted, bears a remote graphic resemblance to the "Bāb al-Salā[ ]" in our text.) Possibly evidence for Vadet's choice, the Tigris was called Nahr al-Salām, whence, according to the *Tāj,* the name "Madinat al-

phant, singing, dancing, and making merry. Then they got up and left, and they stayed away for three days or so. But the elephant keeper began to go about and look for them. ᶜAlī al-Aḥwal said: "The elephant keeper met me and exclaimed, 'Alas, where have you been? I have been looking for you since that day.' 'Nothing is wrong, I hope,' I said. 'Alas,' he replied, 'since that day the elephant has not eaten a thing. So please, by God, go back to him for a while.'" He continued: "So we went back to him and sang songs and made merry, and he resumed eating his fodder as usual."

The author of this book, may God be pleased with him, said: Stories like this are numerous. **[230]** But the examples we have given should be sufficient. Let us turn now to [the chapter on] what is meant by the word *shāhid* (witness) and how it is understood by the people of gnosis. We shall explain what they mean by it because the meaning is obscure and difficult, [even though] the word itself is well known.

Salām" for Baghdād (*Tāj al-ᶜarūs,* VIII, p. 342, s.v. *salm*). There was a Bāb "Salm" in Shiraz, where al-Daylamī spent most of his life, and another in Isfahan (ibid., p. 343).

CHAPTER TWENTY
ON THE MEANING OF THE WORD *SHĀHID*

The word *shāhid* (witness) has two meanings. The first is a witness beyond reproach (*shāhid ᶜadl*) who informs you that his Maker stands apart from all other artisans by his workmanship. For such a witness is the work of a wise artisan who is distinguished from all other wise artisans by his wisdom. The second meaning of *shāhid* is an eye witness (*[shāhid] ḥāḍir*) who informs you that he has recently been at the scene of the universal beauty and that he has been distinguished by his Maker by (the beauty of) his workmanship from all his other works.[1]

Let us consider first the meaning of the words "a witness beyond reproach who informs you that his Maker stands apart from all other artisans by his workmanship." The meaning of this is that works that are out of **[231]** the ordinary point to the uniqueness of their maker in his craft. This is because when one looks at a work that is distinguished from other works, the power of the wisely executed workmanship leads one to recognize the maker of the object. For the beauty that a work acquires through the skill of its maker is something from thc artisan himself. It is something he has given it, not something the work possesses on its own. If it came from the work itself, then it would have been in it before its maker made it. Thus a beautifully patterned silk, were it not for the beauty acquired from its maker, would be merely the spittle of a repugnant worm. But when its maker imparts beauty to it, that beauty is in effect the maker himself.

Understand that when an artisan stands apart from other artisans by his workmanship and is distinguished from any rivals by his skill, then his work is a witness that identifies him to whoever sees it, and a guide to him **[232]** for whoever seeks him. For if someone sees his work, he recognizes it as his without anyone telling him. But if the artisan is not skillful and matchless and does not stand apart from his rivals, then his work is not recognizable as his, because it is ordinary work, and ordinary

---

[1] The practice of some mystics of gazing at a *shāhid,* often a comely youth, as a token of the divine beauty was the subject of considerable controversy. For discussions of the issue, see Ritter, *Das Meer der Seele,* esp. pp. 470–77, and Bell, *Love Theory,* pp. 139–44. On the meanings the word *shāhid* acquired, apparently as a result of the practice, see Redhouse, *A Turkish and English Lexicon,* s.v., and Steingass, *A Comprehensive Persian–English Dictionary,* s.vv. *shāhid* and *shāhid-bāzī.*

pieces of work do not reveal their maker, since they could be the work of any artisan.

Now if this is the case with a skillful artisan and his work among us, how much more will it be so of the Artisan who is distinguished by his work from everything customary and familiar, who transcends the realm of human ability. Once you have grasped this, you will know that the work of the Artisan who is distinguished from others by his work and who transcends the realm of human abilities is an indication of his oneness and his uniqueness in his craft. For he has no equal, and the definition of the one is that which has no like and no equal. Let this be understood.

Now let us turn to the meaning of the second definition, namely, "an eye witness who informs you that he has recently been **[233]** at the scene of the universal beauty and that he has been distinguished by his Maker by (the beauty of) his workmanship from all his other works." Now every beauty is derived from the universal beauty, [which] is near to[2] the Beautiful. However, beauty appears or is hidden in proportion to its proximity to this source or its remoteness from it, as well as in proportion to the coarseness or fineness of the constitution of its locus, the elements of turbidity or clarity in the attributes of the locus, and the thickness or thinness of the veil hung over it. Hence when you see in something a manifest beauty, this tells you two things: first, that it has been present at the scene of the universal beauty and has acquired from it a clear trace, and, second, that the locus of the beauty is free from corrupting elements and has received beauty in a manifest way. This being the case, what we mean by the word *shāhid* in the second sense is one who has been present at the scene, who has been distinguished with favor, and who has come bearing a true report with the token of its veracity. **[234]** For [he has obtained] the solicitude of his Maker, who has distinguished him with comeliness. Understand this well.

The foregoing sums up what comes to our mind concerning the meaning of the word *shāhid*.

All witnesses, then, are alike, except that [beauty] is more intense in some than in others. Indeed it may be so hidden in some that it hardly can be perceived by any rational being, and it may be so manifest in others that it hardly can escape the notice of any irrational animal. Thus a certain poet has said:

---

[2] "[which] is near to": *[alladhī] yaqrub.* The text could conceivably be read simply *bi-qurb,* giving the same meaning, or perhaps "by virtue of proximity to the Beautiful." Cf., however, the parallel passage above (MS, pp. 19–20).

In each and every thing there is a sign of him,
indicating that he is one.

Now we shall leave this subject and proceed, God [willing], to the chapter on the extreme limit of the perfection of love.

CHAPTER TWENTY-ONE
ON THE DEFINITION OF THE PERFECTION OF LOVE

Let it be understood that love is an attribute of the lover as long as it remains valid to assert this quality of him. But when this ceases to be the case, he is translated from the attribute of love to another attribute. When this happens, he is given a new name derived from the attribute to which he has been translated, and he is qualified by a new adjective derived from the state that comes upon him. Thus the old state is subsumed **[235]** in the new state, and he is called drunk, vanquished, extirpated, or subsumed. All this comes about if the lover is translated from love to love, that is, if he proceeds in love to the limit of annihilation through it, for it, and in it.

But if a man, when he proceeds to the limit of love, is translated to the level of gnosis, he is not vanquished by it, or extirpated, nor does he become drunk with it. Rather, the quality of love is subsumed in the quality of gnosis, and he becomes both lover and knower. His level rises above the previous rank so that he comes to despise all the love that has passed in comparison with that which he sees now. He experiences a kind of love different from the earlier kind and becomes one of those to whom love has come after gnosis.[1] Hence love becomes for him a station (*maqām*), whereas previously it was a state (*ḥāl*). This is indeed a very noble station among the people of gnosis, and it is to this that the mystics allude.

Thus Sumnūn, who was among those who had been vanquished **[236]** by love, alluded to it, after reaching gnosis, when he said:

> I thought I had reached in passion
> a limit beyond which I had nowhere to go.
> But when passion and I parted, I remembered what had passed,
> and knew for certain I had only been dallying.

Now among those whose affection proceeds from nature, love ends in loss of reason, bafflement, and an estrangement from other men like the fearfulness of a wild animal; and this leads to their destruction and their death. But such is not the case with divine lovers. For their love reaches its limit either in union (*ittiḥād*) with the Beloved, which is everlasting life, or in the station of unification (*tawḥīd*), which is reaching [the Be-

[1] Cf. MS, p. 106.

loved] through the Beloved and beholding his signs in the beloved Manifestation,[2] as though he were the true essence of every thing, every thing being from him, by him, **[237]** for him, and out of him, and he being in every thing, with every thing, for every thing, by every thing, and out of every thing, and as though he were not by any thing, nor for any thing, nor out of any thing, nor from any thing, nor in any thing, nor being any thing. Understand all this if you wish to have knowledge of the stations of those who love him, so that you may make no mistake regarding that to which you bear witness, nor any denial, lest you be counted among those who speak lies and make false claims. We ask God that we may be truthful in our words and pious in our acts, that we may pass away from our attributes and leave behind our portion in life, and, lastly, that our hearts may be pure and our failings forgiven.

Having made these points, we shall now relate reports to illustrate some of what we have said. But we shall leave the rest of what we have said without illustration for the sake of those who have no need of what we have said or those for whom only some of what we have said is needed to converge with their total knowledge. For they will know the part by the whole, or the whole by the part, or the part [by the part], or the whole by the whole. These **[238]** are words that, spoken at length, confound and baffle the mind, but they are beloved words, worthy to be ransomed with father and mother among those whose concern they are—the noble notables, the many esteemed[3] masters, may God gather us together with them in an abode where eyes cease to weep and hearts are healed, for he is our Protector and forgiving.[4]

Aḥmad b. ᶜAṭāᵓ related that God says: "Those who trust in me are deserving of the perfection of my love. But it has no markers along the way, no end, and no term. Whenever I cause them to experience [one marker, I raise another marker before them of which they have never conceived. They are the ones who look on the world as I look][5] on it. They are the ones who speak among men with my speech as I revealed it to my messenger Muḥammad. And how should their speech not be my speech, when I have inspired them with my proofs?"[6]

Fuḍayl b. ᶜIyāḍ was asked, "When does a man reach the utmost degree in love?" "When the beloved's refusing him favors or granting them to him are the same to him," he replied.

---

[2] "the beloved Manifestation": *al-shāhid al-maḥbūb.* Cf. chapter sixteen, n. 1.

[3] "many esteemed": *al-najl.* Cf. *Tāj al-ᶜarūs,* s.v.

[4] Cf. Koran 7:155.

[5] Cf. MS, p. 195.

[6] Cf. Koran 6:83.

One of the masters said: "When a lover is at the beginning of his experience, all things weep for him because of the gravity **[239]** of that into which he is entering, but when he reaches the end, he weeps for all the people of the earth because of the portion from God they have missed."

We have heard the following verses related from al-Ḥusayn b. Manṣūr, known as al-Ḥallāj:[7]

> I am the one I love, and the one I love is I.
> We are two spirits dwelling in one body.
> Ever since we were bound by the covenant of love,
> our affection has been proverbial among men.
> If you see me, you see him,
> and if you see him, you see us.[8]
> You who desire to know our story,
> if you were to see us, you could not tell us apart.
> His spirit is my spirit and my spirit is his spirit.
> Who has ever seen two spirits abiding in one body?

This is an example of his doctrine of essential union (*ittiḥād*).

Yaḥyā b. Muᶜādh said: "True love is that which does not increase when the beloved is kind and does not diminish when he is harsh."

Aḥmad [b. Abī ᵓl-Ḥawārī] said that he heard Abū Sulaymān (al-Dārānī) say: "I looked towards God for years, and then the door of approaching him was opened for me, and I was shown heaven and hell. But I paid no heed to them, because I was distracted from them by him." **[240]**

Al-Ḥārith al-Muḥāsibī said: "Love inspires a good opinion of the beloved, and the lover flares up with anticipation of the favors he will receive from him. So the ardor of love increases, and yearning cries out, while moans lament. The pangs of love are awakened, the lover's color changes, his limbs despair of life, his body languishes, and his skin turns to goose flesh. At times he cries out, at times he weeps, at times he sighs, at times he is bewildered, at times he is distraught, at times he loses his mind for a short while, or perhaps much longer, and at times he plunges by his acumen to the very depths of understanding and derives from the subtlest gifts [by] the light of discernment [things revealed to him by][9] the Knower of Invisible Things."

---

[7] See on these verses al-Ḥallāj, *Le dîwân d'âl-Hallâj* (ed. and trans. Massignon), pp. 92–93, and Massignon, "Interférences," pp. 239–40.

[8] "us": perhaps to be understood as "me," being plural here only for the sake of the rhyme.

[9] Conjecture for a lacuna in the text pointed out by Vadet.

ᶜAmr b. ᶜUthmān [al-Makkī] said on the subject of the mystical lover's reaching the final goal: "His names are annihilated in earth and in heaven, his qualities and his states are exterminated from the circumstances of sacred and profane, his attributes are obliterated, his life is snatched away, his breath is extirpated, and his traces are effaced, yet without his dying the death of the dead or knowing the survival **[241]** of the living. There remains no name for annihilation, nor any name for survival, nor indeed any name for the survival of anyone in annihilation, save the One, the Unique."

The author of this book said: This is what divine lovers say. What the philosophers have to say about love we shall take up, God willing, in the next chapter, in which we shall consider the deaths of natural lovers.

CHAPTER TWENTY-TWO

ON THOSE WHO DIED OF NATURAL LOVE

Aristotle, being asked about the cause of the passionate lover's falling into a swoon when he looks at his beloved and the cause of his sudden death, replied:[1] "The reason for this is the intense joy of the spirit. By this we mean that the lover may look at his beloved suddenly and his spirit may become agitated inside him out of joy. As a result, his spirit flees and disappears for twenty-four hours. It is when his spirit disappears **[242]** that he faints. At this point he may even be taken for dead and be buried alive. Or perhaps when he looks at his beloved he may heave a deep sigh, and his lifeblood[2] may become throttled inside his pericardium. When the blood collects thus, the heart closes [over it] and does not open until the one afflicted dies. Or perhaps passionate love and thought may wear him down, and he may imagine that were he to see his beloved he would be relieved. But when he sees his beloved suddenly, his soul departs."

Among the stories we have heard about the deaths of natural lovers is the following we heard from Abū ᶜAbd Allāh Aḥmad b. ᶜAbd al-Raḥmān b. Muḥammad al-Hāshimī,[3] who said that he heard Jaᶜfar al-Khuldī say: "One day as I was passing by the door of the bathhouse of a certain estate,[4] I saw two young men remonstrating with each other. As their voices rose, one said to the other, 'What is it you want from me?' 'Your spirit,' the other replied. Then the first young man let out **[243]** a shriek and fell down dead. The other young man fled. The people gathered round and, recognizing the dead youth, carried him back to his house.

---

[1] Cf. MS, pp. 158–59.

[2] See chapter eleven, n. 2.

[3] Abū ᵓl-Sāᵓib ᶜAbd al-Raḥmān b. Muḥammad al-Hāshimī was one of Ibn Khafīf's teachers in *ḥadīth* (al-Daylamī, *Sīrat-i İbn al-Ḫafīf,* p. 208). Perhaps this is his son (Cf. Sobieroj, "Ibn Ḫafīf aš-Šīrāzī," pp. 144–45). On this assumption he was presumably a contemporary of Ibn Khafīf (d. 371/982), and he could very well have met both Jaᶜfar al-Khuldī (d. 348/959) and al-Daylamī. Sobieroj (ibid.) suggests that he is possibly to be identified with the author of a mystical work mentioned by al-Kalābādhī.

[4] "estate": *qaṭīᶜa.* The feudal estates in Baghdad and Samarra are mentioned by al-Yaᶜqūbī (*Kitāb al-buldān* [ed. de Goeje], pp. 243–62).

"Six years later I went on the pilgrimage, and while I was performing the circumambulation I saw the second young man and realized who he was. I drew him to me and asked him, 'Are you not the one to whom such and such happened?' 'Yes,' he answered. Then, taking me by the hand, he brought me out of the circle of pilgrims and asked, 'Did you see me on that day?' 'Yes,' I replied. He wept bitterly and said, 'You should know that that young man used to love me, whereas I used to loathe him. All his life he wanted to make the pilgrimage, and I was the cause of his not going. For this reason I have already made the pilgrimage on his behalf five times, and this is the sixth. However the night before last I was weeping grievously, and when sleep finally came over me, I saw him and greeted him. But he gave me no reply. So I implored him and wept before him. Whereupon he broke into verse, saying: **[244]**

After taking my life, do you weep for me,
after such harshness to me before my death?
O moon, who wasted my body and my heart,
who forsook me and showed me no mercy,
Stop your weeping and cry no more,
For to me what you did was nothing at all."[5]

In Arrajān I heard a sheikh by the name of Abū ʾl-Ḥusayn Muḥammad b. al-Jabahī[6] say: "I made the pilgrimage in a certain year and stayed in a house in the neighborhood of Shiᶜb ᶜAlī.[7] The house belonged to an old woman named Umm ᶜAlī, who had a number of daughters and sisters. One day, while I was sitting on a couch in one of the rooms of the house, I looked up and saw written on the wall with saffron dye two lines of poetry. This is what I read:

They shouted, Let us depart, and I was sure it was
my spirit I heard, wishing to depart this world

---

5 Al-Sarrāj (*Maṣāriᶜ,* I, p. 254) has four verses instead of three. The first verse in our text is made up of the first two in the *Maṣāriᶜ*. The last two verses are fairly similar in both sources. The story, on the other hand, is totally different.

6 On the *nisba* al-Jabahī, see al-Samᶜānī, *al-Ansāb* (Hyderabad), III, p. 199, no. 479.

7 On the ravines (*shiᶜb,* pl. *shiᶜāb*) of Mecca, see al-Yaqūbī, *Kitāb al-buldān,* VII, pp. 314–15.

In the call[8] of the All-Merciful. So I entrusted my beloved[9]
to the one who does not let a friend lose a friend. **[245]**

"'Umm ᶜAlī,' I said, 'who wrote this?' She began to weep, and all the women wept with her. 'Alas, tell me your story,' I entreated them. 'You will have to give us something sweet to eat[10] before we tell you the story,' the old woman replied. So I took out what I had and gave it to them to eat. Then I said to Umm ᶜAlī, 'Now tell me the story,' and this is what she said.

"'Several years ago, when the pilgrims came to stay with us, there was among them a woman from Baghdad who stayed in this very room. We had never seen anyone more beautiful than her, or of better character, before. When the day of departure came and they called for everyone to come out ready to leave, she was sitting there where you are now, and she said, "You Meccans are cruel people. You are neither faithful nor loyal. When I leave you, you will not remember me." "Not so, by God," we replied, "We shall never forget you as long as we live. How could we forget someone like you?" Then she wrote those two lines on the wall and said, "When you read this, remember me, for I shall return to you next year, **[246]** God willing."

"'But the next year she did not come. However among the pilgrims coming from the Yemen was a charming young merchant who stayed in this same room. He read the two verses and asked, "Who wrote this?" "A woman," we said. He asked about her, and we told him what had happened. The young man was fascinated with reading the two verses, and they distracted him from every other concern. He neither ate nor drank. He just kept reading the two verses. We pitied him, and so we said to him, "She promised to return to us this year. Perhaps some matter has deterred her." To this the young man answered, "Then I will stay on. Perhaps she will come next year." So he took leave of his companions and stayed. When the pilgrims went back, he was not among them. He continued on here in the same state as before. How he used to delight in hearing her story whenever we told it to him.

---

[8] "call": *daᶜwa* (MS); conceivably *riᶜya* (keeping) or *raᶜwa,* which is attested as synonymous with *ruᶜwā* in the sense of "forbearance" (root *r-ᶜ-w*), although not in the sense of "mercy" (root *r-ᶜ-y*). Cf. Lane and *Tāj al-ᶜarūs,* s.vv. *r-ᶜ-w, r-ᶜ-y.*

[9] "So I entrusted my beloved": *fa-stawdaᶜtuhū.* We might have expected "entrusted *it,"* with the pronoun *hu* referring to the spirit, but the text has just treated *rūḥ* as feminine twice in the preceding verse.

[10] Although the primary meaning is intended here as well, "something sweet" was and remains a euphemism for a gratuity.

"'We observed his fascination for her and said to ourselves, "This man has become useless. If we efface the verses and he can no longer read them, perhaps he will forget." So we rubbed them off. But when the young man came and looked at the spot, **[247]** he let out a cry and exclaimed, "Alas, why have you done this?" He wept and sobbed so much that we felt sorry for him, and we said, "We only did it out of pity for you." He began to weep so profusely that we feared for him. Indeed his sorrow continued to grow until he fell ill and died.

"'The next year the woman arrived with the pilgrims. She stayed in the same place, and when she looked at the wall she did not see her writing. "Now I know how cruel you Meccans are," she cried, and wrote the verses again with her finger. We wept and said, "Thereby hangs a strange tale." "Tell me,"[11] she said. "You have killed a man with those two verses," we replied. "How?" she asked. So we told her the story of the young man. Filled with grief, she said, "Show me the way to his grave."[11] So we showed her the way, and she visited the grave and said, "I must assist in mourning[12] for him, since he abandoned his people and his homeland for me." So she left the pilgrims and stayed with us.

"'The woman became fascinated with mentioning the young man and hearing about him. No night or day passed without her visiting his grave and weeping for him. Indeed, she went on lamenting, wailing, **[248]** and weeping until the news of her spread, and the people, pitying her, came to look at her in amazement. She went on in this fashion until she fell ill and died of love. Then the people came and said, "Let us bury her at his side." So they buried her beside the young man.'

"I could not believe the woman," Abū ʾl-Ḥusayn continued, "so I said, 'Show me her grave.' She showed me two graves, one next to the other. But I was not convinced until I asked the gravedigger. 'Whose are these two graves?' I inquired. 'These,' he said, 'are the graves of two lovers who fell in love with each other and died of love without ever having met.'" This is the purport of what he (the narrator) said, although his actual words may have been different.

The author of this book [said]: This is among the most amazing reports of this kind I have ever heard. Were not the narrator a reliable authority, I would have doubted him. But I have no doubts about the integrity of the one who gave the account.

Jarīr b. Isḥāq al-Rāfiʿī related the following: "Once I was sitting in a gathering at the house of a friend of mine in Raqqa. With us **[249]** was a young man who was in love with a singing girl. Now the singing girl,

---

[11] The Arabic imperative is masculine plural, not feminine plural.

[12] "assist in mourning": *musāʿada.* Cf. Lane, s.v. *s-ʿ-d.*

who was also with us in the gathering, began to sing these lines:

> The sign of the servility of love
> in lovers is their weeping,
> Especially when the lover
> finds no occasion for his plaint.

'Well done, by God, my lady!' exclaimed the young man, 'Do I have your permission to die?' 'Die,' she said. Whereupon he lowered his head and closed his eyes. We began to shake him, but we found him dead."

From Ibrāhīm al-Kilābī[13] it is related that he said: "I was sitting one day in Basra when a youth in the coarse clothing of a servant passed by me. He seemed anxious as though he were pursuing someone or being pursued. 'What is the matter?' I inquired. 'Are you from Basra?' he asked. 'Yes,' I replied. 'My master has made a vow,' he said, 'that if I bring him a man from Basra he will free me.' 'What does he want?' I asked. 'He is ill,' he answered, 'and I presume he will make you his executor.'

"So I went with him, and he took me into a spacious house with a garden inside. He went into the garden, **[250]** and I followed him. There beneath a tree I saw lying a man who was about to expire. I sat down beside his head and began to speak the name of God. The man started to look about to the right and to the left. Then he fell into such a deep swoon that I said, 'Let us prepare him for burial.' But as [we] were thinking of this, he opened his eyes and broke into verse:

> The man whose abode is far from his homeland,
> who weeps alone in his grief,
> In every revolution of time
> the days multiply his sorrow.

"Then he fainted again, and we thought he was dead. But suddenly a bird called from the trees, and he shuddered in a terrifying manner and again broke into verse:

> Our cares have been increased
> by a lone bird weeping on its branch.

---

13 The similar reports we have found make no mention of this person. One is related from al-Aṣmaᶜī (al-Khaṭīb al-Baghdādī, *Taʾrīkh Baghdād,* XII, pp. 132–33; same source in Mughulṭāy, *al-Wāḍiḥ al-mubīn,* p. 206), while another is related from a group of people of Basra, all of whom saw al-ᶜAbbās b. al-Aḥnaf die (al-Masᶜūdī, *Murūj,* VII, pp. 247–48). Immediately after the report in the *Murūj,* mention is made of the death of the jurist Abū Thawr Ibrāhīm b. Khālid al-Kalbī, whose name resembles that of the narrator here.

What has afflicted me has afflicted him, and he weeps.
Each of us weeps for his beloved.[14]

Then his soul departed, and I asked the youth, 'Who was this man?' 'This was al-ᶜAbbās b. al-Aḥnaf,' he replied."[15] **[251]**

ᶜIkrima related the following: "We went out together with Ibn ᶜAbbās on the last of the three days following the Day of Sacrifice, and we saw some servant boys carrying a young man. They came towards us and stood him in front of Ibn ᶜAbbās. 'Pray for his recovery,' they said. Ibn ᶜAbbās looked at the young man and observed that he had a comely face but a skeletal frame. 'What is the matter with you?' he asked him. To his question the young man replied:

We suffer such agony from the violence of the maladies of love
as would almost melt the soul of a compassionate man.
But the last trace of life in what you see before you
has been preserved, despite great suffering, by a sturdy will.

Then he uttered a single cry and died. Whereupon Ibn ᶜAbbās said, 'Have you ever seen a comelier face, a sturdier will, or a more eloquent tongue than his? [He] was killed by love. [For him] there is neither retaliation nor blood money.'"

[It is also related that] Hind [loved] Bishr before he loved her. Now Hind was a woman of the tribe of Juhayna, while Bishr **[252]** was from the tribe of the Banū ᶜAbd al-ᶜUzzā. Both of them were celebrated for their beauty. Hind concealed her passion until she could endure it no longer. Then she disclosed [what] she was suffering and began to send messages to Bishr in verse. But he rejected her, shunning sin. So she devised a ruse whereby the two of them would meet in a certain place. When she came forward to him and he saw her, he fell in love with her. After that he began to send her messages, but now she disdained him.

How all this ended was that Bishr, having fallen ill and being on the

---

[14] "beloved": *sakan,* either the person (persons) or place in which one finds ease. Both meanings fit the context.

[15] There is disagreement as to where the celebrated amatory poet al-ᶜAbbās b. al-Aḥnaf died, whether in Baghdad, Basra (as here), or the desert (Brockelmann, *GAL,* I, p. 73). Al-Masᶜūdī's version of the story (see n. 13) situates the events somewhere along the pilgrimage route, which makes the poet's request for a man from Basra, which was probably his birthplace, more understandable. While it remains uncertain where al-ᶜAbbās was born, his family belonged to the Arab clan of Ḥanīfa, which was from the district of Basra. Although they emigrated to Khurasan, al-ᶜAbbās's father seems to have returned to Basra. See *EI²,* I, pp. 9b–10b, s.v. "al-ᶜAbbās b. al-Aḥnaf."

point of death, wrote her these verses:

Hind, O splendor and beauty of this world,
    my soul be your ransom, you have settled love in my liver.
With you among them, it would not harm a people,
    were they not to see the light of the sun for eternity.
I pray that you will not seek blood revenge for me,
    O people of Ṭayba,[16] O people **[253]** of piety and rectitude.

She answered him saying:

The All-Merciful knows who was the first
    to sever and cut the bonds of our union.
You had no pity on me, Bishr, when you exposed me to shame
    before the Messenger of God. This is repayment of like for like.
Never again, after us, may two lovers dwell on earth,
    for the God of the Throne decrees with equity.

The reason for her saying this was that Bishr had earlier complained to the Messenger of God.

When Bishr read the poetry he fainted. Those who were with him said, "Let us hurry to Hind and speak to her. Perhaps she will have pity on him." So they went and spoke to her saying, "Spare this man out of fear of God, for we are afraid he will die." "May God give him death, not life!" she replied. At this they left her, saying, "Beyond any doubt **[254]** God will punish Hind for what she has done." Sitting down with Bishr, they told him her answer. Close to death, he spoke these lines:

O Lord, I have been wasted by love,
    and I have become, O Master of the Throne, wholly distraught.
I suffer with a soul ravished by love.
    My friends grumble at me, and my family is weary of me.
O Lord, I perish because of my love
    for Hind, but I pardon her for my murder.
Though she may have done me harm,
    I cannot bear that she be tormented on my account.

Then he uttered a cry and died.

His sister arranged a funeral for him and began to bewail him. Sud-

[16] Ṭayba: a name given in the *ḥadīth* to Medina. Cf. Wensinck, *Concordance,* and *Tāj al-ᶜarūs,* both s.v. "Ṭayba." Bishr is apparently asking the young Muslim community in Medina, to which he belonged, not to come into conflict over his death with Juhayna, Hind's tribe, with whom the Prophet had concluded a treaty after coming to the city. Cf. M. J. Kister, *EI²,* V, pp. 315b–317a, s.v. "Ḳuḍāᶜa."

denly Hind arrived, striking her face in lamentation and saying, "Poor Bishr, he has left his loved ones and his kin! Poor Bishr, **[255]** my liver is in pain for you and is dried up with grief! Poor Bishr, there is nothing in life for me after your death!" She continued to weep in this manner until he was buried and the people had dispersed. Then she threw herself on his grave and broke into verse:

By the House of God, the angle of the Black Stone, and al-Ṣafā,[17]
I rue my broken promises and my broken pledge.
Now that Bishr has passed on,
I too seem to lie beneath the dust in my grave.
I know I shall be carried towards him,
and perhaps I shall meet him in the Garden of Eternity.

Then she uttered a cry and died. After they had washed her and wrapped her in a shroud, they buried her at his side, may God have mercy on them both.

Hishām related the following: "I set out with my camel and came to water among a community of the tribe of Ṭayyiʾ. Now the people who dwelt in the place where the water was found were divided into two groups, and they were having a quarrel.[18] Among them was a young man of Ṭayyiʾ who was ill and a girl [who was talking] off to one side. The young man, hearing what she was saying, raised his voice and cried: **[256]**

Why is the lovely lady not generous?
Is it avarice, or is it aversion?
If you were ill, I would come running
to you. No threat could hold me back.

"The girl heard his voice and started to run towards him. But the womenfolk with her took hold of her. When thc young man saw her, he also ran towards her, but the men held him back too. Somehow the girl managed to make her way to him, and they met and embraced. Then they both fell to the ground dead. At this point an old man came out of one of the tents and stood over them crying, 'We belong to God, and to him we shall return!' Then he said, 'By God, though you were never together

---

[17] al-Ṣafā: one of the two hillocks in Mecca, the other being al-Marwa, between which the ceremony of "running" seven times (*al-saʿy*) takes place during the pilgrimage. (Most of the distance is in fact walked.) Al-Ṣafā and al-Marwa are now within the walls of the Holy Mosque. Cf. the mention of the two places in Koran 2:158.

[18] "and they were having a quarrel": *baynahum daʿwā* (MS: *daʿwa*).

while you were alive, I shall bring you together now that you are dead.' 'Who are these two, old man?' I asked him. 'This was my daughter,' he answered, 'and this was my brother's son.' Then he had them buried in a single grave."[19]

As for Majnūn of the Banū ᶜĀmir and Laylā his beloved, the story of their death has been narrated by a number of authorities, all of whom related it from one of their sheikhs,[20] who said: "I journeyed out into the lands of the Banū ᶜĀmir and met Majnūn. I tracked him until I found him, and then I collected some of his poetry. Now this was after **[257]** he had begun to live in the wilderness like a wild animal. I stayed three days with Majnūn's family and went out to him every day. I would remind him of Laylā and of the poems of Qays b. Dharīḥ, and when he came to his senses I would speak to him and learn some of his poetry. Then I left him.

"A matter that required my attention came up in Syria, and I set out on thc journey. But while I was in the land of Nejd, in the region beyond Taymāᵓ, I was caught in a violent rainstorm. During the storm I perceived a tent off at a distance. So I headed towards it. When I came up to it, I cleared my throat, and a woman spoke to me from within. 'You are most welcome,' she said, 'Be our guest.' So I entered the tent. Their camels and sheep, I noticed, were exceedingly numerous. Then I heard the woman say, 'Ask this guest where he has come from.' 'From Tihāma,' I said. To which she replied, 'Come in, good sir.'

"So I entered an apartment in the tent, and she let down a curtain between herself and me. Then she said, 'Tell me, sir, [in] which regions of Nejd have you traveled?' 'All of them,' I answered. 'Whom did you stay with?' she asked. 'With the Banū ᶜĀmir,' I said. 'With which branch of the **[258]** [Banū] ᶜĀmir?' she continued. 'With the Banū Jaᶜda,' I replied. When she heard this, she broke into tears. Then she said, 'Did you hear anything of a young man among them named Qays, who is known because of his madness as Majnūn?' 'Yes, by God,' I said, 'I heard of him, I went to him, and I watched him wander about in those deserts and steppes, living with the wild animals and never coming to his senses or understanding a thing, except when they mentioned Laylā to him. But whenever they mentioned her to him, he would weep and recite the po-

---

[19] Cf. al-Sarrāj, *Maṣāriᶜ*, I, pp. 110–111.

[20] In other sources identified as one of the sheikhs of the Banū Murra. Cf. al-Sarrāj, *Maṣāriᶜ*, I, p. 33; Abū ᵓl-Faraj al-Iṣfahānī, *Aghānī* (Bulaq), II, p. 13. Dāwūd al-Anṭākī (*Tazyīn al-aswāq*, I, p. 69) has Rabāḥ b. ᶜĀmir of the Banū ᵓl-Ḥarīsh, Laylā's tribe (cf. *Aghānī*, I, p. 183).

etry he had composed about her.'

"Then she raised the curtain that was between us, and I saw a woman as fair as an ostrich egg, thc like of whom my eye had never seen before. She wept so, by God, that I thought her heart had split in two. 'Woman,' I said, 'Fear God and take pity on yourself, for, by God, I said nothing so bad.' [But she would not calm down], nor would she be comforted, [and she remained a long while] in that state. Then she broke into verse:

> Would that I knew, amidst all these misfortunes,
> when Qays will saddle up and return.
> More precious than my life is the one who cannot manage his saddle,
> who, if God did not protect him, would perish. **[259]**

[Then she wept until she fell into a swoon.] When she recovered I said, 'Who are you, my lady?' 'I am the one who brought him ill fortune,'[21] she replied, 'the one who did not requite [him].'" The sheikh added: "By God, I had never seen anything like her grief for him.

"Then I went on to Syria. Once my business there was concluded, I decided to return. On the way back I passed by her again and informed her that I intended to meet Majnūn. She received me as her guest and gave me provisions for the way. Before leaving I asked, 'Do you have anything to convey to him?' 'What I have to convey to him,' she replied, 'no messenger can bear. Just give him my greetings.'

"So I traveled until I reached the lands of the Banū ᶜĀmir. When I inquired about Qays, they said, 'He is still in the same state.' I went off to look for him, and when I found him, I saw his nurse sitting with him and feeding him some food she had brought with her. When he saw me he ran away, and his nurse complained to me, 'By God, you have made him go hungry today.' So I went aside, and he came back to his place. Now when he had settled down, I approached him from behind and said, 'I am a messenger from Laylā.' He turned to me and exclaimed, **[260]** 'Alas, what are you saying? Have you seen Laylā?' 'Yes,' I answered. Thereupon he began to sob so violently that I thought his liver had split in two. Yet he did not shed a single tear. 'What did Laylā say to you,' he asked, 'and how is she?' 'She sends you her greetings,' I replied, 'and I have never seen anything like her grief for you.' After this I recited to him her poetry about him. He wept and then spoke these lines:

> My two friends, if death comes to me, seek
> retaliation from an idle woman with full flesh on her bones.

---

21 "the one who brought him ill fortune": *al-mashʾūma ᶜalayhi* (al-Sarrāj, *Maṣāriᶜ,* I, p. 34; Abū ʾl-Faraj al-Iṣfahānī, *Aghānī,* II, p. 14; Dāwūd al-Anṭākī, *Tazyīn al-aswāq,* I, p. 70) for *al-malūma ᶜalayhi* (MS), "the one to blame."

Do not take in my stead a beautiful but husbandless woman,
for husbandless women are not my equals.
But take in my stead a married woman, with her husband,
vile(?)[22] and ignoble, who ever puts off her creditor.

"Suddenly a gazelle appeared, and he leapt up in pursuit of her. I went off after him and looked for him all day long, but I could not find him. So I went back at the end of the day and told his father what had happened. He and Qays's brothers went out and searched for him for three days. At last they found him dead between some rocks in a ravine. They carried him back, wrapped him in a shroud, and buried him. Thereafter I copied down his poems from a young man with whom he had been close. **[261]**

"Then I decided to return to Syria. When I reached the place where Laylā was, I went to her. 'You are a welcome guest,' she said. I dismounted, and she asked me where I had come from? 'I am the rider,' I told her, 'who visited you on such and such a day and whom you charged to covey your greetings to Majnūn.' 'What has happened to Qays?' she asked. 'Qays is dead, by God,' I answered. At this she let out a cry, and with it her soul departed. I did not leave until they had washed her, wrapped her in a shroud, and, after I had offered prayers for her, buried her, may God have mercy on her."

Having come to the end of this chapter, we shall now turn to [the chapter on] those who killed themselves for love.

---

22 Text uncertain here and at the end of the preceding hemistich.

CHAPTER TWENTY-THREE
ON THOSE WHO KILLED THEMSELVES FOR LOVE

It is related from ᶜAlī b. Jabala that he said: "I went from Samarra to Baghdad with Muḥammad b. Isḥāq b. Ibrāhīm on his barge. He had his morning meal[1] and called for some date wine. Now this was one day after the Persian New Year's Day, and I said, 'O emir, the Tigris is at its highest, and with these waves **[262]** the way they are we are risking disaster.' But he paid no heed to my words and ordered a curtain to be hung in the middle of the vessel. Four slave-girls skilled in singing came out (but remained behind the curtain).[2] Muḥammad called for a pint for himself and another for me. Then he cried, 'O curtain, speak!' At this, one of the slave-girls began to sing to the accompaniment of her lute:

O abandonment, leave love alone! Let love
be sweet for lovers, O abandonment!
What can you want from those whose eyelids are covered
with sores, whose breasts are filled with burning coals,
On whose cheeks the fast flowing tears
seem pearls falling like drops of rain,
Who are struck down on the bridge of passion by their distress,
with whose lives and souls fate plays its games?

"When she was done, Muḥammad exclaimed to her, 'Well done!' and downed his drink, **[263]** as I did mine. Then he called for another for each of us. 'O curtain, speak!' he cried again, and another slave-girl, accompanying herself on a *ṭunbūr,*[3] began to sing:

Have pity on lovers!
I see no one to help them.
How often they are forsaken, reviled,
and beaten, yet they endure.

"'What do lovers do?' a slave-girl who was with her asked. Whereupon the girl who had just sung leapt towards the curtain, tore it apart, and appeared before us like the moon on the night it is full. 'This is what

[1] "had his morning meal": *taghaddā* (in later and modern usage "to have a midday meal").
[2] Cf. al-Masᶜūdī, *Murūj,* VII, p. 227.
[3] A stringed instrument resembling a mandolin.

they do,' she said, and threw herself into the Tigris. Now standing by Muḥammad b. Isḥāq's head was a young Greek slave who was chasing the flies from him. When he saw her and what she had done, he cried:

> It is you [who] have drowned me,
> along with God's decree, if only you knew.

Then he flung himself after her. Never have we seen a bitterer, more troubled, or more amazing day!"[4]

I discovered a report from a certain person of Quraysh who said: "Sulaymān b. ᶜAbd al-Malik[5] was one of the most jealous of all men. No one was ever allowed to see **[264]** even one of his servants or slave-boys, not to mention his slave-girls. Now once when he was holding a public audience, a petition came into his hand containing the following words: 'May God grant the Commander of the Faithful long life and make me his ransom. Should the Commander of the Faithful see fit to have his slave-girl so-and-so sing me two songs, he will do so.' Sulaymān said to his chamberlain, 'Take this petition, find out who presented it, and bring him to me.'

"The chamberlain took the petition and went out to ask after the one who had brought it. He found a young man in appearance like a silver wand, who said, 'It was I.' So he brought him in, and the young man greeted the caliph. Sulaymān returned his greeting and said, 'Woe to you. What moved you to write the like of this petition? Do you not know me?' 'O Commander of the Faithful,' the young man answered, 'your sound judgment and your kindness moved me to write what I wrote.' Sulaymān lowered his head and remained thus until the public had gone.

---

[4] Approximately this same story, together with a version of the following narrative is ascribed to al-Jāḥiẓ, who claims to have taken the barge journey to Baghdad with the military commander Muḥammad b. Ibrāhīm (the paternal uncle of Muḥammad b. Isḥāq b. Ibrāhīm named in this version) after he had been rejected by the caliph al-Mutawakkil as a tutor for one of his sons because of his ugliness. Al-Jāḥiẓ says that he told the story that follows about Sulaymān b. ᶜAbd al-Malik in order to cheer Muḥammad up after the suicide of his two slaves. (Al-Masᶜūdī, *Murūj,* VII, pp. 222–24; Ibn Dāwūd, *Kitāb al-zahra,* pp. 352–54; al-Washshāᵓ, *al-Muwashshā,* pp. 62–64; cf. al-Sarrāj, *Maṣāriᶜ,* I, pp. 113–14, where it is the judge ᶜAbd al-Raḥmān b. Isḥāq who tells the story.) Al-Masᶜūdī (pp. 224–27), Ibn Dāwūd, and al-Washshāᵓ group the second story with the first. The second story is told of Yazīd b. ᶜAbd al-Malik in the *Murūj,* but with a final note that it is also said that the story is about Sulaymān b. ᶜAbd al-Malik, not Yazīd.

[5] Seventh Umayyad caliph (96/715–99/717).

Then he looked up at a servant who was before him and said, 'Bring me so-and-so, with her lute.' Now she was **[265]** one of his concubines.

"In almost no time she swayed in, looking like the moon on the night it is full. She greeted Sulaymān, and he returned her greeting and ordered her to sit down. Then Sulaymān said to the young man, 'Sit down,' and told him, 'Choose the first of your two songs.' It was this song by al-ᶜArjī that he chose:

The lightning flashed out of Nejd and I said to it,
O lightning, I cannot be concerned with you.
A raging, furious enemy spares you the trouble of striking me,
who has in his hand [a sword sparkling (?)] like bubbles [of water].[6]

"When the slave-girl had finished singing, the young man let out such a cry that his soul almost departed with it. He rent his robe so that it became like an open-fronted tunic, and then he fainted. When he came to his senses, Sulaymān said to him, 'Ask for what you wish.' Now he said this hoping that he would ask him for the slave-girl, and intending to give her to him. But the young man replied, 'O Commander of the Faithful, have them bring me a pint of date wine.' Sulaymān had it brought to him and said, 'Choose the second song.' So he chose these verses by someone:[7]

Tomorrow many will weep for us and for you,
and my abode will be yet farther from yours.
If you wish, I will declare all women forbidden to me but you,
and if you wish, I will drink neither sweet water nor saliva.[8] **[266]**

"On hearing these verses, the young man let out another cry. Then he ascended to the top of a dome belonging to Sulaymān that was forty-five cubits high, and, throwing himself down, he landed on his head and was killed. At this Sulaymān exclaimed, '"Surely we belong to God, and to him we shall return!"[9] I have never seen a day like today. Tell me, what

---

[6] The additions are conjectures for a lacuna in the manuscript. Al-Masᶜūdī (*Murūj,* VII, p. 226) has "who has a sword like a lance drawn in his hand." It would be possible to take from this variant the word *maslūlū* (drawn) for our conjecture *maṣqūlū* (sparkling), but it is less suited to the fragment of the hemistich in our manuscript.

[7] These verses, or at least the second, are apparently also by al-ᶜArjī. See *Lisān,* s.v. *b-r-d,* and Lane, s.v. *bard.*

[8] "saliva": *bard,* the meaning being, "I will not taste saliva from any lips but yours." Possibly also, "sleep." (See Lane, s.v. *bard,* where this hemistich is cited.) Possibly again, "cool water" (*Qāmūs,* s.v.).

[9] Echoing Koran 2:156.

shall I do with the girl?' 'Decisions are made by the Commander of the Faithful,' someone replied. Whereupon Sulaymān said, 'By God, I did not show [her] to him with the intention that she should return to my property. Servant boy, take this girl by the hand and deliver her and everything she possesses to the young man's house. And if he does not have a house, then sell her and give the price as alms, with the reward for his soul.'

"So the youth led the girl away by the hand. But when they reached the courtyard of the palace, they came upon a basin thirty cubits deep[10] that had been dug to collect rain water. The slave-girl stood on the edge of it and threw herself in, thus ending her days. Sulaymān was amazed at what she had done and ordered that the two of them be buried in his presence."

We have come to the end of what we intended to say about natural lovers who killed themselves for love. As for **[267]** divine lovers, God has preserved them from such things as are related in these stories. They have been raised from this rank to a level where they sense nothing but their Beloved, and where they seek nothing from him save to be near him. Their love is not fatal. It gives life. The difference between divine lovers and natural lovers is that the latter have stopped at the level of means, and that their love is the result of the love of one nature for another. They do not find contentment in any state, and their love brings them to physical death.

But divine lovers have risen to the world of the spirit and of absolute survival. Their love is such that some of them have been lifted up into heaven and some of them remain alive. Of the latter, some remain alive in their graves, while others are translated from place to place without ever passing away. There is evidence and proof to support all that I have said, and we shall set it forth in the next chapter on the death of divine lovers.

[10] "deep": *ṭūluhā*.

CHAPTER TWENTY-FOUR
ON THE DEATH OF DIVINE LOVERS

Divine lovers are divided into **[268]** five groups. Those in the first group were so vanquished by love that it made them like itself and translated them to its own abode alive, so that they became spiritual beings together with the angels. Those in the second group were given authority to judge over this terrestrial abode and over all persons and things in it. They enjoined good and forbade evil, and they declared things to be lawful or unlawful. Then, when what it had been willed they should do was accomplished, they asked God to take them back to their original places. Those in the third group were translated from place to place and from life to life. They are alive in their tombs, and at times they can be found there, while at others they cannot. Those in the fourth group, after having remained long on earth, asked their Beloved for release from this abode and escape from this prison so as to be joined with him. Those in the fifth group, having passed continually through veil after veil, at length reached the last veil, which was the veil of their selves. When they cast off this veil, the branch was rejoined to the trunk, and that which had emerged out of it **[269]** returned to it. The part was rejoined to the whole, and means were abolished. These, then, are the five groups.

So that it will be easier to remember, we may divide those who belong to these groups into three classes: two of prophets and one of saints (*awliyāʾ*). None of them passed away, however, before choosing to die.

[Section One.]

The first class includes Idrīs, al-Khaḍir, Elijah, and Jesus. In the case of these prophets and those like them, their demise consisted in their being vanquished by the attribute of love to the degree that it made of them spiritual beings like itself. Thus they soared up with the angels and became both celestial and terrestrial, angelic and human.

Idrīs (Enoch),[1] it has been said, was sent to all the people of the earth

---

[1] The usual identification of Idrīs with Enoch is followed by al-Daylamī. Less often Idrīs is identified with Elijah or al-Khaḍir. Among suggestions for the derivation of the name are those of Casanova (Esdras, the Greek form of Ezra), of Nöldeke (Andreas, referring to the apostle Andrew), and of Hartmann (Andreas, referring to the cook of Alexander the Great who became immortal according to the Alexander Romance). See G. Vajda, *EI²,* III, pp. 1030a–31b, s.v. "Idrīs." Al-Daylamī derives the name from the Arabic verb *darasa* (to

in his time[2] and gathered for them all the knowledge of those before him and added to it thirty books.[3] In the Pentateuch it is written that God lifted up Idrīs after three hundred and sixty-five years.[4] He was called Idrīs because of the great number **[270]** of God's books he used to study (*yadrus*). Also, he was the first [man to write] with a pen[5] and the first to sew clothes and to wear them. Before his time men used to wear skins. It is written in the Pentateuch[6] that Enoch was the best of God's servants, and so God lifted him up to himself.[7]

---

study).

[2] According to Muslim belief, prophets before Muḥammad were sent to particular peoples. The inclusion of the words "in his time" here may be meant to distinguish Enoch's particular charge from the universal mission of Muḥammad.

[3] Al-Nadīm (*Fihrist,* trans. Dodge, I, p. 42) gives the same number. In the first century B.C. the Essene copyists of Qumrān put together a Pentateuch of Enoch consisting of the Astronomical Book, the Book of Watchers, the Book of Giants (replaced during the Christian era by the Book of Parables), the Book of Dreams, and the Epistle of Enoch. The Christian reworking has largely survived in an Ethiopic version, which has been edited and translated into English by R. H. Charles (the Book of Enoch). In later Enochic writings the number of the sage's books is given variously as three hundred and sixty-six, three hundred and sixty, and sixty-seven. In the Book of the Secrets of Enoch 68, it is said that Enoch, after handing over his books to his sons, remained another thirty days on earth. See J. T. Milik, ed., *The Books of Enoch,* pp. 1, 76, 111, 124, and R. H. Charles, ed., *The Apocrypha and Pseudepigrapha of the Old Testament in English,* II, pp. 163–277, 469.

[4] Genesis 5:23–24. Cf. Koran 19:56–57, "And mention in the Book Idris; he was a true man, a prophet. We raised him up to a high place."

[5] On Enoch's being the first man to write, cf. the Book of the Secrets of Enoch 33 and 35 (in R. H. Charles, *Apocrypha and Pseudepigrapha,* II, pp. 451–53). The addition in our text here is from Vadet.

[6] We assume that al-Daylamī is thinking here specifically of the books revealed to Moses, although the name *al-Tawrāh* may also refer, as likewise at times in Jewish practice, to the whole of the Jewish scriptures. See al-Tahānawī, *Kashshāf iṣṭilāḥāt al-funūn,* II, p. 1524, s.v. *al-Tawrāh,* and J. Horovitz, *EI¹*, VIII, pp. 706a–707b, s.v. "Tawrāt."

[7] Al-Daylamī's statement reflects a Jewish tradition rooted in the Targums. Genesis 5:24 says, "And Enoch walked with God: and he was not; for God took him." But while the Targum Onkelos uses the same root (*h-l-k*) for "walked" as the Hebrew (Alexander Sperber, *The Pentateuch according to Targum Onkelos,* p. 8), the Targum Neofiti I and Pseudo-Jonathan render the word by an Aramaic verb meaning "to serve" (cf. Roger Le Déaut, *Targum du Pentateuque,* I, pp. 110–111). John Bowker (*The Targums and Rabbinic Literature,* p. 142, n. b) comments that this verb may have been chosen in order to avoid "a possibly

Al-Khaḍir's name was Jeremiah son of Ḥilqīyā.[8] He was a prophet, it is said, who was sent to the Children of Israel. However there is some dispute among the learned as to whether he was a prophet or a saint.[9] It is said[10] that when the Israelites' sins had multiplied, God revealed to him: "I shall destroy the Children of Israel."[11] Whereupon al-Khaḍir wept, put dust on his head, and prayed to God. Then God revealed to him: "By my might, I shall not destroy them until the order comes from you." Al-Khaḍir rejoiced at this and informed the king of the Children of Israel, whose name was Josiah son of Amūṣ.[12] But they continued to increase in evil.

Then God sent to al-Khaḍir an angel in the form of a man of Israel. "O Prophet of God," the angel said, "I wish to consult you in the matter of

---

anthropomorphic expression." Origen's Septuagint also renders the Hebrew verb interpretively, having εὐηρέστησε, "pleased," and seems to be the text on which the author of Hebrews relied in writing of Enoch that "before his translation he had this testimony, that he pleased God" (Hebrews 11:5). Communication from Richard Holton Pierce.

[8] Cf. Jeremiah 1:1. Following the celebrated authority on Jewish and Christian traditions Wahb b. Munabbih (d. 110/728–29 or 114/732–33), Jeremiah, among other Old Testament figures, is connected by Muslim commentators, with the story in Koran 2:259 of a man who passed by a ruined city and, wondering how God could ever restore it, was caused by God to die for a hundred years and then raised up again as a sign that God could bring the dead back to life (cf., e.g., al-Ṭabarī, *Tafsīr* [Maᶜārif], V, pp. 447–54). A similar story is associated with the Ethiopian Ebed-melech mentioned in Jeremiah 39:16–18. There are Jewish traditions that place Ebed-melech among the immortals and Islamic traditions that hold al-Khaḍir to be among them. These facts, it has been suggested, lie behind the belief that Jeremiah is immortal and his identification by Wahb b. Munabbih with al-Khaḍir. See A. J. Wensinck, *The Shorter Encyclopaedia of Islam*, pp. 172b–73a, and G. Vajda, *EI²*, IV, p. 79a–b, both s.v. "Irmiyā."

[9] Jeremiah is not among the prophets mentioned in the Koran, nor is al-Khaḍir. The commentators, however, identify both with Koranic figures. On Jeremiah, see the preceding note. Al-Khaḍir, according to most commentaries, is to be identified with the servant of God whom Moses and his servant encounter in Koran 18:65–82. See A. J. Wensinck, *EI²*, IV, pp. 902b–905b, s.v. "al-Khaḍir (al-Khiḍr)."

[10] Reading *wa-qīla* for MS *qāla,* "[The narrator] said."

[11] Cf. al-Ṭabarī, *Taʾrīkh,* I, p. 550.

[12] We have not made the name of Josiah's father conform to the biblical name (Amon), despite the easy confusion of the letters *ṣād* and *nūn,* because of its occurrence elsewhere with *ṣād.* Cf. al-Ṭabarī, *Taʾrīkh,* I, p. 366.

my family and my kin. **[271]** I have kept close the ties of kinship. I have done good to them and have been generous to them. But this only makes their wickedness increase." "Do good to them, keep close the ties that God has commanded us to keep close, and rejoice at the news of a good event," al-Khaḍir replied. The angel went off and left [him] for some days. Then he came back and repeated what he had said before. Al-Khaḍir answered him as he had the first time.

Thereafter Nebuchadnezzar[13] besieged Jerusalem, and the king[14] came to al-Khaḍir and said, "O Prophet of God, where is that which you promised to us?" "I trust in my Lord," al-Khaḍir answered. Then the angel who had approached him before came to him while he was up on the walls of Jerusalem looking at the encamped army, laughing and joyously awaiting victory. The angel said to him the same words he had said twice before, and al-Khaḍir replied, "Has not the time come for them to abandon their past ways?" "On the contrary, their wickedness has increased," the angel said, "and I ask of you in God's name nothing but that you invoke God against them." At this al-Khaḍir said, "O King of Heaven and Earth, if they are following a course that is good and right, spare them, but if they are following a course that angers thee and are doing deeds that displease thee, destroy them." **[272]** As these words issued from Jeremiah's[15] mouth, God sent down on Jerusalem a thunderbolt from heaven, and the temple burst into flames and nine of the city's gates fell.

When Jeremiah saw this he cried out, and rending his garments and spreading dust on his head, he exclaimed, "O King of Heaven, where is thy promise?" Whereupon a voice called to him, saying, "O Jeremiah, this thing only befell them by your decision." At this Jeremiah understood that the man who had sought his opinion had been a messenger from God. Then he flew away to live with the wild animals, and God prolonged his life. It is he who is sometimes seen in the desert. Following this, Nebuchadnezzar entered Jerusalem.[16]

It is said that al-Khaḍir was of Persian blood, but it is also said that he was an Israelite, and that Elijah was likewise an Israelite and that the two of them used to meet once each year. Al-Khaḍir is also said to have been

---

13 See G. Vajda, *EI*², I, pp. 1297b–98a, s.v. "Bukht-Naṣ(ṣ)ar."

14 The king was no longer Josiah by the biblical accounts. Cf., e.g., II Chronicles 36:1–20.

15 This passage is condensed from al-Ṭabarī, *Taʾrīkh,* I, pp. 550–53, or a similar source. Al-Ṭabarī, for the most part, uses the name Jeremiah (Irmiyā) when mentioning the prophet. Our text substitutes al-Khaḍir when condensing.

16 Al-Ṭabarī (ibid., pp. 553ff.) continues with the history of Nebuchadnezzar.

of royal blood. This has been mentioned by Ibn Jarīr (al-Ṭabarī) in his history, [where he speaks] of the different opinions people hold about him.[17]

Elijah the son of Yāsīn belonged to a people who were excessive in their disobedience. Elijah came to them with signs of prophecy,[18] but these did not avail them. **[273]** So he prayed to his Lord to take him to himself and to deliver him from them. But a voice said to him, "Wait for such and such a day, and then go out to such and such a place. When something comes to you, mount it and do not fear it." So Elijah set out in the company of Elisha,[19] and when he had reached the appointed place, a horse of fire came up and stood before him. Elijah leapt onto it, and the two of them soared away. Elisha called out after him, "Elijah, what do you command me to do?" Elijah prayed for him, and God caused Elisha to remain after him and strengthened him with a like spirit.[20] But God clothed Elijah with feathers, clad him with light, and deprived him of pleasure in eating and drinking. Thus Elijah joined the angels and became both human and angelic, terrestrial and celestial.[21]

The Messiah, Jesus the son of Mary, upon whom be peace, was pursued by the Jews, and one of his companions directed them to him and took for his services thirty pieces of silver.[22] But when they came, they were led to mistake Simon, one of the disciples, for him,[23] and it was he whom they carried off and crucified. He remained (on the cross) for seven days. Then, after the seven days had passed, Jesus' mother Mary,

---

[17] Cf. ibid., pp. 365–76, esp. p. 365. Al-Ṭabarī's report concerning al-Khaḍir's meetings with Elijah mentions only that al-Khaḍir was of Persian blood.

[18] "signs of prophecy": *āyāt.* The Arabic word, which is used to denote the verses of the Koran, may also include the meaning "prophecies."

[19] Al-Ṭabarī (*Taʾrīkh,* I, p. 463) adds "the son of Akhṭūb."

[20] This sentence is missing in the report as related in al-Ṭabarī's *Taʾrīkh* (I, p. 463). Cf. II Kings 2:9: "And Elisha said [to Elijah], I pray thee, let a double portion of thy spirit be upon me," and 2:15: "And when the sons of the prophets which were to view at Jericho saw him [Elisha, after Elijah had been taken up unto heaven], they said, The spirit of Elijah doth rest on Elisha." The "spirit" of prophecy in Islam is the angel of revelation Gabriel, who at various places in the Koran is called "spirit" or "holy spirit." Cf., e.g., Koran 26:192–93; 2:87; 5:110.

[21] Cf. al-Ṭabarī, *Taʾrīkh,* I, pp. 461–64, and the story in II Kings 2:1–13.

[22] This story is also in al-Ṭabarī (*Taʾrīkh,* I, pp. 601–2).

[23] Cf. Koran 4:157 on the crucifixion of Jesus: "Yet they did not slay him, neither crucified him, only a likeness of that was shown to them." Also Matthew 27:32, Mark 15:21, and Luke 23:26, on Simon of Cyrene.

upon whom be peace, **[274]** and a woman he had cured of madness[24] came and sat beneath the cross and wept for him. Suddenly Jesus came up to them and said, "For whom are you weeping?" "For you," they replied. To this he said, "God lifted me up to himself, and nothing but good has befallen me." Then he commanded the disciples [through them][25] to meet him in a certain place, and when they met him, he spoke to them and committed his work to their charge.[26]

Wahb [b. Munabbih] said: "God caused Jesus to pass away for three hours of the day and then lifted him up."[27] The Christians claim that God caused him to pass away for seven hours and then brought him back to life and said to him, "Go down to Mary [Magdalene],[28] for she has wept for you as no one has ever wept for any man." Then he sent him down to her. Moreover, God deprived him of pleasure in eating and drinking, and he soared up with the angels; and he clothed him with feathers and clad him with light, so that he became both human and angelic, celestial and terrestrial.[29]

These men did not wish to die, so God spared them until the end of time. He alone knows what he will do with them thereafter.

Section Two.

The second class was given authority to judge over the [affairs] of men and over their souls. They **[275]** declared things to be lawful or unlawful, and they exhorted men and restrained them. They dwelt among men as long as they deemed their presence among them to be of benefit to them. But when God's will and their charge were accomplished, they asked God to take them back to their original places, and he caused them to pass away and lifted them up to himself. Thereafter they might be seen in their graves, or in the heavens, or in Paradise. Among them are Abraham the Friend of God, Moses, with whom God spoke,[30] Aaron, and Muḥammad the Beloved of God, together with those like them and those near them in rank, may God's blessings be upon them.

When God willed to make Abraham, upon whom be peace, wish to

---

[24] Mary Magdalene. Cf. Mark 16:9.

[25] Cf. al-Ṭabarī, *Taʾrīkh,* I, p. 602.

[26] The biblical parallels are found in Matthew 28:1–20, Mark 16:1–19, and John 20:1–23.

[27] The saying attributed to Wahb ends here. Cf. al-Ṭabarī, *Taʾrīkh,* I, p. 602.

[28] Addition from al-Ṭabarī (ibid.).

[29] This passage is more complete in al-Ṭabarī (ibid., pp. 602–3).

[30] Cf. Koran 4:164: "And unto Moses God spoke directly," and 7:143; also D. B. Macdonald in *EI¹,* IV, p. 699a, s.v. "Kalīm Allāh."

die, an old man came to pay the prophet a visit. Abraham, who never ate except with a guest, sat and ate with him. Now before the old man could manage to put any morsel into his mouth, he would first stick it in his eye or up his nose. "How old are you, old man?" Abraham asked. The old man told him, and as it happened, he was only one year older than Abraham. Abraham said to himself, "If I live yet another year, I will become **[276]** like this. O God, take me to thyself." Then he died.[31]

Nufayl related the following: "When God willed to take the spirit of Abraham, the angel of death came down to him and said, 'Peace be upon you, Abraham.' 'And upon you be peace, O Angel of Death,' he replied, 'Have you come only to summon me or to announce my death?' 'To announce your death,' the angel said, 'so obey.' 'Have you ever seen a friend who causes his friend to die?' Abraham asked." Nufayl continued: "Then the angel of death went away and stood before God and said, 'Didst thou hear, my God, what thy friend said?' But God replied, 'O Angel of Death, go back down to him and say, "Have you ever seen a friend who loathes to meet his friend?"' So the angel went back down to him, and Abraham said, 'Now take my spirit.'"

Of Aaron, who died before the death of Moses, the following is said: "God gave a revelation to Moses, saying: 'I am about to cause Aaron to pass away, so take him to such and such a mountain.' So Moses took Aaron to the place, and he found there trees such as he had never seen before. A house had been built there too, and in it was a bedstead covered with bedding that gave off a pleasing fragrance. **[277]** Now when Aaron saw this, he was delighted and said, 'Moses, I wish to sleep on this bed.' 'Sleep on it,' Moses answered. 'I am afraid the owner of the house may come and be angry with me,' said Aaron. 'I shall protect you from him, so sleep,' Moses replied. But Aaron said, 'Moses, you sleep with me. Then if the owner of the house comes he will be angry with both of us.' When they had both[32] fallen asleep, death clutched Aaron, and he cried, 'My brother, you have betrayed me!' Then he was taken, and the house, the bed, and the trees were all lifted up into the heavens."[33]

As for Moses, he was walking together with his servant[34] Joshua when suddenly a black wind came up. Joshua, when he saw it, thought the Resurrection had come and he clung to Moses. "The Resurrection is at

---

[31] The old man is identified in al-Ṭabarī's narrative as the angel of death (*Taʾrīkh,* I, p. 312).

[32] Cf. ibid., p. 432.

[33] This and the following narratives are in al-Ṭabarī (ibid., pp. 432–33).

[34] Cf. Koran 18:60, 62.

hand," he cried, "and I will cling to the one with whom God spoke." But Moses was snatched away from under his garment, and Joshua was left holding it [in his hand]. Now when Joshua returned with the garment, the Israelites seized him[35] and said, "You have murdered the Prophet of God," and they desired to kill him. But he asked for a delay of three days, which he spent in prayer and humble supplication. Then every man of Israel **[278]** was visited in his sleep and informed that Joshua had not killed Moses, and they were told, "We have lifted him up to ourself."

It is said that Moses was loath to die and that God willed to endear death to him. Therefore the revelation was cut off for a year and six months, and Moses said, "O my God, I can endure no longer. Take me to thyself!" It is also said that the prophethood was transferred to Joshua and that Moses, being in anguish because of this, asked God to grant him death. Likewise it is said that Moses used to live in a simple shelter and drink from a hollowed-out stone in humility before God. One day he left his shelter and passed by a band of angels who were digging a grave of a more delightful greenness and freshness than anything he had ever seen. "O angels of God," he asked them, "for whom are you digging this?" "For a servant who is dear to his Lord," they replied. "This servant must have great standing with God," he exclaimed. Whereupon the angels said to him, "O Chosen One of God, would you like this grave to be yours?" "I would," he answered. "Go down and lie in it," they said, "and turn your face towards God Most High." When he did this, **[279]** he was taken. Then the angels filled in the grave over him. The Messenger of God said: "I passed by Moses' grave and heard him reciting the Torah from the tomb. Then, when I was transported on my Night Journey, I saw him in the fourth heaven."[36]

As for Muḥammad, may God bless him and grant him peace, God revealed these words to him: "He who imposed the Recitation upon thee shall surely restore thee to a place of homing" (28:85). Ibn ᶜAbbās said

---

[35] Or possibly: "took it."

[36] During his Ascension the Prophet is reported to have met one of the earlier messengers of God in each of the seven heavens. Usually he meets Moses in the seventh. Cf. B. Schrieke/J. Horovitz in *EI²,* VII, p. 99b, s.v. "Miᶜrādj." "Fourth" (*al-rābiᶜa*), clear in our manuscript, is graphically and phonologically close to "seventh" (*al-sābiᶜa*) in Arabic. Moses is an example of those who may be seen at times in their graves and at times in the heavens (see MS, p. 275). Cf. the narrative of Moses' death in al-Ṭabarī (*Taʾrīkh,* I, pp. 433–34). On the dual tradition of Moses' having suffered a natural death and his having been assumed into heaven, see R. H. Charles, introduction to the Assumption of Moses, in his *Apocrypha and Pseudepigrapha* (II, pp. 408–9, and p. 408, nn. 1, 2).

that "a place of homing" means Paradise. It has likewise been said that it means Mecca. Ibn ᶜAbbās also said: "The meaning is a secret known only to God and his Messenger." This latter statement from Ibn ᶜAbbās pertains to the real meaning, while his former statement pertains to the exoteric meaning. The exoteric meaning is known to men, but the esoteric meaning is known only to God and to "those firmly rooted in knowledge."[37]

On the matter of the Prophet's having chosen (death), Jābir (b. ᶜAbd Allāh al-Anṣārī) related that he said: "God gave a certain man the choice between living in this world, eating whatever he liked, and meeting his Lord. This man chose to meet his Lord." Hearing this, Abū Bakr, may God be pleased with him, wept and said, "May we ransom you **[280]** with our fathers and ourselves."[38] In another tradition (the narrator) said: "Next to him (Abū Bakr) was a man who said, 'What is it that makes an old man like you weep at God's having given a man a choice and the man's having chosen to meet him?' 'Alas,' replied Abū Bakr, may God be pleased with him, 'the man in question is the Messenger of God.'"[39]

ᶜĀʾisha related the following: "I used to hear that no prophet died before he was given the choice between this world and the next. Then I heard the Messenger of God in his (last) illness, when a hoarseness had come into his voice, say, 'With those whom God has blessed, prophets, just men, martyrs, the righteous; good companions they!' (Koran 4:69), and I thought he had been given the choice between this world and the next." ᶜĀʾisha, may God be pleased with her, also said: "The Messenger of God fainted while his head was on my lap. So I began to stroke his head and to pray for his recovery. But when he regained consciousness he said: 'Not thus. Rather I ask him for the lofty and highest.'" In another version the words are "the highest company."[40] And the Messenger

---

[37] An allusion to Koran 3:7 and 4:162. Cf. in connection with the passage in our text here the author's remarks on the branch being rejoined to the trunk after the casting off of the veil of the self (MS, pp. 268–69).

[38] The same tradition is related above (MS, pp. 200–201).

[39] Cf. the version of this report in *Ṣaḥīḥ Muslim, Faḍāʾil al-ṣaḥāba* (XV, pp. 149–51; trans. ᶜAbdul Ḥamīd Ṣiddīqī, IV, p. 1274, *ḥadīth* 5869) and al-Ṭabarī, *Taʾrīkh,* III, p. 191. See also Zaghlūl, *Mawsūᶜat aṭrāf al-ḥadīth,* III, p. 347.

[40] The second version is closer to that related above (MS, p. 200). The first variant has *al-rafīᶜ al-aᶜlā* and the second *al-rafīq al-aᶜlā.* Cf. the report of the Prophet's death here with the traditions in *Ṣaḥīḥ Muslim, Faḍāʾil al-ṣaḥāba* (XV, pp. 208–9; trans. ᶜAbdul Ḥamīd Ṣiddīqī, IV, pp. 1301–2, *ḥadīths* 5985–90) and al-Ṭabarī, *Taʾrīkh,* III, pp. 196, 199. See also the note in our edition and Zaghlūl, *Mawsūᶜat aṭrāf al-ḥadīth,* VII, p. 40.

of God said: "I am too precious in God's sight for **[281]** him to leave me in my grave more than three days."[41] We have given the explanation of this tradition [in] our book entitled *The Secrets of Knowledge.*[42]

Section Three.

Let us now consider the saints, among whom we shall first cite ᶜUmar b. al-Khaṭṭāb, may God be pleased with him. Saᶜīd b. al-Musayyab related the following: "ᶜUmar b. al-Khaṭṭāb removed[43] from Minā and halted in al-Abṭaḥ, where he made a pile of sand and pebbles and spread the edge of his garment over it. Then he lay down on his back and, raising his hands towards the sky, said, 'O my God, my age is advanced, my strength has waned, and my flock has scattered.[44] So take me to thyself, before I become neglectful and flag in my duty.' Now before the month of Dhū ᵓl-Ḥijja had come to an end, [Abū Luᵓluᵓa][45] stabbed him and he died."

ᶜUthmān, may God be pleased with him, beheld the Messenger of God in his sleep. "Break your fast with us," the Prophet said to him. The morning following that same night ᶜUthmān was buried.[46] From Abū Umāma the following is related: "On the night before his murder the caliph ᶜUthmān, may God be pleased with him, said: 'I saw the Messenger of God, may God bless him, last night **[282]** in this small window. "ᶜUthmān!" he said, "Here am I, O Messenger of God," I answered.

---

41 "more than three days": *fawqa thalāth.* The first word is incomplete in the MS and may be read *qadra thalāth*, "as much as three days." Cf. al-Suyūṭī, *al-Ḥāwī lil-fatāwī,* II, p. 264: "Imām al-Ḥaramayn in the *Nihāya* and al-Rāfiᶜī in his commentary (*al-Sharḥ*) said that it is related from the Prophet that he said: 'I am too precious in my Lord's sight for him to leave in me in my grave after (*baᶜd*) three days.' Imām al-Ḥaramayn added that another version has 'more than two days.' Abū ᵓl-Ḥasan [ᶜAlī b. ᶜUbayd Allāh] b. al-Zāghūnī al-Ḥanbalī cites in one of his books a *ḥadīth* saying, 'God does not leave a prophet in his grave more than half a day.'" Ibn al-Zāghūnī died in 527/1131–32. See al-Dhahabī, *al-ᶜIbar fī khabar man ghabar,* II, p. 252, and *Tāj al-ᶜarūs,* IX, p. 226, s.v. al-Zāghūnī.

42 *Asrār al-maᶜārif.* Not in Sezgin.

43 "removed": *nafara.* The verb is used especially of removing from Minā with the pilgrims in the month of Dhū ᵓl-Ḥijja. Cf. Lane, s.v.

44 "my flock has scattered": *intasharat raᶜīyatī,* reading with Abū Nuᶜaym, *Ḥilya,* I, p. 54. MS and Vadet have *intasharat raghbatī,* "my will [to live] has dissolved (?)".

45 Addition from Vadet.

46 "was buried": *qubira;* perhaps, "was killed" (*qutila*). Cf. the following report on ᶜUthmān's death from Abū Umāma.

"Have they besieged you?" he asked. "Yes, O Messenger of God," I said. "Have they deprived you of food?" he asked. "Yes, O Messenger of God," I said. "Have they made you thirst?" he asked. "Yes, O Messenger of God," I said. "ᶜUthmān," he said to me, "if you wish, I shall pray to God to make you victorious over them, but if you wish, you may break your fast with us." "Then let me break my fast with you," I replied.' ᶜUthmān was killed the next morning."

As for ᶜAlī b. Abī Ṭālib, his son al-Ḥasan, upon whom be peace, said: "ᶜAlī said: 'The Messenger of God, [may God bless] him and his family [and give them peace], appeared to me this night in my sleep, and I said to him, "O Messenger of God, what deviation and contention I have encountered from your community!" "Invoke God against them," he replied. So I said, "O my God, give me in their stead one better for me than them, and give them in my stead one worse for them than me."' Then he went out, and the man struck him down, may God bless him."[47] It is also related [that] on the day of the Battle of Ṣiffīn there occurred an uproar and ᶜAlī b. Abī Ṭālib went out and asked what the matter was. "Muᶜāwiya **[283]** is dead," they replied. But ᶜAlī said, "Muᶜāwiya will not die before he seizes power."

From Shaddād b. Aws it is reported that al-Nuᶜmān b. Qawqal, on the day of the Battle of Uḥud, said, "I adjure thee to let me be killed and enter Paradise," and he was killed. On this the Messenger of God said: "Al-Nuᶜmān adjured God, and God answered him. Indeed, I have seen him walking on the greenery of Paradise, with no trace of his lameness."[48] The author of this book said: Consider how the Messenger of God was together with them in battle, while at the same time he was in Paradise, where he beheld al-Nuᶜmān and the kindness God had bestowed on him. This must be accepted on faith, except by those to whom God has given direct heavenly knowledge, which allows them to dispense with mere assent. Let this be understood.

---

[47] This benediction, usually reserved for prophets, may possibly be a corruption of *wa-ṣallā ʾl-Ḥasanu ᶜalayhi,* "and al-Ḥasan prayed over him." Cf. Ibn Saᶜd, *Ṭabaqāt* (Beirut), III, p. 38. But it is consistent with the benedictions after the name of ᶜAlī elsewhere in al-Daylamī's text. See chapter five, n. 53.

[48] Cf. Ibn Ḥajar, *Iṣāba,* VI, p. 451; also the stories of the deaths of al-Nuᶜmān b. Mālik al-Anṣārī in al-Ṭabarī, *Taʾrīkh,* II, p. 503, and ᶜAbd Allāh b. Jaḥsh in al-Nabhānī, *Jāmiᶜ karāmāt al-awliyāʾ,* I, p. 148. For the paradigmatic form of the Prophet's response, see, e.g., *Sunan Abī Dāwūd, Diyāt* (trans. Ahmad Hasan, III, p. 1289): "Among Allah's servants there are those who, if they adjured Allah, He (Allah) would consent to it." See also the other sources mentioned in Wensinck, *Concordance,* I, p. 159b, s.v. *abarra.*

From Sufyān b. ᶜUyayna it is related that he said: "I halted at the halting place (of the pilgrims on ᶜArafāt) seventy times, and each time I said, 'O my God, O Lord, do not let this be my last time.' But in the seventieth year I was ashamed to ask this of my Lord, mighty and glorious is he." It was in that same year that Sufyān died.

As for Abū Dharr, the mercy of God be upon him, the following is told in a report: "When [his demise] **[284]** drew near, he said to his daughter, 'Look out and tell me whether you can see anyone.' 'I can see no one,' she replied." The report continues: "After a while he sat up and, having ordered her to slaughter a sheep and cook it, said to her, 'When those who will bury me[49] come to you, tell them, "Abū Dharr entreats you not to ride off until you have eaten."' When the pot of meat was thoroughly cooked, he said to her, 'Look out and tell me whether you can see anyone.' 'Yes,' she replied, 'I can see a company of riders approaching.' 'Make me lie in the direction of the kiblah,' he said. When she had done this, he exclaimed, 'In the name of God, by (the will of) God, and in the religion of the Messenger of God!'[50] Then his daughter went out to meet the company of riders, saying, 'May God have mercy on you, come and see to (the burial of) Abū Dharr.' 'Where is he?' they asked. 'There he is,' she said. And he was dead. 'We will gladly do it,' they said, 'It is an honor God has bestowed on us.' Now the company of riders was from Kufa, and among them was ᶜAbd Allāh b. Masᶜūd. As they approached Abū Dharr, Ibn Masᶜūd wept and said, 'The Messenger of God spoke the truth when he said: "He will die alone and be resurrected alone."'"

Ibn Masᶜūd said: **[285]** "When I came to him, I saw a tent that had been sprinkled with musk, and I said to the woman, 'What is this?' She answered me saying, 'He acquired this musk on one of the expeditions in which he took part, and when he was on the point of death, he said, "When a man dies, there are some present who perceive fragrances but who do not eat. So dissolve this musk in water, sprinkle it on the tent, and serve its fragrance to them. And cook this meat, for a company of

---

[49] According to al-Masᶜūdī (*Murūj,* IV, p. 271; ed. Pellat, III, p. 84), Abū Dharr, on being banished, said to ᶜUthmān, "[the Messenger of God] informed me that I would be exiled from Mecca and Medina and would die in al-Rabadha and that a company of men coming from Iraq to the Hejaz would take charge of my burial." Cf. also al-Yaᶜqūbī, *Taʾrīkh,* II, pp. 200–201, where a version of this story similar to that in our text is related, and al-Ṭabarī, *Taʾrīkh,* III, p. 107 (rather different), and IV, pp. 308–9 (again similar).

[50] Words spoken at a Muslim burial service when the body is placed in the grave.

righteous men will come to me and take charge of my burial. Greet them for me.'"" Then Ibn Masᶜūd repeated the saying of the Prophet.[51]

As for Salmān al-Fārisī, his wife Buqayra reported the following: "When he was on the point of death, he called me to him. Now he was in an upper chamber that had four doors. 'Open these doors for me, Buqayra,' he said, 'for today I shall have visitors, but I do not know through which of the doors they will come in to me.' Then he called for musk, water, a bowl, and a robe and said, 'Dissolve this musk in the water.' When I had done what he asked, he said, 'Sprinkle it around my bed, and then go back down and wait. When you look up, you will be able to see me in my bed.' **[286]** But when I looked up to see him, his spirit had already been taken, and he seemed to be lying asleep in his bed."

Regarding Uways [al-Qaranī] the following is told: "When Harim met Uways (after their exchange related in the beginning of the report),[52] he said to him, 'Let me be your companion.' 'No,' Uways responded, 'but when I die, no one shall wrap me in my shroud until you come and shroud me and bury me.' With this they parted. Thereafter Harim searched continuously for Uways. Eventually he entered the city of Damascus, where in the courtyard of the mosque he found a man lying wrapped in a cloak. He went over to him, and, pulling the cloak from his face, discovered him to be Uways. He raised his hand to his head and cried out, 'My poor brother! He died alone and neglected.' 'Who are you,' the people asked, 'and who is this?' 'This is Uways,' he told them, 'and I am Harim b. Ḥayyān.' Now the people had collected the price of two lengths of cloth with which to shroud him. But Harim exclaimed, 'He does not need your two lengths of cloth, for Harim will shroud him at his own expense.' Then he put his hand into a provision bag that had belonged to Uways and found there to his surprise two lengths of cloth **[287]** which he had never seen before. On one was written: 'In the name of God, the Merciful and Compassionate. Immunity from hell granted by God to Uways.' On the other were these words: 'This is a shroud for him from Paradise, may God have mercy on him.'"

Abū ʾl-ᶜAbbās Aḥmad b. Manṣūr,[53] in his work on the masters, said:

---

51 The tradition cited at the end of the preceding paragraph. Or conceivably the entire preceding report is meant.

52 Cf. MS, pp. 153 and, esp., 222–23.

53 Most probably the scholar and benefactor of Sufism Abū ʾl-ᶜAbbās Aḥmad b. Manṣūr (d. 382/992). He was the father of Ibn Khafīf's learned student Abū ᶜAbd Allāh al-Bayṭār and a teacher in *ḥadīth* of Abū Isḥāq al-Kāzarūnī. See the Introduction, pp. xix–xx, lxiii; Junayd Shīrāzī, *Shadd al-izār*, pp. 103–4; and Sobieroj, "Ibn Ḫafīf aš-Šīrāzī," pp. 137, 208.

"Thābit al-Bunānī prayed to God saying, 'If thou hast ever permitted anyone to perform the prayer in his grave, then make me such a man.' On this matter the gypsum miners[54] used to say, 'When we passed by his grave, we could hear his recitations.'"[55]

Ḥumayd al-Ṭawīl said: "When Thābit died, I took charge of placing him in the tomb. Now I had with me a purse belonging to someone else, and I left it in the grave. After the task was done, I remembered it and said to the gravedigger, 'Dig up the grave. I left something in it.' So he dug up the grave, and I took the purse. But then I said to myself, 'Let me see whether his face is turned to the kiblah, for I have heard that the faces of innovators in the faith will be turned away from the kiblah.' I removed **[288]** two of the mud bricks, but I did not see Thābit in the tomb. So I replaced the bricks and went to ᶜAbd Allāh b. Ṭāhir, who was then governor of Basra. 'Where have you come from?' he asked. 'Thābit died,' I answered, 'and I was at his funeral.' 'If you had informed me,' he said, 'I too would have attended his funeral.' 'O emir,' I replied, 'I have seen a wondrous thing.' 'What was that?' he inquired. When I told him the story, he said, 'God is great! Such things I have heard about the men of former times.' Then he said to me, 'Let us be off.' We performed the night prayer, and, taking with us some candles, proceeded to the grave. Ibn Ṭāhir went down into the grave, and I went with him. We removed the bricks but did not see Thābit in the tomb." The report continues: "I asked his daughter, 'What did you use to hear your father say when he was alive?' and she replied, 'He used to say, "O Quickener! O Inheritor![56] Do not leave me alone in my grave."'"

It is reported that Rabīᶜ b. Ḥirāsh, the brother of Ribᶜī b. Ḥirāsh, swore that he would never smile until he knew whether he was in heaven or hell. Indeed no one ever saw him smile to the day he died. But as they were sitting by his body, after having laid him out, covered him with a length of cloth, **[289]** closed his eyes, dug his grave, and brought his shroud, he suddenly raised the cloth, and, flinging it from his face, he turned towards them smiling. "My brother," his brother Ribᶜī asked him, "does one return to life after death?" "Yes," he replied, "I met my Lord, and he received me 'with repose and ease, and my Lord was not angry.'[57] He clothed me with silk and fine brocades." He also said, "More-

---

[54] See chapter fourteen, n. 12.

[55] The same story is related above about Ayyūb al-Sakhtiyānī (MS, pp. 189–90). Cf. chapter fourteen, n. 11.

[56] "Inheritor": that is, of the earth and all those on it. Cf. Koran 19:40.

[57] Quotation from a *ḥadīth* reflecting Koran 56:89. Cf., e.g., Ibn Māja, *Sunan, Zuhd* 31, II, p. 1424, *ḥadīth* 4262.

over, I discovered the matter to be easier than you think, so do not be deceived. But, oh, my beloved Muḥammad is waiting for me in order to perform the burial prayers for me. So I must make haste." Then his soul departed as though it were a pebble cast into water.[58] The narrator continued as follows: "The news of this reached ᶜĀᵓisha, and she said, 'The Messenger of God spoke the truth, as did the brother of the Banū ᶜAbs,[59] for I heard the Messenger of God say: "A man from my community, one of the best of the Followers, will speak after his death."' And Ribᶜī said, 'My brother, [may God have mercy on him], kept vigils more than any of us on cold nights, and he fasted more than any of us on hot days.'"[60]

I found the following in a book by Sheikh Abū ᶜAbd Allāh b. Khafīf, God's mercy be upon him, **[290]** and in his own hand: "It is related from Abū ᶜAbd Allāh Muḥammad b. ᶜAbd al-ᶜAzīz b. Sulaymān that he said: 'Shaᶜwāna al-Ubullīya was sorely grieved at having neglected her devotions because she remained so long distraught by love. Then someone came to her in a dream and said to her:

Let your eyes flow with the tears you were holding back,
for lamentation can cure the grief-stricken.
Be diligent, keep vigils, and fast always and forever,
for wasting away is a trait of the obedient.[61]

After this she returned to her devotions.'

"Muḥammad b. ᶜAbd al-ᶜAzīz continued: 'I told this to Sufyān (al-Thawrī), and he said, "Come, let us go and visit her." Now when she knew that it was Sufyān, she turned her face towards us and, after greeting him, said, "Abū ᶜAbd Allāh, tell me about gnosis. Is it a means between the worshipper and the one he worships?" "Why have you asked me this?" he inquired. "It is just something that came to my mind," she replied. "Allow me not to answer," he said. "You must tell me," she insisted. "It is a means," he said, "a means." **[291]** "Can it be eliminated?"

---

[58] The meaning is apparently "as easily as a pebble cast into water." Cf. Abū Nuᶜaym, *Ḥilya,* IV, p. 368, ll. 15–16. Arberry renders it "with the sound of a pebble cast into water" in his translation of the same story in al-Kalābādhī, *The Doctrine of the Sufis,* pp. 163–64.

[59] The person referred to is either Rabīᶜ, who is addressed with this expression in Abū Nuᶜaym, *Ḥilya,* IV, p. 367, or Ribᶜī, who was the source of the story (ibid.).

[60] Cf. ibid., pp. 367–68.

[61] In the MS these verses are scarcely recognizable as poetry, since the hemistichs are given in different order and two contain additional words. Our emendation is based on Ibn al-Jawzī, *Ṣifat al-ṣafwa,* IV, p. 56.

Sha^cwāna asked. "It can be eliminated in some states, but it is necessary in others," Sufyān replied. Thereupon Sha^cwāna uttered a cry and fell down dead.' Muḥammad b. ᶜAbd al-ᶜAzīz added: 'Sufyān's statement, "It is a means," bears a number of interpretations which will be grasped by those possessed of understanding.'"

When Sahl b. ᶜAbd Allāh [al-Tustarī] died, ᶜUmar b. Wāṣil said: "I went in to wash his body, and he said, 'There is no god but God!' Whereupon I exclaimed, 'You were a marvel during your life, and you are a marvel after your death.'"[62]

Abū ᶜAbd Allāh ᶜAmr b. ᶜUthmān al-Makkī said: "A man among our companions called Abū Bakr al-Zaqqāq[63] related to us from another of our companions, who was one of those who used to preach before the people, that he said: 'I used to preach before the people every Friday, and a certain man dressed in tattered clothing always used to come to hear me. He would sit at the back of the congregation and weep profusely. After a time I noticed that he had stopped coming, but I did not know whom to ask about him. However an old woman came to me and said, "That poverty-stricken **[292]** man who loved you so says to you, 'I should like you to visit me because I am ill.'" So I accompanied her to one of the slums of Baghdad and went in to him, only to find that the illness had brought him near his end. When he saw me, he rejoiced and said, "I did not think you would arrive in time." "I did not know where to find you," I replied. To this he said, "What you say is true. Do you think that if I weep, you will weep?" "I do not know," I answered. At this he burst into tears, and his weeping caused me to weep so violently I feared I might die. Then he said to me, "Wait with me. I shall die now, and you will help the old woman to conceal[64] my bodily form. But watch for me in your sleep, for I shall avail you." Hardly had he finished speaking these words when he died.'

"The preacher continued: 'So I said to the old woman, "Do you have a hoe?" "What will you do with a hoe?" she asked. "I shall dig his grave," I answered. "He himself dug his grave more than twenty years ago," [she said]. After this exchange, the old woman and I carried him to the well to wash his corpse. But suddenly there was a knock **[293]** at the door.

---

62 The lack of an introduction giving the source of this report suggests that it may belong to the quotation from Ibn Khafīf contained in the two preceding paragraphs.

63 See n. 65.

64 "to conceal": *muwārāt,* a Koranic usage. Cf. Koran 5:31, "Then God sent a crow, scratching the ground, to show him [Cain] how to conceal his brother's unseemly corpse."

When the old woman opened the door, we beheld a horseman dressed in more beautiful apparel and with a more beautiful [face] than anyone we had ever seen. "Is the man dead?" he asked. "Yes," I replied. "Take these," he said, giving me some aromatics and a shroud. Then he rolled up his sleeves and said, "Pour some water on my hands so that I may wash him." After he had washed him, he perfumed him for burial and wrapped him in the shroud. Then he said to me, "Step forward and lead the funeral prayers for him. It is you who should do this." When we had recited the prayers, the horseman left with no further delay. I remained puzzled by the horseman, for I had failed to ask him who he was. Moreover, I forgot that the dead man had said to me, "Watch for me in your sleep." A year passed before I remembered it.

"'One Thursday night I put on clean, unsullied garments, perfumed myself, and spent the entire night before the prayer niche. A little before daybreak, sleep came over me, and I dreamt that the Resurrection was at hand. Someone was calling, "Where are those who rehearse the name of God? Where are those who praise him? Where are those who are content? Where are those who love?" **[294]** Now whenever he called for a group, a man came forward, and a banner was tied for him and a company of people followed him. Then a group whose name I have forgotten was called, and the man I had helped to bury came forward. His face was as beautiful as the moon on the night it is full. He was given the banner that had been tied for him, and a great company of people followed him. I started to run after them, but I could not catch them. When the man reached the gates of Paradise, he was met with mounts and servants. Those who were with him dispersed to their abodes, but he mounted an animal and was led to a magnificent palace. I followed him in, but lost my way because of the many doors, sitting-niches, and rooms within it. I saw no one, and no one received me. Suddenly a wind so strong it almost carried me off began to blow through the rooms and chambers. Never had I known a more pleasant or more fragrant breeze.

"'Then there appeared to me an august personage with a beautiful face, the light of which dazzled my eyes. "What are you doing here?" he asked me, "Is it allowable for you to enter someone else's house?" **[295]** "The master of the house has commanded me to come to him," I answered. "He is too busy to see you," he replied. "And who are you, please?" I asked. "I am the angel of the winds of mercy," he said, "and I have been commanded to cause the winds of mercy to blow in this palace." As I was speaking to him, suddenly the man I had helped to bury came up to me. "I am so-and-so," he said, "What made you come so late?" "I forgot what you told me," I answered. Then he turned to one of his servants and said, "Take him by the hand and see that he has a noble return." So he took me by the hand and I awoke.'"[65]

ᶜAmr (b. ᶜUthmān) also said: "Abū Saᶜīd al-Kharrāz related to me from a certain pious man of Baghdad that he said: 'I heard someone say to me in a dream, "After you perform the midday prayer, go to such and such a place in the cemetery and join in the funeral prayers at a particular burial, and your sins will be forgiven." So I went there and continued to take part in funeral prayers until shortly before sunset. Just as I decided to leave, **[296]** I saw a coffin being borne by three men and a woman. "If my dream had any meaning," I said to myself, "this must be the funeral," and I went over and took the place of the woman. "Lead the funeral prayer for him," she said to me. So I stepped forward and led the prayer. Then we carried him to the grave. The woman asked me to go down into the grave, so I did. Now the shroud had come loose around his head, and it suddenly fell from his face. His features were a ghastly gray. "Truly I shall avail you," he said to me. At this I fell down in a swoon, and they brought me out of the grave and buried him.'"

Muḥammad b. Manṣūr[66] related that Abū ᶜImrān told him the following: "I was walking behind Fatḥ al-Mawṣilī, and I heard him say, 'O my God, how long wilt thou leave me to wander in the ways of this world? Has not the time come for the lover to see his Beloved?'" He added: "Not a week passed before he died."

Our teacher, Abū ᶜAbd Allāh (b. Khafīf), may God's mercy be upon him, related the following: "When I went to Mecca and attended a gathering held by Abū ᵓl-Ḥasan al-Muzayyin (the Barber)[67] at which **[297]** a

---

[65] The narrator of this report, Abū Bakr al-Zaqqāq (d. 290/903), on whom see Abū Nuᶜaym, *Ḥilya,* X, p. 344, relates the comments of Abū Saᶜīd al-Kharrāz on a dream he had just awoken from in al-Sulamī, *Ṭabaqāt al-ṣūfiya* (ed. Pedersen), p. 225. The next report in our text, apparently related by ᶜAmr b. ᶜUthmān directly from al-Kharrāz, is also about a dream.

[66] The reference may be to Muḥammad b. Manṣūr al-Ṭūsī (d. 254/868 or 256/870), on whom see Ibn Ḥajar, *Tahdhīb* IX, pp. 472–73, Abū Nuᶜaym, *Ḥilya,* X, pp. 216–19, and al-Nabhānī, *Jāmiᶜ karāmāt al-awliyāᵓ,* I, p. 169. Conceivably, despite the apparent anachronism, *Aḥmad* b. Manṣūr (d. 382), mentioned above (MS, p. 287) and below (MS, p. 299), is meant. Fatḥ al-Mawṣilī died in 220/835.

[67] On al-Muzayyin (d. 328/939–40), the first of Ibn Khafīf's teachers in Mecca listed by al-Daylamī in his *Sīrat-i İbn al-Ḫafīf,* see *Sīrat,* pp. 51–59, and, e.g., al-Sulamī, *Ṭabaqāt al-ṣūfiya* (ed. Pedersen, Leiden, 1960), pp. 396–400, and Ibn al-Jawzī, *Ṣifat al-ṣafwa,* II, pp. 265–66. Sobieroj ("Ibn Ḫafīf aš-Šīrāzī," p. 58) summarizes the reports about him in al-Daylamī's *Sīrat.*

group of dervishes were present, he said to me: 'When Abū Yaᶜqūb al-Aqṭaᶜ was on the point of death, I was present along with a group of dervishes.[68] Now one of those who were sitting there said to me, "Raise his eyelid and dictate to him the profession of faith." Then (Abū Yaᶜqūb himself) opened[69] his eye, and I said to him, "Say, 'There is no god but God.'" He looked up into my eyes and said, "Do you mean me?" "Yes," I replied. Whereupon he said, "By the might of him who never tastes death, there is no longer any veil between him and me except the veil of might." No sooner had he said this than he died.'" Our teacher added: "Whenever Abū ᵓl-Ḥasan told this story, he would take hold of his beard and say, 'A cupper like me dictate the profession of faith to the saints of God!'"

Ibn Khafīf also related this: "Someone once came to me and said, 'A certain woman of the Mubārakiyūn,' they being a pastoral people in Fārs,[70] 'desires you to go and visit her so that she may ask you a question.' Now she was the wife of one of their chieftains and could not go out. So I went **[298]** to her, and she said, 'Teacher, I wish to ask you about a matter that has baffled us.' 'Ask,' I replied. 'We had in our tribe a boy,' she said, 'who used to tend the flocks. He was constantly fasting, and when he went out to tend the sheep he would let them graze where they pleased and make himself an oratory of stones where he would stay and perform his prayers. He hardly ever spoke, and when he came back at night he would not mix with us or banter with the other boys. One day he came down with a fever, and we had him lie down and rest outside the tents.[71] The men went out about their business, and we remained in the tents alone. Sometime later in the day we saw the boy rising off the ground, and we cried, "There is no god but God!" We were frightened and seized with terror. He floated higher and higher, and his mother ran out to catch hold of him, but she could not reach him. So he floated up, with us looking on stupefied, until he disappeared into the sky.

"'We told the men when they returned, and they went out looking for him for three days, scouring the valleys **[299]** and the mountain paths,[72]

---

68 Al-Daylamī also relates this story in his *Sīrat-i Ibn al-Ḫafīf* (pp. 51–52), but the introduction is different.

69 "(Abū Yaᶜqūb himself) opened": The passage in al-Daylamī's *Sīrat* (p. 51) reads: "[Those there] said to me, 'If he opens his eye, dictate to him the profession of faith.' So when he opened his eye I dictated it to him."

70 The Mubārakīya were a Kurdish tribe in Fārs. Cf. al-Iṣṭakhrī, *Masālik al-mamālik,* pp. 114–15, and Ibn Ḥawqal, *Ṣūrat al-arḍ,* pp. 270–71.

71 "tents": *buyūt;* possibly, "houses."

72 "mountain paths": *shiᶜāb;* also, "ravines." The reading is from Vadet for

in the hope that he might have come down somewhere. But he was not to be found, and nothing has been heard of him since. We are baffled by this matter.'" Our teacher continued: "I hesitated as though pondering the matter, and she said, 'Perhaps you doubt my story.' Then, calling over a group of women, she asked, 'What happened to the boy?' They all described the events just as she had." Our teacher concluded: "[To this day][73] I still ponder this story."

Among the reports which we have received from Aḥmad b. Manṣūr in his work on the masters[74] is this: "The following is related of Muḥammad b. ᶜAbd al-Raḥmān, that is, Abū Jaᶜfar al-ᶜImāmī, a well-known dervish [of] Raqqa who sustained himself with food that had been discarded by others. One day he passed by the door of al-Ḥasan al-ᶜArīḍī, a notable of Raqqa. Now al-Ḥasan had a slave-girl whom he had bought for a hundred thousand dirhams, and she happened to be singing this verse:

> You see them struck down on the bridge of love,[75]
> and the bridge quakes from their agony.

"'Abū [ᶜAlī]!'[76] Abū Jaᶜfar called out. Al-Ḥasan looked down to him **[300]** from the palace and signaled to those present to be quiet, thinking the man was rebuking them. 'Abū Jaᶜfar,' he asked, 'what is it you wish?' 'I entreat you by God,' Abū Jaᶜfar answered, 'to command the girl to sing that again.' The gathering regained its cheerful mood, and the girl began to sing the line again and again. Abū Jaᶜfar shrieked and threw himself to the ground. His body remained quaking for a while, and then he died, The slave-girl clutched her garments and threw them off. Then she struck her lute against the floor and smashed it to bits. 'My master,' she exclaimed, 'I have repented to God and will sin no more.' 'I am in greater need of repentance than you,' he replied, 'To doubt (after such a sign) is the mark of an unbeliever.' So they both repented and spent the remainder of their days worshipping God."

The author of this book, ᶜAlī b. Muḥammad, may God's mercy be upon him, said: Stories like these, were we to try to relate them all, would be many indeed. Those we have mentioned should be ample and sufficient for our purpose here.

ᶜishā in the manuscript.

[73] Conjecture for a possible lacuna in the text.

[74] Cf. MS, p. 287.

[75] Cf. MS, p. 262, the last of the four verses.

[76] Vadet's addition. Men named Ḥasan are commonly called Abū ᶜAlī.

Now we ask God for success in all our affairs, a good issue at our death, everlasting joy **[301]** upon meeting our Lord, and forgiveness for all our sins at our reckoning. For all this is in his hands and subject to his power.

And may God bless our lord Muḥammad, and his family,
and his good and virtuous Companions,
all together, to the Day of Judgment,
and grant them peace.

BIBLIOGRAPHY

Transliteration of names and titles in the bibliography follows the Library of Congress system, but not always the LC name form.

ʿAbd al-Qādir, ʿAlī Ḥasan. *The Life, Personality and Writings of al-Junayd. See* al-Junayd ibn Muḥammad, Abū al-Qāsim.

Abū Dāwūd Sulaymān ibn al-Ashʿath al-Sijistānī. *Sunan Abī Dāwūd* (any numbered edition). See also the trans. of the *Sunan* of Abū Dāwūd by Ahmad Hasan. Lahore: Sh. Muhammad Ashraf, 1984.

Abū Ḥayyān al-Tawḥīdī, ʿAlī ibn Muḥammad. *Al-Muqābasāt.* Ed. Ḥasan al-Sandūbī. Cairo: al-Maktabah al-Tijārīyah al-Kubrā, 1348/1929.

———. *Thalāth rasāʾil.* Ed. Ibrāhīm al-Kīlānī. Damascus: Institut Français de Damas, 1951.

Abū al-Faraj al-Iṣfahānī (LC: al-Iṣbahānī), ʿAlī ibn al-Ḥusayn, *Kitāb al-aghānī.* Būlāq, 1285/1868–69.

Abū Maʿshar, Jaʿfar ibn Muḥammad. *Kitāb al-mudkhal al-kabīr. See* Sezgin, *GAS,* VII, pp. 141–42.

———. *Kitāb al-uṣūl. See* Sezgin, *GAS,* VII, pp. 147, 152–53.

Abū Nuʿaym Aḥmad ibn ʿAbd Allāh al-Iṣfahānī. *Ḥilyat al-awliyāʾ.* Cairo: Maktabat al-Khānjī and Maṭbaʿat al-Saʿādah, 1351/1932–1357/1938.

Abū Sulaymān al-Manṭiqī al-Sijistānī. *See* al-Sijistānī, Muḥammad ibn Ṭāhir.

Adab al-mulūk fī bayān ḥaqāʾiq al-taṣawwuf. Ed. Bernd Radtke. Beiruter Texte und Studien, vol. 37. Beirut: Franz Steiner Verlag Stuttgart, 1991.

Akhbār al-Ḥallāj. Ed. and French trans. Louis Massignon and Paul Kraus. Paris: Éditions Larose, 1936.

Allan, James W. *Persian Metal Technology 700–1300 AD.* Oxford Oriental Monographs, no. 2. London: Ithaca Press, 1979.

Allard, Michel. *Le problème des attributs divins dans la doctrine d'al-Ašʿarī et de ses premiers grands disciples.* Beirut: Imprimerie Catholique, 1965.

ʿAnqā Shāh Maqṣūd Pīr Uwaysī, Muḥammad Ṣādiq (LC: ʿAnqā, Ṣādiq). *Min al-fikr al-ṣūfī al-īrānī al-muʿāṣir.* Trans. al-Sibāʿī Muḥammad al-Sibāʿī and Ibrāhīm al-Dusūqī Shitā. Cairo: Dār al-Thaqāfah lil-Ṭibāʿah wa-al-Nashr, [1975].

al-Anṭākī, Dāwūd ibn ʿUmar. *See* Dāwūd ibn ʿUmar al-Anṭākī.

Arberry, A. J. *The Koran Interpreted. See* Koran.

Aristotle. *De anima.*

———. *De generatione et corruptione.*

———. *Eudemian Ethics.*

al-Ashʿarī, Abū al-Ḥasan ʿAlī ibn Ismāʿīl. *Maqālāt al-Islāmīyīn wa-ikhtilāf al-muṣallīn.* Ed. Hellmut Ritter. Istanbul: Maṭbaʿat al-Dawlah, 1929–30.

al-ʿAskarī, Abū Hilāl al-Ḥasan ibn ʿAlī. *Jamharat al-amthāl.* On margin of al-Maydānī, *Majmaʿ al-amthāl.* [Cairo]: al-Maṭbaʿah al-Khayrīyah, 1310 A.H.

Badawī, ʿAbd al-Raḥmān. *Shahīdat al-ʿishq al-ilāhī.* Cairo: Maktabat al-Nahḍah al-Miṣrīyah, 1962.

Baqlī, *See* Rūzbihān ibn Abī Naṣr Baqlī Shīrāzī.

al-Bayḍāwī, ᶜAbd Allāh ibn ᶜUmar. *Beidhawii Commentarius in Coranum* (*Anwār al-tanzīl wa-asrār al-taʾwīl*). Ed. H. O. Fleischer. Leipzig: Guil. Vogel, 1846–48.

———. *Tafsīr* = *Beidhawii Commentarius in Coranum.*

Bell, Joseph Norment. "Avicenna's *Treatise on Love* and the Nonphilosophical Muslim Tradition." *Der Islam* 63 (1986): 73–89.

———. *Love Theory in Later Ḥanbalite Islam.* Albany: State University of New York Press, 1979.

———. "'Say It Again and Make Me Your Slave': Notes on al-Daylamī's Seventh Sign of Man's Love for God." In *Culture and Memory in Medieval Islam: Essays in Honour of Wilferd Madelung,* ed. Farhad Daftary and Josef W. Meri (London, New York: I. B. Tauris Publishers in association with The Institute of Ismaili Studies, 2003), pp. 190–209.

Biesterfeldt, Hans Hinrich, and Dimitri Gutas. "The Malady of Love," *Journal of the American Oriental Society* 104 (1984): 21–55.

Boll, Franz Johannes. *Sphaera.* Hildesheim: Georg Olms, 1967.

Bowker, John. *The Targums and Rabbinic Literature.* London: Cambridge University Press, 1969.

Böwering, Gerhard. *The Mystical Vision of Existence in Classical Islam: the Qurʾānic Hermeneutics of the Ṣūfī Sahl al-Tustarī (d. 283/896).* Studien zur Sprache, Geschichte und Kultur des islamischen Orients, Neue Folge, vol. 9. Berlin, New York: Walter de Gruyter, 1979.

Brockelmann, Carl. *GAL = Geschichte der arabischen Litteratur.* 2nd ed. Vols. I, II. Leiden: E. J. Brill, 1943, 1949.

———. *S = Geschichte der arabischen Litteratur.* Supplementbände I-III. Leiden: E. J. Brill, 1937–42.

Caspari, Carl Paul. *A Grammar of the Arabic Language.* Ed. and trans. William Wright. Cambridge: Cambridge University Press, 1955.

Charles, Robert Henry, ed. *The Apocrypha and Pseudepigrapha of the Old Testament in English.* Vol. II. Oxford: Clarendon Press, 1913.

Dāwūd (LC: Dāʾūd) ibn ᶜUmar al-Anṭākī. *Tazyīn al-aswāq.* Cairo, 1291/1874.

al-Daylamī, Abū al-Ḥasan ᶜAlī ibn Muḥammad. *Kitāb ᶜaṭf al-alif al-maʾlūf ᶜalā al-lām al-maᶜṭūf.* Ed. Jean-Claude Vadet. Cairo: Imprimerie de l'Institut Français d'Archéologie Orientale, 1962.

———. *Kitāb ᶜaṭf al-alif al-maʾlūf ᶜalā al-lām al-maᶜṭūf.* Ed. Hassan Mahmood Abdul Latif Al Shafie and Joseph Norment Bell. Forthcoming.

———. *Sīrat al-Shaykh al-Kabīr Abī ᶜAbd Allāh Muḥammad ibn Khafīf al-Shīrāzī.* Arabic translation of Annemarie Schimmel's edition and her introduction by Ibrāhīm al-Dusūqī Shitā. Cairo: al-Hayʾah al-ᶜĀmmah li-Shuʾūn al-Maṭābiᶜ al-Amīrīyah, 1977.

———. *Sīrat-i Abū ᶜAbdullāh İbn al-Ḫafīf aṣ-Şīrāzī.* Persian translation by Ibn Junayd al-Shīrāzī. Ed. Annemarie Schimmel Tarı. Ankara Üniversitesi İlâhiyat Fakültesi Yayınlarından, no. 12. Ankara: Türk Tarih Kurumu Basımevi, 1955.

———. *Le traité d'amour mystique d'al-Daylami.* French trans. by Jean-Claude

Vadet of al-Daylamī's *Kitāb ᶜatf al-alif.* Hautes Études Orientales, no. 13. Geneva: Librairie Droz, 1980.

al-Dhahabī, Muḥammad ibn Aḥmad. *Al-ᶜIbar fī khabar man ghabar.* Ed. Salāḥ al-Dīn al-Munajjid and Fuᵓād Sayyid. Kuwait, 1960–.

———. *Kitāb tadhkirat al-ḥuffāẓ.* Hyderabad: Dāᵓirat al-Maᶜārif al-ᶜUthmānīyah, 1390/1970.

———. *Mīzān al-iᶜtidāl.* [Cairo], 1325/1907–8.

———. *Mīzān al-iᶜtidāl.* Ed. ᶜAlī Muḥammad al-Bijāwī. Cairo: ᶜĪsā al-Bābī al-Ḥalabī, 1382/1963–64. Unless otherwise noted, references are to this edition.

Diogenes Laertius. *Lives of Eminent Philosophers* (*Vitae et sententiae philosophorum*). With English trans. by R. D. Hicks. Loeb Classical Library, no. 184. Cambridge: Harvard University Press, 1950.

EI¹ = The Encyclopaedia of Islam. 1st ed. Photomechanical reprint. Leiden: E. J. Brill, 1987. (The volumes of the original edition have been subdivided in the reprint, although the pagination has been retained. References to volume numbers in our notes are to the reprinted edition.)

EI² = The Encyclopaedia of Islam. 2nd ed. Leiden: E. J. Brill, 1960–.

Ernst, Carl W. *Rūzbihān Baqlī: Mysticism and the Rhetoric of Sainthood in Persian Sufism.* Richmond, Surrey: Curzon Press, 1996.

———. "Rūzbihān Baqlī on Love as 'Essential Desire.'" In *Gott ist schön und Er liebt die Schönheit/God is Beautiful and Loves Beauty: Festschrift für Annemarie Schimmel,* ed. Alma Giese and J. Christoph Bürgel (Bern: Peter Lang, 1994), pp. 181–89.

———. "The Stages of Love in Early Persian Sufism from Rābiᶜa to Rūzbihān." In *Classical Persian Sufism from its Origins to Rumi,* ed. Leonard Lewisohn (London: Khaniqahi Nimatullahi, 1994), pp. 435–55. Also in *Sufi* 14 (1992): 16–23.

al-Fīrūzābādī, Muḥammad ibn Yaᶜqūb. *Al-Qāmūs al-muḥīṭ.* Cairo, 1863–64.

al-Ghazālī (LC: al-Ghazzālī), Abū Ḥāmid. *Iḥyāᵓ ᶜulūm al-dīn.* Cairo: Maṭbaᶜat Lajnat Nashr al-Thaqāfah al-Islāmīyah, 1356/1937–1357/1938. Unless otherwise noted, references are to this edition.

———. *Iḥyāᵓ ᶜulūm al-dīn.* On margin: ᶜAbd al-Raḥīm ibn al-Ḥusayn al-ᶜIrāqī, *Al-Mughnī ᶜan ḥaml al-asfār fī al-asfār fī takhrīj mā fī al-Iḥyāᵓ min al-akhbār.* Cairo: al-Maktabah al-Tijārīyah al-Kubrā and Maṭbaᶜat al-Istiqāmah, n.d.

Giffen, Lois Anita. *Theory of Profane Love among the Arabs: the Development of the Genre.* New York and London: New York University Press and London University Press, 1971.

Gutas, Dimitri, and Hans Hinrich Biesterfeldt. *See* Biesterfeldt, Hans Hinrich, and Dimitri Gutas.

al-Ḥalabī, Shihāb al-Dīn Maḥmūd ibn Sulaymān ibn Fahd. *Manāzil al-aḥbāb wa-manāzih al-albāb.* MS Top Kapı, Ahmet III, 2471.

al-Ḥallāj, al-Ḥusayn ibn Manṣūr. *Le dîwân d'âl-Hallâj.* Ed. and trans. Louis Massignon. New edition with additions and corrections. Paris: Librairie Orientaliste Paul Geuthner, 1955.

———. *Kitâb al-ṭawâsîn.* Ed. Louis Massignon. Paris: Librairie Paul

Geuthner, 1913.

———. *Kitāb al-ṭawāsīn*. Ed. Paul Nwyia. *Mélanges de l'Université Saint-Joseph,* 47(1972): 183–238.

al-Hamdānī, al-Ḥasan ibn Aḥmad *called* Ibn al-Ḥāʾik. *Kitāb al-jawharatayn al-ʿatīqatayn.* Ed. with German trans. Christopher Toll. Studia Semitica Upsaliensia, no. 1. Uppsala: [Almquist & Wiksell), 1968.

al-Haythamī, Nūr al-Dīn ʿAlī ibn Abī Bakr. *Majmaʿ al-zawāʾid wa-manbaʿ al-fawāʾid.* Beirut: Dār al-Kutub al-ʿIlmīyah, 1408/1988.

al-Hujwīrī, ʿAlī ibn ʿUthmān al-Jullābī. *Kashf al-maḥjūb.* Ed. V. A. Zhukovskii. Zabān va Farhang-i Īrān, no. 89. Tehran: Kitābkhānah-i Ṭahūrī, 1358/1979 (reprint of Leningrad, 1926).

———. *The Kashf al-maḥjúb.* Trans. (abridged) Reynold Nicholson. E. J. W. Gibb Memorial, no. 17. London: Luzac, 1936.

al-Ḥuṣrī, Ibrāhīm ibn ʿAlī. *Zahr al-ādāb.* Ed. ʿAlī Muḥammad al-Bijāwī. Cairo: ʿĪsā al-Bābī al-Ḥalabī, 1372/1953.

———. *Zahr al-ādāb.* Ed. Zakī Mubārak, reedited by Muḥammad Muḥyī al-Dīn ʿAbd al-Ḥamīd. Beirut: Dār al-Jīl, 1972.

Ibn Abī Ḥajalah, Aḥmad ibn Yaḥyā. *Dīwān al-ṣabābah.* On margin of Dāwūd al-Anṭākī, *Tazyīn al-aswāq*. Cairo, 1291/1874.

Ibn Abī Uṣaybiʿah, Aḥmad ibn al-Qāsim. *ʿUyūn al-anbāʾ fī ṭabaqāt al-aṭibbāʾ*. Cairo: al-Maṭbaʿah al-Wahbīyah, 1882.

Ibn Abī Yaʿlā, Abū al-Ḥusayn Muḥammad ibn Muḥammad. *Ṭabaqāt al-Ḥanābilah.* Ed. Muḥammad Ḥāmid al-Fiqī. Cairo: Maṭbaʿat al-Sunnah al-Muḥammadīyah, 1371/1952.

Ibn ʿAdī, ʿAbd Allāh. *Al-Kāmil fī ḍuʿafāʾ al-rijāl.* Beirut: Dār al-Fikr, 1404/1984.

Ibn al-ʿArabī, Muḥyī al-Dīn. *Al-Futūḥāt al-Makkīyah.* Ed. ʿUthmān Yaḥyā. Cairo: al-Hayʾah al-Miṣrīyah al-ʿĀmmah lil-Kitāb, 1392/1972–.

———. *Tarjumān al-ashwāq*. Beirut: Dār Ṣādir, Dār Bayrūt, 1381/1961. (LC transliterates *Turjumān al-ashwāq.*)

———. *The Tarjumán al-ashwáq*. Ed. and trans. with an abridged translation of the author's commentary by Reynold A. Nicholson. London: Royal Asiatic Society, 1911.

Ibn al-Athīr, ʿIzz al-Dīn. *Usd al-ghābah fī maʿrifat al-ṣaḥābah.* Cairo: al-Shaʿb, n.d.

Ibn al-Dabbāgh (LC: al-Dabbāgh), ʿAbd al-Raḥmān ibn Muḥammad al-Anṣārī. *Kitāb mashāriq anwār al-qulūb.* Ed. H. Ritter. Beirut: Dār Ṣādir, Dār Bayrūt, 1379/1959.

Ibn al-Jawzī, Abū al-Faraj ʿAbd al-Raḥmān ibn ʿAlī. *Dhamm al-hawā.* Ed. Muṣṭafā ʿAbd al-Wāḥid. Cairo: Dār al-Kutub al-Ḥadīthah, 1381/1962.

———. *Kitāb al-mawḍūʿāt.* Ed. ʿAbd al-Raḥmān Muḥammad ʿUthmān. Medina: al-Maktabah al-Salafīyah, 1386/1966–1388/1968.

———. *Al-Muntaẓam fī taʾrīkh al-mulūk wa-al-umam.* Vol. VI. 1st ed. Hyderabad: Dāʾirat al-Maʿārif al-ʿUthmānīyah, 1357/1938–39.

———. *Ṣifat al-ṣafwah.* Ed. Maḥmūd Fākhūrī and Muḥammad Rawās Qalʿahjī.

Aleppo: Dār al-Wa^c^y; Cairo: Maṭba^c^at al-Nahḍah al-Jadīdah, ca. 1970–.
———. *Talbīs Iblīs*. Ed. Muḥammad Munīr al-Dimashqī. Cairo: Idārat al-Ṭibā^c^ah al-Munīrīyah, 1928.
Ibn al-Nadīm. *See* al-Nadīm.
Ibn al-Qaṭṭān al-Jurjānī. *See* Ibn ^c^Adī, ^c^Abd Allāh.
Ibn al-Qifṭī. *See* al-Qifṭī, ^c^Alī ibn Yūsuf.
Ibn ^c^Asākir, ^c^Alī ibn al-Ḥasan. *Ta^ɔ^rīkh madīnat Dimashq*. N.p.: Dār al-Bashīr lil-Nashr wa-al-Tawzī^c^, n.d.
Ibn Baṭṭah, ^c^Ubayd Allāh b. Muḥammad. *Al-Sharḥ wa-al-ibānah ^c^alā uṣūl al-sunnah wa-al-diyānah* (*La profession de foi d'Ibn Baṭṭa*). Ed. with introduction and French translation by Henri Laoust. Damascus: Institut Français de Damas, 1958.
Ibn Dāwūd al-Ẓāhirī. *See* Muḥammad ibn Dāwūd al-Iṣfahānī.
Ibn Farḥūn, Ibrāhīm b. ^c^Alī. *Al-Dībāj al-mudhahhab (al-mudhhab) fī ma^c^rifat a^c^yān ^c^ulamā^ɔ^ al-madhhab*. Ed. Muḥammad al-Aḥmadī Abū al-Nūr. Cairo: Dār al-Turāth lil-Ṭab^c^ wa-al-Nashr, [1975?].
Ibn Ḥajar al-^c^Asqalānī, Aḥmad ibn ^c^Alī. *Al-Iṣābah fī tamyīz al-ṣaḥābah*. Calcutta: Asiatic Society of Bengal, 1856–88.
———. *Al-Iṣābah fī tamyīz al-ṣaḥābah*. Ed. ^c^Alī Muḥammad al-Bijāwī. Cairo: Dār Nahḍat Miṣr, 1970–. Unless otherwise noted, references are to this edition.
———. *Kitāb lisān al-Mīzān*. Hyderabad: Dā^ɔ^irat al-Ma^c^ārif al-Niẓāmīyah, 1329/1911–1331/1913.S
———. *Tahdhīb al-Tahdhīb*. Hyderabad: Dā^ɔ^irat al-Ma^c^ārif al-Niẓāmīyah, 1325–27/1907–9.
Ibn Ḥawqal, Abū al-Qāsim Muḥammad. *Kitāb ṣūrat al-arḍ*. Ed. J. H. Kramers. Bibliotheca Geographorum Arabicorum, vol. 2. Leiden: E. J. Brill, 1967.
Ibn Ḥazm, ^c^Alī ibn Aḥmad. *The Ring of the Dove: a Treatise on the Art and Practice of Arab Love (= Ṭawq al-ḥamāmah)*. Trans. A. J. Arberry. London: Luzac, 1953.
Ibn Kathīr, Ismā^c^īl ibn ^c^Umar. *Al-Bidāyah wa-al-nihāyah*. 2nd ed. Beirut: Maktabat al-Ma^c^ārif, 1977.
———. *Tafsīr al-Qur^ɔ^ān al-^c^aẓīm*. Beirut: Dār al-Andalus, 1385/1966.
Ibn Khallikān, Aḥmad ibn Muḥammad. *Wafayāt al-a^c^yān*. Ed. Muḥammad Muḥyī al-Dīn ^c^Abd al-Ḥamīd. Cairo: Maktabat al-Nahḍah al-Miṣrīyah, 1948 (vols. II-VI), 1964 (vol. I).
Ibn Khayr al-Ishbīlī. *See* al-Ishbīlī, Muḥammad ibn Khayr.
Ibn Mājah. *Sunan*. Ed. Muḥammad Fu^ɔ^ād ^c^Abd al-Bāqī. N.p.: Dār Iḥyā^ɔ^ al-Turāth al-^c^Arabī, 1395/1975.
Ibn Manẓūr, Muḥammad ibn Mukarram. *Lisān al-^c^Arab*. Būlāq, 1300/1882–1308/1891.
Ibn Qayyim al-Jawzīyah, Muḥammad ibn Abī Bakr. *Rawḍat al-muḥibbīn wa-nuzhat al-mushtāqīn*. Ed. Aḥmad ^c^Ubayd. Cairo: Maṭba^c^at al-Sa^c^ādah, 1375/1956.
Ibn Sa^c^d, Muḥammad. *Al-Ṭabaqāt al-kubrā*. Ed. Eduard Sachau. Leiden: E. J.

Brill, 1905–40.
———. *Al-Ṭabaqāt al-kubrā.* Beirut: Dār Ṣādir, 1957–68.
Ibn Taymīyah, Aḥmad ibn ᶜAbd al-Ḥalīm. *Al-Fatwā al-Ḥamawīyah al-kubrā.* Beirut: Dār al-Kutub al-ᶜIlmīyah, ca. 1984.
al-ᶜIrāqī, ᶜAbd al-Raḥīm ibn al-Ḥusayn. *Al-Mughnī ᶜan ḥaml al-asfār fī al-asfār fī takhrīj mā fī al-Iḥyāᵓ min al-akhbār.* On margin of al-Ghazālī, *Iḥyāᵓ ᶜulūm al-dīn.* Various editions used. *See* al-Ghazālī.
al-Ishbīlī, Muḥammad ibn Khayr. *Fahrasah.* Ed. Franciscus Codera and J. Ribera Tarrago. Beirut: The Trading Office, 1963.
al-Iṣṭakhrī. *Kitāb masālik al-mamālik.* Ed. M. J. de Goeje. Bibliotheca Geographorum Arabicorum, vol. 1. Leiden: E. J. Brill, 1967.
al-Jāḥiẓ. *Al-Bayān wa-al-tabyīn.* Ed. ᶜAbd al-Salām Muḥammad Hārūn. Cairo: Maktabat al-Khānjī, 1380/1960–1381/1961.
Jāmī. *Nafaḥāt al-uns.* Ed. Mahdī Tawḥīdīpūr. Tehran: Kitābfurūshī-i Saᶜdī, 1336/1958.
al-Junayd ibn Muḥammad, Abū al-Qāsim. The *Life, Personality and Writings of al-Junayd.* With an edition and translation of his writings by Ali Hassan Abdel-Kader. E. J. W. Gibb Memorial, n. s. 22. London: Luzac, 1976.
Junayd Shīrāzī. *Shadd al-izār fī ḥaṭṭ al-awzār ᶜan zuwwār al-mazār.* Ed. Muḥammad Qazvīnī and ᶜAbbās Iqbāl. Tehran: Chāpkhānah-i Majlis, 1328/1949–50.
al-Jurjānī, ᶜAlī ibn Muḥammad, al-Sayyid al-Sharīf. *Kitāb al-taᶜrīfāt* (LC: *Definitiones*). Ed. G. Flügel. Leipzig: F. C. G. Vogel, 1845.
al-Kalābādhī, Abū Bakr ibn Abī Isḥāq Muḥammad b. Ibrāhīm. *The Doctrine of the Ṣūfīs* (*Kitāb al-taᶜarruf li-madhhab ahl al-taṣawwuf*). Trans. A. J. Arberry. Cambridge: Cambridge University Press, 1935.
Kazimirski = A. de Biberstein Kazimirski, *Dictionnaire arabe-français.* Nouvelle édition. Paris: G. P. Maisonneuve, 1960.
al-Khaṭīb al-Baghdādī, Abū Bakr Aḥmad ibn ᶜAlī. *Taᵓrīkh Baghdād.* Cairo: Maktabat al-Khānjī and Maṭbaᶜat al-Saᶜādah, 1349/1931
Koran (trans. Arberry) = Arthur J. Arberry. *The Koran Interpreted.* New York: Macmillan, 1955.
Koran (trans. Maulānā Muḥammad ᶜAlī) = Maulānā Muḥammad ᶜAlī. *The Holy Qurᵓān, Arabic Text, Translation and Commentary.* 4th ed. Lahore: Aḥmadiyyah Anjuman Ishāᶜat Islām, 1951.
Koran (trans. Pickthall) = Marmaduke William Pickthall. *The Meaning of the Glorious Koran.* London: Allen & Unwin, [1957]. Bilingual edition. Cairo: Dār al-Kitāb al-Miṣrī, Beirut: Dār al-Kitāb al-Lubnānī, n.d.
Kraus, Paul, ed. *Akhbār al-Ḥallāj. See Akhbār al-Ḥallāj.*
Lane = Edward W. Lane, *An Arabic-English Lexicon.* Book I, Parts 1–8 and Supplement. Ed. Stanley Lane-Poole. London: Williams and Norgate, 1863–93.
Laoust, Henri. *La profession de foi d'Ibn Baṭṭa. See* Ibn Baṭṭa, *Kitāb al-sharḥ wa-al-ibānah.*
LC = Library of Congress.
Leclerc, Lucien. *Histoire de la médecine arabe.* Burt Franklin, n.d. (= Paris: E.

Leroux, 1876).

Le Déaut, Roger, trans. *Targum du Pentateuque.* Tome I. Genèse. Sources Chrétiennes, no. 245. Paris: Les Éditions du Cerf, 1978. (LC catalogues under Bible. O. T. Pentateuch. French. Le Déaut – Robert. 1978.)

Lisān = Ibn Manẓūr, *Lisān al-ᶜArab.*

Maḥmūd ibn Sulaymān ibn Fahd. *See* al-Ḥalabī, Shihāb al-Dīn.

Maḥmūd ibn ᶜUthmān. *Firdaws al-murshidīyah fī asrār al-ṣamadīyah.* Ed. Īrāj Afshār. Tehran: Kitābkhānah-i Dānish, 1333/1954.

———. *Firdaws al-murshidīyah fī asrār al-ṣamadīyah* (*Die Vita des Scheich Abū Isḥāq al-Kāzarūnī*). Ed. Fritz Meier. Bibliotheca Islamica, vol. 14. Leipzig: F. A. Brockhaus, 1948.

al-Makkī, Abū Ṭālib Muḥammad ibn ᶜAlī. *ᶜIlm al-qulūb.* Ed. ᶜAbd al-Qādir Aḥmad ᶜAṭāᵓ. Cairo: Maktabat al-Qāhirah, 1348/1964.

Marᶜī ibn Yūsuf ibn Abī Bakr al-Karmī. *Munyat al-muḥibbīn wa-bughyat al-ᶜāshiqīn.* MS Dār al-Kutub, Adab 6252.

Massignon, Louis, ed. *Akhbār al-Ḥallāj. See Akhbār al-Ḥallāj.*

———. *Essai sur les origines du lexique technique de la mystique musulmane,* New edition. Paris: Librairie Philosophique J. Vrin, 1954.

———. "Interférences philosophiques et percées métaphysiques dans la mystique hallagienne: notion de 'l'essentiel désir.'" In Louis Massignon, *Opera minora,* II (Beirut: Dar al-Maaref, 1963), pp. 226–53.

———. *La passion d'al-Hosayn-ibn-Mansour al-Hallaj.* Paris: Librairie Orientaliste Paul Geuthner, 1922.

———. *La passion de Husayn Ibn Mansûr Hallâj.* New edition. [Paris]: Gallimard, 1975.

———. *The Passion of al-Hallāj.* Trans. Herbert Mason. Bollingen Series, no. 98. Princeton: Princeton University Press, 1982.

———. *Salmān Pāk and the Spiritual Beginnings of Iranian Islām.* Translated from the French by Jamshedji Maneckji Unvala. Bombay, 1955.

al-Masᶜūdī. *Murūj al-dhahab wa-maᶜādin al-jawhar.* Édition Barbier de Meynard et Pavet de Courteille revue et corrigée par Charles Pellat. Publications de l'Université Libanaise, Section des Études Historiques, no. 11. Beirut, 1966–79.

———. *Les prairies d'or* (*Murūj al-dhahab*). Arabic text with French translation by C. Barbier de Meynard and Pavet de Courteille. Paris: Imprimerie Nationale, 1861–77. Unless otherwise noted, references are to this edition.

al-Maydānī, Aḥmad ibn Muḥammad. *Majmaᶜ al-amthāl.* Ed. Muḥammad Abū al-Faḍl Ibrāhīm. Cairo: ᶜĪsā al-Bābī al-Ḥalabī, [1978].

Meier, Fritz. *Abū Saᶜīd-i Abū l-Ḫayr (357–440/967–1049) Wirklichkeit und Legende.* Acta Iranica, 3rd series, vol. 4. Leiden: E J. Brill, 1976.

Milik, Jósef Tadeusz, ed. *The Books of Enoch: Aramaic Fragments of Qumrân Cave 4.* With the collaboration of Matthew Black. Oxford: Clarendon Press, 1976.

al-Mubarrad, Muḥammad ibn Yazīd. *Al-Kāmil.* Ed. Muḥammad Abū al-Faḍl Ibrāhīm and al-Sayyid Shiḥātah. Cairo: Maṭbaᶜat Nahdat Miṣr, n.d.

Mughulṭāy, ᶜAlāᵓ al-Dīn. *Al-Wāḍiḥ al-mubīn fī dhikr man ustushhida min al-*

muḥibbīn. Mughulṭai's Biographical Dictionary of the Martyrs of Love. Part I. Ed. Otto Spies. Delhi, 1936.

Muḥammad ibn Dāwūd al-Iṣfahānī. *Al-Nisf al-awwal min "Kitāb al-zahrah"* (The first half of *Kitāb al-zahrah*). Ed. A. R. Nykl with Ibrāhīm Ṭūqān. Studies in Ancient Oriental Civilization, no. 6. Chicago: University of Chicago Press, 1932.

al-Murtaḍā al-Zabīdī. *Sharḥ al-Qāmūs al-musammā Tāj al-ᶜarūs.* Cairo: al-Maṭbaᶜah al-Khayrīyah, 1306–7/1888–90.

Muslim ibn al-Ḥajjāj al-Qushayrī. *Ṣaḥīh Muslim.* English translation by ᶜAbdul Ḥamīd Ṣiddīqī. Lahore: Sh. Muhammad Ashraf, 1976.

———. *Ṣaḥīḥ Muslim bi-sharḥ al-Nawawī* (Muslim's *Ṣaḥīḥ* with the commentary of al-Nawawī). Cairo: al-Maṭbaᶜah al-Miṣrīyah bil-Azhar, 1347/1929–1349/1930.

al-Muttaqī, ᶜAlī ibn ᶜAbd al-Malik al-Hindī. *Kanz al-ᶜummāl fī sunan al-aqwāl wa-al-afᶜāl.* Ed. Bakrī Ḥayyānī, Ṣafwat al-Saqqā, [and Ḥasan Razzūq]; indexes Nadīm Marᶜashlī and Usāmah Marᶜashlī. Beirut: Muᵓassasat al-Risālah, 1409/1989.

al-Nabhānī, Yūsuf ibn Ismāᶜīl. *Jāmiᶜ karāmāt al-awliyāᵓ.* Ed. Ibrāhīm ᶜAṭwah ᶜAwaḍ. Cairo: Muṣṭafā al-Bābī al-Ḥalabī, 1394/1974.

al-Nadīm (LC: Ibn al-Nadīm), Muḥammad ibn Isḥāq. *The Fihrist of al-Nadīm.* Ed. and trans. Bayard Dodge. New York and London: Columbia University Press, 1970.

———. *Kitāb al-fihrist.* Ed. G. Flügel. Leipzig: F. C. W. Vogel, 1871–72.

———. *Kitāb al-fihrist.* Ed. G. Flügel. Reprint of Leipzig, 1871–72. Beirut: Khayat's, 1964.

al-Nawawī. *Riyāḍ al-ṣāliḥīn.* Cairo: al-Maṭbaᶜah al-Yūsufīyah, n.d.

al-Nīsābūrī (al-Naysābūrī), al-Ḥasan ibn Muḥammad. *ᶜUqalāᵓ al-majānīn.* Ed. Wajīh Fāris al-Kaylānī. Cairo: al-Maṭbaᶜah al-ᶜArabīyah, 1343/1924.

Pape, Wilhelm and Benseler, G. *Wörterbuch der griechischen Eigennamen.* Graz: Akademische Druck und Verlagsanstalt, 1959.

Ptolemy. *Tetrabiblos.* Edited and translated by F. E. Robbins. The Loeb Classical Library. London: Heinemann, 1948.

Ptolemy, 2nd cent. *Kitāb al-thamarah* (*Centiloquium*). *See* Sezgin, *GAS,* VII, pp. 44–46.

Qāmūs = al-Fīrūzābādī, Muḥammad ibn Yaᶜqūb. *Al-Qāmūs al-muḥīṭ.* Cairo, 1863–64.

al-Qifṭī, ᶜAlī ibn Yūsuf. *Taᵓrīkh al-ḥukamāᵓ = Ibn al-Qifṭī's Ta'rīf al-ḥukamā'.* Ed. Julius Lippert. Leipzig: Dieterich'sche Verlagsbuchhandlung (Theodor Weicher), 1903.

al-Qushayrī, ᶜAbd al-Karīm ibn Hawāzin. *Laṭāᵓif al-ishārāt.* 2nd ed. Cairo: al-Hayᵓah al-Miṣrīyah al-ᶜĀmmah lil-Kitāb, 1981–83.

———. *Al-Risālah al-Qushayrīyah.* Cairo: Muḥammad ᶜAlī Ṣubayḥ, 1386/1966. References to edition of 1966 without volume number are to this edition.

———. *Al-Risālah al-Qushayrīyah.* Ed. ᶜAbd al-Ḥalīm Maḥmūd and Maḥmūd ibn al-Sharīf. 2 vols. Cairo: Dār al-Kutub al-Ḥadīthah, [1966].

———. *Al-Risālah al-Qushayrīyah.* Text with marginal notes from the commentary of Zakarīyā al-Anṣārī. Cairo: Dār al-Kutub al-ᶜArabīyah al-Kubrā, 1330/1912.

Redhouse, James W. (James William), Sir. *A Turkish and English Lexicon.* Constantinople: H. Matteosian, 1921.

Ritter, Hellmut. *Das Meer der Seele.* Leiden: E. J. Brill, 1955.

———. "Philologika. VII. Arabische und persische Schriften über die profane und die mystische Liebe." *Der Islam* 21 (1933): 84–109.

Rosenthal, Franz. "On the Knowledge of Plato's Philosophy in the Islamic World." *Islamic Culture* 14 (1940): 387–422.

Rūzbihān ibn Abī Naṣr Baqlī Shīrāzī. *Le dévoilement des secrets et les apparitions des lumières: journal spirituel du maître de Shîrâz.* Trans. of *Kashf al-asrār* by Paul Ballanfat. Paris: Éditions du Seuil, 1996.

———. *Rūzbihān al-Baḳlī ve Kitāb kaşf al-asrār'ı ile farsça bâzı şiirleri.* Ed. Nazif Hoca. Istanbul: Edebiyat Fakültesi Matbaası, 1971.

———. *Kitāb-i ᶜabhar al-ᶜāshiqīn* (*Le jasmin des fidèles d'amour*). Edited with French translation of the first chapter by Henry Corbin and Moh. Mo'in. Tehran: Département d'Iranologie de l'Institut Franco-Iranien, 1958; Paris: Adrien-Maisonneuve, 1958.

———. *Kitāb mashrab al-arwāḥ.* Ed. Nazif M. Hoca. İstanbul Üniversitesi Edebiyat Fakültesi Yayınları, no. 1876. Istanbul: Edebiyat Fakültesi Matbaası, 1974.

———. *Manṭiq al-asrār.* Copies of pages from MSS Mashhad 156 (catalogue I, 48), fols. 110b–111b; Massignon, Paris, fols. 56b–57b; Tashkent (entitled *Tafsīr al-shaṭḥīyāt bi-lisān al-ṣūfīyah*), fols. unnumbered. All were kindly provided by Carl W. Ernst. Cf. his Rūzbihān Baqlī, pp. 155 and 159, n. 8.

———. *Sharḥ-i shaṭḥīyāt* (*Commentaire sur les paradoxes des soufis*). Ed. Henry Corbin. Tehran: Département d'Iranologie de l'Institut Franco-Iranien, 1966; Paris: Adrien-Maisonneuve, 1966.

———. *The Unveiling of Secrets: Diary of a Sufi Master.* Trans. of *Kashf al-asrār* by Carl W. Ernst. Chapel Hill, N.C.: Parvardigar Press, 1997.

al-Ṣābiʾ, Abū al-Ḥasan al-Hilāl ibn al-Muḥassin. *Kitāb tuḥfat al-umarāʾ fī taʾrīkh al-wuzarāʾ.* Beirut: Maṭbaᶜat al-Ābāʾ al-Yasūᶜīyīn, 1904.

al-Samᶜānī, ᶜAbd al-Karīm ibn Muḥammad. *Al-Ansāb.* Ed. ᶜAbd al-Raḥmān ibn Yaḥyā al-Muᶜallimī al-Yamānī. Hyderabad: Dāʾirat al-Maᶜārif al-ᶜUthmānīyah, 1962–.

al-Sarrāj al-Qāriʾ, Jaᶜfar ibn Aḥmad. *Maṣāriᶜ al-ᶜushshāq.* Beirut: Dār Bayrūt, Dār Ṣādir, 1378/1958. Unless otherwise noted, references are to this edition.

———. *Maṣāriᶜ al-ᶜushshāq.* Constantinople: Maṭbaᶜat al-Jawāʾib, 1301 A.H.

———. *Maṣāriᶜ al-ᶜushshāq.* Ed. Muḥammad Badr al-Dīn al-Naᶜsānī. Cairo: Maṭbaᶜat al-Saᶜādah, 1335/1907.

al-Sarrāj al-Ṭūsī, Abū Naṣr ᶜAbd Allāh ibn ᶜAlī. *The Kitáb al-lumaᶜ fi ʾl-taṣawwuf.* Ed. Reynold Alleyne Nicholson. E. J. W. Gibb Memorial, no. 22. Leyden: E. J. Brill, London: Luzac & Co., 1914.

Schimmel, Annemarie. *Mystical Dimensions of Islam.* Chapel Hill: The University of North Carolina Press, 1975.

Sezgin = Fuat Sezgin, *GAS*.

Sezgin, Fuat. *GAS* = *Geschichte des arabischen Schrifttums*. Leiden: E. J. Brill, 1967–.

Shādhān ibn Baḥr. *Mudhākarāt Abī Ma*ᶜ*shar* (= *Kitāb [Abī Ma*ᶜ*shar fī] asrār* ᶜ*ilm al-nujūm*). *See* Sezgin, GAS, VII, pp. 15, 147.

al-Sharīf al-Murtaḍā, ᶜAlam al-Hudā ᶜAlī ibn al-Ḥusayn, *Dīwān al-Sharīf al-Murtaḍā*. Ed. Rashīd al-Ṣaffār. [Cairo]: ᶜĪsā al-Bābī al-Ḥalābī, 1958.

al-Shiblī, Abū Bakr. *Dīwān Abī Bakr al-Shiblī*. Ed. Kāmil Muṣṭafā al-Shaybī. Baghdad: Dār al-Taḍāmun, 1386/1967.

Shīrāzī, Abū al-ᶜAbbās Aḥmad ibn Abī al-Khayr Zarkūb. *See* Zarkūb Shīrāzī, Muᶜīn al-Dīn.

The Shorter Encyclopaedia of Islam. Ithaca: Cornell University Press, 1961.

al-Sijistānī, Muḥammad ibn Ṭāhir, Abū Sulaymān al-Manṭiqī. *Ṣiwān al-ḥikma wa-thalāth rasāʾil*. Ed. ᶜAbd al-Raḥmān Badawī. Tehran: Bunyād-i Farhang-i Īrān, 1974.

Sīrat = al-Daylamī, Abū al-Ḥasan ᶜAlī ibn Muḥammad. *Sīrat-i Abū* ᶜ*Abdullāh Ibn al-Ḫafīf aṣ-Ṣīrāzī*.

Sobieroj, Florian. "Ibn Ḫafīf aš-Šīrāzī und seine Schrift zur Novizenerziehung (Kitāb al-Iqtiṣād)". Doctoral dissertation, Albert-Ludwigs-Universität zu Freiburg. Freiburg, 1992. Subsequently published in the series Beiruter Texte und Studien (vol. 57) of the Orient-Institut of the Deutsche Morgenländische Gesellschaft (Beirut: In Kommission bei Franz Steiner Verlag, 1998).

Sperber, Alexander. *The Pentateuch according to Targum Onkelos* (= *The Bible in Aramaic. Vol. I*). Leiden E. J. Brill, 1959. (LC catalogues under Bible. O. T. Aramaic 1959.)

Steingass, Francis Joseph. *A Comprehensive Persian–English Dictionary*. Reprint. Beirut: Librairie du Liban, 1975.

al-Subkī, Tāj al-Dīn ᶜAbd al-Wahhāb ibn ᶜAlī. *Ṭabaqāt al-Shāfi*ᶜ*īyah al-kubrā*. Ed. Maḥmūd Muhammad al-Ṭanāḥī and ᶜAbd al-Fattāḥ al-Ḥilw. [Cairo]: ᶜĪsā al-Bābī al-Ḥalabī, 1964–76.

Sunan Abī Dāwūd. See Abū Dāwūd Sulaymān ibn al-Ashᶜath al-Sijistānī. *Sunan Abī Dāwūd*.

al-Sukkarī, Abū Saᶜīd al-Ḥasan ibn al-Ḥusayn. *Kitāb sharḥ ash*ᶜ*ār al-Hudhalīyīn*. Ed. ᶜAbd al-Sattār Aḥmad Farrāj. Cairo: Maktabat Dār al-ᶜUrūbah, 1963–65.

al-Sulamī, Abū ᶜAbd al-Raḥmān Muḥammad ibn al-Ḥusayn. *Kitāb ṭabaqāt al-ṣūfīyah*. Ed. Johannes Pedersen. Leiden: E. J. Brill, 1960.

al-Suyūṭī. *Al-Ḥāwī lil-fatāwī*. Beirut: Dār al-Kutub al-ᶜIlmīyah, 1403/1983.

———. *Bughyat al-wu*ᶜ*āh fī ṭabaqāt al-lughawīyīn wa-al-nuḥāh*. Ed. Muḥammad Abū al-Faḍl Ibrāhīm. Cairo: ᶜĪsā al-Bābī al-Ḥalabī, 1384/1964–65.

———. *Al-Jāmi*ᶜ *al-ṣaghīr*. Cairo, 1330 A.H.

———. *Lubb al-lubāb fī taḥrīr al-ansāb*. Ed. Pieter Johannes Veth. Leiden: S. & J. Luchtmans, 1842; reprint Baghdad: Maktabat al-Muthannā, n.d.

al-Ṭabarī. *Jāmi^c al-bayān.* Cairo: Muṣṭafā al-Bābī al-Ḥalabī, 1954–68.

———. *Tafsīr al-Ṭabarī Jāmi^c al-bayān.* Ed. Maḥmūd Muḥammad Shākir. Cairo: Dār al-Ma^cārif, 1961–.

———. *Ta^ɔrīkh al-rusul wa-al-mulūk.* Ed. Muḥammad Abū al-Faḍl Ibrāhīm. Cairo: Dār al-Ma^cārif, 1960–69.

al-Tahānawī, Muḥammad ^cAlā^ɔ ibn ^cAlī. *Kashshāf iṣṭilāḥāt al-funūn.* Ed. Mawlawies Mohammed Wajih, Abd al-Haqq, and Gholam Kadir under the supervision of Aloys Sprenger and W. Nassau Lees. Calcutta: W. N. Lees' Press, 1862; reprint with Persian introduction Tehran: Maktabat Khayyām wa-Shurakāhu, 1967.

Tāj al-^carūs = al-Murtaḍā al-Zabīdī, *Sharḥ al-Qāmūs.*

Takeshita, Masataka. "Continuity and Change in the Tradition of Shirazi Love Mysticism—A Comparison between Daylamī's *^cAṭf al-Alif* and Rūzbihān Baqlī's *^cAbhar al-^cĀshiqīn.*" *Orient* 23 (1987): 113–31.

al-Tanūkhī, al-Muḥassin ibn ^cAlī, Abū ^cAlī. *Nishwār al-muḥāḍarah wa-akhbār al-mudhākarah.* Ed. ^cAbbūd al-Shāljī. [Beirut: Maṭābi^c Dār Ṣādir], 1971–73.

al-Tustarī, Sahl ibn ^cAbd Allāh. *Tafsīr al-Qur^ɔān al-^caẓīm.* Cairo: Maṭba^cat al-Sa^cādah, 1326/1908.

Vadet, Jean-Claude. Edition = *Kitāb ^cAṭf al-alif al-ma^ɔlūf ^calā al-lām al-ma^cṭūf. See* al-Daylamī.

———. Translation = *Le traité d'amour mystique d'al-Daylami. See* al-Daylamī.

Virgil. *Aeneid.*

Ullmann, Manfred. *Wörterbuch der klassischen arabischen Sprache.* Wiesbaden: Otto Harrassowitz, 1970–.

Walzer, Richard. "Aristotle, Galen, and Palladius on Love." In Richard Walzer, *Greek into Arabic,* pp. 48–59. Originally published under the title "Fragmenta graeca in litteris arabicis 1. Palladios and Aristotle" in *Journal of the Royal Asiatic Society,* 1939, pp. 407–22.

———. *Greek into Arabic; Essays on Islamic Philosophy.* Oxford: Bruno Cassirer, 1962.

———. "New Light on the Arabic Translations of Aristotle." In Richard Walzer, *Greek into Arabic,* pp. 60–113.

al-Washshā^ɔ, Muḥammad ibn Aḥmad ibn Isḥāq. *Kitāb al-muwashshā.* Ed. Rudolph E. Brünnow. Leiden: E. J. Brill, 1866.

Wehr, Hans. *A Dictionary of Modern Written Arabic.* Ed. by J Milton Cowan. 4th ed. Wiesbaden: Otto Harrassowitz, 1979.

Wehrli, Fritz. *Die Schule des Aristoteles: Texte und Kommentar.* Basel: Benno Schwabe & Co., Verlag, 1944–59.

Wensinck, Arent Jan. *Concordance et indices de la tradition musulmane.* Leiden: E. J. Brill 1936–.

Wright = Carl Paul Caspari, *A Grammar of the Arabic Language,* trans. William Wright.

al-Ya^cqūbī, Aḥmad ibn Abī Ya^cqūb. *Ibn-Wādih qui dicitur al-Ja^cqubī Historiae* (= *Ta^ɔrīkh*). Ed. M. Th. Houtsma. Leiden: E. J. Brill, 1969.

———. *Kitāb al-buldān.* Ed. M. J. de Goeje. Bibliotheca Geographorum Arabicorum, vol. 7. Leiden: E. J. Brill, 1967.

Yāqūt ibn ᶜAbd Allāh al-Ḥamawī. *Muᶜjam al-buldān. = Jacut's geographisches Wörterbuch.* Ed. Ferdinand Wüstenfeld. Leipzig: F. A Brockhaus, 1866–1870; reprint Tehran: Maktabat al-Asadī, 1965.

———. *Muᶜjam al-udabāʾ* (*Irshād al-arīb*). Ed. Aḥmad Farīd Rifāᶜī Bak. Cairo: Maktabat ᶜĪsā al-Bābī al-Ḥalabī, Dār al-Maʾmūn, n.d.

Zaghlūl, Abū Hājar Muḥammad al-Saᶜīd ibn Basyūnī. *Mawsūᶜat aṭrāf al-ḥadīth al-nabawī al-sharīf.* 1st ed. Beirut: ᶜĀlam al-Turāth, 1419/1989.

al-Zamakhsharī, Maḥmūd ibn ᶜUmar. *Al-Kashshāf.* Cairo: Muṣṭafā al-Bābī al-Ḥalabī, 1966–68.

Zarkūb Shīrāzī, Muᶜīn al-Dīn. *Shīrāznāmah.* Ed. Bahman Karīmī. Tehran: Kitābkhānah'hā-yi Aḥmadī va-Maᶜrifat-i Shīrāzī, 1310/1931.

al-Ziriklī, Khayr al-Dīn. *Al-Aᶜlām.* 2nd printing. n.p., n.d.

INDEX OF PERSONS, PEOPLES, AND PLACES

References are to pages of the manuscript.